ACC. No: 02315883

# MICHAEL OF ROMANIA

*For Chris and Alex*

# Michael of Romania

## The King and the Country

Ivor Porter

SUTTON PUBLISHING

First published in the United Kingdom in 2005 by
Sutton Publishing Limited · Phoenix Mill
Thrupp · Stroud · Gloucestershire · GL5 2BU

Copyright © Ivor Porter, 2005

All rights reserved. No part of this publication may be reproduced, stored in a retrieval system, or transmitted, in any form, or by any means, electronic, mechanical, photocopying, recording or otherwise, without the prior permission of the publisher and copyright holder.

Ivor Porter has asserted the moral right to be identified as the author of this work.

British Library Cataloguing in Publication Data
A catalogue record for this book is available from the British Library.

ISBN 0-7509-3847-1

Typeset in 10.5/14pt Sabon.
Typesetting and origination by
Sutton Publishing Limited.
Printed and bound in England by
J.H. Haynes & Co. Ltd, Sparkford.

# Contents

| | |
|---|---|
| *List of Illustrations* | vii |
| *Acknowledgements* | ix |
| *Preface* | xi |
| *Chronology* | xv |
| *Map: Frontiers of Romania 1878–1942* | xxii |

PART ONE: FAMILY, CHILDHOOD AND ADOLESCENCE:
25 OCTOBER 1921–6 SEPTEMBER 1940

| | | |
|---|---|---|
| One | A Mother 'what makes me laugh': Papa in Exile | 1 |
| Two | A Flamboyant Father and his Mistress: Mama in Exile | 20 |
| Three | The Loss of Greater Romania: King Carol II Abdicates | 42 |

PART TWO: TOWARDS THE *COUP D'ETAT*:
SEPTEMBER 1940–AUGUST 1944

| | | |
|---|---|---|
| Four | King Michael and the pro-German Dictator | 61 |
| Five | King Michael's Decision to Break with the Axis | 83 |
| Six | The *Coup d'Etat* | 98 |
| Seven | Romanian Army Drive Out the Germans: Soviet Army 'Liberates' Bucharest | 111 |

PART THREE: SOVIET OCCUPATION:
SEPTEMBER 1944–3 JANUARY 1948

| | | |
|---|---|---|
| Eight | Vyshinsky Imposes a Communist Government | 125 |
| Nine | King Michael Goes on Strike: the West Dithers | 142 |
| Ten | Royal Wedding in London: Royal Engagement in Switzerland | 160 |

| | | |
|---|---|---|
| Eleven | An Illegal Abdication | 177 |

**PART FOUR: EXILE: JANUARY 1948–DECEMBER 1989**

| | | |
|---|---|---|
| Twelve | The Wedding of King Michael and Princess Anne of Bourbon Parma | 191 |
| Thirteen | Searching for an Identity, Working for Romania, Making a Living | 205 |
| Fourteen | The Romanian Uprising of 1989 | 226 |

**PART FIVE: ROMANIA TRAPPED IN ITS COMMUNIST PAST – AFTER 1989**

| | | |
|---|---|---|
| Fifteen | A Government of Reluctant Democrats | 239 |
| Sixteen | The Easter Visit | 252 |
| Seventeen | President Iliescu Loses an Election | 263 |
| Eighteen | King Michael Returns to Romania | 273 |
| | *Genealogical Tables* | 287 |
| | *Principal Romanians* | 293 |
| | *Royal Residences* | 300 |
| | *Notes* | 301 |
| | *Bibliography* | 312 |
| | *Index* | 314 |

## List of Illustrations

1 Three Generations: King Carol I, Crown Prince Ferdinand, Prince Carol.
2 Elizabeth of Wied, Queen of Romania, in peasant dress.
3 Queen Marie of Romania.
4 Prince Michael on the beach at Mamaia.
5 Crown Prince Carol, Crown Princess Helen, Prince Michael and dog.
6 King Michael with his cousin Prince Philip of Greece (later Duke of Edinburgh) 1928.
7 Princess Elisabeta, Queen of Greece.
8 Princess Maria 'Mignon', Queen of Yugoslavia.
9 Princess Ileana, Archduchess of Austria.
10 On the anniversary of King Ferdinand's death, the Royal Family attend a memorial service at Curtea de Argeş.
11 Crown Prince Michael during the State Visit to London in November 1938.
12 Memorial service for Queen Marie at Curtea de Argeş, January 1939. With the Royal Family is the Patriarch Miron Cristea.
13 King Michael, Queen Helen, Madame Antonescu, Mihai Antonescu and Baron Ion Mocsoni-Styrcea.
14 The house at Săvârşin.
15 Group in front of King Michael's twin-engined Fokker Wolf at Săvârşin in 1946.
16 The Royal Palace and Casa Nouă after the German bombing.
17 King Michael's first press conference after the *coup d'état*.
18 The Moscow Three Power Commission at Sinaia, 8 January 1946.
19 Prime Minister Groza, King Michael and Marshal Tolbukhin.
20 Princess Anne of Bourbon Parma saying goodbye at Lausanne station.
21 Juliu Maniu.
22 Dinu Brătianu.
23 Marshal Antonescu during his trial.
24 Gheorghe Tătărescu.
25 King Michael and Princess Anne at Athens airport before their wedding.

26  Princess Margarita and Mr Radu Duda after their wedding.
27  President Nicolae Ceauşescu.
28  President Ion Iliescu.
29  President-elect Emil Constantinescu.
30  King Michael in Romania on 28 February 1997.

Every effort has been made to trace copyright holders. The author and Sutton Publishing apologise for any unintentional omissions and would be pleased, if any such case should arise, to add an appropriate acknowledgement in future editions.

# Acknowledgements

I am most grateful to His Majesty King Michael, the only constitutional monarch who had the opportunity of leading his people in person during the Second World War, for his help and understanding during the writing of this book. I was given access to the archives of the royal family including a wealth of family letters and documentation and to Queen Helen's diaries which are a gold mine of perceptive comments on the events – national and domestic – of their daily lives. The conversations I was able to have with King Michael and Queen Anne and with the Crown Princess Margarita and, more recently, with Prince Radu have given me invaluable glimpses of their lives during the turmoil of wartime Romania and what has followed.

I should like to mention in particular Peter Day, David Horbury and Professor Dennis Deletant. Also Rebecca Haynes, Cameron Pyke, Oliver Corderoy, Antonia Till, Alexandra Whiting and Ilinca Bossy who first suggested the book.

I owe much to Arthur Gould Lee whose books *Crown against Sickle* and *Helen, Queen Mother of Romania* have the immediacy of having been written in the 1940s. I have also drawn from historical accounts, biographies and diaries of the period, particularly those published in Romanian and not available to the English reader. I am grateful to all those Romanians who answered the many questions I was asking: Ana Blăndiana, Ioana Ieronim, Constantin Brâncovan, Eleodor Focșeneanu, Rica Georgescu, Gabirel Liiceanu, Ion Mocsoni-Styrcea, Cristian Mititelu, Nelly Pilat, Annie Samuelli, Jacques Vergotti and Lascar Zamfirescu – there must be many others. For the illustrations to John Wimbles, Johnny and Ioana Troiano, Jacques Vergotti, the Romanian Cultural Centre, Reuters, AP, the *Daily Telegraph* Syndication, the *Evening Standard* and to the officials of the newspaper section of the British Library at Colindale who have been very helpful in our search for photograph copyright holders.

I should like to thank the Royal Geographical Society for their help with the map and the London Library for their help on the Danish Royal Family.

My gratitude goes in particular, to Caroline Dawnay, my literary agent, and to Jaqueline Mitchell and Elizabeth Stone, my editors.

Though I hesitate to say it, I suspect that Katerina, my wife, has done as much as anyone to help the book.

# Preface

Michael's parents – the Crown Prince Carol of Romania and the Princess Helen of Greece and Denmark – were married at the Metropolitan Cathedral in Athens on 10 March 1921. While they made their way to Romania via Constantinople at the beginning of May, Queen Marie of Romania prepared a handsome apartment for them in Cotroceni Palace, the family home in Bucharest, which they declined. They would go to Sinaia in the mountains as soon as they could and if they were to spend any time at Cotroceni it would, Carol said, be in the quarters he had had as a boy – 'a staircase' Helen called it – 'and three rooms' where they could be on their own.[1]

Meanwhile, Queen Marie wrote optimistic letters to her cousin, Queen Sophie of Greece, telling her how lovely her daughter 'Sitta' looked on every occasion and what an excellent influence she was having on Carol.

> I hope I may say they are happy. I am sure they are . . . Carol is awfully proud of her but because of the painful situation he had got himself into formerly, he has not been able to rejoice over the joy his people had over his marriage.[2]

King Carol I, founder of the Romanian dynasty, had bought the estate above Sinaia in the Carpathian Mountains as a refuge from the marshy humidity of the capital. At the top of his estate he had built the castle of Peleş, an ambling construction influenced by Byzantium but in the style of the German Renaissance, and named it after the stream running through the valley whose magic his wife, Queen Elizabeth, described in her children's fairy tales under her pen name Carmen Sylva. Lower down the mountain he built a smaller castle with the diminutive name of Pelişor for his nephew, the Crown Prince Ferdinand, and his British-born wife Marie. A delightful makeshift chalet called Foişor was used by the family while the two castles were being built, and by the 1920s this had become the favourite summer home for the younger generation. It was here that Princess Helen decided to have her baby. She threw out the antler chairs and made Foişor cosy with comfortable English furniture. Carol was often kept busy in the capital, she wrote to her mother, but 'rushes up to Sinaia whenever he can'. Nevertheless, she was lonely.

She had only two real friends in Sinaia, Rosa her Greek maid, and Billie the Alsatian dog inherited from her favourite brother, Alexander. It was Alexander who had given her her pet name of 'Sitta', the nearest he could get to calling her 'sister' when he had been a little boy. He had died less than a year before and she still missed him dreadfully.

Princess Helen's homesickness shows in the letters she wrote to her mother: they are full of unhappy criticism of almost everyone and everything around her. After the comparatively simple and informal atmosphere in which she had been brought up she found the Romanian court pompous, oppressive and, at the same time, run down. During the First World War the Germans had occupied Cotroceni and had left the garden a wilderness. The servants, with a major revolution going on across the Russian frontier, were rebellious and walked out whenever they felt like it. The silver, she noted, was only cleaned once a month. Yet neither the brilliant 'Missy', as Queen Marie, her mother-in-law, was called in the family, nor the scholarly 'Nando', her father-in-law, seemed to care much about such things.[3]

The baby showed signs of being early, and when Louros, the Greek family doctor, arrived in mid-October Helen was hoping that the birth would not occur on the 25th, the anniversary of Alexander's death. Yet that was the date of Michael's birth. Queen Marie, who administered the chloroform, wrote in characteristically dramatic language, 'It was a terrible battle . . . the room looked like a slaughterhouse',[4] and two days later Carol was still sending telegrams to assure their relatives that 'after very anxious days Louros was obliged to make operation and thanks to his skill Sitta and boy out of danger'.[5]

Next day Princess Helen was sitting up in bed asking her father, King Constantine of Greece, in a shaky pencilled letter to be Michael's godfather.[6] Constantine had just returned from a disastrous Greek campaign against the Turks in Asia Minor, his hopes and his health shattered. She knew that he might not reply, for that was how he was.

Queen Sophie paid them a fleeting visit but since by then her grandson was already eight days old and her daughter making a good recovery, she returned to her husband. On 29 November Helen wrote to her:

> The little General is getting on beautifully . . . However much you find him like Carol his forehead is like Papa with little dents on each side which pleases me very much.[7]

In December she and Carol moved into their Bucharest house – a present from the city council – in the handsome, tree-lined Chaussée Kiselev. On the 17th, King Constantine – probably prodded by his mother, the energetic dowager Queen Olga, who had just returned to Athens from a trip to Sandringham and Paris – wrote to her saying that he would be flattered and pleased to be Michael's godfather. 'When are you coming, I'd a sort of impression you were coming for Christmas and now I'm rather disappointed. I hope you'll be able to come soon.'[8]

This letter decided her. Although she suspected that the King and Queen counted on her to leave Carol to his own devices as little as possible, she obtained permission to take the heir to the throne out of the country as soon as he had been christened. She wished to show her baby to her family and to see for herself how sick her father really was.

The baby was baptised 'Mihai' on the afternoon of 10 January 1922 and at the *vin d'honneur* which followed, the British Minister offered the King and Queen and the prince's parents 'every possible wish for the future welfare and prosperity of the eventual heir to the Romanian throne'.[9] No one at that time could have foreseen the turbulent and stricken life that awaited him.

Following the World War treaty settlements, Prince Michael's birthplace was roughly at the centre of the new Greater Romania he could be expected one day to rule. To the west Transylvania stretched deep into the central European plain. To the east lay the two principalities of the Old Kingdom – Wallachia, south to the Danube and south-east to the great delta and the Black Sea – and Moldavia – including the rich wheatlands of Bessarabia – north and north-east to the frontiers of Poland and the Ukraine. Yet before Prince Michael had reached the age of eighteen Romania would be forced to return Bessarabia to the Soviet Union and her beloved Transylvania to Hungary.

His bringing up was to be grotesque. Little of his childhood would be spent with both parents, most of it at court with his flamboyant father, his father's mistress, Madame Lupescu, and a sycophantic and corrupt *camarilla*. Yet Princess Helen would worry unnecessarily about their influence on her son. He turned out to be a man who could smell corruption a mile away and suffered all his life from an overriding sense of duty.

King Michael did not hesitate to use what powers he had when his country was threatened. In his early twenties he would personally lead an anti-German *coup d'état* which was to take Romania out of the Axis. For three years, with the Red Army already in occupation, he would then hold on to some degree of constitutional democracy until Stalin was forced to show his hand, to reveal, as

Churchill noted, 'the pattern of things to come'. During his exile in England and Switzerland he would ride the roller-coaster of Anglo-American cold-war policies towards Eastern Europe while he and his wife, the Princess Anne of Bourbon Parma, tried to bring up five children on what they could earn from market gardening and a chicken farm; he also worked as test pilot for Lear Aircraft and later as a reluctant Wall Street stockbroker.

I first met King Michael on the night of his *coup* – a tall, serious young man of 22 who had just performed one of the most courageous individual acts of the war and was probably still on a bit of a high though not showing it, merely saying to us 'I hope I have done the right thing.' King Michael's reserve in later life is partly the result of a dreadful childhood and lack of recognition for what he had done as an adult. He sometimes lacks spontaneity. Sometimes he leaves a silence to be interpreted. Yet he can be frank about himself. He is a man of great integrity and in spite of what he has suffered never cynical. He is determined but also patient; his mother sometimes reacted violently in her diary to his coolness and apparent disregard for the risks they were taking. His handling of the agents sent in by Hitler and Stalin was a severe test of character which he passed with flying colours. He is not attracted by the pomp and circumstance of monarchy, feeling, he once told me, that there 'seems always to be something missing' on such occasions. He has a daughter who once told the head of the Romanian Monarchist Party that the best thing he could do for her father would be to dissolve it.

King Michael was the first king of his line to speak Romanian as his mother tongue, and his empathy with the Romanian people was genuine and life-long. When he was a child, their affection was to help restore the confidence his father seemed bent on undermining. After a long, enforced exile he would be allowed to return for only a few days to his country. He was greeted in Bucharest by an immense crowd. He told them, as no communist leader would have dared to do, 'I love you' and, although consecutive administrations had spent forty-four years trying to rubbish the monarchy, they believed him.

NOTE ON PRONUNCIATION

The accented vowels and consonants are pronounced roughly as follows: ă as the 'u' in 'cut'; â as the 'u' in 'cull'; ţ as the 'ts' in 'tsar'; and ş as the 's' in 'sugar'.

# *Chronology*

| | |
|---|---|
| 10 May 1866 | The principalities of Wallachia and Moldavia, still under Turkish suzerainty, invite Prince Karl of Hohenzollern-Sigmaringen to be first foreign and constitutional ruler, 10 May becomes National Day. |
| 29 June 1866 | A constitution is adopted by Parliament. |
| 3 November 1869 | Prince Carol (his name in Romanian) marries the German Princess Elizabeth of Wied. One child, Maria, 1870–4. |
| 12 April 1877 | War breaks out between Russia and Turkey. |
| 28 November 1877 | Prince Carol at head of Romanian and Russian troops defeats Osman Pasha at Plevna. |
| June 1878 | Congress of Berlin confirms Romania's independence. |
| 10 May 1881 | Romania proclaimed a kingdom. |
| 19 April 1889 | King Carol's nephew, Prince Ferdinand of Hohenzollern-Sigmaringen, brought to Romania as Crown Prince. |
| 29 December 1892 | Prince Ferdinand marries the English Princess Marie, daughter of the Duke of Edinburgh, granddaughter of Queen Victoria. |
| 15 October 1893 | Prince Carol (to become King Carol II) born to Ferdinand and Marie. |
| 27 September 1914 | Death of King Carol I; Ferdinand and Marie become King and Queen and Carol Crown Prince. |
| 14 August 1916 | Romania enters the war on the side of the Allies. The Central Powers occupy the capital. The Royal Family and Government move north to Iaşi, capital of Moldavia. |
| May 1917 | King Ferdinand goes to the front and promises his peasant soldiers land and a larger part in public affairs. |
| Summer 1917 | Romanian victories at Mărăşeşti and other key places. |
| Autumn 1917 | Russia, Romania's only ally in the region, plunged into revolution and ceases hostilities. |
| 24 April 1918 | Romania signs a treaty with the Central Powers. |

| | |
|---|---|
| 13 September 1918 | Without the King's consent Crown Prince Carol marries Ioana Lambrino, a commoner. |
| 9 January, 1919 | The marriage is dissolved. The relationship continues and Carol renounces his right to the throne. |
| 7 January 1920 | Prince Carol promises his parents never to see Ioana Lambrino alone again. |
| 8 January 1920 | Prince Carol's illegitimate son, Mircea Grigore Lambrino, is born. |
| 10 March 1921 | Prince Carol marries Princess Helen of Greece and Denmark. |
| 25 October 1921 | Birth of Prince Michael, future King of Romania. |
| 15 October 1922 | The coronation of King Ferdinand and Queen Marie takes place in Alba Julia. |
| 28 March 1923 | A new constitution is approved by Parliament. |
| 30 December 1925 | Prince Carol exiles himself with his mistress Elena Lupescu; renounces his right to the throne. King Ferdinand accepts; Prince Michael becomes successor. |
| 20 July 1927 | Death of King Ferdinand. Michael, aged five, becomes king. |
| 21 July 1928 | Prince Carol and Queen Helen are divorced. |
| 6 June 1930 | Prince Carol returns to Romania; proclaimed king on 8 June. |
| 1 November 1932 | Princess Helen is exiled and goes to live in Florence; Michael remains with his father and Madame Lupescu. |
| 10 February 1938 | King Carol replaces the 1923 constitution by a royal dictatorship. |
| March–August 1940 | Under pressure from Hitler and Stalin, Romania cedes Bessarabia and Bukovina to the USSR, Dobrugea to Bulgaria and North West Transylvania to Hungary. |
| September 1940 | King Carol cedes the royal prerogatives to General Ion Antonescu; abdicates in favour of his son. Michael becomes king for the second time and his mother, as 'Queen Mother', returns to Romania. Antonescu forms a government with the Iron Guard, an extreme right-wing movement. |
| 20–27 January 1941 | The Iron Guard attempt to take over the country; Antonescu defeats them. |
| 22 June 1941 | Antonescu, allied with Germany, declares war on the USSR without consulting the King. He recovers |

## Chronology

|                       |                                                                                                                                                                                                                                                     |
| --------------------- | ----------------------------------------------------------------------------------------------------------------------------------------------------------------------------------------------------------------------------------------------------- |
|                       | Bessarabia but becomes involved in Hitler's ideological war with the USSR proper. Puts his faith in Hitler and sacrifices Romanian troops to the Führer's cause.                                                                                      |
| 1 January 1943        | New year broadcast: King Michael criticises Romania's involvement in Hitler's war. He builds up a Resistance group with leaders of the democratic parties and has a radio link with Allied headquarters in the Middle East.                          |
| 23 August 1944        | King Michael's *coup d'état* overthrows Antonescu, takes Romania out of the Axis and shortens the war.                                                                                                                                                |
| 12 September 1944     | Romania signs an armistice with the three Allies.                                                                                                                                                                                                     |
| 6 March 1945          | Deputy Foreign Minister Vyshinsky during a visit to Bucharest forces King Michael to appoint a communist-controlled government under the premiership of Petru Groza, leader of a minor communist satellite party.                                    |
| 17 July–2 August 1945 | The three Allies meet in Potsdam and announce that a peace treaty would only be concluded in Romania with a recognised democratic government.                                                                                                         |
| 21 August 1945        | Petru Groza refuses to resign; King Michael goes on strike. He asks the three Allies to advise him on how to meet the Potsdam conditions.                                                                                                             |
| 8 November 1945       | A large demonstration on the King's name-day is fired upon. London and Washington are unable to give the King effective support against Moscow; he abandons his strike, and Groza and his communist government remain in power.                      |
| 19 November 1946      | Rigged Romanian elections.                                                                                                                                                                                                                            |
| 1 December 1946       | The King opens Parliament.                                                                                                                                                                                                                            |
| 10 February 1947      | Romania signs a peace treaty with the three Allies.                                                                                                                                                                                                   |
| November 1947         | King Michael and Queen Helen attend the wedding of Princess Elizabeth and Philip, Duke of Edinburgh in London. The King falls in love with Princess Anne of Bourbon Parma and they are unofficially engaged.                                          |
| 21 December 1947      | King Michael and Queen Helen arrive in Bucharest. Romanian Communist Party under great pressure from Moscow to get rid of the monarchy.                                                                                                               |
| 30 December 1947      | Petru Groza and Gheorghe Gheorghiu-Dej, leader of the Communist Party, force King Michael to sign an abdication.                                                                                                                                      |

| | |
|---|---|
| 3 January 1948 | King Michael and Queen Helen leave Romania for exile in Switzerland. |
| January 1948 | London and Washington recognise the People's Republic of Romania. |
| 20 February 1948 | Romanian Government strips King Michael of his citizenship. |
| 4 March–8 April 1948 | King Michael and Queen Helen visit the UK and USA. |
| 28 March 1948 | Romanian Government obtains a 98 per cent electoral victory. |
| 17 May 1948 | Romanian Government announces a decree nationalising King Michael's property in Romania. |
| 10 June 1948 | The wedding of King Michael and Princess Anne in Athens. |
| August 1948 | Romania's traditional Siguranţa [Secret Service] replaced by the Securitate. |
| January 1949 | Romania's gendarmerie replaced by a communist miliţia. |
| 26 March 1949 | First child, Margarita, born. |
| 3 May 1949 | Romanian National Committee in exile holds first meeting with ex-prime minister as chairman. Unable to operate as an entity. Chairman ex-prime minister Rădescu. |
| 14 September 1950 | Rădescu and his followers leave the National Committee. The King entrusts the chairmanship to Constantin Vişoianu, an ex-Foreign Minister. |
| 15 November 1950 | Second child, Helen, born. |
| 31 December 1950 | King Michael makes his first BBC broadcast to Romania. |
| February 1951 | US government offers the King an annual income and an estate in America; he declines. |
| April 1951 | While visiting Queen Helen in Florence Princess Elizabeth and her husband suggest that their cousins might like to live in England. |
| May 1951 | Lease taken on flat in Bramshill Hall near Reading. |
| 11 June 1951 | In Paris King Michael opens a cultural centre for Romanian students in exile. |
| July 1952 | Royal family move from Bramshill Hall to Ayot St Lawrence. Later they build up a successful chicken farm. |
| 1952 | In Romania Gheorghiu-Dej neutralises his rivals; becomes Prime Minister as well as First Secretary of the Communist Party. |

| | |
|---|---|
| 28 February 1953 | Third child, Irina, born. |
| 3 April 1953 | King Carol II dies of a heart attack. |
| September 1954 | Lear of Lear Aviation invites King Michael to join his Geneva firm. The King accepts. They move to Versoix, near Geneva. |
| September 1957 | The Lear firm closes. |
| 29 October 1957 | Fourth child, Sophie, is born. |
| 14 January 1958 | The King finds finance for his project to manufacture electronic equipment for automation. |
| July 1962 | King Michael's firm, Metravel S.A., is in danger of being swamped by German and Japanese industry. |
| 6 March 1964 | King Paul of Greece, one of Michael's best friends, dies. |
| May 1964 | King Michael joins the Droulia stockbrokers in New York. Youngest daughter, Maria, born in Copenhagen. |
| 19 March 1965 | In Romania Gheorghiu-Dej dies and is replaced by Nicolae Ceauşescu. In 1968 he openly opposes the Soviet invasion of Czechoslovakia. |
| 1972 | Membership of the Romanian National Committee is down to four. |
| 1974 | Vişoianu resigns from the National Committee. |
| 1975 | Funds for the National Committee and the University Foundation in Paris dry up. |
| 1976 | Royal family move to a more comfortable villa in Versoix. |
| 1978 | Nicolae Ceauşescu and his wife pay a state visit to London. The promotion of their personality cult is soon to become the Securitate's principal occupation. |
| 1979 | Queen Helen, who is becoming frail, moves from Florence to Lausanne. |
| 1979 | The King becomes aware that the communist hold on some East European countries is weakening; urges Romanians to prepare once more for liberation. |
| 1986 | The King has his first interview for many years with Radio Free Europe. |
| Autumn 1989 | Romania's neighbours, encouraged by Gorbachev, overthrow their Communist *régimes*. |
| 16 December 1989 | Romania's revolt begins in Timişoara. |
| 25 December 1989 | Ceauşescu and his wife are executed. A provisional government is set up by a group of |

|  |  |
|---|---|
|  | communist *apparatchiks* who had quarrelled with Ceaușescu. Led by Ion Iliescu, they call themselves The National Salvation Front. The democratic leaders after years of imprisonment or exile can offer little effective opposition. |
| April 1990 | Iliescu's Government give King Michael a visa, but refuse to allow him to visit Romania for Easter. |
| 20 May 1990 | The National Salvation Front easily win the elections. |
| 24 December 1990 | The King and Queen Anne visiting the tombs of his ancestors at Curtea de Argeș, are stopped on the road by Romanian Securitate agents and despatched back to Switzerland. |
| 1990 | Princess Margarita sets up a charity for the health and well-being of children and old people. |
| 1991 | The King visits England, the USA and France, talks to distinguished audiences on the problems facing Eastern Europe and Romania. |
| 1 June 1991 | Anniversary of Antonescu's execution. Romanian Parliament stands for a minute's silence. |
| 8 December 1991 | A new Romanian constitution becomes law. |
| 25 April 1992 | The King attends Resurrection Mass at Putna monastery; visits Bucharest and Curtea de Argeș. Huge crowds turn out to greet him; banned from Romania for the rest of Ion Iliescu's presidency. Misses 50th anniversary of his *coup d'état* and 75th anniversary of the union of Transylvania with the Old Kingdom. |
| 27 November 1992 | At the first elections under the new constitution Iliescu is elected president and his party wins most seats in Parliament. For the first time extreme right-wing parties are also represented in parliament. |
| March 1993 | Queen Anne visits Romania without the King. |
| 7–8 May 1995 | King Michael attends the celebration in London of the 50th anniversary of VE Day. |
| 11 November 1995 | Death of Corneliu Coposu. |
| June 1996 | Princess Margarita and Mr Radu Duda become engaged. |
| July 1996 | Queen Anne, accompanied by Princess Margarita and Mr Duda, pays a twelve-day visit to Romania. |
| 21 September 1996 | Princess Margarita and Mr Radu Duda married by the Metropolitan Damaskinos in Orthodox church in Lausanne. |

# Chronology

| | |
|---|---|
| 3 November 1996 | The Democratic Convention led by Emil Constantinescu defeat Ion Iliescu's party in the parliamentary election. |
| 18 November 1996 | Constantinescu defeats Iliescu in the presidential election. |
| 28 February 1997 | Under the new centrist *régime* of Constantinescu the King pays his first visit to Romania for five years. Agrees to campaign for Romania's entry into NATO. |
| Spring/Summer 1997 | King Michael promotes Romania's case for joining NATO in Belgium, Denmark, Luxemburg, the Netherlands, Norway and the United Kingdom. Partly for US domestic reasons, it is not selected. |
| 28 August 1997 | Constantinescu appeals to Romanians to support his drive against corruption. |
| 30 December 1997 | King Michael expresses his wish that Princess Margarita should inherit his rights and prerogatives. |
| 19 December 1999 | In a millennium speech King Michael attacks the type of republicanism forced on the Romanian people in 1990, which was intended to stifle democracy. |
| 10 December 2000 | Constantinescu withdraws from the presidential election and Iliescu is challenged by Tudor, leader of the extreme right-wing party; the King warns Romanians that voting for him will keep Romania out of Europe for decades. |
| 18 May 2001 | The King and Queen visit Romania. The King meets President Iliescu, who for some months has been working for a reconciliation. |
| 10 July 2001 | Law grants special rights to ex-heads of state, including King Michael. |
| Summer 2002 | King Michael again campaigns for Romanian accession to NATO. |
| September 2002 | Prince Radu appointed roving ambassador to promote Romania's long-term interests. A delicate operation. |
| March 2004 | Romana joins NATO. |
| 21 October 2004 | Government adopts bill – still to be approved by Parliament – under which King Michael would be compensated for loss of the Peleş estate. |
| December 2004 | Traian Băsescu, representing the Democratic Alliance, elected President and appoints Liberal Prime Minister. |

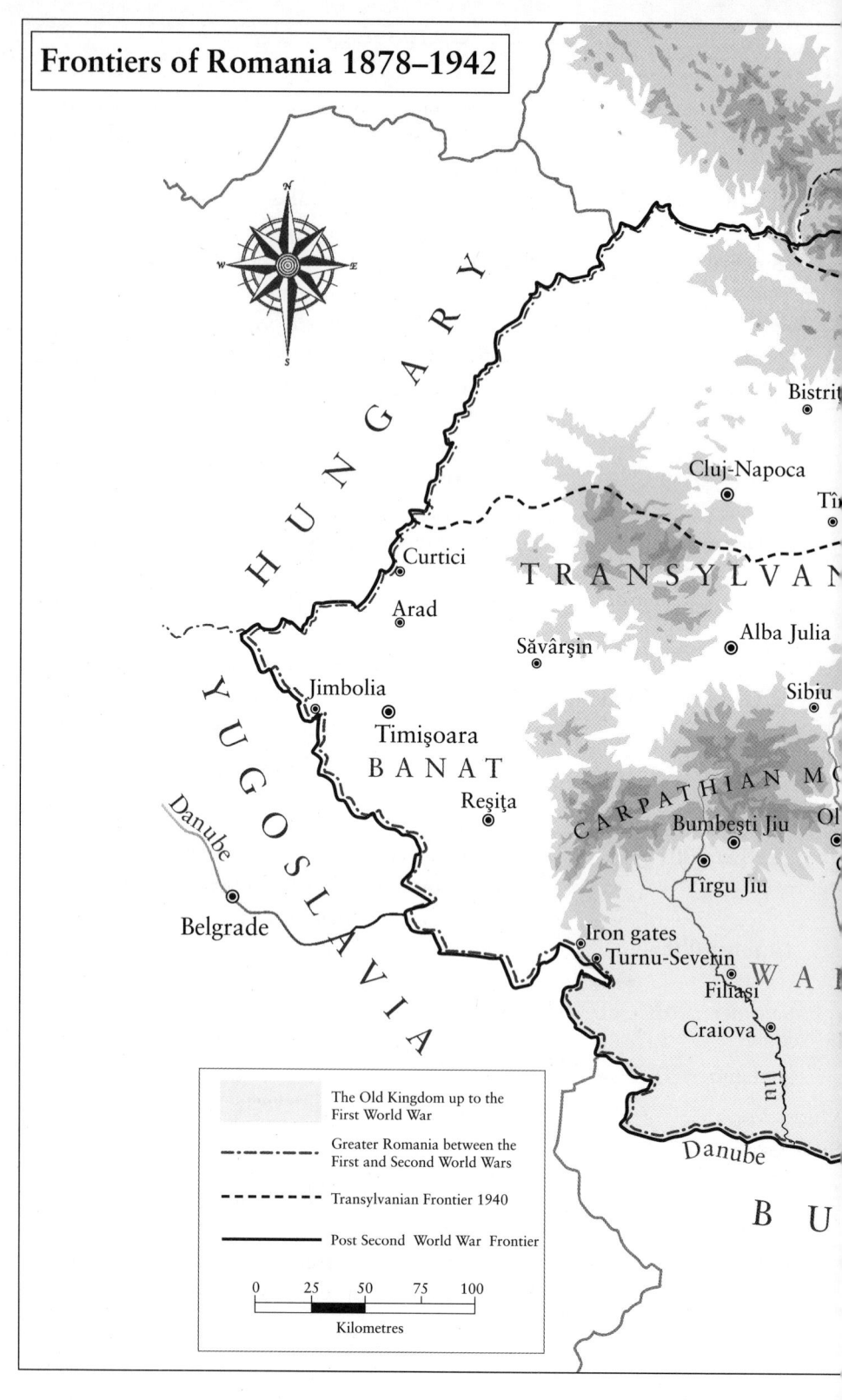

# PART ONE

Family, Childhood and Adolescence:
25 October 1921–6 September 1940

## ONE

### A Mother 'what makes me laugh': Papa in Exile

Romanians are of Romano/Dacian descent with an important Slavonic influence. They are the only Latin people east of the Adriatic and are mostly of the Orthodox rite. They inhabit Transylvania, Wallachia, and Moldavia, including Bessarabia.

When, during the early years of the second millennium, Romanian nobles (known as *boiers*) gave way to Magyar domination of Transylvania and emigrated with their followers to establish the principalities of Wallachia and Moldavia, they left behind Romanians who, although the largest ethnic group in the province, were without leaders or influence and found themselves at the bottom of the hierarchical pile of Hungarians, Saxons, Secklers and later Austrians. They were to remain so until autonomy for subjugated ethnic groups became part of European thinking in the nineteenth century. On the other hand Romanians of Wallachia and Moldavia – later known as the 'Old Kingdom' – were for most of their history directly ruled by Romanians. The boier elected by his peers as ruling prince had absolute powers, and the intrigue and corruption germane to this system produced a chronically unstable society and, with notable exceptions, a mediocre ruling class. During the relatively easy-going suzerainty of the Turks from the fifteenth to nineteenth centuries the Porte only sent in their own Greek Phanariot governors when they feared a Russian invasion of the principalities, which eventually took place in 1769.

During the nineteenth century, Romania's more progressive boiers and intellectuals were active in the European revolutions of 1848, were stimulated by the explosion of nationalism among their Transylvanian kinsmen and began to see all Romanians as part of Latin Europe. They looked to France for support and France, recognising the strategic value of a sphere of influence in this combustible region, reciprocated. In 1866 the two principalities, who, with the help of Napoleon III and Queen Victoria, had already achieved *de facto* union within the Ottoman empire, felt that the time had come to adopt a hereditary constitutional monarchy. In March their prime minister, Ion Brătianu, approached Prince Karl of Hohenzollern Sigmaringen, the older, Catholic branch of the Hohenzollern family. The King of Prussia was nervous about the reaction of the Great Powers to this further step towards Romanian independence. Bismarck, however, was optimistic and when Napoleon III let it be known discreetly that he too was in favour, Prince Karl decided to face Europe and the Sultan with a fait accompli. He obtained a Swiss passport under another name, bought a second class ticket to Odessa, wore glasses he did not need and as the Danube steamer docked at Turnu Severin and with the captain shouting for him to come back he jumped ashore from the gangway into his new country. He was 27.

In July 1866, Prince Carol, his Romanian name, gave his people a constitution based on the progressive one Belgium had adopted in 1831. It was to remain in force for fifty-seven years. It provided for a hereditary, foreign, constitutional monarchy with precisely circumscribed prerogatives. Civic rights were guaranteed though universal education for instance, was at the time no more than an expression of intent. By the end of Carol's reign it had improved sufficiently for male universal suffrage to become a credible proposition. In 1869 the disciplined, hard working Prince Carol married the somewhat fey Princess Elizabeth of Wied whose principal contribution to her new country was her – and through her – European recognition of Romania's cultural tradition. Their only child, Maria, was born in August 1870 but four years later died of scarlet fever. Relations deteriorated between them and in April 1889 Prince Carol brought to Romania a reluctant nephew, Prince Ferdinand of Hohenzollern-Sigmaringen, to be his heir.

King Michael has pointed out that when Prince Carol took the oath 'to rule as a constitutional monarch' his Romanian subjects attached more importance to the word 'rule' than to the word 'constitutional'.[1] A mid-nineteenth-century constitutional monarch in Eastern Europe was expected not only to lead his troops into battle, but also to take the initiative in peacetime administrative matters.

During the next half-century Romania, under his reign, became the most successful of the emerging south-ast European states, exporting grain, developing its large oil reserves, producing respected poets, playwrights, painters, historians, sculptors, composers and the only President of the League of Nations to hold that office twice running.

Within a decade Prince Carol had turned his tattered peasant army into a competent force of 50,000 men. In 1877 he led a successful Russian/Romanian attack against Osman Pasha's formidable defences at Plevna. Thus at the Berlin Congress of the Great Powers, Romania was awarded independence from Ottoman suzerainty and in 1881 Carol I crowned himself king with the heavy Plevna crown of iron melted down from Turkish canon.

To balance the unrelenting threat from Russia, in 1883 King Carol concluded a defence pact with the Austrian Empire, the only great power ready to do so, but a power which for centuries had dominated the Romanians of Transylvania and like Russia was one of Romania's traditional enemies. The treaty was later signed by Germany and Italy. Parliaments were not told of its existence, but on the outbreak of the First World War it blew up in the King's face. The royal family were split. Queen Elizabeth rallied in support of her husband. Only the British-born Princess Marie, granddaughter of Queen Victoria, daughter of Alfred, Duke of Edinburgh, wife of Crown Prince Ferdinand, King Carol's nephew, supported the Entente but she had the backing of almost all Romanians. At the critical Crown Council meeting on 3 August 1914 the King was supported by only one minister. The Liberal Prime Minister, Ionel Brătianu, son of the Ion Brătianu who had invited Karl Hohenzollern to Romania, announced that on such an important issue the Government would follow the will of the people and would remain neutral until ready to join the Allies.[2]

King Carol I died suddenly less than two months later. He had given his country a stability and prosperity it had never previously known. Though an autocrat committed by treaty and family to the Central European Powers, he had respected his people's wishes to join the Allies. Unlike his wife, who under the pen name of Carmen Sylva put Romanian culture on the European map and was probably better known in European intellectual and artistic circles than her husband, the King, totally committed to duty, was hard-headed and austere. Yet he had a sufficiently good eye to buy El Grecos at his personal expense for the castle of Peleș at a time when El Greco was unfashionable and obscure.

After King Carol's death Prince Ferdinand and Princess Marie became King and Queen of Romania, and their son Carol, the future father of Prince Michael, became Crown Prince. By the year 1940, when Michael had reached the age of 18, his father had provoked four constitutional crises which were to be responsible for much of his unhappiness and frustration in later life. The first of these occurred just over three years before Michael was born.

When she joined the hostilities in the summer of 1916, the war went badly for Romania. Her Russian ally, which should have been supporting her advance into Transylvania, was on the verge of a revolution. The Germans occupied Bucharest and the royal family and government fled to Iaşi, capital of Moldavia on the Russian border, ravaged by starvation and black typhus, during the coldest winter for fifty years.

Michael's English-born grandmother, Queen Marie, organised Red Cross work. She refused to wear gloves when working with typhus patients and inspired everyone she met with her own absolute confidence that the Allies would eventually win this war. King Ferdinand knew that in such dreadful conditions his peasant soldiers could not be expected to resist Bolshevik propaganda from across the frontier. In early May 1917 he went to the front and, in his stilted Romanian, electrified the army by promising them land – he, he said, would be the first to give it – and a larger part in public affairs.[3] At the second battle of Mărăşeşti the Romanian army, without the support of their Russian ally, held the combined German and Austrian forces, saved Odessa and possibly Moscow.

However, in November that year, Lenin concluded an armistice with the Central Powers and Romania, now isolated, had to choose either a separate peace with Germany or dismemberment. She chose the former, and Queen Marie had a blistering row with her husband, telling him that abdication would have been more honourable than acceptance of a German diktat. She may not have been in love with him but she respected and was very fond of 'Nando'. She knew how bitterly he, a Hohenzollern, regretted having allowed himself to be talked into an alliance with the Entente, which had brought his country to its knees. But his word once given was kept. And he had never once blamed his wife, who had pressed him hard to support the Entente rather than the Central Powers.

It was during this summer of 1918, when Romania was on the brink of destruction and his parents under the most severe stress of their lives, that Prince Carol dropped his first little bombshell.

This tall, fair-haired young man with a moustache and a nervous way with a cigarette had been unable to find for himself a satisfactory wartime activity. He was popular with the army but it was the Queen, not the Crown Prince, who had become the soldier's hero. At the age of 21 Prince Carol had a good mind and was a natural administrator. He realised, unlike many of his class, that the Great War marked a major turning point for European attitudes. But he lacked the essential self-discipline, the sense of duty and loyalty which were to be so outstanding among his son's qualities and which by the end of the war would win so much respect for his own father.

When not with his unit he spent much of his time with Ioana Lambrino, another refugee from Bucharest who was living in Iași with her mother. Ioana – known to her friends as Zizi – was attractive, determined, popular and intelligent, and one evening in June 1918 Carol dropped in on a small party at the Lambrino flat and proposed to her. No, he replied to one of her first questions, he had not asked the King's permission but felt sure that, faced with a *fait accompli*, he would do nothing about it; the post-war world would be very different from his father's, and royal families, too, must learn to be modern. On 2 September 1918 they eloped and were married on the 13th in Odessa. He was 23, she a year younger. He telegraphed the news to his father and the family and government were thrown into panic.

When, in 1866, Romanians had chosen a hereditary monarchy it was understood that a member of the royal family – and in particular the Crown Prince – would obtain the approval of the King and the government in power before marrying. His father, faced with the same problem, had given up the woman he loved – also a Romanian – rather than endanger the dynasty.

Anti-dynastic feeling had already grown alarmingly since Romania's separate peace with Germany and the Conservative Prime Minister, a good friend of the Lambrinos, now recommended that the succession should pass immediately to Carol's younger brother Nicholas. Queen Marie objected. Nicholas, she argued, did not have sufficient drive. Carol must somehow be saved. The couple were enticed back to Romania. Ioana was despatched to Ciuc in the Carpathian Mountains to live with her grandmother. Carol was condemned by the King to seventy-five days' confinement at the remote monastery of Horaița.

Isolated there, the Prince seems for the first time to have realised the immense damage his behaviour could do his country, particularly during the eventual peace conference that would decide Romania's future. When, on 15 September 1918, only four days after his arrival, Brigadier Râmniceanu, who acted as both warden and ADC, suggested that should the marriage be annulled he could still obtain an undertaking that would allow him to return to Ioana after the war, Carol showed some interest. On the 18th, returning exhausted and depressed from a long walk in the forest, he found his mother's buccaneering Canadian friend Colonel Boyle waiting for him, and after a long and difficult talk he agreed to the Râmniceanu formula. When he asked what precisely his relations with Ioana Lambrino would be during the period between the formal separation and the conclusion of a peace treaty, he was told that this would be at the King's discretion. He took this to mean that they would not be allowed to meet at all but was already too far committed and demoralised to put up any resistance. The day his parents paid him their first visit, bringing his little sister Ileana with them, he and his father had little of substance to discuss; everything had already been settled.[4]

Prince Carol's first letter had not reached Ioana Lambrino, and his letter of 29 September telling her that he had agreed to an 'official separation' until the end of the war, with no possibility of seeing each other until then, came as a great shock. However, she quickly discovered a safe way of communicating, and they exchanged passionate letters. She warned him to trust none of the people around him and that a 'legal separation' meant an 'absolute separation': the public could not be kept in a state of uncertainty until the end of the war. 'You must choose between the Crown and me.' In her letter of 2 November she reminded him, in desperation, that, since they were adults the marriage could only be annulled with the formal agreement of at least one of them.[5]

When Allied victories in Western Europe forced the Germans to withdraw from Romania, Carol was released so that he could take part in the Iaşi Armistice celebrations. Ioana Lambrino travelled down in a freezing, unlit, flea-ridden railway carriage, reaching Iaşi at two in the morning and walking through the snow to her mother's flat with somebody carrying her luggage. On Armistice Day Carol saw her in the street as she watched his carriage drive by and she wrote to him, 'je n'admets pas cette vie ridicule – toi dans ton palais et moi, ta femme, dans ma chambre vide et froide'.[6] A few days later, Prince Carol had a brief, emotional meeting with her at the house of one of his mother's ladies-in-waiting. He admitted that on Armistice Day he had given Prince Barbu Stirbey, one of the King's closest advisers, his written consent to an annulment of the marriage but promised that once peace had been concluded they would remarry. Next day he joined a new regiment and on 1 December 1918 took part in the parade of Allied troops formally re-entering the capital with the King and Queen riding side by side at their head.

On 9 January 1919, the civil court at Ilfov annulled the marriage of Prince Carol and Miss Lambrino in their absence. 'No' the Minister of War had told Ioana Lambrino two days before in Iaşi, she could not be Carol's mistress, there must be no child by them at least until Carol was suitably married, and she would be kept under close surveillance.[7] Yet surprisingly we find her back in Bucharest by the end of the month, asking Carol to bring sugar, flour, nuts and ten kilos of benzine for the parquets and all his love that evening, telling him, 'I love you madly but that does not prevent me from seeing the gulf which is opening between us.'[8] Carol's latest affair, with a young milliner sponsored by a hard-headed older man who threatened him with exposure, could well have persuaded the authorities that their Crown Prince was for the moment safer in Ioana Lambrino's arms than out of them. The couple were given unexpected freedom. Carol came to her house most evenings, listening to the gramophone, playing bridge with friends. She had the use of his car when he could not accompany her. When in June she became pregnant, she wrote to him, 'Since you so much desire it and beg me to keep the child, I shall resign myself and obey you.'[9]

The King asked his son to serve on a mission to the Far East. Carol shot himself in the leg and Queen Marie wrote in her diary, 'For the first time I nearly hated my son.'[10] The couple were banished to Prince Carol's house at Mănăstirea on the sweltering Danube delta and, in spite of the discomfort, seem to have spent a happy few months together. When the Hungarians attacked the Romanian army in Transylvania and Carol was instructed to rejoin his regiment, he obeyed but only after a period of arrant insubordination. He wrote a letter to the King, with copies to the leaders of all political parties, renouncing his right to the throne on behalf of himself and his heirs, together with his present rights as Crown Prince. The letter was ignored. In November he tried unsuccessfully to rally support from the presidents of the two legislative assemblies. Then over the Christmas holiday he quite unexpectedly collapsed and on 7 January 1920, in his parents' railway carriage at Bistrița, undertook never to see Ioana Lambrino alone again. He never did. Next day her son was born, just twelve months after the annulment of the marriage, and according to the birth certificate he was named Mircea Grigore Lambrino. The space for the father's name had been left blank, as was usual for illegitimate children.

Within a month Prince Carol had departed on a prolonged tour of the Far East and when he returned in October 1920, just a year before Michael's birth, he was far less of a love-sick outcast. At a banquet given in his honour at Peleș castle, he spoke extremely well and both Romanians and foreign diplomats expressed to the British Minister their hope that he had now freed himself from his domestic entanglements and would devote himself to the service of the state.

On 17 August, during his absence abroad, the Assembly had closed the loophole he had discovered in the Family Statutes by making it a legal obligation for members of the royal family to obtain the King's permission before marrying.[11] It was part of a new trend, which would grow in Europe, to give legal force to conventions that were previously considered to be matters of honour.

Michael's paternal grandparents, King Ferdinand and Queen Marie of Romania, had had a hard war but their support for the Allies had not wavered and they had emerged the shaken but victorious rulers of a Greater Romania. Michael's maternal grandparents, King Constantine and Queen Sophie of Greece, had also suffered during the war but the outcome for them had been disastrous.

King Constantine was the eldest son of King George I* – the first of the Danish line to reign in Greece – and of the Grand Duchess Olga of Russia. He married Princess Sophie, daughter of the enlightened Emperor Frederick of Germany and of 'Vicky', Queen Victoria's eldest daughter, and they had three sons, George, Paul and Alexander, and three daughters, Helen – to be Michael's mother – Irene and Katherine. When his father was assassinated in 1913 during the Balkan wars, Constantine as commander of the Greek forces had already almost doubled the size of his country and at the end of hostilities returned to Athens not only as the new King of the Hellenes but also as a Greek hero. The Greek dynasty at that time seemed secure, yet within four years was to be in tatters.

To the anger of his brother-in-law, the Kaiser, Constantine declared Greece's neutrality in the First World War. The majority of Greeks supported the Entente and when in October 1914 Turkey joined the German camp, the Greek Prime Minister, Eleftheros Venizelos, saw an opportunity of realising the dream of every Greek nationalist of the old school – the final defeat of Turkey and the renaissance of a Byzantine empire with Constantinople as its capital. The King did not agree, if only because Russia would never allow Constantinople to fall into anyone's hands but theirs. When, in October 1915, Bulgaria attacked Serbia, with which Greece had a mutual defence treaty, and King Constantine still refused to enter the war, Venizelos, without consulting him, invited the Allies to use Salonica as a base for Serbia's military support. Parliament supported Venizelos. The King removed Venizelos from office and henceforth was to find himself taking less and less account of Parliament and the electoral mandate.

By now the British and French governments had tagged King Constantine as pro-German and neither Lord Kitchener, the Tsar, nor King George V could change their minds. An Anglo-French force occupied Salonica. British and French warships shelled Athens and the naval blockade systematically starved

---

\* The 19-year-old Prince William, second son of Christian IX of Denmark, was proclaimed King George I of the Hellenes in March 1863, three years before the 27-year-old Prince Karl became Prince Carol of the united provinces of Wallachia and Moldavia.

out regions of Greece loyal to the King. On 10 June 1917 the French diplomatic representative in Athens, speaking on behalf of the Allies, demanded that King Constantine abdicate on the grounds that he had violated his oath to rule as a constitutional monarch. The King went into exile in Switzerland and was succeeded not by the Crown Prince George, whom the Allies also considered to be Germanophile, but by the inexperienced 23-year-old Prince Alexander.

By the year 1920 the Greek and Romanian royal families, who in many ways were so dissimilar, showed signs of drawing together, though this was undoubtedly due largely to Queen Marie's determination to find suitable spouses for her two most difficult children, Carol and Elisabeta.

Crown Prince George of Greece had proposed to Princess Elisabeta in 1914. Now, he proposed again and, to Queen Marie's delight, she accepted. Unlike Carol, he was an impeccable son, if anything a little too nice and straightforward for Elisabeta, who, according to her mother, 'is curiously silent and seldom expresses what she feels'.[12]

Since the exiled Greek family were without travel documents, Carol returned from his Far Eastern trip via Lucerne to escort Prince George to Bucharest for the official betrothal ceremony and at Queen Marie's suggestion his two eldest sisters, Helen and Irene, accompanied them.[13] Though Queen Sophie was not enthusiastic, her husband saw this as an opportunity to show the world that at least his children were no longer treated as pariahs. The three Greek guests were given charming rooms in the royal castle at Sinaia. George thought Carol 'ein guter Kerl, hard working and full of plans for the army and country',[14] whereas Helen thought him a retiring and not very affable character. But on 25 October 1920, their stay in Romania was cut short by news that their brother Alexander – King of Greece for just over three years – had died in Athens. During his reign he had not even been allowed to telephone his family in exile. His closest companion had been Miss Aspasia Manos, daughter of Colonel Petros Manos, Master of the King's Horse, whom he had married in November 1919. Now, only a year later, he had died horribly from blood poisoning, nursed through seven operations by his pregnant wife and with none of his family allowed back to see him.

The day after news of Alexander's death reached Sinaia Queen Marie was informed that her mother had died in Coburg. She left immediately and invited Helen and Irene to accompany her as far as Switzerland. To her great surprise, Carol, at the very last minute, asked to go with them. In Switzerland he saw rather more of Helen and before returning home asked King Constantine's permission to marry her.

Princess Helen's parents were not enthusiastic about their daughter's attachment to someone with Carol's reputation and, having had little experience of young men outside her family, she found it difficult to make up her mind. Her life had been turned upside down by Carol's proposal and grief for her favourite brother, but also because the Greeks had suddenly made a U-turn in favour of the monarchy.

Following King Constantine's exile in 1917, Greece had joined the Allied drive to liberate Macedonia and Serbia, and by July 1920, with considerable Allied logistical help, had penetrated Asia Minor as far as the Sea of Marmora. Venizelos had all but achieved his dream of a new Byzantium. After King Alexander's death, he offered the throne to Prince Paul, and when Paul refused it on the grounds that his father was already King of Greece, Venizelos called for elections to settle the matter once and for all. He was at the peak of his career and could not have doubted that the Greek people would support him in this new confrontation with the royal family. Yet he was so badly defeated by the unpredictable Greeks that he immediately left the country. King Constantine, somewhat taken aback by what had happened and conscious of his difficult relations with the Powers, hesitated, and it was not until a Greek plebiscite on 5 December again went overwhelmingly in his favour that he decided to return. Princess Helen wrote to a friend that while she felt she could love Carol, it was the thought of having to face life in Athens again without Alexander that had decided her to marry him.

King Constantine finally agreed to the marriage on condition that his future son-in-law had 'quite finished' with Zizi Lambrino.[15] The assurance was given and in November Carol sent a characteristically self-centred farewell to Ioana Lambrino telling her that he was engaged to a princess, which was all against his principles, and that she had agreed to console his deeply wounded heart.

On 10 March 1921 Crown Prince Carol of Romania and Princess Helen of Greece were married in Athens, only twelve days after Crown Prince George of Greece and Princess Elisabeta of Romania had been married in Bucharest. Yet King Constantine was still an outcast in Europe and King Ferdinand decided that, out of deference to the Allied Powers, he could not go to Athens as King Constantine's guest. He therefore absented himself from the marriage of his eldest son.

On 25 October 1921 Prince Michael was born into an unstable Europe – at the end of the war the three great empires of Russia, Austria and Turkey had collapsed. He was also born into a country which was radically different from pre-war Romania. Following the post-war accession of Bessarabia, Bukovina and Transylvania, it had doubled in size and ethnic complexity. Moreover, as a consequence of King Ferdinand's promise to his soldiers in May 1917, the long political era dominated by the Conservative and the Liberal parties had come to an end. Eighteen months before Michael's birth, two-thirds of the largest estates, including the agricultural land of the Royal Domains, had been distributedto the peasantry who would in future play a part in the country's political life. The Conservative Party of great landowners had been virtually destroyed.

Romania's Social Democratic Party had in 1920 split on familiar lines, those who supported affiliation with the Soviet Comintern becoming the Romanian Communist Party – which was to be made illegal in 1924 – and the majority remaining loyal to Social Democracy but never coming to power. There was no Romanian extreme right-wing party in 1921. A terrorist organisation led by the charismatic Corneliu Codreanu had pledged itself to destroy Jews, communists, corruption and the parliamentary system but in normal times it would have remained on the fringe of Romanian politics. As it was, the rise of the Nazi cult in Central Europe ensured that by the late 1930s it had named itself the Iron Guard, with assassins operating within a secure cell structure, with representation in the National Assembly and by the end of the decade links with the German National Socialists.

But in 1921, when Prince Michael was born, the only effective opposition to the Liberal Party seemed to fall to two parties who were strangers to Old Kingdom politics. One of these was the Peasant Party recently formed to represent the extensive new peasant franchise and led by a schoolmaster called Ion Mihalache. The other, Juliu Maniu's National Party of Transylvanian Romanians, dated back to the 1880s and drew its strength from centuries of Romanian resistance to Austro-Hungarian domination. On 1 December 1918, over a thousand National Party delegates met in the ancient Transylvanian city of Alba Julia, proclaimed their union with the Old Kingdom and despatched a delegation to so inform King Ferdinand in Bucharest.

The King recognised the constitutional value of a strong Opposition and, in any case, rather liked Juliu Maniu, a relatively poor man with little regard for favours, a Catholic like himself though of the Uniate Orthodox rite. However, under the influence of Queen Marie, Știrbey and Brătianu, he was to keep the Liberals in power for almost a decade. The fiery Ionel Brătianu and the analytical Prince Știrbey had shown a loyalty during the roughest moments of the war which had not yet become obvious in the unconventional behaviour of the newcomers, Maniu and Mihalache. Moreover, Prince Știrbey had been the first Romanian to recognise in the Queen, when she was still the 'butterfly'

Crown Princess of the early 1900s,* the intelligence and gallantry which was to serve Romania so well in the desperate years to come. He was her greatest admirer and became her life-long lover.

Maniu and Mihalache were enraged by what they saw as a conspiracy to keep them out of power, and unfortunately their mistrust of the Liberals and Liberal influence with the Crown became obsessive. Although for generations Maniu's Transylvanian Party had fought for union under a single Crown with Romanians of the Old Kingdom, they shunned the coronation ceremony of King Ferdinand and Queen Marie which took place on 15 October 1922 in the Transylvanian town of Alba Julia. Although in 1923 Brătianu produced a sound constitution for an enlarged postwar Romania, now including many citizens who had no historical links with the one of 1866, Maniu's conviction that he was incapable of being fair to Transylvanian interests became so widespread that instead of setting a seal on the new territorial unity of the Romanian people it inflamed their differences and temporarily weakened the Crown's unifying role. When in 1925 Prince Carol dropped his second constitutional bombshell and his father this time decided that he was unfit to become king, the Opposition leaders convinced themselves that Carol had been the victim of a plot engineered by Brătianu and Ştirbey. It was a misjudgement that was to do lasting harm to the country and to Michael personally. Even eighteen years later during the Second World War, when the adult King Michael, together with Juliu Maniu and the brother of Ionel Brătianu, attempted a *coup d'état* that would enable Romania to break with the Axis, he had to carry a heavy burden inherited from his father and the politics of the 1920s.

When Princess Helen took her baby to Athens in January 1922 to see her family Michael had so delighted King Constantine that occasionally when the three of them were alone together, she caught glimpses of the man she had known as a child. But now he was sick in body and spirit. He had never recovered from a muffed wartime operation on his lung and had suffered yet another haemorrhage during the *Te Deum* celebrated just before he left for the front. He had been persuaded to follow Venizelos's policy and drive deep into Kemal Ataturk's territory in Asia Minor. But the Allies, who were by now having second thoughts about the destruction of Turkey, had suspended their

---

* After being manoeuvred into marriage with Prince Ferdinand when she was just 17, Princess Marie was kept in virtual isolation until after the birth of her second child. When she obtained a little more freedom Queen Victoria's daughter 'Vicky' described her as 'beautiful and gifted' and compared her to a butterfly 'which sometimes burns her pretty wings'. 'Butterfly' became her nickname in the family.

logistical support of the Greek army and, when he turned to them for advice, they coldly told him 'to hold on'. Princess Helen, who could not be sure of seeing her father alive again, extended her stay for three months. It was tactless of her at the beginning of her marriage and, to make matters worse, she finally returned to Romania in April 1922 accompanied by her sister Irina.

Michael by now was 'grunting, spitting and screaming with laughter, a real joy'.[16] In July Princess Helen asked her mother to lend her the family play-pen. 'Instead of crawling he rolls when he wants to get somewhere & then drags himself up and tries to stand. St John* is afraid of his hurting himself & if I have to order one from England it wld cost about a million.'[17] In August he started to say Mama – 'so pleased with himself he screams it out all day. He gets such laughing fits over everything, he holds his breath like other children do with crying fits.'[18]

But the immense pleasure Michael gave her was marred by a rumour she had first heard while in Greece, that her husband was having an affair with a Romanian officer's wife called Elena Lupescu.

During the first shock she had told her mother 'if I were to live my life over again I should certainly not marry'.[19] Later she seemed to accept a marriage which, though unlikely to improve, need not deteriorate further. If Carol wanted mistresses, she decided, she would not be the first woman to find herself in that position. She would concentrate on bringing up Michael and fulfilling her duties as crown princess. For a time she seemed happier, more in tune with her life in Romania. On 8 June 1922 she attended the marriage of Carol's second sister, Marie, to Alexander, King of Yugoslavia but for her the highlight of the wedding was when the Infante Alfonso of Spain told her that the Duke of York, who was representing his father King George V at the ceremony, had admitted to being ashamed of how her father had been treated by the Allies.[20]

That autumn the fortunes of the Greek royal family collapsed for the second time. In August the Greek army, exhausted after a year of 'hanging on' without Allied support, suffered a shattering defeat. The Turks then sacked Smyrna with a brutality that shocked Europe. Greek army anti-monarchists held the King responsible and on 26 September 1922 he abdicated in favour of his son the Crown Prince George and again left for exile, this time in Sicily. King George had no influence with the Greek Revolutionary Committee and only a last-minute intervention by the British Foreign Office saved Prince Andrew** from execution. Immediately after the Romanian coronation Princess Helen

---

\* Miss St John had been Princess Helen's nanny and was now Michael's.
\*\* Father of the Duke of Edinburgh, who had been in command of the Greek 12th Army division.

and her sister Irene joined their parents in Palermo, leaving Michael, who was twelve months old, to spend Christmas with his father and grandparents.

On 11 January 1923 King Constantine died of a heart attack. Prince Carol left immediately for Palermo to represent the Romanian family. But King George was not allowed to attend his father's funeral, nor to hold a service in Greece, nor even to fly the palace flag at half-mast. 'How cruel it is', Queen Marie wrote to Queen Sophie, 'to think that you were not yet hit hard enough.'[21]

When Princess Helen returned from Palermo in the spring of 1923, all Bucharest was buzzing with what was known as 'the Lupescu affair'. Queen Marie and her husband blamed Princess Helen for her apparent inability or unwillingness to take Carol in hand. She had been out of the country for nine of the first twenty-four months of her marriage and when in Romania she was accompanied either by her sister Irene, her younger sister Katherine, or, after her father's death, by her mother, of whom Queen Marie once said, 'her conventionality, her preconceived ideas, tastes and prejudices withered all joie de vivre in her. She always felt defeated, so she attracted defeat.'[22] Her clannish family, Queen Marie rightly suspected, were helping to distance Helen from Carol. The palace wags muttered 'here comes Carol and his wives' and the Queen herself referred to her son as 'Carol and Co.'.

When, in July 1924, Prince Carol and his wife went on holiday to London and, after calling briefly at Florence to see her family, returned to Sinaia on their own, Marie wrote to Queen Sophie:

> I do miss Tim [the family nickname for Princess Irene]. It seems so strange to see Sitta without her shadow.
>
> Of course it is not a bad thing for Sitta and Carol to be a little together without any other member of the family, a thing they have never been since they married hardly, and have a little bit of a quiet time together with their splendid Mihai.[23]

They were not together for long. When Carol suggested that they renew normal married relations, Helen felt unable to agree. After staying with her mother for a while, in November she was back in Foişor writing that she was feeling 'lonely and horrid and miserable'.[24] Carol was on a tour of inspection which would be followed by a week's shooting and then another stint of inspection.

> Baby has become insufferable & is nasty and disagreeable with me. If he develops in character like some of his relations have, I refuse to have any more to do with him. . . . St John is in despair about it and says I don't see him enough. I suppose it's true.[25]

A month later Michael, according to his mother, had become 'very amiable again and talks fluently at last and has grown up expressions', along with odd phrases he had picked up from Shakespearean stories his nurse read to him. Overnight his mother became 'Sitta' and 'My Fair Lady'.

> It's too impertinent and when he gets anything he spits . . . Uncle Pa gave him a sweet little dog, a cocker. He promptly called it Mumbo & wld not hear of any other name. They are inseparable & he is full of cuts and scratches & bruises from playing with it.[26]

When Michael was three his mother turned the dining room into a playroom.[27] He was a sturdy and intelligent little boy who could already use a camera competently. A year later he began to ride. His first languages were English and Romanian, which he spoke equally well. He was a determined child and when he locked himself in his room and in spite of all cajoling and threats refused to come out, the door had finally to be forced.

According to his mother's diary, once when he found a half-drowned cat in a ditch he held it out to his mother with 'My heart bleeds to see him thus.' At church one day with Queen Marie and his mother, he refused to take communion. When Helen lifted him to the altar he shook his head and told them firmly that he never took wine in the morning. This was the little boy who when he was five would be plunged by his father into the second domestic and constitutional crisis of King Ferdinand's reign.

Michael hid his feelings from anyone but his nurse and his mother 'what makes me laugh' [*sic*] and this tendency became more pronounced as he grew up. In spite of all the protection that Miss St John and his parents gave him, an intelligent and sensitive boy of four must have been aware of the tension building up between his mother and father. His first memory of his mother was in a chapel of the Patriarchy, which she visited quite often and always took him with her.

> I turned my head and was suddenly looking at her and I saw her crying in front of the icon. Later I did not dare to ask her why she was crying. I knew more or less what it was about. Since then I have never been able to get that picture out of my memory. That was my oldest memory of mama. It was at a time when I went every evening to her bedroom to say my prayers and whenever I was beside her I remembered seeing her crying at the icon.[28]

The seeds of Prince Carol's estrangement from his parents were more complex. He had had a governess who let him see that she did not approve of his mother and later a Swiss tutor whose republicanism amounted to little more than an endless diatribe against everything Hohenzollern. Carol was also inflamed by an intense hatred of the two men – Știrbey and Brătianu – who were closest to his parents – Prince Știrbey because he was his mother's lover and Brătianu who, since he became premier in January 1922, had, he felt, missed no opportunity to denigrate him. When in 1924 his parents went on a tour of Western Europe, the Crown Prince was excluded from the *ad interim* Regency Council and he was never able to discover whether this had been done with his father's consent. After Brătianu had indirectly accused an Air Force procurement commission headed by Prince Carol of corruption and on Carol's insistence an official inquiry had been set up which found all members of the commission innocent of any misconduct, the ensuing scandal split the country into pro- and anti-Carol camps: an attack on the Liberal Party would henceforth often carry an echo intended for the ears of the King and Queen.

However, the principal cause of the looming dynastic crisis was not political but rather the Crown Prince's relationship with Madame Lupescu. But for her, the first woman he had met capable of holding him, Prince Carol would probably have continued to live with Princess Helen, having vicarious affairs which posed no threat to the dynasty and a running battle with Brătianu, which would have petered out soon after his father's death two years later.

In 1925 Elena Lupescu[29] was 29, two years younger than Carol. Her father was Jewish and, in order to be allowed to own a chemist's shop, he had Romanianised his name of Wolff to Lupescu (pertaining to a wolf). Elena went to a convent school. By 1912 the old man had set up a novelty and perfume shop in Iași and she must have been there at the same time as Carol and Zizi Lambrino. Elenuța, as she was known in the family, was distinguished by her colouring rather than her features. She had red-gold hair, a dead white skin, and heavily lidded eyes. In Iași she was a great success with many of the officers and in 1916 married Lt Tampeanu.

She set out to meet Prince Carol at the King Carol I Foundation of which he was honorary president. He was intrigued and by 1923 attached.

In the autumn of 1925, Carol told his wife that this was not an affair but a lasting relationship. He confided in his parents shortly before his mother's birthday on 29 October. Although, when speaking with his father he implied that his mother's relationship with Prince Știrbey justified his own behaviour, he must have known that Barbu Știrbey was no threat to the dynasty. He must have often seen them together (as an ADC described them), discussing something while gazing absentmindedly at the crowd, noticeable only for their extraordinary charm and distinction, at ease with each other as Carol would never be in public with Madame Lupescu.

The King did not banish Elena Lupescu, and when she asked for a passport to travel abroad it was promptly granted. She would presumably have found it difficult to return.

In November 1925, when Alexandra, the English Queen Mother, died, Prince Carol was the appropriate person to represent his father at the funeral. King Ferdinand vaguely hoped that the change of scene and going into 'these very royal circles' would make him see things differently.[30] Carol, who hedged when they urged him to be back for Christmas, was, his mother said, 'in such a state of nerves that neither Papa, I nor Sitta dared go beyond a certain limit because we were afraid that he might do something desperate'.[31] He was seen off at the station by the whole family, travelling part of the way with Queen Sophie at the end of one of her interminable visits and being, she remembered later, particularly kind and attentive. He attended the funeral on 27 November, spent a week with the British royal family, was cheerful with his young sister Ileana when he saw her at her school and seemed to assume that they would be travelling back to Bucharest together for Christmas. Then, on 4 December, he telephoned her to say that he would not be able to make it. He had arranged for his motor to be delivered to Paris, where he now joined Elena Lupescu and drove with her to Milan.

On Monday, 21 December, Princess Helen received a badly typed letter from her husband dated the 12th. His mother, he wrote, had described him as 'an object of disdain and scandal for everybody'. 'I can't go on occupying a situation which I'm considered not worthy of. Perhaps morally they are right, humanly certainly not. I can't live like an intangible idol I'm not made that way.'[32] He enclosed letters for his mother and father which she immediately took to Queen Marie. 'Bald, cold, expressionless letters' Queen Marie called them, 'no excuses, not even a regret, no message to his boy.'[33]

> We sent for H.M. All three we sat there as though struck by lightning. I was expecting Barbo [Prince Barbu Știrbey]. He came. When we told him he nearly collapsed. Brătianu . . . came at 10 2 [*sic*].[34]

In the letter to his father Carol had described his decision, for which he gave no explanation, as 'irrevocable'. He had asked to be allowed to renounce his prerogatives as crown prince, to be removed from the royal family and to be given a name under which he could create a new civil status. He undertook not to return to Romania for ten years. Ferdinand told Hiottu, Minister of the Royal Court, that this time he would accept his son's renunciation.

When Hiottu went to Milan on 24 December his instructions were precise. Should Prince Carol show signs of a serious psychological crisis – meaning that he was not aware of the consequences of his action – then he should be asked to return alone to Sinaia within 24 hours and to put himself under the King's orders. If, however, it was clear to Hiottu that Carol had indeed taken a properly thought-out and 'irrevocable' decision, then the undertaking he had given in his letter should be incorporated in a formal declaration which should include a phrase by which Carol would renounce those rights which under the laws of the country would then pass from him to his son, Michael. After satisfying himself about Prince Carol's mental condition Hiottu asked him to copy out and sign the following declaration:

> I declare through the present act my willingness to renounce irrevocably all my rights, titles and prerogatives, which are mine by virtue of the constitution and the statutes of the royal family, in the capacity of Prince and heir to the throne and member of the royal family. I renounce these rights in favour of my son Michael. I hereby declare that I shall have no further claims to the throne and obligate myself, for the good of the country, not to return to Romania for a period of ten years and, even after that time, only with the explicit consent of my sovereign, the King.[35]

On receiving confirmation that the document had been signed, the King called a special meeting of the Crown Council for 31 December.

King Ferdinand received the principal political leaders individually before the meeting. Iorga, who was joint president with Maniu of the National Party, told his sovereign that by refusing any further negotiation with Prince Carol he had become 'the victim of the biggest stupidity ever perpetrated on the country'. When the King protested that he had acted on his own free will, Iorga replied, 'under the influence of two men (Brătianu and Ştirbey) to whom I shall never offer my hand for the part they have played in this act'.

Maniu proposed a characteristically long and tortuous procedure which the King turned down, knowing that it would open the whole issue to public debate.[36]

Mihalache advised prudence in a matter involving such 'incalculable dangers for the future', but he had nothing further to say when the King described his son as 'a rotten branch in the Dynasty that must be cut off to save the Crown'.

Opening the proceedings, King Ferdinand told the Crown Council that had Prince Carol's act not been without precedent he would still have illusions and hopes. As it was, he would be disloyal to the tradition of his House and his past and would be acting against his feelings as King and Romanian if he did not unhesitatingly follow the dictates of his duty to the Crown and accept the renunciation. He therefore asked the country's leaders to support him and to help explain to the country why he had accepted Prince Carol's renunciation and had recognised Prince Michael as the Crown Prince of Romania.[37]

During the debate Brătianu proposed a regency, should this become necessary, composed of Prince Nicholas, the Patriarch Miron Cristea and Gheorghe Buzdugan, Chief Justice of the Court of Appeal. This was approved.

Next day, 1 January 1926, the *Monitor Oficial* informed a shocked Romania that Crown Prince Carol's 'irrevocable renunciation to the succession to the throne and of all prerogatives appertaining to that rank, including membership of the Royal Family', had been accepted.[38]

On 4 January 1926 Parliament debated the Crown Council's findings and adopted a bill accepting their decision and the consequent proclamation of Prince Michael as Crown Prince of Romania. This 'Act of 4 January' would be at the centre of the constitutional struggle which dominated the next five years.

'A hellish week,' Helen wrote to her mother. 'Imagine our Christmas. The Butterflies have taken our little one to Sinaia & I will go on the 1st.' They had told Michael that his father was ill in Paris but he still went looking for him in his bedroom.[39]

On Christmas Eve Helen wrote to her husband, imploring him

> think everything over again because don't forget, whatever people say, you are popular here, specially with the army. Has a man the right to do this thing vis a vis of his God and his country?[40]

Carol's reply seemed categoric. He could not change his decision, especially after his father had sent him a message which was in the form of an ultimatum. He himself had proposed that he should be banished for ten years but had never supposed that they would accept it. The case was not so grave for the country as the first time\* because there was Michael and, therefore, constitutional continuity. He asked her to forgive him

> for all the harm I've done to you and all the sorrow I've given you. Poor baby but hees [*sic*] small enough and he'll be able to forget his Papa that others have not found worthy of him.
>
> Thank you again for having been a real and helpful friend to me.
>
> With ever so much love and kisses. A big hug kiss perhaps the last I'll ever be allowed to send to Baby.[41]

---

\* Prince Carol was referring to his marriage with Miss Lambrino.

# TWO

## A Flamboyant Father and his Mistress: Mama in Exile

The day before the parliamentary Act of 4 January 1926 Princess Helen had written a conciliatory letter to her husband which she had asked him to keep to himself and to destroy. He did neither. She told him that she should have thrown the letters he had asked her to give his parents onto the fire. She admitted that when he had suggested returning to normal married life after their holiday in London she should not have said 'no' so categorically. When she had heard of the Crown Council's decision, she had fought, she said, 'like a wild tiger' to have the process postponed.[1]

In a letter to her mother she describes her mother-in-law as 'false, heartless and scheming' and the King little better since he was under the influence of Ştirbey, 'who is everything that is vile on God's earth'. What Carol did, he did openly: 'Poor boy, all I can feel for him is the deepest pity . . . will see him secretly for a day if I can.'[2] A month later her brother George describes her as 'skin and bones'.[3] She was not allowed to go abroad in case she got in touch with Carol; she did not leave the house because people stared at her, and for a time the family were afraid that she was heading for a complete break-down.

'Carol Caraiman', Prince Carol's rarely used new name, was treated generously. When Ioana Lambrino filed a ten-million-franc suit for desertion in the French courts the Romanian Legation in Paris was instructed to give the Prince all help necessary to win the case. His substantial income from private property was paid regularly into his Paris bank. His Paris house was in the smart suburb of Neuilly and, for weekends, Madame Lupescu bought the Château de Coesmes in Normandy. They enjoyed a cosy domesticity.[4] Carol read books on archeology and military matters, she detective stories. He did not care for night clubs, was a bad dancer and, in any case, Madame Lupescu hardly ever touched alcohol.

Over tea one afternoon Queen Marie confided to the British Minister that, while she had to be careful not to go too far, she would continue to oppose her husband's inclination to favour the Transylvanian party led by Juliu Maniu.[5] King Ferdinand who had a longer political vision than his Liberal advisers, saw the constitutional advantage of a valid Opposition and in March 1926 he tried to appoint a coalition of Opposition parties under Maniu's premiership. Overnight Queen Marie and Prince Știrbey persuaded him that only the Liberals, or General Averescu's People's Party, which toed the Liberal line, could be trusted to keep Carol out of the country. Next morning Maniu was putting the finishing touches to his coalition cabinet when he was told that Averescu had just left the Palace, having been asked to form a government entirely of his own party.*

Maniu and Mihalache reacted to what they saw as another example of Liberal chicanery by joining forces and forming the National Peasant Party led by Maniu, with Mihalache as his deputy. 'This is what His Majesty wanted', Vaida Voevod, a senior member of the National Peasant Party, remarked – 'large homogeneous parties, the Liberal Party and our party'.[6] True, but the last thing King Ferdinand would want was an Opposition committed, by their hatred of Carol's enemies, to letting him return on his own terms. A long regency, which, with Carol no longer the heir, seemed likely, would be unpopular but, until his son had demonstrated convincingly that he was fit to rule, he must at all costs be prevented from usurping his grandson's throne. In August King Ferdinand visited his son privately in Paris with the promise that he would forgive him if he would give up Madame Lupescu and return to his wife. Carol, however, was unrelenting, drawing on Princess Helen's private letter of 3 January to argue with his father that he, not his wife, was the wronged party, and informing his wife that, whether or not she wanted a divorce, he was now going to take the necessary steps to obtain one.

When in November rumours began to circulate about King Ferdinand's health, party rivalry over the Act of 4 January flared up again. Queen Marie returned early from a tour of the United States. On 9 December Princess Helen wrote to her mother: 'Ferdinand has cancer. As soon as Missy returned, the doctors told her. The people guessed the truth. Intrigues raging. Hartman of Paris made an exploratory operation but could not remove it.'[7] In January, if he was strong enough to go to Paris, they would start radium treatment.

Princess Helen dreaded the unwanted advice concerning Michael that would inevitably accompany a regency, but seems to have held her own. Twelve months later the British Minister would still be able to inform London that

---

\* General Averescu, the hero of Mărășești, had gone into politics after the war.

'Prince Michael is being brought up with absolute simplicity and the Princess has closed her doors to all newspaper reporters and film agents.'[8]

Michael was by now writing short essays about dogs, cats and chalk, and on the opposite page of his exercise book personal notes such as 'Tomorrow I am going to Cotroceni to play with the electric car.' On one page he wrote 'God made Adam and Eve' and immediately below – what really mattered – 'I can drive the Buick very well and fast'.[9]

He was a reserved and observant child and greatly missed his father. His mother made sure that he mentioned him every evening in his prayers. Carol sent him messages and presents – a pedal car for Easter – but this was not enough. Entering a room and recognising one of the Air Force officers there he said, to everyone's embarrassment, 'This is the officer who used to work with Daddy, but when will Daddy come?'[10] When, therefore, Queen Sophie suggested that she have Alexander's daughter, Alexandra,* to stay, Princess Helen jumped at the idea: it would do Michael 'a world of good', she thought, to have a child his own age to play with instead of always grown-ups.

The visit did not go well. Alexandra was, according to Princess Helen, terribly spoiled; her nanny had been encouraged always to give way to her. 'For Michael', Princess Helen noted, 'excellent to be treated like that & has already subdued and improved him but sorry for her if this bringing up continues.'[11] Three weeks later

> They were fighting like cats and dogs . . . meals were absolutely impossible. Food flew round the room . . . Driving to Cotroceni in the same carriage was also an impossibility, the thumping, yelling, crying and quarelling became the talk of the town as nothing wld stop them. . . . I have watched Sandra and I have watched Michael and both are equally to blame. She hits and pinches him & runs away laughing for protection so he thumps out at her. On their own they are perfect angels.[12]

As King Ferdinand's death drew closer, so did the Carlist threat. King Ferdinand and Juliu Maniu sent simultaneous messages to Carol, the former repeating the conditions he had offered him in August, the latter assuring him that if he left Madame Lupescu the National Peasant Party would institute action for the annulment of the Act of 4 January 1926.[13] Carol, however, remained uncompromising and in May 1927, when his father was dying, he attempted a *coup d'état* to coincide with a National Peasant rally

---

\* Princess Alexandra was to marry King Peter of Yugoslavia in 1944.

to be held at Alba Julia. He was staying with English friends at the time and was about to climb into his plane at Croydon airport, when Home Office agents moved in to stop him and to impound copies of the manifesto he intended to scatter over the Alba Julia meeting. The British declared him *persona non grata*. The Romanian Government thanked them for their prompt action. Queen Marie wrote a letter of apology to King George V. Juliu Maniu demonstrated his remarkable authority over his followers by preventing the adoption of any resolution at the Alba Julia assembly which would strengthen the Prince's case.

Averescu, who was by now employing unacceptably harsh measures against Carol's supporters, was on 22 June replaced by Ionel Brătianu as Prime Minister, a move which must have given the King more peace of mind during the closing days of his life. Princess Helen, though she despised Brătianu's electoral methods, was also reassured by his return to power. His unscrupulousness plus his determination to keep Carol permanently at bay was the best defence she could hope for for Michael and herself.[14]

One of King Ferdinand's last official acts was to send a letter to the new Prime Minister in which he prayed for a country which would be able, under the rule of his grandson Michael, to consolidate and prosper. He called upon Carol to do everything in his power to allow this to happen.[15]

In July, Princess Helen and her son, who, after Alexandra's visit had gone down to Queen Marie's house near the beautiful beaches of Mamaia, returned to Bucharest and on the 14th drove up to Sinaia. Michael remembers once seeing his grandfather lying on a *chaise-longue* in a small pavilion which, when he became too ill to walk, had been built for him on a flat piece of grass outside Pelişor. But that had been earlier. By now, Princess Helen noted, the King was difficult to understand. She cancelled their return to Mamaia. King Ferdinand's nephew, Friedel, head of the house of Hohenzollern-Sigmaringen, was on his way from Germany. The King had not asked for Carol.

In a letter to her mother Princess Helen describes how different members of the family coped with their grief.

> Mignon [she wrote] is very sweet to him and after she has been with him for ten minutes, she says 'now let's go up and have a good laugh'.
> They went to 'Petalutra's'* room to listen to her new gramophone. She has all Beethoven symphonies and the music and knowing that he is dying become one . . . Moments when P cries unrestrainedly in front of everybody.

---

\*   Greek for 'butterfly'.

Such a curious mixture . . . Lady Dragon* arrives Monday. She will be shocked at the difference but I don't suppose she will show anything. Before she left she told me quite naturally 'I can't be sorry for Papa when I am with him, he is no more the father I knew, he has a different face, voice, manner & figure so how can I be sorry for someone I don't know. Only when I am not with him I remember him as he was. Then I cry.'

Towards evening on the 18th July he seemed a little better & rather talkative, though it was mostly unintelligible. Next day he was half asleep until at about 2 o'clock in the morning of the 20th when he asked the nurse to call A. Ma. who was in the next room. She came immediately as she was not asleep & he said to her quite quietly 'I am so tired I don't know what to do & I feel if I go to sleep I will be much better.' She put her arms round him & he went to sleep, that is to say he passed away so quietly with his head on her shoulder, & fancy she only remarked he was dead because he began to grow cold.[16]

According to Raoul Bossy, newly appointed Secretary General of the Regency, at a hastily summoned meeting of ministers and court officials, Ioan Duca, Minister of the Interior, proposed that the official *communiqué* should say that King Ferdinand died in the arms of Queen Marie – although, in fact, when the last rites were being given the family, after so many hours of anxiety and exhaustion, were resting on the first floor. The proposal was agreed since 'it will make a good impression on the public'[17] and Princess Helen had chosen to use the more comfortable version in her letter to her mother.

To reduce the risk of Carlist disorders Ionel Brătianu arranged for the funeral to take place four days later. King George II of Greece, now estranged from Princess Elisabeta and living mostly in London, could not get there in time. Carol asked permission to attend and was refused.

Michael was proclaimed king a few hours after the King's death and when he asked next morning why people were calling him 'Your Majesty', his quick-witted mother replied 'It's just another nickname, dear.' They travelled down from Sinaia for the swearing in of the Regents at 2 o'clock that afternoon.

When the Speaker of the packed House announced 'His Majesty the King', there appeared 'a little boy with his hair brushed, dressed in white and holding the hand of his mother who was wearing full mourning'.[18] Michael recognised the applause – from which members of the Opposition parties refrained – with one of his little salutes. Then, seated on a raised chair, he watched while the

---

\* Princess Helen's name for Princess Elisabeta.

three Regents each laid his hand on a huge Bible and swore allegiance to the new King and the constitution.

A press photograph of King Michael emerging from the Parliament building frowning and concentrating on something was given the caption 'The Young King's Concern about his New Responsibilities'. According to his mother, his attention had divided three ways during the proceedings – between the cheering inside the Parliament, the firing of canon outside and the piece of plaster on his knee. The photographer, she thought, had probably caught him while he was counting the steps and trying not to walk on the cracks.

A week after the parliamentary Act of 4 January 1926, King Ferdinand had added a codicil to his will by which he revoked that part of the inheritance which he had left to his eldest son[19] – mainly the property at Sinaia – and left it instead to Michael with a provision that during his minority Queen Marie should enjoy its use and income. Princess Helen, the only member of the family without any personal fortune, was not mentioned in the will but during the apportioning of the estate Queen Marie obtained the agreement of the rest of the family that the palace at Mamaia should be made over to her.[20] Marie also made Peleş available for Princess Helen to decorate and use for herself and her son. In a letter of 11 August 1927, her brother George writes that Helen is arranging Carmen Sylva's old room for herself. Michael would live just above in rooms overlooking the drive and the big lawn.

When Parliament reassembled in mid-October 1927 it was expected to run for the full four-year parliamentary term and, with its Liberal majority, to guarantee Carol's exile. Yet, within weeks, the whole political scene changed dramatically. Soon after his father's death Carol had declared his right to 'respond to an appeal by the people',[21] and when Ionel Brătianu suddenly died of blood poisoning on 24 November 1927 the second major obstacle to his return had been removed. In effect the great Brătianu dynasty had come to an end. Vintila Brătianu, who replaced him as premier and leader of the party, lacked the overriding ambition, arrogance and determination which had made his brother Ionel such a dominant figure.

Carol renewed his campaign for a divorce, informing the new premier that Princess Helen had had a lover before they were married – a blatant lie – sending Queen Marie a copy of Princess Helen's letter of 3 January 1926. Maniu, Ştirbey and Vintila Brătianu decided that this vilification of Princess Helen must stop. The marriage was dissolved on 21 July 1928.

Vintila Brătianu inherited his brother's chauvinistic economic policy which had aroused such bad feeling abroad that after a disastrous harvest he was unable to raise a desperately needed international loan. By the summer of 1928 public opinion had begun to swing in favour of Maniu. He even had the support of Queen Marie who had recognised that the growing dissatisfaction with the Liberal Party in Romania and abroad could become a threat to the dynasty. In the winter of 1928 Maniu, after spending almost a decade in the wilderness, was invited by the Regency to form an administration, and elections on 12 December, though they were scrupulously fair, gave his party 78 per cent of the votes returned.

In normal circumstances Juliu Maniu, with such a large parliamentary majority, might well have revived the prosperity, the morale and the image of his country. The world economic slump of 1929, the absence of an adult monarch as head of state together with the inadequacy of the Regency were largely responsible for his failure. He went a long way towards cleaning up the administration: certainly he and his close advisers were incorruptible. But before he could reverse his predecessors' economic policies Romania was struck by the first wave of the American depression. In the spring of 1929 foreign investors were already drawing in their horns and very soon the whole of Eastern Europe would be trying to survive with the very protectionist policies that Maniu had aimed to get rid of. Raoul Bossy, admittedly no friend of Maniu, described Romania at that time as 'a boat without an oarsman being driven by the wind'.[22]

The week following the death on 7 October 1929 of Gheorghe Buzdugan, third Regent after Prince Nicholas and the sixty-year-old Patriarch Miron Cristea, was to become a turning point for Carol's ambitions. The Prince remarked at the time that 'this unexpected occurrence allows Maniu to resolve my question by my joining the Regency'.[23] Maniu, if he had the same objective in mind, was prepared to overlook the fact that Prince Carol with his foot in the door would not be satisfied with a Regency post. Brătianu, when proposing the three Regents at the Crown Council meeting of December 1925, had assumed that since he himself would still be in control, theirs would be a purely representational function. Had Maniu wished to seize the opportunity of Buzdugan's death to strengthen the Regency he would have encouraged Queen Marie to join and give it the authority it so badly needed. Instead he invited her in terms that she considered insulting and then appointed in her place a nonentity called Sărățianu.

The Regency lost all credibility and public opinion swung abruptly in favour of the Carlists. Only Vintila Brătianu and his immediate supporters were putting up any resistance to Carol's return. Averescu – at one time known for his unshakable support of the Act of 4 January – had by now a permanent link man with the Prince. Professor Iorga, leader of the rump National Party, lectured regularly at the Sorbonne and saw Prince Carol quite often in Paris. Maniu forbade 'alarmism' without any success. Only the Iron Guard showed vision when they welcomed Carol's return as a means of creating a climate favourable to the liquidation of party-political democracy in Romania.

On 12 April 1930 Prince Carol sent Maniu a message warning him that he had until the end of the month to decide whether to help him. He sent another at the end of May to say that he no longer needed his help. He knew a few kind words would break down the barrier with his mother. He could exploit dissension within the National Peasant and Liberal parties. The Regency Council was ineffective. There was no insurmountable barrier between him and his son's throne.

Although Queen Marie would have preferred a more talkative grandchild she grew very fond of Michael and when he was older became his close confidant. But although he was taken every morning to see her at Cotroceni she knew very well that Helen preferred him to see her side of the family. In 1928 cousins Dolla, Margarita and Philip (later the Duke of Edinburgh) – Prince Andrew's children – came to stay in Mamaia. The following year it was Prince Paul of Yugoslavia, his wife Olga, and their two little boys. Olga, eldest daughter of Princess Helen's Uncle Nicholas and sister of Princess Marina, later Duchess of Kent, was to be one of 'Sitta's' closest friends during the dreadful years that followed her ex-husband's return.

Mr Hill came out in 1929 to tutor Michael and the boy seemed to do well with him. The young King Michael accepted without fuss ceremonies that went with his new status. In Arthur Gould Lee's words, 'He would watch parading troops with interest, generally returning their salutes and never intimating that he might be tired. Sometimes he would ask his mother whether he could go and play now and when she had to say no he never showed resentment.'[24]

Back in Bucharest rumours were rife and many National Peasants believed that so long as they obtained credit for engineering Carol's accession to the throne he would adopt their party as wholeheartedly as King Ferdinand had adopted the Liberals. Their leader was less sanguine. For his drive and administrative ability Maniu wanted the Prince in the Regency but not necessarily on the throne. During the preparatory negotiations in Paris, Maniu's agents had, therefore, attached three conditions to his return. He must accept the post of Principal Regent. He must break completely with his mistress. He must undertake a reconciliation with his ex-wife. Prince Carol agreed to all three, though not in writing.

While Madame Lupescu in the Neuilly house could listen to these negotiations from an adjoining room, Princess Helen in Bucharest, whose fate and that of her son hung no less than Madame Lupescu's on the outcome of the talks, was kept completely in the dark. Maniu, who clearly knew little about Princess Helen, feared – in his own words – that, had he confided in her, she would have exploited his trust, perhaps even started a civil war.

On Tuesday, 3 June 1930 Carol left Paris by car. Next day Maniu was told of the Prince's proposed return and sent back a message advising him to wait until the spring. On Thursday the 5th Michael's grandmother left for a fortnight's visit to Germany timed to include the passion play at Oberammergau: Maniu was informed that Carol would arrive at 1800 hr the following day.

Prince Carol took off from Munich next morning, 6 June, flew over Austria and Hungary without incident but the pilot had to come down not far from Cluj owing to shortage of oil. When he failed to arrive on time at Group 11 HQ where he was expected, the Air Force sent out a plane which soon located him. When Carol's plane again had to land he transferred to the Air Force plane for the rest of his journey. Over Bucharest it was by now too dark to land at the little plateau near Cotroceni and he switched to Baneasă, where the runway could be illuminated. He touched down at 2205 – four hours late, a muffled-up figure whom nobody met or immediately recognised. After feeling some qualms about his vulnerability, he was finally driven to Cotroceni, where Prince Nicholas embraced him warmly.

One of Prince Carol's first moves was to telephone Maniu and announce 'Mr Maniu, I've arrived.'

Maniu welcomed him; they awaited him, he said, at the Presidency of the Council of Ministers, where he would be a guest of the Government. Carol hesitated, then said that he had better stay where he was. But he would like to speak to Maniu. Their first meeting on 6 June 1930 took place, therefore, not on the Prime Minister's ground but on Carol's.

Carol began by saying that since Romania's political situation was growing worse he would like to help the country recover.

Maniu replied that personally he could take no action that would dethrone King Michael, to whom he had sworn an oath of allegiance. However, he proposed certain conditions which, if fulfilled, would make it possible for the Government to abrogate the Act of 4 January 1926 so that the throne could revert to King Ferdinand's eldest son.

First, Prince Carol should become a member of the Regency, probably in place of Sărățeanu. Second, he must fulfil the undertaking he had given during the Paris negotiations, that is, restore his marriage with Princess Helen and separate from Madame Lupescu. Princess Helen was mother of the present king and according to all constitutional and social usage she should become queen. In any case she could not be replaced by a royal mistress who, given the experience of other countries, would mix directly in politics. Moreover, when he became king he must accept all the limitations which the basic law of the country had put in the way of an authoritarian monarchical *régime*.

Carol, who knew that the Prime Minister could use the laws in force to expel him, limited himself to saying that though he saw the situation differently he was ready to accept these formulas in principle. He would be happy to serve on the Regency though he reserved the right to become king after at most six months.

Maniu must have left the Palace knowing that Carol's undertakings would be worthless. Prince Carol, for his part, had noted that in spite of his forceful arguments, Maniu had accepted his arrival without a murmur. He was therefore to spend the rest of the night strengthening his position with political leaders who attached less importance than Maniu to constitutional and ethical niceties. He won over Ion Mihalache, deputy leader of the National Peasant Party, and Professor Gheorghe Brătianu, leader of the dissenting Young Liberals. He talked to influential military figures and the leaders of the smaller political parties. Next morning, 7 June, he told Maniu that since he now had the support of the army and Parliament he would forthwith seek both the annulment of the Act of 4 January and his proclamation as king. Newspapers were already carrying banner headlines 'Long Live the Saviour of the Greater Romania'. King Michael asked his mother why there were so many flowers and so much bunting in the streets.

Princess Helen broke her rule never to criticise her ex-husband in front of their son; he was now eight and she told him, as best she could, what had happened. But if he came back 'like a sneak', Michael asked, why had he been allowed to stay? When she said that in some countries he might have been killed, Michael, who by now did not remember his father, said that that might have been best.[25] During lunch on 6 June he asked three questions: Did those ministers come to see you to talk about that? What does Granny think about it? And Uncle Nicky? The answers she felt she could not give him were that Maniu and his ministers had not confided in her, that Granny had sent her son a telegram of congratulation from Oberammergau, and that Uncle Nicky had, for his own reasons, been at the centre of the plot. It was becoming clear by now that the proposed annulment of the 1926 Act would be interpreted as passing the succession directly from Ferdinand to Carol – as if Michael had never been king. His father was now to take over, and later sell even the private property – the pictures and some small factories in the Prahova valley – that King Ferdinand had inherited from King Carol I and had bequeathed to Michael in the codicil to his will.

Flowers and letters of condolence began to arrive at Kiselev, and the moody Elisabeta of Greece called on Helen and was sweet and understanding. Carol had been to see the family that morning, and when he had started to rave against his ex-wife, she had cut him short with, 'People having your character always hate the person they have hurt most.'[26]

When Miron Cristea told Prince Carol in a private audience that the Regents should not be forced to violate their oath to King Michael, he replied that he, too, would violate it should he become first regent and then king. 'Better', he told Cristea, 'that you gentlemen violate your oath than that I violate mine.'[27] Early that morning Maniu had failed to obtain his cabinet's approval for the conditions he had put to the Prince at Cotroceni. In the afternoon a group of some thirty parliamentarians came to express the hope that the National Peasant Party would not make difficulties about the restoration of Prince Carol. They were greeted by his deputy, Ion Mihalache. Knowing that he was beaten, Maniu decided to protect his personal reputation for integrity and resign rather than break his oath to King Michael. The post of prime minister could be filled temporarily by his deputy Mihalache or, if absolutely necessary, by the Foreign Minister, Mironescu.

Mironescu – once described as a man with an eternal smile on his lips, a jovial moustache as white as a head of beer – 'took me by the arms in my office', said Raoul Bossy, 'and whispered in my ear "What unexpected things are happening. For twenty four hours I must be prime minister . . . I would have rather that Mihalache had carried the burden but he refused because of the question of the oath – a pure formality"'.[28] At nine that evening Mironescu and his ministers swore their allegiance to King Michael in the presence of the three Regents and so became the government that would betray him the following day.

At 11 o'clock next morning, 8 June, the Senate and the Lower House met separately and, as expected, decided to annul the Act of 4 January 1926 and, as a form of compensation, to accord the title of Mare Voevod de Alba Julia to Prince Michael.

At a joint meeting of both Houses that afternoon, with the public gallery packed and Princess Helen and her son listening to the proceedings on their wireless set, not a single political leader opposed the motion that the Act of 4 January 1926 be anulled and for the throne to pass directly to 'the rightful heir of King Ferdinand'. When the vote was taken at 3 o'clock there was only one dissenter – a Liberal who had ignored his party's order to stay away. The Patriarch had disappeared for a moment, leaving his vicar to vote on his behalf.

Mironescu then left for Cotroceni and escorted Carol, accompanied by Prince Nicholas, through rapturous crowds back to the Parliament. After being sworn in, the King addressed the assembly of both Houses. He had been forced in 1926, he told them, to give up his privileges as Crown Prince by people who had tried to break the link between himself and everything Romanian. Yet he had not returned with the idea of revenge. He asked all Romanians without distinction of political opinion to gather round the throne and work for the prosperity of the country. He omitted some flattering references to his ex-wife which the speech-writers had inserted to win him additional support but his speech was, nevertheless, acclaimed with tremendous applause.

It had taken four years and five months to destroy the Act of 4 January 1926, which had been intended to protect the country, the throne and the child king from Carol's irresponsibility. Michael listened fascinated to his father's voice. His mother was shocked by Carol's duplicity, particularly when he quoted from the Bible and made protestations of patriotism. She knew that he had broken his voluntary pledge not to return to the country for ten years and that, since a king could only be replaced constitutionally by death or abdication, the whole afternoon's ceremony had been no more than a dressed-up *coup d'état*. 'People', she told her diary, 'who were insulting Carol only a few days ago were scratching [*sic*] and bowing and creeping before him, calling him saviour.'[29] In a country which she considered to be without any effective communal morality, she felt isolated and afraid, knowing that she and her son had virtually no defence against Carol's deep-seated resentment.

Within two hours of taking the oath King Carol came to Princess Helen's house in Chaussée Kiselev. Elisabeta had already warned her that her ex-husband wanted the boy to live with him, and when Prince Nicholas burst in to tell her that Carol expected Michael at the palace she was horrified. The least Carol could do, she told Nicholas, was to come and see the child in her own house. Nicholas, who had always been afraid of his elder brother, agreed to give him her message and a quarter of an hour later he telephoned to say that Carol would come immediately.

> Suddenly Nicky arrived, he can be charming when he wants to, he kissed me & told me not to give way & put his arm round me & just couldnt have been nicer. He told me Carol was coming with Elisabeta . . . suddenly we

heard the door open downstairs . . . then he appeared looking just as usual, in uniform. He came towards me quite naturally and shook hands & said 'hallo'! The first impression I had was why didnt he kiss my hand & what a funny thing it was to say 'hallo.' Then I realised we were standing opposite each other speechless so I said, 'Carol the only thing for us to do is to be friends for the child's sake.' He said 'I quite agree, and let us not talk about the past.' Then he sat down on the arm of a chair & lit a cigarette. I could see he was agitated & was trying to hide it. I went upstairs to fetch Michael. Poor little thing, I had prepared him for the interview, but I could see he was rather frightened. He kept on looking at me anxiously and said 'Mummy what should I do.' I told him it would be quite alright and he must just be natural & answer Papa's questions. My legs were trembling so, I could hardly walk. When we came into the room Carol rushed at him & kissed him saying 'of course you know who I am.' Then he knelt down before him & stared into his eyes for quite five minutes without saying a word . . . I wonder why this family must always be so theatrical.[30]

Today, King Michael still remembers this meeting.

I knew that he existed. I had seen photographs of him but I could make no connection between him as a person and what I knew of him. I would have liked to go into hiding somewhere. If I had been a snail I would have gone right back into my shell. It seems that Princess Elizabeth was also there. Mama had gone over to a window and was crying. . . . That is my first memory of my father. It seemed to me that he was happy, and happy because of me.[31]

When King Carol said he would now take the boy back to the Palace, the paralysed Princess Helen could only ask him, since it was his bedtime, not to keep him too long. Then he asked to see his tutor – an odd thing to do, she thought, at this moment, though 'finesse and manners have never been his strong point'.[32] Michael went up to get his hat and brought Mr Hill down with him, and after he had exchanged a few banalities with the tutor he took Michael. When Princess Helen saw her son going away with him, her self-control gave way and she rushed into her room.

Michael drove with his father and Aunt Elisabeta to the Palace in Calea Victoriei. They went out on an upstairs balcony, standing all together for the crowds in Piața Palatului to see. The people cheered madly, many in the half-light mistaking Elisabeta for Helen and assuming that a reconciliation had already taken place. Next day she received messages of gratitude for her sacrifice on the country's behalf.

> I long to pack up and leave immediately [she told her diary], but what about poor darling little Michael. He keeps on repeating Mummy, please don't let Papa take me away from you. Yesterday he came to my room during the pause in his lessons & said 'I just wanted to ask you how you are feeling Mummy & to see if you were crying.'[33]

A few days later King George V and Queen Mary returned from Sandringham to London and invited Helen's brother George for tea. He had already had a talk with Titulescu, the distinguished Romanian Minister in London, but judging from the letter he wrote to his sister on 11 June they had only reached a general conclusion about the advice to give her. It was Queen Mary who provided a firm and detailed programme for Helen. At the start of the meeting in Buckingham Palace, 'U. Georgie was absolutely livid and made such a noise, that a footman opened the door to see if any accident had happened.' When the King had quietened down, Queen Mary helped Helen's brother to bring the conversation round to practicalities. They both agreed that although anyone in Helen's position would think seriously of 'leaving the country and chucking everything', this was not what they would advise. To remain and become queen, though a great sacrifice,

> would at least allow you to be near Baby and insure you financially. Also they hope it would push Butterfly back into the background. Then U. Georgie added 'her great sacrifice would perhaps save that bl . . . dy dynasty for that country of immoral . . . (can't say the word).
> A. May said that by reconciliation she understood that you both should be on speaking terms, that you should appear together for opening of Parliament, court functions and state occasions. Apart from that she said you ought to be allowed to live in your own house, have your own household and separate fortune. You ought to be able to have complete freedom to arrange your private life as you chose. She added that all this was far from an ideal life, one she would wish for nobody. But that you probably would be one of the very few ones to stand it. Then U. Georgie bellowed out: 'I don't approve of it really, but I suppose there is nothing else to be done. But don't let that d . . . d . . . give her a kiss, he can content himself in kissing her hand!' . . . He was really touching all he said about you. I was astonished to see again how very well informed he seemed to be.[34]

The day after Queen Mary, her choleric husband and King George II of Greece had discussed the advantages and disadvantages for Princess Helen of becoming Queen of Romania, she herself, over tea with Prince Nicholas in Bucharest, was beginning to doubt whether she would be given that choice. The King, Prince Nicholas told her, requested a letter from her in which she would admit that it was she, not her ex-husband, who was resisting a reconciliation. This, Nicholas explained, would move public pressure from Carol to her. When she sent King Carol a letter which made the admission he had required of her but also made it clear that this had been done under pressure, the King's revenge was immediate. That evening the family were to gather at the station to welcome – in Queen Marie's own words when speaking to the press – a mother who had cut short her European tour 'to be of service to her son in the great and heavy task that is before him'.[35] Princess Helen was now ordered not to appear at the station but to have Michael ready to accompany his father. So the little boy stood on the platform with his Aunt Elisabeta and Uncle Nicholas, knowing that his mother should have been there, watching his grandmother greet his father in an embrace so theatrical that it was featured in the *Evening Standard* next day. 'Carol', Queen Marie noticed as they drove away from the station, 'was proud and a little shy. Micky was dumb.'[36]

Princess Helen, who had gone to bed early, 'feeling as if she had been beaten round the town', was told next day that the King had decided that she would be known not as 'Her Majesty the Queen', but simply as 'Her Majesty'. Carol, Nicholas explained, 'was in a blue funk' about the whole thing and hoped that by suppressing the queen bit he would stand a better chance of safeguarding his divorce.[37] Meanwhile the King, having forbidden her to discuss the question of a reconciliation, was spreading his own version unchecked, and in the *Daily Telegraph* of 13 June we read, 'it is stated that Princess Helen's resistance to the idea of a reconciliation is weakening. It is popularly expected that Queen Marie's return will see this effected within a few days.'

When Prince Nicholas asked her to lunch with her ex-husband so that they could have a frank talk, particularly about Michael's upbringing, Carol entertained her with such a boisterous account of his flight back to Romania that she had no opportunity to tackle him about Michael. She was even left with the impression that reconciliation might still be possible and had he offered it that day on terms similar to those suggested by Queen Mary in London she might well have accepted rather than run any further risk of losing her son. She simply did not know where she stood with Carol.

During June 1930, until Princess Helen took Michael up to Peleş Castle for the summer, relations between her and the King were probably as amiable as they would ever be. The day Michael sat the end of school year examinations – which went well – Carol told them over lunch how busy he was and when Michael had gone to his room, talked to Helen about his hopes and plans. Another day he described to her the Order of Suffering, a medal which would portray him with a cross and a crown of thorns as a reminder of his great suffering in exile. He seemed vulnerable that afternoon and she felt able to put in a word for some of the people he had treated rather brutally since his return.[38] Another time she sat speechless while he told her that 'Magda' Lupescu had refused to marry him until 'the day she saw him reinstalled in his rightful position, dealing out punishments to those who had made him suffer'.[39]

But when they appeared together for the first time in public at Curtea de Argeş, the ancient Transylvanian city where members of the royal family are buried, on the anniversary of King Ferdinand's death King Carol ignored her, passing through doors ahead of her. He behaved naturally so long as the family were unobserved, but the moment they were exposed to the people again he acted out the part of a man who had begged for forgiveness and reconciliation and had been spurned by a hard-hearted woman who had no interest in the good of the country. On the train, his compartment door was left open so that all the family and household could see the elaborately framed photograph of Madame Lupescu on his table.

King Carol and his brother Nicholas moved into Foişor on 1 August for the summer and Princess Helen's life became a nightmare. Michael met his father at Sinaia station and twenty minutes later ran excitedly into her room saying 'Look, Mummy, what a beautiful watch Papa has given me and he says it is from the nice lady whose photograph he has next to his bed and when I said thank you he said, "you must not thank me, you must thank her, and, you know, she lives in Paris!" Who is she?' he asked, and two days later 'Is she Papa's wife?'[40]

Again Carol pressed her to admit in public that it was she who prevented the annulment of their divorce, this time in front of Maniu and his Foreign Secretary, Titulescu, whom he had invited to lunch. Again she refused and when she finally summoned up courage to ask Carol whether some serious reason prevented him from agreeing to annul the divorce, he burst out, 'For me it is a question of either taking my luggage and leaving the country or of the divorce remaining intact.'[41] It was not true, as Princess Helen thought possible, that he had already married his mistress. But Madame Lupescu was on the Orient Express heading for Bucharest and would spend the rest of August hidden in Foişor seeing no one but Carol, who by now seemed to be trapped painfully between his mistress and world opinion.

A week later Princess Helen and her son left for her house in Mamaia by the sea[42] and when two months later they returned to Bucharest the new *régime* was already installed. The old palace staff had been replaced within weeks of Carol's arrival and a friend from his days in exile, Puiu Dumitrescu, appointed to the newly created post of the King's Private Secretary. Madame Lupescu was already attracting her personal *camarilla*, in which Dumitrescu was to play a prominent part. When the King had lied to him about Madame Lupescu's return, Juliu Maniu had resigned and had been replaced by the more amenable Gheorghe Mironescu. The policy the Liberal Party had pursued with such determination for the last four and a half years was already in tatters. King Carol was setting up his personal intelligence service. Ştirbey was spied on continuously but was careful to say nothing that could be interpreted as 'plotting'. His family moved to Switzerland. From the day of her arrival from Germany Carol had ensured that his mother would have no political role in Romania. Within a few months she was under pressure to exile herself in her house at Balcic in the remote province of Dobrugea.

As for Princess Helen, her house was under permanent police surveillance, her visitors' book examined daily. She was forbidden to meet politicians or appear on public occasions. Her expense allowance was cut and – since Prince Michael was too young to drink wine – her cellar removed. She was not permitted to fly her flag on her car. She, for her part, no longer shielded her ex-husband, and when forbidden to see foreign representatives in Bucharest, she made sure that the Japanese Minister knew why his appointment had been cancelled.

Although, to satisfy public opinion, Michael was allowed to sleep in his mother's house, King Carol seemed determined to demolish her plans for his education. He now spent most of his day at the Palace. 'He leaves at 11,' his mother noted in her diary, 'and returns at half past seven. He is only permitted to have his two hours of Romanian lessons from 8.30 to 10.30. Everything else has been scrapped, no preparation, no more English, no carpentry, no botany, no French, nothing.'[43] His tutor was not allowed to accompany him into the Palace, where he appears to have spent most of the day with the chauffeurs. He was taught not to say 'please' and 'thank you' which his father thought effeminate. 'Papa is mad', Michael told his mother.[44]

On 25 October, his ninth birthday, Michael, following family tradition, joined the army. He wore the uniform with beret that Carol had designed for his regiment – the Mountain Chasseurs – and six other cadets and two officers came home with him to pay their respects to Princess Helen.

Queen Marie was warned not to ask Princess Helen to her birthday party and Michael said to his Romanian teacher, 'One day I am going to tell Papa what an absolutely horrid man he is.'[45] Princess Helen was ordered to absent herself from the annual palace Christmas party but Michael brought her presents – little boxes and odds and ends, she described them, 'to make you happy because you are always so sad'.[46] She decorated a small Christmas tree but Michael was made to spend the entire holiday at Sinaia. Carol undoubtedly felt that his son should be taken out of the rarefied atmosphere of his mother's household, but Queen Marie was scandalised at his behaviour and in a letter of 31 March wrote:

> He allows him to smoke and swear. He teaches him to be rude and greedy, allows him to listen to dreadful conversations, and has put him in the company of precocious young girls instead of with boys his own age.[47]

Princess Helen did not have permission to go to Foișor but when Michael caught flu, she defied Carol, walked in past the guard and sat with her son in his room for half an hour while Elisabeta kept Carol at bay.

This standing up to him, Queen Marie warned her, would only make things worse. Although Carol had told his sister, Elisabeta, that his ex-wife must eventually leave the country of her own free will and without Michael, for the moment he made her life as unbearable as he could by keeping her in a kind of limbo. Michael, at the time, could not understand why his father was using him to hurt his mother. Now he thinks that it was part of a programme pursued by Madame Lupescu and others to keep his mother out of the Palace and to throw the dynasty off balance.

King George V of England had written to her mother at the end of December 1930 advising Helen to break out of the terrible situation she was in. While she remained in Romania, he said, she would be miserable, bullied by Carol, and her health would finally break under the strain. She might then be forced to leave in a hurry. Better that she plan now to leave under conditions acceptable to her – that is, in a dignified way and with the sympathy of all decent people. 'And if in the future he really became mad & was kicked out, she might return again to her son, who knows?'[48]

Such was King George's dislike for Carol that he was not prepared to approach him personally. However, his advice, everyone agreed, was sound. By the spring of 1931, Princess Helen was beginning to see that by remaining in Romania she was in danger of putting her own feelings before the interests of her child. He was at the centre of the struggle between her and her ex-husband and, by witnessing his mother's humiliation almost daily, he was being destroyed. A solid legal agreement must be negotiated between her and King Carol whereby, should she agree to live abroad, she would have access to her son, have enough to live on and a proper title. And since this could not be done by a Romanian, a foreign mediator who would not be brow-beaten by Carol must be found. It was Mignon's husband, the dry-humoured King Alexander of Yugoslavia who, in May 1931, offered to take on the unenviable task. It would, nevertheless, take a stormy eighteen months to produce an agreement which would ensure a sound academic education for Michael and for his mother an independent life away from the horrors of her existence in Romania.

As soon as negotiations with King Alexander began to take shape King Carol realised that the whole thing would be debated at length in Parliament under the cynical eye of the foreign press. Although he had confided to King Alexander that life was impossible for him so long as his ex-wife remained in Romania, he now let it be known that he had never intended her to reside abroad, only to travel more frequently. King Alexander played his hand. Princess Helen took a few months' holiday in London and Paris and on the day before Michael's birthday was met on the station platform by a little boy who looked thinner after his tonsil operation and whose first question was 'don't you think Papa would marry you again now that you have been away so long?'[49]

Five weeks later, she had to leave him again and go urgently to the hospital in Frankfurt where her mother, Queen Sophie, died on 13 January 1932.

In February, 1932 her son wrote:

Dear Mama,
Will you please excuse me for not having written since so long but only to day have I found out where you are.
I was very so very sad about Amamas death and I thought so much of you.
I'm so pleased that you liked my photo . . . I had very good and nice xmas hollydays [sic] in Sinaia.
The snow was so good that I made a lot of winter sports and really got on very well with skying [sic] etc.[50]

In her own letter of condolence of 14 January Queen Marie confirmed that Michael was getting on well with his skiing and that she saw him daily.

> He is less shy, more communicative but says little about his feelings. I speak to him about you as often as I can but feeling a certain mystery about things. I suppose he is instinctively careful.[51]

On 17 February Princess Helen, working through her lawyer and with help from Princess Elisabeta, concluded an agreement with King Carol which gave her the right to visit Romania, her arrivals and departures to be approved by the King, and allowed Michael to visit her abroad for six weeks each year. She returned to Romania at the end of March and was expelled for no apparent reason five weeks later. 'Decidedly the red lady and her associates must be rampant again,' Queen Marie wrote to her. 'What about the boy? How sad it all is and how unsatisfactory and full of despair.'[52]

At the end of September 1932, Michael was due to visit his mother in London for the agreed six-week holiday. The February agreement was again put to the test and this time an international scandal ensued which nearly cost Princess Helen her son.

He was accompanied by two ADCs who had instructions to report regularly to his father. With the authority of a Canute, Carol forbade photographs or other press coverage of Michael's visit and when, within days, the English newspapers had published pictures of his ex-wife and son shopping together, he accused Helen of purposely flouting his wishes. He ordered Michael to return to Bucharest and only the fact that they were expected for tea at Buckingham Palace prevented his immediate departure. Carol had also given orders that Michael was to wear shorts throughout the visit. By then he was almost eleven and tall for his age, and Princess Helen, feeling that it would be rude to take him to tea in short trousers, bought him a suit.

When they returned from Buckingham Palace to the hotel the senior of the two ADCs told Princess Helen that he had reported the incident of the long trousers to Bucharest and had had instructions to return with Michael immediately. At this her patience snapped. She gave an interview to the *Daily Mail*, 'in the hope that public opinion would help me to preserve the rights which I claim as a mother'. The *Mail*'s piece of 4 October 1932 was severe about Carol but nothing to what the *Sunday Express* published on the 9th. 'King Carol the Cad' blazed across the page, who would be 'kicked out of England a second time should he ever set foot here in future'. Carol was thrown into a terrible rage which was not improved when Elisabeta told him that should he wish them to stop calling him 'cad', all he had to do was to behave differently.

To escape the British press, Princess Helen left London for Florence, from where she telephoned her lady-in-waiting, Madame Catargi, in Bucharest to say that she would be back for Michael's birthday less than a week away. She was by now fighting mad and ready to take risks. When the British Minister in Rome was instructed to visit her in Florence and try to persuade her to delay her return until the tensions created by the anti-Carol press campaign had subsided, he got nowhere. Princess Helen called Carol a liar. Should she not obtain her rights in her own country, she would take her case to the International Court of Justice at The Hague.[53]

Foreign Minister Titulescu met Princess Helen with flowers at the small Baneasă station on the outskirts of Bucharest from where she was escorted under heavy military guard to her house on Chaussée Kiselev and there spent the 25th with Michael.

When, in September 1932, Vaida-Voevod resigned as the third Peasant Party prime minister after Mironescu and Iorga, the National Peasant Party still had a large majority in Parliament and King Carol felt that he could not avoid appointing the far less amenable Juliu Maniu. Princess Helen knew that only a three-pronged agreement to which the Romanian Government was a party had any chance of holding Carol to his word, and that only Maniu had the authority and integrity to promote such an arrangement. She made an appointment with the Prime Minister. She also called on Princess Elisabeta, her sister-in-law, who accused her of having behaved 'abominably' ' by not warning her of what she intended to do in London'. To this, 'Sitta' replied that as the February agreement she had concluded with Carol had not been kept, she had felt at liberty in London to defend herself as she thought best. The conversation deteriorated until Elisabeta finally asked her to leave and, as they walked from the balcony through the sitting room and the conversation became even more heated, Elisabeta suddenly turned in a fury, slapped her face and told her to go to hell. Writing to Princess Olga about the incident, Princess Helen said that she replied 'Thank you,' and succeeded in closing the door quietly behind her.[54]

The palace *camarilla* were by now amassing large fortunes and the King's popularity, even with the army, had plummeted. Women friends of Princess Helen dared not meet her for fear of ruining their husbands' careers. The King's agents fed the newspapers with wild, baseless rumours of her attempted suicides. When, about three weeks after her arrival, two sympathetic politicians called on her – though her lady-in-waiting sent them away immediately – Carol ordered her to leave the country.

She was allowed to see Michael on the afternoon of her departure, but he does not remember the meeting. It was 'something very vague, more an atmosphere of danger, not the fact in itself. Certainly her departure was very hard because my memory has rejected it. I know this much, that suddenly I saw her no more.'[55]

In the evening she was escorted to the station by the Chief of Police, an old friend, who guided her to her carriage with a big electric torch. The whole place was in darkness. Apart from her lady-in-waiting, he was the only human being near her. The station staff had withdrawn and the passengers were confined in the train behind drawn blinds. She had left Miss St John behind, ostensibly to look after the house, and she hoped, to maintain contact between herself and her son.

Princess Helen had had two principal reasons for returning to Bucharest against the advice of Maniu and Titulescu. One was to keep her promise to spend Michael's birthday with him. The other was to arrange something definitive for their future. Unlike Iorga, whom she had approached during his premiership, Maniu took her request seriously. Among her papers is a document of 24 October, probably drawn up by her lawyer, Antoniade, which suggested that in any agreement reached with her, her allowance should be reduced until the Romanian economy had picked up. Maniu responded within a week and the following conditions, which he had already cleared with the King, were drawn up in order to 'complete the accord of February 1932 and to put an end to present and future disagreements of whatever nature'. On 1 November 1932 the agreement was signed by Princess Helen and by Iuliu Maniu on behalf of the Romanian government, and she left for Florence soon afterwards.

> 'Her Majesty Elena' had the right to visit Romania; her arrivals and departures would be approved by the King and have the government's consent. When in Romania she could be visited by Michael as often as possible taking into account circumstances and having in mind his studies.
> Should she spend less than six months in the country she would have the right to receive Michael for visits in Switzerland, totalling not more than two months. Visits to countries other than Switzerland would require the prior approval of the King and government.
> Princess Helen would receive a civil list payable directly by the Ministry of Finance. Her house at Mamaia had been purchased by the state. She would contribute to the upkeep of the Kiselev house.
> Articles 5 and 20 of the Statutes of the Royal Family would be amended accordingly.[56]

Although the agreement, in accordance with Carol's decree, named her 'Her Majesty Elena', she wished to be and was normally known as Her Royal Highness Princess Helen of Romania. The new agreement more or less held. Princess Helen did not return to Romania during King Carol's reign but every year for the next eight years her son spent about two months with her in Florence.

# THREE

## *The Loss of Greater Romania:*
## *King Carol II Abdicates*

Michael's cocoon of selected adults and children had exploded, exposing him to eleven Romanian boys of his own age and to the grubby materialism and corruption of those who had followed Madame Lupescu into the King's household.

Possibly the best thing King Carol did for his son was to set up this palace school of twelve boys, eleven companions selected from the different regions of the country he would one day rule. Sons of a diplomat, an engine driver, a Saxon school teacher, etc., gathered in one of the palace reception rooms early in 1933, first to be briefed by the headmaster, an army general, and then to stand in order of height while the Crown Prince, who was as shy as any of them, walked down the line and shook hands with his future schoolmates.[1]

The Director of the Institut Français in Bucharest taught them French. There was no English since it was already one of the Prince's first languages. They learned musical appreciation and the piano. The art master was a professional painter. According to Lascar Zamfirescu, the diplomat's son, Michael came top in mathematics, but his favourite teachers were Ion Conea for geography and Gheorghe Lazar for history. The curriculum, though based on the state *baccalauréat*, had been tailored under King Carol's supervision to emphasise Romanian studies. Political discussion in school was forbidden.

Classes were held in one of the neighbouring houses that King Carol I had bought when the Palace was built. Eleven students entered from the street, one from the palace garden – a handy security arrangement. They sat in two rows of six and classes lasted from eight until two. Some afternoons they played basketball and Michael, being tall for his age, was good at the game. The atmosphere was disciplined and friendly. There was no corporal punishment and the headmaster, Zamfirescu says, was as nice as 'warm bread'.[2]

Prince Michael was the only student given lessons in practical engineering. Every Friday morning he went to the Ford garage, put on overalls and worked under the supervision of trained mechanics. Although he was not to be given university training he became an excellent self-taught engineer.

The pupils also had annual field studies. One year they followed a river to its source, another year they visited Oltenean monasteries. It was his father's idea, and according to Michael the most interesting part of their school work.

The teachers were not only told to treat Michael like everyone else, they were sometimes ordered to treat him unfairly. For instance, he was given, a very poor mark for a history essay he felt to be one of his best. After class, he went to Mr Lazar, his teacher, and asked what was wrong with it. Nothing, was the reply. It was a very good essay, but Lazar had been instructed to give him a bad mark.[3] It was an extraordinary thing to do to a boy who showed no sign of becoming swollen-headed in any way. Michael now believes that such incidents were motivated by jealousy rather than a father's desire to instil sobriety into his son.[4]

Some years later Baroness van der Hoven left a convincing verbal snapshot of father and son. Carol was telling her of a clause he had found in the 1866 constitution which, he thought, would justify a dictatorial *régime* when Michael walked into his office.

> He smiled as he looked up at his son who made his way across the room in that quiet, measured step of his. What a contrast to the determined, impetuous man who held the fate of Romania in his strong hands. There was thought and method in the boy. He was quiet and reserved. One could see he thought things out for himself and his opinions would not be easily swayed, but there was a certain gentleness in his expression, a lazy good-heartedness in his smile.[5]

When the boys went home to their parents – or relatives if they were from the provinces – Michael returned to his father at the Casa Nouă, a two-storey house built behind the Palace. The King's rooms were on the first floor. On the ground floor were Michael's room, a dining room and sitting room but no kitchen; food was brought in from the main building.

Michael caught his first glimpse of Madame Lupescu when he was coming out of the Palace one morning by a back door. She was about to leave Casa Nouă but when she spotted him she stepped back into the house and slammed the door.[6] It was such a traumatic moment for Michael that he mentioned it to a boy whose parents, unknown to him, were friends of Madame Lupescu – for she, too, had had her say in the selection of Michael's schoolmates.

> Two days later my father summoned me and told me that he knew all about it and considered that this was the moment for me, too, to get to know her.

He took me to the drawing room and there she was . . . At first I was upset by the idea of having to meet her. With time I realised that she was a vulgar person – I don't quite know how to put it – with a loud and strident nature. . . . I did not find her beautiful. . . . she brought with her a feeling of unease. In her presence you felt yourself diminished; even when she tried to be nice she did it with a kind of aggressivity. She was like someone who dressed only in striking colours. . . . Any good feelings I might have developed towards her were killed off when my father asked me to treat Madame Magda Lupescu as my own mother. I forget which year this was but I was an adolescent – and you do not recommend an alternative mother to an adolescent with such levity, with such disregard for a certain feeling for what is right.[7]

The King appointed a Colonel Grigorescu to give him constant company. 'I rather remember the moments when I tried to be alone to think of Mama, than those spent with Col. Grigorescu.'[8] However, school and life with his classmates eased, he said, the harshness of what was to him an unnatural separation:

It was good with them, we were friendly together, we amused ourselves. But when I returned home everything was grey. I waited for the evening to come with a kind of uneasiness, for as soon as it was evening Magda Lupescu appeared. Whether I liked it or not I would see her. I could not wait to go to Florence.[9]

At home in Bucharest he was ignored. When he tried to say something his father more often than not told him to 'shut up'.

In Florence with mama I was no longer lonely. . . . Until then I seemed to break with reality, with life. I could pour out my unhappiness. She was an extraordinary confidante. She knew how to listen, not for one moment did her thoughts stray while we were talking.[10]

According to a friend who once met Madame Lupescu, she was the kind of professional woman who, today, would become an executive in a large enterprise. But Prince Michael saw her daily and knew the other side of his father's 'Duduia' – the small, vicious side.

When Zamfirescu spent part of his holiday with them in Florence and was unwise enough to say in Bucharest how much he had enjoyed it, he was requested – though this would have been his final year before the *baccalauréat* – to leave the school immediately.

On one occasion King Carol took the Prime Minister for a picnic in his rather special Rolls Royce which he would not allow Michael to drive:

> Something happened to bring on a crise de nerfs. She began to shout, to threaten to jump out of the car. And when the car had stopped, she screamed that she would go no further until my father handed over the wheel to me. The scandal went on until she had had her way. She wanted to humiliate him in front of the Prime Minister.[11]

To Michael she was repulsive; she created painful situations from which there seemed no escape. Once, when he and his father were fishing for crayfish while Magda Lupescu lay in the sun, Michael took a crayfish by its whiskers and twirled it above her, and purposely let it fall into her lap where it pinched her with its claws.[12]

At official functions Magda Lupescu had a curtained box on the balcony. There she served caviar and champagne to friends and to the more circumspect guests who excused themselves for a few minutes to go upstairs and pay their respects. The two largest industrialists in the country, Auşnit and Malaxa, played poker regularly with the King and the 'First Lady', their sole purpose being to let her win enough money to protect their industries from nationalisation.[13] On the other hand when General Ion Antonescu – who was to play such an important part in King Michael's life – realised that she was present, he promptly left the Palace with his wife.

Lupescu exerted her influence partly through a cavalry officer called Ernest Urdăreanu who had joined the Household in 1931, had become head of the palace garage and then Madame Lupescu's regular chauffeur. His sleek appearance and sharp thinking had appealed to her and, two years later, when Puiu Dumitrescu was finally dismissed, Urdăreanu replaced him as King Carol's Private Secretary. He subsequently became Marshal, then Minister, of the Royal Court, and the most powerful person in the country after Madame Lupescu and the King himself. According to King Michael he was without scruple. 'He had a dark nature and played an ambiguous part in the relationship between my father and Madame Lupescu.'[14]

One night, after a film at Peleş, they were about to drive down the hill to Foişor, Michael at the wheel, Magda Lupescu next to him, the King sitting behind, when Urdăreanu walked over to say goodnight.

He tapped at her window and when she half-opened it he dropped a small packet onto her lap. In it was an emerald the size of this coffee cup and mounted too. 'What is this?' she asked, and Urdăreanu replied 'Pour vous.' I do not know whether it was a present from him or from someone else, but it was a stone worth millions.[15]

Michael's father was a good administrator, a well-read man who worked hard to raise the cultural standard of the country. New books of quality were published at cut prices. Technical books with small circulation were subsidised. By 1936 he had established some 15,000 cultural centres throughout the countryside. According to King Michael, 'The Royal Foundation for Literature and Arts created by King Ferdinand knew in Carol's reign a brilliance it had not experienced until then.'[16]

He had a genuine interest in the welfare of the peasant, but the long-term benefit of his reforms and modernisation is not easy to assess. Bucharestians smiled at the idea of ambulatory baths moving from village to village and peasant women being instructed how best to preserve vitamins in vegetables they had already had to sell to pay for such essentials as oil and salt. Carol's favourite project, the Straja Țării – a scout and guide movement with a Romanian rather than an international character to which every youth, including Michael, belonged – was in many ways similar to contemporary fascist youth movements. As King Michael once remarked, 'My father had caught the spirit of the time.'[17]

He used his so-called Aviation Tax, levied on every letter posted in Romania, to build a new wing onto the Bucharest palace. He amassed a huge personal fortune, much of which he sent abroad and those Romanians who could have given him disinterested advice and loyalty were neither attracted by, nor encouraged to attend, the court of ubiquitous marble in Calea Victoriei. King Michael believes that had all politicians taken a stand his father would have behaved differently. 'But', he adds, 'the liaison between the King and Magda Lupescu was not merely a sentimental question. The political implications went much deeper and were more difficult to identify than we realised. Personal interests were far too great for some men not to approve and encourage the King's weakness.'[18]

His mother and grandmother were afraid that Michael might be tainted by this corruption. They need not have worried. His main problem, he once told his grandmother, was how to be even civil to someone like Puiu Dumitrescu. He grew up to be a difficult man to con.

At first, Michael did not seem even to trust his grandmother, 'a queer, stolid little fellow', she calls him, 'and it is not easy to discover what he feels, sometimes one wonders if he <u>does</u> feel'.[19] Once only he 'suddenly let me look into his generally tightly closed heart and mind and I realised how sad it all was'.[20] In December 1934, when he was 13, she was allowed to spend two days with him and found that he had come on a lot, was very nice, interested in books, art, music, and had a good sense of humour.

King Carol treated every member of his family except possibly his sister Elisabeta as enemies, and was particularly cruel to his mother. Queen Marie had lost her personal fortune during the war and, on his return, Carol took away the private revenues King Ferdinand had left her. He dismissed members of her household without consulting her, spied on her and – most insulting – made Urdăreanu a middle-man for any contact she might wish to have with the Government.

His attitude, Queen Marie told him in a long letter written a few months before she died, was a great mistake, for 'a King's family is the wood that protects the central tree'.[21] Carol had already made it clear that he neither needed nor welcomed his family's protection and when, in 1940, he was forced into exile his son was the only member of the family to see him off at the station.

For Michael's holidays with his mother in Florence King Carol would draw up rules – petty and sometimes harsh – to ensure that they never felt free of his authority. He even steamed open a letter Michael's mother had asked him to take back to his grandmother. The two ADCs who accompanied him were briefed to treat Princess Helen as a person without official status. It is typical of King Michael that, even as a boy, although he bitterly resented their behaviour towards his mother, he did not blame the ADCs for carrying out his father's instructions. However, Michael had suspected from the beginning that Madame Lupescu was the main reason for his mother's exile, and he hated it whenever they even spoke her name. 'I wanted no one to see that I knew what had happened between my parents. . . . In a way I reckoned that anyone who did, had something against me.'[22]

During the first two years of her exile in Florence, renting a house with her brother Paul and her sisters Irene and Katherine, Princess Helen always hoped that eventually Michael would have a real home to come to. After the sale of the Mamaia house she was able to buy a fifteenth-century villa in the grounds of the monastery of San Domenico. It was a fine house with useful dependencies. The garden was large but the gardeners could be shared with the monastery. She brought out her furniture from Bucharest, some of it Italian, of the same period as the villa. She installed a swimming pool for the hot summers. She worked closely with the architects and with her exceptional talent for decoration she produced a beautiful interior. She called her house the Villa Sparta after the title of the Greek Crown Prince. It was to become Michael's true home as a boy and later a second home for his wife and children.

On the political side King Carol had four main enemies – Juliu Maniu, Dinu Brătianu, Nicolae Titulescu and General Ion Antonescu, who in 1940 would be instrumental in his abdication.

The King undermined Maniu's leadership of the National Peasant Party by supporting his rival, Vaida-Voevod. He used similar tactics to sideline the Brătianus. When Ion Duca, the Liberal Prime Minister, was assassinated by the Iron Guard at the end of 1933, the King appointed not Dinu Brătianu, who had succeeded his brother Vintila as leader of the party, but instead Gheorge Tătărescu, an arch-opportunist and yes-man whom Maniu and Brătianu would later hold primarily responsible for the collapse of parliamentary democracy in Romania. Moreover, he managed to keep Tătărescu in power for the next four years.

Nicolae Titulescu, who belonged to no political party, was one of Romania's most distinguished foreign ministers and twice-running president of the League of Nations. He was the principal East European exponent of collective security through a network of mutual assistance treaties linked to the West European powers. He treated Tătărescu and the corrupt administration in Bucharest with contempt, and in February 1934 reached an agreement with Maniu, Brătianu and Mihalache committing them all to stand together against what he saw as 'the Hitlerisation of Romania'. He forced the King to get rid of Puiu Dumitrescu and continued to be a thorn in the side of the Lupescu *camarilla* until the summer of 1936, by which time the Western Powers had demonstrated their inability to stand up to Hitler and it was no longer realistic for Romania to rely on them.Titulescu was sacked and for the next four years King Carol tried to strike a balance between the Entente and Germany.

In the New Year of 1937 King Carol's mistrust of Queen Helen seriously endangered their son's life.

Michael's friend Philip, Prince Andrew's son, spent part of the Christmas holiday at Villa Sparta. Soon after he left, Michael developed a bad bout of bronchitis. On 19 January he told his father on the telephone that he felt better but next day he was in such pain that his mother called her doctor. Acute appendicitis was diagnosed but, as he was a minor, he could not be operated on without the agreement of both parents. When the ADCs telephoned

Bucharest, King Carol, who assumed Michael's illness to be a manoeuvre by his mother to keep him longer in Florence, gave a categorical no. The delay had become dangerous for Michael. The ADCs were frantic, but only after a long telephone conversation which almost ended in tears did one of them finally obtain the King's permission. Michael was rushed to hospital. There was no time for a general anaesthetic and since the surgeon began to operate before the local anaesthetic had had time to take full effect he was in some pain. Michael said later,

> I understood less and less my father's actions whenever they had to do with relations with mama. He behaved as if someone always wished to deceive him. The deceit did not come from my mother and certainly not from me. I think that to some extent he realised how different we were, that God had made us in such a way that no sides of our character or way of seeing life would ever meet.[23]

On 1 February 1937 he was declared convalescent. Although he was still only fifteen, in May that year he represented his father at the Coronation of King George VI and Queen Elizabeth and so paved the way for his father's acceptance by the British royal family. He stayed at Buckingham Palace for the official period of the coronation, and then with Grigorcea, the Romanian Minister in London, to attend the Royal Naval Review at Spithead.

> He is shy and rather silent [Queen Marie wrote to her 'American friend'], and has instinctive tact. He knows wonderfully how to hold his peace. They liked him very much when he went to London for the Coronation. It had been my idea to send him, although he was so young; but I so wanted that something quite unspoilt should come from Roumania whose name has been too often dragged through the mire.[24]

In July, King Carol followed up Michael's official visit to Britain by an unofficial visit of his own. He was received by the King and had talks with the Prime Minister and Foreign Minister and a state visit to London was planned for November 1938.

On 25 October 1937, when he was 16, Prince Michael became an army officer in a ceremony which included a short service and an impressive march-past. Michael remembers the event though, as he put it, he does not take naturally to ceremony. 'It seems to me that, just at that moment, something essential escapes me.'[25]

On 9 January 1938 Michael again represented his father abroad, this time at the marriage in Athens of his uncle, Crown Prince Paul of Greece, to Princess Frederika of Hanover. Prince Paul's elder brother, King George II of Greece, had been called back to the throne in November 1935, after twelve years of exile.

In Romania, as had already happened in Greece and Yugoslavia, parliamentary government was drawing to a close. When, in December 1937, Tătărescu's government failed to obtain the necessary 40 per cent of the votes required to stay in office, King Carol passed over the National Peasant Party which had done better than any of the other Opposition parties and appointed Octavian Goga, leader of the extreme right-wing National Christian Party, with only 9 per cent of the vote. General Antonescu was made Minister of Defence and Călinescu, the small, one-eyed, competent Moldavian lawyer Minister of the Interior. Over the next few months Goga's rabid anti-Semitic campaign provoked such violent reaction in the British press that the state visit to London was postponed until November. On 10 February Goga had to resign and a government, which still included Antonescu and Călinescu, was formed under the Patriarch Miron Cristea. Ten days later a new constitution was published and accepted by the Romanian people with – the British Minister reported – 'almost Hitlerian unanimity'. The King could now nominate half the Senate and prorogue Parliament for as long as twelve months. Legislation would in future be initiated mainly by the Crown and the Legislative Chamber reconstituted on a corporative basis.

A spate of restrictive legislation followed. The traditional parties were abolished; the only legal party would, in future, be the King's National Renaissance Front. The Crown Council was given special powers. The press was controlled, new governors appointed, the judicial system reorganised, trial by jury abolished.

Political conventions, King Michael said later, were breaking down: 'it was no longer shameful to kick a few rules aside'. For this reason, he said, the two leaders of the historical parties quite rightly wanted nothing more to do with his father. More serious, he added, politics throughout almost the whole of Europe had begun to practise cynicism.[26]

The boys of Prince Michael's school had to learn the new constitution by heart but had no right to discuss it. A boy of 16, he saw his father as a selfish and often very unkind man but one who worked hard for his country – certainly not for its destruction. Today, he is of the opinion that he was working for royal absolutism from the moment he returned to Romania in 1930, because he believed – as did many Romanians – that the replacement of political parties by a concentration of power in himself would be for the country's benefit. But when he dispensed with the political parties he disabled one of the best constitutions in Europe. The historical parties were, King Michael said later, 'the single great political force to promote freedom of opinion. I can affirm that the moment my father renounced collaboration with them, in that moment he cut the branch from under his feet.'[27]

Queen Marie had suffered for some time from a disease of the liver, and when King Carol finally allowed her to go to the Stormer clinic in Dresden, Princess Helen visited her. After talking to the doctors who described her treatment in Romania as verging on the criminal, she realised that her mother-in-law was dying. When she saw her a few months later Queen Marie told her that she was better and was returning to Romania. By 'better' she only meant that the haemorrhaging had stopped.

Carol refused to let her fly home so she travelled by train with the summer heat beating down on her carriage and Dr Stormer administering oxygen and arranging for water to be sprayed on the roof at stations where this was possible. The bleeding started again and when she reached Sinaia on the morning of 17 July 1938 she was already very weak. She had asked that no one should meet her, but Carol, Michael and Elisabeta were at the station. Knowing that in Romania she would not be allowed to write to him, she had already sent the exiled Barbu Știrbey her farewell letter.

When she suffered another severe haemorrhage during the night, Carol and Elisabeta decided to call Ileana, Nicholas and Mignon, though none of them had by then any chance of reaching their mother before she died. Nor was she allowed to say goodbye to Zwiedenek, the head of her household who had accepted demotion in order to help her ride out the humiliation of her son's reign. The dreadful Miron Cristea pronounced a short prayer. She died in Pelișor on the afternoon of 18 July 1938 at 5.38.

Michael had left her to go up to Foișor for a few minutes but, soon after half-past five, he was called back. He ran down the hill and paused for a moment in the ante-room to the old nursery where his grandmother lay. He heard his father discussing the *communiqué* with Urdăreanu, insisting that Michael's name should not appear among those present at her death. He knew that his father's preoccupation with getting this detail right had more to do with his want of love for 'Amama' and himself than with any concern he might have had for the truth.[28]

In the funeral procession the Crown Prince walked behind his father. He noticed how small the coffin looked on its gun carriage and was old enough to be aware of the petty spitefulness, so unlike his grandmother, that had surrounded her dying and death.

The representational side of the state visit to London in November went well. The King was awarded the Order of the Garter, Prince Michael the Order of the Bath and Madame Lupescu had been persuaded to remain in Paris.

In the train going down to Dover King Carol remarked that, on the political side, other countries seemed to act while the English were still talking. But only two months after Munich and Chamberlain's promise of 'peace in our time' he could have had little hope of persuading the British Government to buy oil and wheat – Romania's only source of hard currency – at above world prices with the sole object of denying Hitler these essential wartime products. Berlin, too, had anticipated Chamberlain's reaction. Carol, on his way home, spent a few days with his cousin, Prince Frederick of Hohenzollern, at Sigmaringen, and had lunch with Hitler. While Michael tried out the latest Mercedes on the mountain roads around Hitler's eyrie, Carol laid the foundation with Hitler and Goering for an agreement to be signed in March 1939 – the month Hitler completed his occupation of Czechoslovakia. There was a hitch in this new German/Romanian relationship when, on arriving home and being told that the Iron Guard had committed another assassination, the King ordered that Codreanu, its head, be promptly executed. Berlin reacted strongly but not for long: the prospective treaty meant too much to them. It would provide for the supply of Skoda armaments in exchange for Romanian oil, essential to Hitler's war. It would open the way for some degree of German control over Romania's economic and military establishments and become part of Hitler's tailor-made plan to make Romania his main staging post for the invasion of the USSR. The British and French, with Romanian agreement, were preparing to sabotage the oil wells the moment German troops crossed the Polish/Romanian frontier. But Romania, unlike Poland, was to be taken by infiltration, not invasion, and with the minimum of violence or risk to the oil.

Members of the King's National Renaissance Front – which included all senators and government ministers – were put into a semi-military, sky-blue uniform and expected to greet their king with the Roman salute. The elections of June 1939 went smoothly. The Front provided 86 deputies to represent agricultural and industrial workers, 86 to represent industry and commerce and 86 to represent professional occupations. When Brătianu and Maniu informed the President of the Senate that they did not accept the validity of the new parliament their letter was returned.[29] In July, nine senators, including

Brătianu, Maniu and Mihalache, who refused to wear the National Renaissance Front uniform, were deprived of the right to sit in Parliament. Miron Cristea died in March 1939 and was replaced by the genuinely anti-Nazi Armand Călinescu. Six months later, on 21 September 1939, members of the extreme right-wing Iron Guard assassinated Călinescu. King Carol was so distraught by the loss of one of the few men of quality left to him that he called Michael upstairs and gave him the news personally. 'He was in awful shape, gone to pieces. He was lying on his bed and was probably frightened too about the Iron Guard.'[30] The King's reaction to the murder certainly showed signs of panic. The murderers were arrested, taken to the site of the assassination, executed, and their bodies left there for 24 hours. Within days over 400 summary executions of Legionary sympathisers had been carried out in Romania – a bloodbath on which Maniu commented, 'Only barbarous countries or those in a state of dissolution take such measures.'[31]

On 10 May 1940, the day Churchill was made Prime Minister, the Wehrmacht attacked the Low Countries. Within three weeks Belgium had capitulated and British troops had been driven out of the continent via Dunkirk. On 2 June King Carol appointed the pro-German Ion Gigurtu Foreign Minister – a distinct lurch away from his policy of neutrality. On the 14th the Germans occupied Paris and Romanians wept openly on the streets of Bucharest. Romania was cornered now between Germany and the USSR and her collapse became part of the temporary accord between the two great dictatorships which Hitler needed before he struck. On 26 June Moscow gave Romania 24 hours to cede Bessarabia, Northern Bukovina and the province of Herţa. Russia's interest in Bessarabia – but not Bukovina – had been recognised in the secret protocol to the Molotov/Ribbentrop agreement of 23 August 1939 and Hitler advised King Carol to agree to Stalin's demands in full.

Still under the tension of his *baccalauréat* exam, Prince Michael waited in the ante-room for news of the Crown Council's decision. When the door opened, Iorga came over to him and in a loud voice said to his pupil, 'They are all traitors.'[32] They had yielded. Army morale plummeted. General Antonescu was cashiered and put under house arrest at Bistriţa monastery for publicly holding the King responsible for the loss of the eastern territories.

On 4 July 1940 Gigurtu replaced the long-serving Tătărescu as Prime Minister and was himself replaced at Foreign Affairs by Manoilescu, another pro-German and active member of Madame Lupescu's *camarilla*. The fall of Paris on 22 June had cut Carol off from any possible Western military or diplomatic support. Bessarabia and Bukovina had been lost in circumstances that deprived him of an independent foreign policy: in future his *rapprochement* with Germany would be unconditional.[33] Forty British oil engineers and their families were expelled, together with the whole staff of the British Institute. On 22 June a pathetic attempt was made to put new life into the King's party by renaming it The Party of the Nation, and he was reduced to sending Hitler messages pleading with him to prevent Bulgaria and Hungary 'extending demands beyond the limits of natural justice'.

The Führer, however, was determined to settle Romania's revisionist problems speedily. Under the Craiova agreement of 7 September Romania released the Dobrugea to Bulgaria with the minimum of fuss. However, the loss of Transylvania, which was now threatened, would be a national tragedy for Romania. Hitler and Mussolini were already considering a Hungarian memorandum on the problem and Bossy had been told by his German colleague in Rome that the Transylvanian problem was for Germans not a question of justice or an ethnic problem; it was simply a matter of *realpolitik*.

When representatives of Germany, Italy, Hungary and Romania met in Vienna on 29 August, Manoilescu was told that by ten that evening Romania must decide whether to accept or refuse arbitration by the Axis Powers. There would be no negotiation. Acceptance would guarantee the territorial integrity of what was left of Romania. Refusal would make her an enemy of the Axis and she would be destroyed. At 3.40 a.m. the Crown Council agreed by a vote of 19 to 11 to accept the arbitration and a member of the Romanian delegation remarked, 'It is a staggering tragedy to be imposed on a country which has not been defeated, is not even in a state of war.'[34]

When the principals met at the Belvedere at 4 o'clock next day, 30 August 1940, Manoilescu asked to be allowed to make a statement and was told that he might do so after Ribbentrop had spoken. When Ribbentrop had announced that roughly two-fifths of the province had been delivered to Hungary, he again asked to speak and was told that he should first sign the protocol of acceptance. After the signing ceremony he was told that his statement would now be otiose. The Romanian Minister to Berlin flew to Bucharest and handed the arbitration document with map to the King.

The national humiliation of such a massive loss of territory was devastating. Transylvania was on the point of insurrection. Several generals defied orders to withdraw. Street demonstrations throughout the country grew in size and anger. Although the democratic structure of Romania had been destroyed, many Romanians looked for leadership to Juliu Maniu, the acknowledged leader both of Romanian Transylvanians and of opposition to King Carol. Had he at this moment challenged the Vienna agreement, known in Romania as the

'Vienna Diktat', the army and people might well have rallied to him. The Romanian army would have been a match for the Hungarian and, since Hitler could not afford prolonged warfare in what was to be the springboard for his invasion of the USSR, the German army would almost certainly have been forced to intervene. Open conflict with Germany – however short-lived – might have won for Romania at the very start of the war the kind of Allied respect that Poland was to enjoy.

But for all his moral courage and committment to democracy, Juliu Maniu was – in Clare Hollingworth's words – 'the last conceivable person to ride the wind and direct the storm'.[35] The country had to wait another three years, until King Michael was old enough to assume leadership, before a military rising against Nazi Germany could become a realistic objective.

On Sunday, 1 September, Michael's father was in a terrible state and he and Madame Lupescu came down to Michael's room after lunch to listen for an hour or so to his gramophone records which, Michael thought, helped him. That evening 'Duduia' was dining in town and would be late home but, instead of staying up to talk with his son, Carol took his anxieties to bed early.

On the 3rd, the Iron Guard attacked the radio and telephone headquarters in Bucharest and key buildings in other parts of the country. A *putsch* was feared and Urdăreanu told the King of a growing feeling in the country that only Antonescu could now restore order. Madame Lupescu was deeply suspicious of her old enemy but General Mihail, the Chief of Staff, assured Carol that despite his outspokenness Antonescu was absolutely loyal.

Antonescu had in fact left the Bistriţa monastery, his *domicile forcée*, two days before. In Ploieşti he had met Maniu and Brătianu who had proposed that in a coalition government of the National Peasant and Liberal parties the General should take the portfolios of War and Home Affairs. They would not, however, serve under the present king and they urged him to make this clear to Carol. The same point was made to him by Horia Sima who had suceeded Codreanu as leader of the Iron Guard when the latter, on the King's orders, had been executed in 1938 while 'trying to escape' from prison.

Antonescu came to the Palace on the evening of the 3rd, and, as was normal practice, had a brief talk with Urdăreanu before the audience. King Michael has since asked himself whether Antonescu took this opportunity to put pressure on his father's right-hand man who by then was extremely vulnerable. If true, it could explain Urdăreanu's unexpected collapse two days later.[36] During his audience Antonescu did not go so far as the leaders of the historic parties had wished but he warned the King that, if he were to form a government, he would require a free hand.

On leaving the Palace Antonescu made a critical decision. He had promised to meet Maniu and Brătianu after the audience. If he continued as their go-between and persuaded the King to step down in favour of his son, the two major democratic parties would revert to a parliamentary government in which he would be given a portfolio. But since Romania was still a dictatorship General Ion Antonescu thought he could serve his country far more effectively other than by taking orders from Mr Maniu. He decided to call on Fabricius, the German Minister, to seek his advice on forming a government with the Iron Guard. Fabricius, who had been impressed by Antonescu when he was Minister of Defence, suggested that he now assume dictatorial powers and get rid of the hated palace entourage. That evening the Minister informed Berlin that in Antonescu he believed they had found their man.

When he took the oath at around midday on the 4th, Ion Antonescu knew that he was swearing allegiance to a man whose prerogatives he must acquire if he were to 'save' his country in cooperation with the Reich. Later that afternoon, after reporting his failure to form a government with either the democratic leaders or Horia Sima, he warned the King that unless he were given full powers he could not continue. King Carol, becoming desperate in a rapidly deteriorating situation over which he seemed to have no control, convinced himself that he could always withdraw this delegation of royal power should Antonescu prove unsatisfactory. He therefore consented.

Mihai (Ica) Antonescu, a lawyer, and distant relative who had frequently visited the General in Bistriţa, was to play an important part in Romania's affairs during the next four years. That night he helped draft the decree which transferred most of the King's prerogatives to Antonescu. In the early hours of the 5th, Carol signed this document which suspended the 1938 constitution, dissolved Parliament and gave Antonescu full powers to conduct public affairs. The appointment of ministers and under-secretaries would, in future, require Antonescu's countersignature. The King would still be head of the army but could not be sure how effective this would prove in a conflict between Antonescu and himself. In his own words, Antonescu 'would become the complete ruler of the country, I remaining a simple figurehead with mere decorative rights'.[37]

Antonescu had now realised the first part of the Fabricius plan. He had still to get rid of King Carol and his entourage. That day, Thursday the 5th, the riots continued, the demonstrations swelled, morale in the Palace dropped and Urdăreanu became more and more pessimistic. Very late that night Antonescu's

ADC brought the King a one-page letter. His father, King Michael says, read it and, without a word passed it to Urdăreanu. Urdăreanu, who seemed by then to have given up, glanced through it and said, 'Well, there's nothing more to be done. We must sign.'[38] Antonescu had written that his attempts to recruit for his government 'men of true patriotism and principle' had failed because they, 'like the Army and the whole Country, were asking for the King's abdication'.[39] King Carol, isolated in the Palace, may not have heard the snappy little verse circulating in Bucharest:

| Rusilor am dat un pic, | I've given the Russians a bit, |
| Las pe Mama in Balcic, | I've left Mama at Balcic, |
| Ungurii sunt in Avrig, | The Hungarians are at Avrig, |
| Nu-i numic. | That's nothing. |
| Fie tronul cît de mic | However small the throne may be |
| Eu nu abdic.[40] | I shall not abdicate.* |

The King's advisers dithered over Antonescu's letter and Carol made up his mind only after General Coroamă, head of the Palace Guard, made it clear that he would refuse to give the order to shoot Antonescu and after he heard that Fabricius had asked whether he would be leaving for Sigmaringen or for some other destination. Antonescu sent his ADC to the Palace at 5 a.m. to say that the King had until 6 a.m. to abdicate.[41]

For Urdăreanu and Madame Lupescu the King's decision to leave the country must have been a relief, since their lives were now at risk in Romania. For Michael, however, it was like the end of the world. If his father, who in Michael's eyes was so experienced and powerful, could not succeed, how, he asked himself, could he? The loneliness, the idea of being left in the hands of a man like Antonescu, who had already betrayed his father, frightened him. Duduia's fussing over him irritated him. His father lectured him about the duty of a prince who must 'overcome human pain and inconvenience must keep the standard of the Dynasty and of Romania flying'.[42] What Michael wanted to hear at this critical hour was something less theatrical, more ordinary and personal. He longed for a gesture of love from his father.

Later he said of his father, 'He was an unusual man, with a remarkable culture – and nevertheless he had never understood that during all these years – and particularly now – I might have need of him.'[43] Even during those last few

---

\* Avrig is near Sibiu in Transylvania. In accordance with her wishes, Queen Marie's heart was buried at 'Stella Maris', her Balcic house in southern Dobrugea.

hours he was too busy working with Ernest Urdăreanu to spend any time alone with his son.

'In all this drama', Carol wrote, 'the most moving figure was little Michael, he remained alone, the victim of circumstances, powerless and without experience in the midst of this pack of wolves and hyenas. He was the only one to fight the abdication with might and main.'[44]

In the proclamation which was drafted during the small hours of Friday the 6th, King Carol delegated what was left of his prerogatives to the Crown Prince and asked the country to give Michael 'all the great support he would need to get over this difficult period'.

Then Michael went to his room. 'I was tired, the presence of Magda Lupescu was more tiring than anything else. I don't know whether I slept three hours when the telephone wakened me and a voice – I think it was Urdăreanu's – told me to get ready quickly because Antonescu was coming to the Palace for the swearing in ceremony.'[45]

He waited in the ADCs' room and when Antonescu emerged from his audience he came straight up to Michael and said, 'General Antonescu guarantees the situation.' He had this curious way of speaking of himself in the third person, which Michael could not explain. He was grateful to him for one thing, however. Antonescu decided to ask his mother to return to Romania.[46]

In the absence of a parliament representing the Romanian people, Michael signed the written form of the oath in the presence of Antonescu, the Patriarch Nicodim and Judge Lupu, the presiding judge of the highest court of appeal. Then Antonescu swore allegiance to the new king and after this simple ceremony suggested that Michael should show himself to the crowd. Arthur Lee describes what King Michael saw when he stepped onto the balcony.

> The square was filled with people, thousands of Legionary Greenshirts among them. Many had been there all night and they now burst into a wild roar of welcome. Urged by Antonescu, Michael stepped forward and saluted, again and again. But his face bore no smile of response or pleasure at the continuous acclamation, for he could not reconcile their applause for him with their hatred for his father. Emotion choked him as, prompted by Antonescu, he once more acknowledged the cheers. Then abruptly he turned and re-entered the room.[47]

According to Buhman, King Carol's Private Secretary, at 9.30 the King said goodbye to the palace staff assembled in the Throne Room. He was 'well composed. His face showed no emotions.' He went round the room shaking hands, but without saying anything... Then Michael entered. His face was also 'like stone.' As he shook Buhman's hand, Buhman was unable to control his emotion any longer...[48]

Urdăreanu organised the departure. Carol agreed that his old friend, Puiu Filiti, brother of one of his early loves who was a close friend of Ioana Lambrino, could go with them. Everyone was now on edge, anxious to get away. The industrialist Malaxa refused to speak to Madame Lupescu or Urdăreanu on the telephone and only Vaida-Voevod and Iorga came to bid Carol goodbye, the latter offering to act as a kind of regent for Michael while he was so young. Tătărescu, whose career Carol had done so much to promote, stayed away.

After dinner Carol, Michael and Madame Lupescu sat together and Madame Lupescu remarked that the hardest part for Michael would be to avoid coming into conflict with Antonescu while not allowing himself to be 'dragged through the mire'.[49]

When they were ready to go, Antonescu sent a message that Michael should not accompany his father to the station. Michael ignored it. At 3.30 a.m. the streets were quiet. Gendarmes lined the Chaussée and surrounded the station but did not salute. Antonescu, who was to have accompanied Carol to the frontier, was not there; he had detailed a Colonel Dragomir to replace him. Michael's Aunt Elisabeta was not there either. Though neither Michael nor his father knew that this would be the last time they would ever see each other, the waiting was terrible. When, finally, the carriage started to move down the platform, the figure at the open window felt more than ever at this moment that he was leaving his son 'in the hands of the enemy'. Michael, in a turmoil of bitterness and love, was on the verge of tears.

In the battle of wills that would now ensue between the 18-year-old king and Ion Antonescu, the 58-year-old, pro-German autocrat, King Michael had few of the prerogatives normally attributed to an East European monarch at that time. Like his grandmother, Queen Marie, during the First World War, he drew strength from a certainty that the Romanian people supported him, and that in the long run, against all the odds, the Allies would win.

# PART TWO

Towards the *Coup d'Etat*:
September 1940–August 1944

---

## FOUR

### King Michael and the pro-German Dictator

On 6 September 1940 Princess Helen wrote in her diary:

> All world seems falling about my ears. Carol has abdicated. Michael is King. Antonescu dictator. Latter wired me come at once. Am shattered. . . . Oh how dif. it will be.[1]

Although her eight years of exile in Florence had been distressing, particularly her separation from her son, she would miss the freedom to mix only with people she liked and trusted. Her contempt for Madame Lupescu, the enthusiasm with which Romanians had helped Carol usurp Michael's throne in 1930, his subsequent treatment of her and his son, Elisabeta slapping her face – suddenly it had all become part of her life again.

On 12 September 1940 Raoul Bossy, the Romanian Minister in Rome, was instructed to go to Florence and invite Princess Helen to return to Romania as Queen Mother with the title of 'Majesty'. He should accompany her as far as the Italian frontier. Bossy, whose diary includes a full account of his meeting with the Queen Mother, found her as beautiful and charming as she had been ten years before, although, when he addressed her as 'Your Majesty', she grimaced and pointed out that when Carol became king they were already divorced. When he insisted that Romanians needed a queen to look up to and that her authority and influence would be that much greater if she had the title of Queen Mother she replied 'Do you really think so? Well then call me as you want!'[2]

Michael's father, Princess Helen said, had neglected his son's education in politics and current affairs. Michael had even had to bribe servants to get him a newspaper. Whereas Carol had been experienced, Michael was quite unprepared for the job he was now to undertake. She could, when he was younger, have helped him with his studies but, she reminded Bossy, 'they drove me out'. Now, she believed, it was too late. To this Raoul Bossy replied, 'You were very much needed, Ma'am, when your son was a child but I am afraid your presence is just as necessary now to help the young King, who is quite alone, with not a single member of the family near him.'[3]

Later, she spoke more positively about her return. She would have a modest court, more like the one she had known as a girl in Athens. She hoped, she said, to visit Florence and to bring Michael with her, and when Bossy was prompted to reply, 'I don't think any of us want to make our Queen a prisoner,' he misled her, albeit unwittingly.

While she was prepared, she said, to return for Michael's sake, the agony of her previous experience in Romania seemed never to be long out of her thoughts. Later during their conversation she told Bossy:

The Romanians did no wrong to me. Not even Carol, he was quite decent to me. It is only the horrid Lupescu, who was jealous and tried to suppress me, even in the heart of my child . . . You know she taught the child that, once he is married, he can still keep a lady-friend, because it is always done. She used to tell him 'If ever you want something from your father, ask it through me, as I make him do whatever I want to.' She used always to come to his room, and when he was ill in bed she sat on his bed. The child hated her.[4]

Michael met his mother at the frontier town of Jimbolia on 14 September 1940. Antonescu boarded the train next morning and, as they drove with him in an open landau from the station to attend a *Te Deum* at the cathedral, they were welcomed by a large crowd of cheering and weeping people among whom members of the Iron Guard, as Michael pointed out to her, were easily recognisable by their green shirts. Antonescu seemed glad about their popularity, remarking that with his mother's help the young king, he felt sure, could regain public esteem for the throne. Queen Helen had been surprised by the warmth of her welcome at every little railway station on the way from the frontier to Bucharest. It had not occurred to her that Romanians remembered the dignity with which she had endured her humiliation under Carol or that, in Olivia Manning's words, she had become the 'symbol of the country's exiled morality'.[5]

Next day Michael took her round the new palace wing, the cost of which his father had charged to his infamous 'Aviation Tax'. Ghastly, she thought it, the taste of an ocean liner and less practical, a criminal waste of the nation's money.[6] But she liked the city centre, the handsome Boulevard Brătianu and, to the north of the Chaussée Kiselev, the new quarter of town houses and shady streets. Carol had drained the marshes, created artificial lakes, and at night you now heard gipsy orchestras playing in the garden restaurants that had sprung up around them.

They did not wish to live in Casa Nouă, where Michael had spent eight years with his father and Madame Lupescu. The family castle at Cotroceni was in a dreadful state but they preferred to make a few of its rooms habitable to use as their Bucharest base while spending most of their time in the mountains at Sinaia. Foişor, the little chalet where Michael had been born, had burned down while Princess Helen was in exile but they would move into the bigger, less attractive Foişor that had replaced it. Queen Helen started work on Cotroceni, supervising repairs and choosing furniture, with the help of Madame Kopkov who, for as long as anyone could remember, had been guardian of the palaces. Then, in the early morning of 10 November, Romania suffered one of her worst earthquakes and Cotroceni was so badly damaged that they had to abandon their plan. Princess Elisabeta offered them her town house just off the Chaussée Kiselev but they preferred in the end to make do with Casa Nouă until the Germans destroyed it on 24 August 1944.

King Michael's prerogatives had been further reduced after his father's departure. He still had the right to issue currency, confer decorations, receive and accredit foreign ambassadors and to nominate prime ministers but not to nominate government ministers and under-secretaries, or to initiate amendments to the constitution. As head of state he had the right of pardon and amnesty, but it was the 'Conducator' – General (later Marshal) Antonescu – who was recognised by the Führer as both head of state and supreme commander of the army. It was he who ran the country and whose suspicious bullying nature, small-mindedness and habit of denigrating Michael were to make their lives so miserable.

As the trauma of his father's abdication wore off, Michael saw that the puritanical, irascible little General had a simplistic honesty that had been missing at his father's court. However, the General had been so obsessed by King Carol's egotism and lack of civic responsibility that he seemed to overlook the possibility that Michael might become a man and king of a very different kind. He often referred to himself in the third person and treated Prince Michael as a child who owed his throne and even his life to the 'inspired intervention of General Antonescu'. He spied on the royal household and anyone whose loyalty to himself was in doubt he got rid of.

> It is clear to me [King Michael said fifty years later], that the Marshal was of an unhappy nature. A suspicious man who sees enemies everywhere, who felt the need to supervise both large and small matters, whose restlessness gave him no time to enjoy a natural life, Antonescu was for ever talking about honour but I believe that at heart he did not consider anyone to be honourable except himself. This probably caused him a lot of suffering.[7]

Antonescu never briefed the King. On the contrary, he systematically isolated him from news of national and international developments, rarely discussed current events with him except in terms of his own prowess. After his father's departure, Michael said, he had learned the truth about many things which had previously been hidden from him but this, he knew, was not enough. Given the threat of an Iron Guard revolt and the increasing involvement of the country with Hitler's military ambitions, he must prepare himself to take decisions and actions[8] which were as yet beyond him. Even a small initiative by him could, he knew, be snuffed out, if not by the General then by his own lack of confidence and experience. On 2 October 1940 his mother wrote, 'Am so morally tired can hardly go on. Are real prisoners. Poor little M. sits in my room till small hours in the morning talking everything over. Awful seeing him suffer so.'[9] 'Poor little' Michael had by then lost all his boyish chubbiness and was over six feet tall.

It was nearly twenty years since Princess Helen had first come to live in Romania, a young bride with her mother's somewhat negative attitude to life and her father's belief that women should not interest themselves in politics. Her exile in Florence had given her the taste of a larger life and her experience with Carol had toughened her. She returned to Romania in 1940 a mature woman with a greater appreciation of the joy of living and a touch of steel along with the charm and active concern for other people which comes through so strongly in her diaries. When Carol asks for her help she shows no sympathy. When he sends his best wishes for 1941 she despises him for humiliating himself with her.[10]

Queen Helen would continue to be her son's most trusted adviser. Despite her remarks to Raoul Bossy in Florence, in the autumn of 1940 she resumed the role she had played until her exile. She engaged constitutional historians to instruct her son in the basic laws from which a king and his governments drew their legitimacy. His occasional audiences were in practice conducted by her. When later they enraged the Führer and Marshal Antonescu by opposing Romania's involvement in the Russian campaign it was she who at first took most of the knocks. She was finally able to shake her son out of depression and torpor, for Michael possessed sound judgement of people and an obstinacy and independence of spirit which were to prove critical to his survival. Early in 1943 we shall find him taking decisions which were unshakeable though rarely, he told me many years later, without first talking things over with his mother.

On 6 September 1940 Michael had taken his oath of loyalty to the Romanian nation, swearing to protect the laws of the state, to protect and defend its future and the integrity of Romanian territory – words to which, he said later, he would refer in times of national or personal crisis for the rest of his life.[11] On that same day Antonescu abolished the Crown Council. Next day he abolished King Carol's beloved youth movement, Straja Țărei, and on the 9th his National Party. King Carol's 1938 constitution was suspended on 6 September 1940. Since the 1923 constitution providing for a constitutional monarchy was not restored until after King Michael's *coup d'état* of August 1944, Antonescu's four-year *régime* seems, therefore, to have been of a provisional nature subject to no legal framework. Nevertheless, the Conducator recognised the *de facto* validity of the 1923 constitution, distinguishing, for instance, between decrees which he could himself sign and those of a constitutional nature or concerning him personally which required the King's signature.[12] When, therefore, on 14 September Romania became an Iron Guard state, this was declared by royal decree, as was the reinstatement of Antonescu into the army and his promotion to Army Corps General.

Horia Sima, head of the Iron Guard, was made the Conducator's deputy. The lawyer Mihai (Ica) Antonescu became Minister of Justice. Juliu Maniu and Dinu Brătianu refused to participate in the Government but allowed members of their parties to accept posts on a personal basis. Most ministries were held by military personnel well known to Antonescu but, against the advice of the two democratic leaders, he entrusted some of the key portfolios to Legionaries with no administrative experience and whose loyalty to him was suspect.

Lunch on his nineteenth birthday must for Michael have been a pretty dull affair, the guests being the Antonescus, all the members of the court, and his Aunt Elisabeta looking, his mother thought, pathetically old, 'covered precious jewels, frightful clothes, black teeth, no beauty left'. She hugged Helen, 'trembling all over', asked her forgiveness for the slapping incident – 'one does things sometimes when one is irresponsible' – and invited them to lunch two days later.[13]

Princess Elisabeta lived in a large Italianate villa set back from the Chaussée Kiselev and adjoining the new lakes. They were met at the door by Scanavi, her lover, administrator of her Banloc estates in Transylvania and former banker to her ex-husband, King George II of Greece. He disappeared when they went in to lunch and the Princess was 'frightfully amiable, for a witch'.[14] At half past two they were able to leave and drive back to the mountains.

King Michael and his mother were convinced that the Iron Guard aimed to take over the country while Romanians were still recovering from the shock of the abdication. Moreover, after giving them so much executive power General Antonescu might well not be able to stop them. They were afraid for Antonescu's life and Queen Helen was particularly sorry for his wife. They must also have known that without the General their own lives would be more exposed to Iron Guard violence. Indeed, the Legionaries seemed to be flexing their muscles when they commandeered the King's name-day ceremony of 8 November. According to the British Minister they first moved it, at the last minute, from Bucharest to Iași where their movement had been created and then, before the assembled diplomatic corps, they turned it into a Legionary jamboree in which King Michael was forced to participate.[15] Queen Helen notes, 'Endless speeches and march past. Lunch at 4 pm. Spoke to all German and Italian generals. Did my best.' And to cap it all, when they returned to Sinaia they found an official guard of honour waiting on the station platform. 'Idiotic,' she noted; it was the kind of fuss they disliked.[16]

Antonescu had appointed members of the Iron Guard to be Minister of the Interior and Prefect of Police, and these set up a force of Legionary irregulars with the combined powers of police, judge and executioner. In November a group entered Jilava prison and killed sixty-five politicians awaiting trial for their alleged involvement in the death of Corneliu Codreanu. They brutally murdered Michael's old professor, Nicolae Iorga, and the economist Mădgearu, Secretary General of the National Peasant Party. The King was shattered by these murders, aggravated as they were by the fact that, although the assassins were known to the government, no arrests were made. It seemed clear that General Antonescu was losing control. Michael telephoned the news to his mother, who was taking a short break in Florence.

When she returned on the Sunday before Christmas she brought her son bad news of a different kind. She had been invited with her sister Irene, the Duchess of Aosta, to meet Hitler informally on 14 December at Berchtesgarten, and seeing this as an opportunity to help her two countries – Greece and Romania

– she had accepted. Hitler had not forgiven Mussolini for invading Greece on 28 October and thus starting a diversionary campaign during his preparations for the far more important invasion of Russia. She was therefore able to speak frankly to him about her native country. Romania, however, was a different story. Hitler seemed to consider it already his. As for King Michael, no one, he said, was fit to rule until he was at least forty years old. 'It is your task', he had told her, 'to see he is prepared in the right way. Until then he must be guided by Antonescu.'[17]

Early in the new year Antonescu tried to placate the Iron Guard with an impressive funeral procession headed by himself and Fabricius, the German Minister, and culminating in the reburial with great ceremony of Corneliu Codreanu. King Michael did not attend. On 14 January 1941 Antonescu paid a visit to Hitler and left with the impression that the Führer now valued him more than the Iron Guard. However, since German assessments of the Iron Guard varied from one government department to another and since non-governmental German associations could also influence Hitler's thinking, neither Antonescu nor Horia Sima could be sure which one would have Berlin's ultimate support. Horia Sima, who had the tactical advantage of being both the Iron Guard leader and Antonescu's deputy, declined on this occasion to accompany the General to Germany – presumably in order to make final arrangements for his armed revolt. It began a week later.

On Wednesday 22 January the Legionaries, who had already stockpiled ample food and ammunition, occupied the Prefecture, the Broadcasting Station and the Telephone Exchange. General Sănătescu, the capital's military commander, was at first hamstrung by not knowing German intentions. In Hitler's war strategy, however, a stable Romania was preferable to a Romania led by Nazi fanatics and at the end of a telephone conversation between Hitler and Fabricius the latter was assured that the German army would support Antonescu.* Sănătescu suppressed the revolt in four days, though not before the Legionaries had murdered eight hundred Jews. On the 27th Queen Helen noted in her diary, 'Those swine tore their teeth out for gold fillings and massacred them naked in fields on edge of town. Makes one quite sick.'[18] Churchill minuted Eden, the Foreign Secretary, that it might be as well to let General Antonescu know that if such 'a vile act' occurred again the Allies

---

* An enquiry ordered by Ribbentrop after the Iron Guard revolt revealed that despite the Führer's instructions and unknown to the Minister, the representative of the German Security Services had hidden nine Iron Guard leaders in Legation premises and refused to disclose Horia Sima's hiding place.

would hold him and his immediate circle personally responsible 'in life and limb'.[19] Sima escaped to Germany. Mihai (Ica) Antonescu replaced him as the General's deputy and also became Minister for Foreign Affairs. After an existence of only five months, the National Legionary State was dissolved by royal decree on 14 February 1941.

One incident during the revolt illustrated the risk Antonescu took by denying the young king reliable advisers and information. Early in October 1940 Antonescu had appointed as ADC in the royal household one Mircea Tomescu, who turned out to be an Iron Guard sympathiser. In Sinaia on the morning of 23 January 1941 Tomescu had the Queen Mother wakened and told that since General Antonescu was cornered in his presidency, Horia Sima had decided that unless the King agreed to act as mediator he was determined to fight on to the end. Michael, who had had no official briefing about the course of the conflict in Bucharest, seized on what seemed to be an opportunity of doing something useful for his country and left immediately for the capital. When Antonescu heard what was happening and realised that should the Legionaries kidnap the King he could be traded for his own capitulation, he ordered the royal party to be stopped.

At the road-block Michael seemed to take his defeat quite coolly, told the cars to turn round and headed back up the mountain. But it was yet another humiliation at the hands of the bigoted old man. His friends helped to take his mind off what had happened, skiing with him all morning, playing pranks on the teachers during their afternoon period at Peleş, but a few days later Queen Helen noted

> Am rather worried about Michael. Seems irritable and flatly refuses to go to bed till impossible hours. Looks pale and puffy. I feel that he is not living the life he ought to be and it seems impossible to do anything as there is just nobody at court who understands the first word of what a boy in his position needs. Am in despair about it.[20]

Antonescu learnt no lesson from this incident. He continued to humiliate the young king, to isolate him and to starve him of information. On 20 February, without informing King Michael, he replaced the head of the royal military household by a General Mardari. Next day, when inviting Michael and his mother to lunch with the newly appointed German Minister Baron Manfred von Killinger (a party man with a reputation for brutality), he warned them that while the Queen Mother could be accompanied by her lady-in-waiting there would not be room at the table for the King's ADC as von Killinger was bringing his own. 'That is how he treats Michael', Queen Helen commented. 'Unheard-of behaviour.'[21]

On 25 January 1941, the British Minister, Sir Reginald Hoare, who already had London's permission to leave the country with his legation as soon as convenient, sent a letter to the Foreign Office reporting on a conversation a friend of his had had with King Michael and the Queen Mother and ending:

> I record the above, not because the views of King Michael or of the Queen Mother are at the moment of any significance, but because the King may well prove a more permanent factor in the politics of this country than any of the politicians. At some future time His Majesty's character and general background may therefore acquire a new importance. But the outlook for the poor boy is pretty black![22]

Yet in March things unexpectedly brightened for King Michael. At lunch with the Antonescus they met Lt Jacques Vergotti and when a few days later Queen Helen asked whether Antonescu would release him to become the King's ADC, the General agreed. It was a surprising appointment for Antonescu to make but he liked Vergotti and knew that he wanted the post. The King and his mother were delighted. In a household which had become antipathetic here at last was a man they could trust, who like themselves had no doubt that Britain would win the war, who disliked the way Jews were being treated in Romania and abhorred the idea of a Europe completely under Nazi domination. He had a chalet not far from Sinaia where they could go after skiing. He knew good little *bodegas* and mountain walks and was like a breath of normality after the stiffness and general unpleasantness that characterised the Household.

When he saw what an isolated life the King was leading, Vergotti persuaded his friend Colonel Petre Lazăr, another member of the royal military household who at one time had taught Vergotti at military school, to give occasional lectures in the Palace. It was a break with routine. At the Queen's suggestion he also invited them to a small party at his Poiana chalet where they met friends of Vergotti, Prince George Sturdza and his Norwegian wife, who promptly invited them to Moldavia for a shoot.

The outcome of Vergotti's unconventionality was predictable. Mardari complained to Madame Antonescu that he was behaving above his station. The rumour was spread that the Queen had been seen driving alone with him and on 25 May she noted:

Was so upset after convs. with Nelly.* I knew something like this would come sooner or later, of course. How is one to stand this 'life'. Never felt so depressed. Also M. is a hopeless case – won't take interest in anything – all despairing.[23]

This was a *cri de coeur* from a woman who, on top of everything else, was being forced to play hostess to German officers on their way south to wreak havoc on Greece and her family. Her son's apparently cool, almost laconic reaction to what was going on was the same defence which he had used as a boy when living at his father's court. He would arrive late for meetings with senior German officers and not bother to apologise. Sometimes he did not appear at dinner and he spent more and more time alone higher up the mountains at a little house which they called Stana Rocată, 'the Royal Sheepfold'.

Then occurred Antonescu's crowning insult. At 1 a.m. on 22 June the King called his mother to say that Romania had been at war with the USSR since midnight. He had been told officially not by Antonescu or his deputy but by a regimental colonel he knew. The King telephoned Mihai Antonescu:

asked him 'What is this? Is it true?' 'Yes, it's true,' he replied. 'But why did you tell me nothing about it?' 'I thought you would know from the newspapers.' All this mixed up with a lot of senseless verbiage in his attempt to avoid giving me a direct answer.[24]

Yet had the Antonescus not behaved so arrogantly, had the King been associated in any way with the invasion of the USSR, his hand would have been greatly weakened in his dealings with the Allies after his *coup* of 1944.

Since the immediate object of Antonescu's invasion of the USSR alongside the Reichswehr was to recover Bessarabia and Bukovina, he had at that time the support of the whole country, including the King. Yet Antonescu was clearly a favourite of Hitler's. He had been the first leader among Germany's allies to be entrusted with the date of the operation, code-named 'Barbarossa'.[25] The Army Group 'Antonescu' under his command included the German 11th Army alongside the Romanian 3rd and 4th Armies. There was already a danger that such a special relationship with the man he expected to become the master of Europe could go to his head. King Michael, Juliu Maniu and Dinu Brătianu all warned him that they would strongly oppose an invasion by Romania of the

---

* Madame Nelly Catargi had accompanied Princess Helen as her lady-in-waiting during the latter's exile in Florence and remained with her for the rest of the Queen's life.

USSR proper. The Soviet Union, they argued, had become an ally of Britain and Britain was Romania's natural ally. Romania had no place in Hitler's war. Hitler sought *lebensraum* in the USSR. Romania, after the recovery of the eastern provinces, had, they considered, no justifiable territorial ambition there. They failed to stop him.

Antonescu once wrote to Maniu, 'You are for a democratic and parliamentary *régime* and for a foreign policy alongside the western powers. I am for a state, national dictatorship at home and a foreign policy alongside the Axis powers.' The King believes that this mentality rather than any military consideration explains why Antonescu crossed the Dniester after retaking Bessarabia and, against the advice of his Chief of the General Staff, pursued an ideological war that cost many Romanian lives. It was this commitment to dictatorship at home and to Germany's foreign policy abroad that led him to believe that whatever the circumstances – even when the Führer consistently betrayed his undertaking to defend Romania's territorial integrity – he himself must keep the word he had given to Adolf Hitler.[26] This obsession seems to have worsened as the war, from the German point of view, deteriorated.

Yet in earlier days, when Ion Antonescu met Juliu Maniu fairly regularly to discuss the future of their country, relations between these two ideological opposites reflected a nationalist, pragmatic approach which was characteristic of Romanians of that time. They both, for instance, despised King Carol II for the damage he had done Romania. They both feared Russian occupation more than anything else. They each expected unswerving support from their patrons – Germany in Antonescu's case, Britain in Maniu's – which, in the circumstances, was unrealistic. Antonescu respected the fact that Maniu enjoyed a wide political support which he knew he himself would never have. In those early days he seemed even to treat Maniu's Resistance activities as a kind of insurance for the country should his own policies fail. When Maniu established a radio link with SOE, Antonescu, despite considerable German pressure, refused to eliminate him. When a small party of British parachutists was captured at the end of 1943 Maniu immediately claimed responsibility for them and they were not handed over to the Germans. The morning after Ion Antonescu's arrest Maniu told the author that he was not a traitor though now he would be treated as one. He was just too limited in his outlook to be allowed to remain in power.

For nearly three weeks Antonescu refused to arrange for King Michael to visit his troops in Bessarabia and Bukovina. 'Makes such a bad impression,' his mother commented, believing that the delay was intentional.[27] Then, on the evening of 8 July, Mihai Antonescu finally telephoned with characteristic discourtesy to say that he should be ready in two hours to accompany General

Antonescu to the front. This first glimpse of the eastern front was a harrowing experience for a 19-year-old and told him much about the conduct of the war in the Romanian sector. He had to stand by while Antonescu cursed at an aged reserve officer riding on a bullock cart while his men marched. If he were too old to carry out his duties, Antonescu shouted, he had better shoot himself. The King watched for an hour through binoculars, Antonescu at his side, while Romanian soldiers advanced and were destroyed by enemy guns. He understood now why German staff officers accused the General of recklessly wasting his men and, although he was snubbed for referring to this during the drive back to the railhead, Queen Helen noted in her diary that Romanian soldiers were being killed in masses due to lack of organisation, training and field hospitals.[28] During August and September of that year, 1941, Romanians – while contributing 12 per cent of the total Axis forces fighting on the eastern front – were suffering 30 per cent of the losses.[29]

By 26 July, the Army Group 'Antonescu' had retaken Bessarabia and Northern Bukovina. It was then disbanded and Romanian troops were regrouped in preparation for crossing the Dniester into the USSR proper. Under an agreement dated 19 August 1941 the territory between the Dniester and the Bug rivers known as Transniestria would, when occupied, be administered by the Romanians.

On 22 August 1941 the King promoted Antonescu to the rank of Marshal for his part in the recovery of Bessarabia and Northern Bukovina. Owing to pressure from the troops at the front, he broke with his decision not to be associated with the campaign once it had crossed the frontier of what he considered to be historically Romanian territory. Towards the end of August he visited Romanian troops beyond the Dniester and was again appalled by their conditions.

Antonescu had known that traditional Romanian military training on the French model of static defence would prove useless against tanks on the Russian steppes and, before the invasion began, had arranged for German instructors to give his men a brief course in modern warfare. It was quite inadequate for the battlefields of the eastern front and, judging by a report made to President Roosevelt by the American General Hurley after a tour of the Stalingrad front in December 1942, conditions for Romanian soldiers continued to worsen.

> The Romanian troops, judging by the dead we saw on the field and by the appearance of the prisoners, were far below the standard of the Soviet troops. The Romanians were equipped for the most part with second-rate

arms and horse-drawn artillery. Throughout the entire salient we were hardly ever out of view of dead horses and dead Romanian soldiers.[30]

Romanian peasants had virtually no experience of mechanical transport. Romanian officers showed great physical courage but their textbook tactics were outdated. Many senior commanders felt, like the King, that after the recovery of Bessarabia and Bukovina the war in the USSR was no longer serving their country's interests. By 1942 many were making unauthorised withdrawals to conserve their men, in part for humanitarian reasons but also with an eye to the eventual recovery of Northern Transylvania. Few of them after 1941 believed that Germany would win the war.

Antonescu was the exception. The road to Transylvania, he repeatedly told the King, lay through Russia; unquestioning Romanian support of Germany would be rewarded by a victorious Führer at the peace settlement.[31] Between the years 1941 and 1944 he therefore contributed front-line troops of never less than six and as many as thirty divisions. When the advance was made into the Ukraine the Germans suggested that the 4th Romanian army should take Odessa. Antonescu was delighted, honoured to be treated as an equal by the Führer. As Romania's war gradually became Antonescu's war, the latter's personal honour, it seemed to Michael, increasingly took priority over military considerations. The 4th Army, which had 4,821 officers before the operation, lost 4,599 during the three assaults on Odessa;[32] the Romanian middle class was not large enough to replace the dead. On 16 October 1941 Sănătescu's 4th Army Corps were the first to enter a city which historically, the Queen Mother noted, was of no interest to Romania. 'Strategically', the King was to comment, 'Odessa was possibly an important point on the war-map, but not on our war-map, on the German.'[33]

Relations between the Antonescus and the royal family deteriorated rapidly after the Romanian army crossed the Dniester. When the King and his mother stopped one day to exchange a few words over his garden wall with Gunther, the American Minister, Mihai Antonescu was sent to complain – as if they were plotting with the USA.[34] On another occasion the Marshal asked for an audience only in order to reproach them with working against him, criticising him to their guests. 'Of all the lies', Queen Helen exclaimed. 'I told him that as he never gives himself the trouble to keep in touch with us and I haven't heard a word from him in three months it is quite natural that these rumours should be spread.'[35] She believed that Antonescu used Michael only because Romanians were attached to the dynasty and that he would never show him any genuine consideration. Given the ratio of power between the Crown and the dictator, Michael had to accept this treatment. When Antonescu arranged a victory parade on the King's name-day to celebrate the fall of Odessa, Michael saw this as nothing more than an attempt to revive Romanian enthusiasm for the war which had waned badly since the recovery of the eastern provinces. Yet he felt obliged to attend. He accepted the Order of Mihai Viteazul from Antonescu, received Marshal Keitel – though he refused to entertain him at home – and stood on the podium during the military parade. But he made it quite clear that the only part of the whole business that really interested him was the opportunity it gave him to be with his own officers and men and to decorate them and the regimental flags for the bravery and self-sacrifice they had shown in a war which he knew they should not be fighting.

It was the beginning of a period of intense frustration and depression for King Michael. He and his mother had to deal daily with Germans – some decent professional soldiers, others committed Nazis. The young King was under continual pressure from senior members of his household to toe the Antonescu line. From the time that Odessa fell to the Romanian army to the time, a year later, when the Axis suffered the Stalingrad disaster the King had to witness the German advance on two fronts – the central front and southwards deep into the Caucasus, knowing that in the process Romanian troops were being sacrificed in their tens of thousands. It was a particularly severe test for a young man who for the time being could do nothing to help his people, and it left him seemingly more determined than ever to take Romania out of the Axis.

The growing Nazi influence in Romania was brought home to King Michael by the vicious treatment of Romanian Jews, particularly in Bessarabia, North Bukovina and North Moldavia, where they were being shipped in large numbers by goods wagons to camps east of the Dniester. Of the 150,000 deported before August 1944, about 50,000 survived. When Alexander Safran, the young Chief Rabbi, finally succeeded in seeing Antonescu in October 1941 and appealed for mercy the Marshal fell into one of his uncontrollable rages. The Patriarch Nicodim told him that 'yids' merited only the contempt of 'good Romanians' and in no case the trust or compassion of 'good Christians'. Safran shouted, 'Do you not understand that you are speaking of tens of thousands of absolutely innocent beings? Do you not think that you will be called one day before the Supreme Judge to render an account of what was committed in Romania under your eyes, you a man of the church?' By then he was kneeling and Nicodim lifted him up muttering 'What can I do?' What he did do was to see the Queen Mother. Safran was already in touch with the King and Queen

Helen, the only people, he said, who – apart from the Papal Nuncio – always received him in a friendly way. They now invited to dine at the Palace the Patriarch, the Marshal, Mihai Antonescu and, since the export of Jews was mainly a German affair, von Killinger. They hoped for a civilised discussion, but when Queen Helen asked von Killinger to show compassion for these innocent people he replied so rudely that, as the Patriarch reacted to the insult and then turned to Antonescu for support, the latter had to respond. The outcome was a slowing down of the Jewish convoys and postponement of those not already on their way.[36]

Michael protested about the massacre of Jewish hostages at Odessa – reprisal for the destruction by Soviet partisans of Romanian army headquarters. He obtained the release of Dr Filderman, head of the Romanian Jewish community. But although the treatment of Romanian Jews, along with the unnecessary slaughter of Romanian troops, would continue to be a principal point of dissension between him and the Marshal, it was his mother who earned the title of 'Jew lover' in Berlin. Her open defence of the Jewish community was as much a threat to her safety as was her son's preparation for Antonescu's downfall to his. Five decades later Queen Helen was to be recognised by the Israeli authorities as a Righteous Gentile Among Nations.[37]

In the winter of 1941 the King and Queen Mother were trapped into meeting Hitler. When, in October, Queen Helen told Mihai Antonescu, the Foreign Minister, that she would like to pay a visit to Florence, he immediately agreed and, much to her surprise, suggested that the King should accompany her. Against their wishes the Government arranged for them to travel through Germany instead of Hungary and, at the last minute, when they could not refuse, they received an invitation to lunch with the Führer. They were greatly embarrassed. It was one thing the year before for Queen Helen and her sister to see Hitler informally, but quite another for the King of Romania to pay him a courtesy visit, one which he had no way of explaining to his cousin King George VI or to Allied governments. It was the Romanian Foreign Minister's doing. On the wave of the Odessa victory he had thought to extract from Germany a firm undertaking that Northern Transylvania would be returned after the war and had felt that to have the King in Berlin when he made his *démarche* would give it greater authority. Like so many of Mihai Antonescu's adventures into foreign policy, it failed. The Führer had no intention of letting Romania off the hook.

The lunch had clearly not been Hitler's idea and was strained. While Queen Helen, who spoke good German, kept up a reasonable flow of conversation, the Führer was distant with the young King. Michael could not get out of his mind Hitler's remark to his mother the year before that he was too young to rule and should be guided by Marshal Antonescu. He could think of nothing to say that would not lead to an argument, but he has left us a vivid account of the Führer's behaviour.

> You could not have a normal conversation with Hitler not even at the level of simple politeness. When something happened to interest him you saw his eyes light up and he took off. He talked a lot, was agitated . . . During the meal an officer came in and reported that something wonderful had happened at the front to which he did not react at all. Probably the interruption was stage-managed.
> 
> Quite suddenly he hit the table with the palm of his hand and said that he guaranteed that the United States would never enter the war. He held forth. At first it was painful. But, since you were obliged to listen, in the end it left an impression. I do not mean a pleasant one. He howled like a savage. I don't know how he is in personal conversations. In official ones he wants to impress you at any price – and then he rambles, ignores the people in front of him, as if addressing a crowd. If you paid attention you saw that he was speaking passionately about things you could read in any Nazi newspaper.[38]

Jacques Vergotti, the ADC accompanying them, noted that in the train to Florence Queen Helen was wearing an orchid that Hitler had offered her. He had also given her a small jar of pervitin tablets, a wonderful anti-depressant without which he had said he could not live.[39]

They had lunch in Rome with the King and Queen of Italy. They had an audience with Pope Pius XII, who assured them that he would convey their concern about the treatment of Jews in Romania and Transniestria to the Papal Nuncio in Turkey, Monseignor Angelo Roncalli, the future Pope John XXIII, the Vatican official responsible for the Black Sea area.[40]

Having been forced to call on Hitler, King Michael could hardly refuse an invitation from Mussolini, who was agreeable and amusing. 'Everyone around Mussolini', the King wrote later, 'was friendly. Hitler was cold – Mussolini was the opposite. He liked to think of himself as the father of a family, a popular leader who went on cross-country runs with his men.'[41] A day later they heard of the Japanese attack on Pearl Harbor and, with this resounding blow to the Führer's guarantee of a neutral USA ringing in their ears, they travelled from Rome to their beloved Florence and the Villa Sparta. They returned to Bucharest on 19 December 1941 in time for Christmas, bringing with them an Italian lamp – a present for the Marshal.

By then the German army had only reached the outskirts of Leningrad and was still twenty miles from Moscow. They had not foreseen such a scarcity of hard-topped roads, had badly underestimated the number of Russian divisions, and now their troops were even without proper winter clothing. The older, ideologically minded Russian generals were being replaced by young professionals and, worse for German and Romanian commanders in the field, the Führer had taken personal charge of the campaign.

Hitler decreed their 1942 objective to be not Moscow, but Donetz coal and Caucasian oil. Stalingrad, on the bend of the Volga, would be taken as flanking cover for the main operation.

By mid-May 1942 German and Romanian troops had taken most of the Crimea. Sevastopol fell on 4 July. Kleist's 1st Panzer division swept down into the Caucasus, but early in September shortage of fuel, thickly forested mountains and Russian harassment brought it to a halt.

By the third week in August von Paulus's 6th Army had established bridgeheads on the Don and was ready to begin the last stage of the attack on Stalingrad. But when German and Romanian soldiers penetrated the suburbs they found themselves without room to manoeuvre and up against workers' units fighting fanatically for their homes and factories. By mid-November their morale had been shot to pieces. Asian troops from the Eastern Soviets and equipment from factories beyond the Urals and from Britain and the USA had begun to appear. When the rivers froze over, the Russians counter-attacked and, despite a courageous attempt by von Manstein to save the 6th Army, von Paulus was forced to surrender on 31 January 1943. By mid-January 1943 the Red Army had cleared the whole Caucasus area, including the Crimea. The Führer's front line now re-formed west of the Dnieper.[42]

If the involvement of Romania in Hitler's war with the USSR was the main issue of contention between King Michael and Marshal Antonescu, the Marshal's interference with the royal household was the greatest irritant. When in January 1942 he wanted to replace all their ADCs with war invalids, the King and his mother decided that only someone with the authority of a Marshal of the Royal Court could put a stop to this kind of thing. Antonescu agreed to the appointment, but in January 1942 selected a certain Rosetti (Toto) Solescu, brother-in-law of von Paulus and a solid pro-German who would back the Conducator against the King on virtually every issue. Solescu joined Mardari's campaign to get rid of Jacques Vergotti and by May had succeeded in having him posted to the front. Even Vergotti's friend, the meticulously correct Petre Lazăr, was forced to leave the King's household and return to teaching. In his memoirs, Vergotti describes the atmosphere as so tense that he could not call at Foişor to say goodbye to the King and Queen. Instead, knowing that they would have to change clothes in Bucharest for the Independence Day parade, he waited for them in the palace garage.[43] Vergotti had been the only ADC the King and his mother could trust not to report on their conversations to the Marshal. After he left they no longer invited the ADCs to eat with them.

When 'Toto' Solescu brought the King the 'good news' that after Vergotti's departure Marshal Antonescu was now ready to restore friendly relations with the royal family, in her diary Queen Helen simply called him a 'nincompoop'. But when Antonescu asked the King to give up the Predeal chalet he had inherited from the Gunthers so that it would be available for von Killinger, and Solescu backed Antonescu over this too, it was the last straw. The King had his way. Mardari resigned in June, Solescu in July.

During that same summer of 1942 Marshal Antonescu had a long bout of sickness and since no one seemed to know for sure what was wrong, it was widely believed that he was the victim of a poisoning attempt. Madame Antonescu begged the Queen Mother to visit him while he was in such low spirits, which she did. They always had one thing at least to talk about – their love of English gardens. Meanwhile King Michael was seeing more of Mihai Antonescu, the Marshal's deputy and Foreign Minister, who during the Marshal's illness had taken over many of his duties. The two men, he concluded, could not have been more different. Ion Antonescu stuck to his views, however misconceived. Mihai Antonescu, at heart an anglophile, was so flexible that he won the respect of neither the Germans nor the Allies.

Without the Marshal, his namesake's ineptitude as Foreign Minister became apparent. Having failed in the winter of 1941 to obtain from Hitler an assurance regarding the return of Transylvania, he now planned a Transylvanian policy so outrageously anti-Hungarian that Berlin and Rome demanded its immediate retraction. King Michael said that had the Marshal been able to find a soldier with a properly structured idea of international politics, he would have replaced his Foreign Minister. Nevertheless, the King added, Mihai Antonescu was a very well-informed man: 'his culture was solid and sometimes it seemed to me that he had no need to be unctuous'.[44]

Even at the peak of Axis military success in the summer of 1942, the King never hid his scepticism about the assumption of a German victory or his anger that Romanians should be so involved with the wrong side. When Mihai Antonescu enthused over occupation of the Crimea and the popularity of the war, Michael said they were 'sitting on the lid of a boiling kettle which could fly off at any moment'.[45] Nevertheless, in July the ambitious Mihai Antonescu took advantage of the Marshal's absence to arrange to accompany the King on what he saw as a major propaganda victory tour of the Romanian front. Had King Michael had competent and loyal advisers in his household, he would have been forewarned. As it was, Queen Helen recorded in her diary that Mihai Antonescu arrived at the airport late.'Bigelet* was still chewing remains of breakfast and had a voice like the morning after the night before', 'Bigelet beaming to be accompanying M'. Killinger appeared with a crowd of satellites and Michael was very angry indeed when he discovered that he would be joined by these high-ranking Germans and a plane-load of journalists. Sevastopol had fallen only a few weeks before. Axis fortunes were at their summit and King Michael resented being used as 'a kind of icing on the cake'.[46] He made his views clear on the occupation of Transniestria by refusing to let the Junker land at Odessa, the pride of the Romanian army. He then made a tour of Romanian troops in the Crimea with the minimum publicity.[47]

Vergotti, who had been unable to see the King during this visit to the front, obtained permission from his commanding officer to return to Sinaia for a few days and, under cover of presenting the King with a captured jeep, to try to correct the misinformation he would have been given about the condition of the Romanian troops. After a furious dash to Sinaia, filling jerry cans with petrol at German posts, taking pervatin to keep awake, driving much too fast for his sergeant's liking, he had some hours with the King, who was delighted with the Willis jeep but who did not need the briefing. He had seen for himself the state of the Romanian soldiers and their discontent at the way they were treated by the Germans. They drove the jeep up to Stana and, while trying out some Russian ammunition Vergotti had brought back, the King spoke angrily of the war, of the risk Hitler took by splitting the enormously long front into one advancing southwards and one eastwards, of his anxiety about the fate of Romanian foot-soldiers, sent originally a few hundred kilometres to liberate Bessarabia and North Bukovina but now following German motorised units deep into the Caucasus and to the banks of the Volga. Later, when he begged the Marshal to withdraw Romanian troops from the Crimea before it was too late, he was ignored. Either Antonescu had put his trust in the Führer's promise of a spring offensive or else he had by then surrendered to the Germans so much control over the Romanian army that he was in no position to take

---

* In private the King and his mother referred to Marshal Ion Antonescu as 'Bige' and his deputy, Mihai (Ica) Antonescu, as 'Bigelet'.

independent action. At Stalingrad alone Romania was to lose about 140,000 men, representing over half their active divisions.[48]

It was during this summer of 1942 that a nucleus of resistance to the Antonescu *régime* began to form around the King. In March Baron Mocsoni* had recommended his adopted son for employment in the King's household – the highly intelligent, highly strung Baron Ionel Mocsoni Styrcea became Head of Chancery to the Marshal of the Court Solescu, and three months later, when Solescu left, was made acting Marshal. In July Dumitriu Negel, a man the King liked, became Administrator of the Royal Estates. King Michael could now count on at least three members of the household – Styrcea, Negel and Ionniţiu, his old schoolmate who had stayed with them for Christmas 1940 and had later become his Private Secretary. That same summer King Michael became acquainted with Niculescu Buzeşti, who as head of the communications department of the Ministry of Foreign Affairs was able to provide secure communications between Maniu and the men he had been able to place in the Legations of neutral capitals – in particular Stockholm and Lisbon. King Michael and Queen Helen met Buzeşti when lunching at the Swedish Legation on 7 June. Though she probably did not yet know of his subversive activities, the Queen Mother noted, 'Seems man of the future',[49] and when, on the 18th, Styrcea brought him to Sinaia for lunch and the King drove them to Predeal, 'Most interesting conversation'. 'Buzel', as she already called him in her diary, lunched again on 13 July. During the next few months the King, using Niculescu Buzeşti as his link, established working relations with Juliu Maniu and, through him, Dinu Brătianu, the leaders of Romania's two historic parties which unofficially still represented the views of the majority of Romanians. At the end of the year he was thus in a position to make a declaration on behalf of the Romanian people which challenged the assumption that Romanian participation in Germany's war with the USSR was to her benefit. However, for security reasons he would not work with Maniu and Brătianu face to face for another two years.

During the autumn and winter of 1942 morale in the pro-German camp dropped. The Marshal was out of action. Towards the end of August his deputy, Mihai Antonescu, seemed to go a little insane, making up violently to Queen Helen and 'drivelling on', in her words, about his love for Michael. On the King's name-day they had news of the Allied victory in North Africa, and a fortnight later the Russians were known to be advancing on a wide front that

---

* Baron Mocsoni was the only member of King Carol's household kept on by King Michael and the Queen Mother.

might well encircle the Romanian armies. On 16 November Queen Helen notes that Mihai Antonescu 'seems quite conscious of what fate is in store for him and is rather anxious about it'. When Marshal Ion Antonescu, who by then was recovering, flew at her for not understanding how essential it was for the world's good for Germany to win, she simply wrote, 'Ass'.[50] She saw little of Michael, who now had supper regularly at the little house at Stana. On his twenty-first birthday she did not see him all day except for lunch. Two days before she had noted in her diary 'My life here is only an existence.'

Towards the end of the year the King bought Săvârșin, a house in the far west of Transylvania, a night's train journey from Sinaia and more or less out of range of government spies. It was a charming two-storey eighteenth-century wooden house with five guest rooms, useful outbuildings, a park of about 20 hectares and woods up into the neighbouring valleys. The house, which had belonged to the Hungarian Count Hunyadi, was very run down and it was over a year – with Queen Helen jollying along the local workmen – before they were able to move in.

When the King and Queen Mother went to the Antonescus for lunch on Christmas Day they were surprised to hear the Marshal cursing German strategy and holding it responsible for the terrible things that were happening to the Romanian armies. His mother joined in, Michael did not. He had a nasty little surprise for Antonescu and the Führer which he intended to insert into his annual new year broadcast to the nation.

By the end of 1942, the King has since explained, it was clear that something concrete had to be done to leave the Axis.

> What was happening was a real scandal with our army in Russia, our losses beginning to horrify us . . . while the responsibility for the lives of so many Romanians fell to the charge of a single man. Any ordinary man would have felt it his duty to protest. The leaders of the historical parties were as angry as I was but their power to influence events had been reduced to the minimum . . . By the end of the year 1942 the idea of a joint action to bring the country out of the war had already crystallised.[51]

Concrete action was taken by King Michael when in this 1943 new year address he called for Romania to discontinue the war alongside Hitler. In effect he was sending a message to the Allies on behalf of himself, the political leaders, many in the army and a large part of the civilian population. Von Killinger protested violently. The Marshal was furious and Hitler, desperate to restore army morale on the eastern front, blamed the Marshal for this unpardonable 'stab in the back'. Such a deliberate flouting of Axis policy could not have been made without the agreement of the man delivering the speech, yet Antonescu chose to blame the Queen Mother.[52] He, the Führer and von Killinger still saw the King as a mere spokesman and fortunately they would continue to underestimate him to the very end.

Although the extraordinarily tight security of King Michael's preparations for his anti-German volte-face in such a gossip-ridden place as Bucharest was something of a miracle, it is doubtful whether he could have succeeded without the help of the blind prejudice of the German and Romanian establishments. He was seen as no more than a youth whose dissolute father had discredited and humiliated the monarchy – someone, therefore, who could be ignored without risk. Hitler had spoken of him as too young to rule during his meeting with Queen Helen in 1940. The King himself was to be taken aback when during his last meeting with Antonescu on the afternoon of 23 August 1944 it became apparent that the Marshal still saw him as the boy he had first met in his father's palace four years before.

These attitudes provided the best security the plotters could have hoped for. Had the Führer been better informed by his representatives in Bucharest, had Ion Antonescu been less egocentric, more aware of Michael's potential, the magic circle of muddled thinking that protected them to the end would have evaporated. When von Killinger stormed into the Palace on the night of the King's *coup* to demand what had happened to Marshal Antonescu, he seemed to be unaware that King Michael, not Marshal Antonescu, was the legitimate and true head of state and commander-in-chief of the army. But the Romanian army was aware of it; that night even the most pro-German generals obeyed the King's orders without question.

# FIVE

## King Michael's Decision to Break with the Axis

Of the senior members of the royal household, Marshal Antonescu trusted the articulate and openly anglophile Ionel Mocsoni Styrcea least. Styrcea, he believed, was chiefly responsible with Queen Helen for the young King's new year broadcast and he was determined to be rid of him.

On the say-so, therefore, of one of his ADCs he accused Styrcea of arranging for King Michael to meet Maniu on the way home from a shooting holiday in Bukovina. He ordered his immediate despatch to the front. King Michael and his mother, who were marking trees at Săvârşin when they heard the news, took the night train back to Bucharest and, when an attempt was made next day to arrest Styrcea, they gave him and his wife sanctuary in Casa Nouă.

The Marshal's charge was based on a lie; the only contact the King had with the Resistance leader was indirect, mainly through Niculescu Buzeşti. At first he was prepared to compromise but, when Antonescu rudely turned down two proposals, he let it be known that rather than put up with any more of this behaviour he would leave the country. 'M. didn't give in', his mother noted in her diary. 'It will strengthen him if he wins this grim battle. The first time he has seriously put his foot down.'[1] The King's battalion of guards was put on the alert, their house became a kind of fortress and the siege lasted four days. Then on the morning of 12 February 1943 Mihai Antonescu telephoned to say that the King's last offer to make Styrcea administrator of the Săvârşin estate had now been accepted and everything arranged according to his wishes.

Nevertheless, the campaign against Styrcea continued. Colonel Codreanu, appointed by Antonescu to head the military household, sent the Marshal a memorandum complaining that Styrcea had obstructed access of the military household to the King. On 24 February Antonescu countersigned this and sent it to King Michael, who annotated it carefully, refuting Codreanu's accusation point by point and concluding, 'Consequently Colonel Codreanu can no longer remain chief of the Military Household.'[2]

Colonel Codreanu resigned from both the Household and the army and the infuriated Marshal sent Michael what he described as a 'letter of correction' reminding him that he was no more than a figurehead and threatening to hold a plebiscite, a vote of confidence which would enable him to banish the royal family. However, Antonescu had made a grave mistake as Romanians held the King and Queen Mother in far greater esteem than him. When he realised this he panicked lest his letter become public, and issued a hasty decree under which anyone divulging, without permission, the contents of any letter of his or of the King or of any minister would be imprisoned for five to ten years. It was a humiliating climb-down for the Marshal.[3] In the new year of 1943 the King had raised his standard for both enemies and allies to see. But the row over Ionel Styrcea six weeks later had been a man-to-man joust, a turning point in their relationship. Antonescu would in future be chary of trying to bully him.

The Germans also put pressure on the King. Von Killinger told a meeting of the German–Romanian Friendship Union in Bucharest that action would be taken against 'those who would raise their hands against Nazism' – a direct, public challenge to King Michael. The King had also received anonymous threats that he could meet with an accident. When Michael's cousin Albrecht, the composer, paid them a visit with the object, Queen Helen believed, of reporting on them to Berlin, he warned her that, should Michael's behaviour force Antonescu to take extreme measures, there could be no question of Germany supporting the monarchy. 'As if it would ever occur to us that Germany would!' she commented to her diary that evening. Nevertheless, it was during that spring of 1943 that King Michael began to consider preparations for an eventual escape from Romania should this become necessary.

Meanwhile the quixotic Marshal Antonescu had decided to replace Colonel Codreanu by a general, a friend and a cavalry officer like himself – the man who had suppressed the Iron Guard uprising of February 1941. When called on 6 March from the front General Sănătescu arrived in Bucharest briefed to discuss the military situation and was taken aback when the Marshal first lectured him about the importance of surrounding the young king with experienced advisers, then offered him the royal military household. During the consequent audience at the Palace the Queen gave him a frank account of the King's constitutional position and the Marshal's attitude to him, and Sănătescu saw that to act as a buffer between this young man and his old army friend would not be easy. He accepted the post but asked that the head of the military household be given the same grade as the Marshal of the Court and that he retain his position of Army Commander. The King agreed to both requests.[4]

At first General Sănătescu thought that the disagreement between the Marshal and the King stemmed from trifles, a shooting party in Bukovina when he was invited by people of whom the Marshal did not approve. He later realised that his two masters were fighting over matters of principle and ideology which ran far deeper than the trouble over Ionel Styrcea.

General Sănătescu decided to live in Bucharest where he had access to the Ministry of the Interior and General Staff. He received copies of their daily operational bulletins and during his weekly visits to Sinaia was able to ensure that the King was for the first time properly briefed. The National Day celebration on 10 May gave him his first taste of the Marshal's erratic behaviour. During the military parade, while, in Sănătescu's words, troops rode by in trucks giving the impression of motorised units, Antonescu was amicable. Yet he failed to attend the lunch at the Palace to which he, his wife and Mihai Antonescu had been invited. The Marshal had fallen into a rage because, after the procession, the King had not asked him to ride in the royal car and, according to Mihai Antonescu (who arrived very upset at the Palace at 2 o'clock), because a protocol official of the Foreign Ministry, thinking that the Marshal would wish to go home after the parade to change for the lunch, had had his car positioned for a quick getaway rather than for driving through cheering crowds behind the royal car. Antonescu had accused Mihai Antonescu of conniving with the Palace to humiliate him. 'As if this were the moment for such trivialities', commented Sănătescu in his diary, 'but he is probably aware of the disaster he has landed the country in and every little thing upsets him'.[5] On this occasion the King and his mother took the Marshal's behaviour in their stride. 'What do we care', she wrote in her diary, 'Old B. is so hated.'[6]

The Marshal had always isolated King Michael from the armed forces except on purely representational occasions when he considered the monarch's presence appropriate. General Sănătescu took steps to correct this policy. In June 1943, for instance, he arranged for the King and Queen Helen to visit a fighter squadron based in Galați and was amazed at Michael's detailed knowledge of aero-engines. They stayed for an impromptu lunch at the officers' mess where the food, said Sănătescu, was about what they were used to at home.

Another man had joined the King's small, loyal group. During his visit to the Crimea in the summer of 1942 his pilot, Udriski, had cured him of air-sickness by offering him the controls. King Michael had not forgotten this gesture and had asked him to Foișor. After lunch, while the Queen and Nelly Catargi, her lady-in-waiting, were going through copies of *House & Garden* looking for ideas for Săvârșin, the King took Udriski in the caterpillar car for a drive through a heavy thunderstorm. They enjoyed each other's company. Udriski, the King felt, was one of the very few people he had met to whom intrigue never seemed to occur.

It was the juxtaposition of Udriski and Săvârşin that gave him the idea of learning secretly to fly a Junker 52 which was big enough to carry the people who would be in most danger if he should have to leave the country. He would keep it near Săvârşin. The house was not yet habitable but he could stay with Ionel Styrcea who, as the administrator, lived nearby. He arranged for the use of some common land at the village of Värädia de Mures which, despite the hazard of grazing cows, made a good enough landing strip. At that time they also had a Klemm 35 trainer monoplane and a small plane which Udriski used for aerobatics.

The authorities knew that King Michael often flew with Udriski in a Klemm 35 but apparently it did not occur to them that in August 1943 he began to have flying lessons. He made his first solo flight after twenty days' instruction – a red-letter day for Michael. He built up his flying hours at every opportunity and, so as not to alert the authorities, took his physical examination at the end rather than the beginning of the course. In September 1943 he obtained his military flying permit. After this he could never understand why Antonescu, although he made life difficult enough for Udriski because his wife was Jewish, allowed him to stay on as unofficial pilot to the royal house.

The Queen Mother, too, sought relaxation in flying and after a tense lunch at Banloc with Princess Elisabeta, she drove straight to the airfield and flew with Udriski for half an hour.

On 28 August 1943 they received a sharp warning. King Boris of Bulgaria, who had rescinded the deportation order issued by his pro-fascist government and so saved a community of 50,000 Jews from the gas chambers, had died suddenly in suspicious circumstances. Sănătescu represented the King at the funeral and when Princess Mafalda of Italy, after visiting her widowed sister in Sofia, passed through the local Săvârşin station at 5 o'clock one morning Michael went to talk with her for a few minutes. 'Poor little thing', wrote his mother. 'She knew nothing but so courageous.'[7] The Princess had not been told of the armistice Marshal Badoglio had signed the day before with the Allies. When her train reached Germany she was arrested as an enemy of the Reich and sent to Buchanwald concentration camp where she died without seeing her husband or children again.

Michael was not intimidated. When on 12 September German Special Forces released Mussolini from his Allied prison, Romania became the first country, after Germany, to recognise his new Republic. Yet the King refused to receive the dictator's diplomatic representative. 'There was a king in Italy,' he said, 'and this man did not represent him. He stayed in Bucharest but I did not accept his letter of credence.'[8]

On Michael's birthday his mother wrote 'He is 22. May god build up this poor country with his help.'⁹ At his request there was no parade that day. On 26 November he attended the official opening of the new academic year at Bucharest University and was given an ovation. The Marshal, as Sănătescu remarked, had had the good sense to stay away.

By Christmas they had moved into Săvârşin and on Christmas Day invited Madame Pacioga (an English nurse whom Queen Helen liked very much), Ionel and Bielle Styrcea, Buzeşti and Victor Pogoneanu. Michael's Great Dane had died some months before and for Christmas his mother gave him an Alsatian called Azo. Two days later he admitted to her that for months he had had a double hernia and thought that perhaps he should do something about it. It took six weeks in those days to recover from such an operation and, to pass the time, he reverted to his boyhood interest – photography – experimenting with colour and 35mm ciné film and soundtrack.

At the beginning of 1943 the King had made public his opposition to the Axis. A year later he had a small group of people ready to risk their lives in a *coup* against the Germans. They included his mother, Ionel Styrcea and his wife, Sănătescu, Mircea Ionniţiu, Colonel Robert Bossy, brother of Raoul Bossy, who had joined the King's Household, Niculescu Buzeşti and Victor Pogoneanu, Buzeşti's colleague at the Ministry of Foreign Affairs. Pogoneanu was paralysed, in a wheel-chair, and would later show incredible courage when faced by totalitarian brutality. The King had now to produce a proper command with enough military and political vision and expertise to make a *coup* possible.

After the British expeditionary force had, in May 1940, been driven out of mainland Europe, Churchill knew that, if only for demographic reasons, Britain alone could not produce an army capable of defeating Hitler. Even if the USA entered the conflict it would take some years to build up an effective invasion force. Meanwhile, however, he could 'set Europe ablaze' by training and equipping the Resistance fighters who, he believed, would now spring up in every occupied country and, to this end he created in August 1940 an organisation known as the Special Operations Executive (SOE).

After the Vienna Diktat (under which Romania lost much of Transylvania to Hungary), Maniu concluded a limited agreement with SOE and a year later when Antonescu committed Romania to Hitler's war in the Soviet Union, he began to prepare for a much larger national uprising. By the end of 1943 he had courier and radio communication with SOE headquarters in Cairo and had placed his men in key posts in the Romanian army, administration and diplomatic service. He had absolute confidence that after the war Churchill would abide by the terms of the Atlantic Charter* and ensure the return of democracy to his country. Although King Michael had a more realistic understanding of Great Power politics, neither man could know that by the end of 1943 Churchill would become the weakest of the three Allies, that US/Soviet insistence on applying the doctrine of unconditional surrender to German satellites regardless of their pro-Allied sympathies had denied him the political room for manoeuvre he had enjoyed in Eastern Europe, and that the Teheran summit of November 1943 had finally ruled out the landing of an expeditionary force in the region. Queen Helen came near to the truth when she noted in her diary:

> News from the Allies confirms what I was always sure of, namely that this country does not interest them except as an enemy. Their only answer to every appeal is unconditional surrender.[10]

She could have added that, when Churchill called on East European countries to 'work their passage home', 'home' now meant Moscow, not London.

Late in 1943, Juliu Maniu informed British Middle East Headquarters that he intended to send out an envoy to negotiate in secret an armistice with the Allies. Maniu was counting on British support but the Allies had quite a different agenda in mind. A Romanian *coup d'état* timed to occur shortly before the Normandy landings – which were planned at that time for early May – and a simultaneous Soviet offensive on the eastern front would cause the Wehrmacht the maximum of embarrassment. Should the *coup* fail, the cost to Germany of men and material needed to occupy Romania would still justify the attempt. But to meet this timing prolonged negotiations must be avoided. A small SOE mission led by Colonel Gardine de Chastelain, a friend of Maniu, and including myself was despatched to Romania to inform the Resistance leader that the three Allies stood solidly together and that since Romania had become a Soviet affair Maniu's delegate to the armistice talks would deal primarily with the Soviet, not the British, representative. Should he prevaricate over the terms offered, these could be withdrawn and harsher ones imposed after Hitler's defeat. Unfortunately, this SOE mission was captured before it

---

* Concluded on 12 August 1941 by Churchill and Roosevelt. The principles to be applied after the war would include the right of peoples to choose the form of government under which they would live.

could brief Maniu, and Maniu's misplaced optimism about the help he could expect from his 'friend' Churchill accounted in large part for the collapse of the talks.

These were to take place in Cairo and, since Maniu's envoy could not travel abroad without Marshal Antonescu's permission and since Mihai Antonescu as Minister of Foreign Affairs would issue his passport, Maniu had to take both the Marshal and his deputy into his confidence. It was a typically Romanian situation. Marshal Antonescu was himself somewhat uneasy about the outcome of his attachment to Nazi Germany. He had allowed Mihai Antonescu to put out peace feelers but these had come to nothing. He had briefed Romanian diplomats going to neutral countries to let it be known that, although he would not surrender unconditionally to the Soviet Union, should an Anglo-American force land in the Balkans and approach the Romanian frontier, he would willingly give them substantial material support. So long as he was not publicly associated with the Cairo operation Antonescu was content to let it proceed.

Maniu's first choice to represent him at the Cairo meeting – Constantin Vişoianu, a diplomat, a Titulescu prodigy in whom he had complete confidence – was considered too leftist by Mihai Antonescu. He was replaced, at the Marshal's suggestion, by the highly experienced and respected Prince Barbu Ştirbey. Maniu and Ştirbey had both suffered under King Carol's *régime* and had similar views on Antonescu's policies. But Maniu could not forget that during the 1920s Barbu Ştirbey and Ionel Brătianu had kept him out of office by what he considered to be unworthy means. Maniu had reservations about Ştirbey and insisted that Vişoianu should join him as soon as the Cairo talks got under way.

This was broadly the picture when, on 14 February 1944, Niculescu Buzeşti went to Sinaia to brief the King on the Ştirbey mission. Michael was recovering well from the operation he had had on 10 January and at the end of February he held the first of many meetings at the Casa Nouă to discuss practical ways of putting an end to Antonescu's disastrous war policy.

The British and American representatives in Cairo hoped to have Moscow's draft of the Armistice before Prince Ştirbey arrived. But Soviet bureaucracy was sluggish and Ştirbey was kept waiting in Ankara, a hotbed of intrigue where the British had no powers of censorship. On 14 March the *Daily Mail* followed by the BBC announced that Ştirbey, with the Marshal's approval, was on his way to negotiate Romania's exit from the war. There was panic in Bucharest. Five days later, on 19 March, the Germans occupied Hungary while the Regent Horthy was visiting Hitler at Berchtesgarten and, when on the 23rd the Antonescus were summoned to a meeting with Hitler, many Romanians awaited the same fate for Romania. The King, at Buzești's request, went down to Bucharest to satisfy himself that, if this happened, everything possible had been done to ensure the safety of Maniu and Brătianu. He also asked General Sănătescu to sound out political and military leaders about the possibility of carrying out a *coup* in the Marshal's absence.

General Sănătescu reported at that evening's meeting that the political and military leaders he had approached were uncertain how to proceed. Most of them thought that the King should organise opposition to the Germans but were not ready to back him openly. The generals believed that with so many German troops in the country a military operation would certainly lead to occupation. The King was not convinced. German troops were continually on the move between their bases in Romania and the front line and it was difficult therefore to assess their strength in Romania at any one time. Estimates based on the number of rations claimed by the German authorities were naturally inflated. 'It's always the way', remarked Queen Helen later. 'All swear fidelity but the moment Sweetie appeals all retire gracefully saying if only one had told them before but this certainly wasn't the moment to act.'[11] Sănătescu, himself, probably agreed with the generals. He found ample boldness and initiative among his young plotters but had to suppress some of their wilder schemes.

After the news leak Prince Știrbey had proceeded to Cairo and since there was still no text of the armistice agreement he was asked to open the first session on 17 March.* He took this opportunity to express a view which may have sounded strange coming from Maniu's representative but which the Western delegates found unexpectedly realistic. Only the Marshal, whom the Germans did not suspect and whose orders would be carried out without question by Romanian troops, could, he said, carry out a succesful *coup* at this time. A *coup* by Maniu would be hazardous and would, in any case, require substantial Allied material support. Romania, he added, knew that she was defeated and he hoped that her treatment by the Allies would be in accordance with the principles of the Atlantic Charter.

Prince Știrbey knew that Maniu refused to go down in history as the man who had signed away Romania's claim to Bessarabia, but he made the personal suggestion that, should the Russians hold a plebiscite while in occupation of the province, the result would be 'a foregone conclusion'. When questioned by

---

* Prince Știrbey was grateful to a member of the British delegation for warning him of this possibility.

Novikov, the Soviet ambassador, on the question of 'Allied military support', he said that he had had in mind Soviet landings at the port of Constanṭa. What he really hoped for was an Anglo-American landing. Although this had been ruled out at the Teheran summit, Allied security had been so effective that Romanian gossip continued to thrive on it, and for the next twelve months up to nineteen German divisions were immobilised in the Balkans awaiting it.

London and Washington found Ştirbey's proposals 'unobjectionable'; Molotov argued that since Ştirbey did not seem to represent Maniu and since Maniu appeared to be a tool of Antonescu they could not take Ştirbey's statements seriously.

Prince Ştirbey was in a difficult position. He saw on arrival in Cairo that he could expect no special treatment from the British, who considered Romania to be primarily Russia's problem. Nor could he be explicit with Maniu because all telegrams exchanged between Cairo and Bucharest were automatically copied to the three delegations and were therefore seen in Moscow. Juliu Maniu had never really trusted Prince Ştirbey and in these circumstances absence of communication or understanding between them was total.

The Germans seemed unconcerned about the armistice talks; although 'Margaretha 11' – a contingency plan for the occupation of Romania – had been ready since January they saw no reason to implement it. Ribbentrop remarked to Mihai Antonescu during his visit to Germany that British relations with Russia had gone so far beyond the point of no return that nothing could come of the Ştirbey mission. Britain's Romanian policy had indeed been subsumed into her Soviet policy. She had no longer anything to offer Romania.

As the Red Army advanced into Bessarabia, Moldavian refugees poured into Bucharest. On 23 March the Romanian Service of the BBC warned Romanians that, at this eleventh hour, unless they broke with the Axis immediately they would be bombed to destruction. The Antonescus returned from Germany just before lunchtime on 25 March and the Marshal saw the King in audience the following day. In King Michael's words, he talked a good deal of the 'usual rot' but one clear fact had emerged from the visit: although the Red Army now had a firm hold on Bessarabia and was moving into Bukovina, Hitler was not preparing to counter-attack and German commanders were afraid to tell the Führer just how bad things were at the front. As he was leaving, Antonescu mentioned that, at the moment, there were virtually no German troops in Romania. So much for the generals, Michael thought, and then, as if reading his mind, the Marshal added very forcibly that anyone attempting an operation against Hitler would be suppressed.

On 28 March a meeting of the King's group discussed first Ştirbey's latest telegram. There was still no draft text of an armistice and Ştirbey's suggestion that they might as well accept the Armistice, text unseen, was unacceptable. Maniu and Brătianu, the King was told, were ready to advise him but not actively to support him. Maniu wanted him to revive the Crown Council and Michael was naturally attracted by anything that would give him a legitimate voice in state affairs. But as Sănătescu argued at the meeting, a Crown Council would inevitably involve the King in Resistance politics, which could lead to German occupation and loss of the freedom of movement necessary to carry out the *coup*. The Germans must continue to associate Romanian Resistance exclusively with Juliu Maniu and to feel confident, therefore, that the Marshal had the situation under control. To this the meeting agreed.

Finally they discussed the Marshal's visit to Germany. The King asked Sănătescu, Negel and Styrcea to put to Mihai Antonescu the proposition that, since Germany had not respected her undertaking to defend Romanian territory, Romania had no further obligation towards the Führer.

At a working lunch at Casa Nouă on 30 March 1944, to which the King invited the Marshal, Mihai Antonescu and Sănătescu, the divergence between Mihai Antonescu and Ion Antonescu became clearer. The former spoke out for an armistice, the latter for strengthening the line Romanian forces were now holding. It would be a great achievement, the Marshal said, if this could be held until the end of the war – 'beyond which', Sănătescu noted in his diary, 'the Marshal never sees'.[12]

That night the King's meeting included Queen Helen. They briefly discussed the stagnation of the Cairo conference and then turned to what they all considered to be a far more difficult nut to crack – the *coup* itself. The Germans were hard and numerous and no one would have precise information about their strength. Sănătescu was still worried about the impetuous courage of some of his young friends, and after the meeting he noted, 'We must wait a little and analyse everything carefully to avoid pitching ourselves into an adventure.'[13] He had a pretty good idea by now that the King would be the only man ready to face up to Antonescu and his admiration and liking for Michael had grown enormously during the last year. King Michael trusted Sănătescu and, since the post of Marshal of the Royal Court was still empty, he made the General titular Marshal as well as head of the military household so that he could see political as well as military personalities without arousing suspicion.

During the first week of April 1944 two events had a direct bearing on the King's preparations. On 2 April Molotov assured Romanians over Moscow radio that his government had no intention of taking Romanian territory or changing its political or social systems. Two days later began the consistent bombing of Romania by US and British aircraft, the RAF by night, the USAF by day.

If Molotov's assurance were genuine, King Michael could feel reasonably confident that should the *coup* be successful Romania would return to a parliamentary democracy after the war. On 6 April what they thought to be a highly confidential telegram was despatched under Maniu's signature asking Știrbey to take discreet soundings about the possibility of the two Western Allies associating themselves publicly with Molotov's statement. The violence of Eden's reaction to this 'impertinent' questioning of Moscow's word should have warned them that Molotov had seen his telegram. The King himself did not at that point lose all faith in Molotov's assurance, but Eden's outburst together with the beginning of the Anglo-American bombing were proof enough for him that in future Romania could expect no particular sympathy from the West.

The King, his mother, Buzești and Sănătescu were having lunch on the 4th when the bombing of Bucharest started and, when Michael went onto the roof to watch the raid, he picked up a piece of still-warm shrapnel. The windows on one side of the Palace were shattered. At Cotroceni the washhouse and Madame Kopkov's apartment were destroyed. Sănătescu reported 500 civilians killed and 1,200 wounded. Perhaps, Michael thought, this might persuade the Marshal that Romania had no place in this world conflict. The bombing of their home towns together with the unopposed advance of the Red Army into Romanian territory was already affecting morale at the front and for the first time German soldiers were seen drunk on the streets of the capital. When King Michael called Mihai Antonescu to the Palace to ask what was being done about the proposal made to him on the evening of 28 March, Ica assured him that the Marshal had been won over. The Marshal had in fact spoken to Hitler some months before on the lines suggested by the King, but to no effect.

Though he would still depend on Maniu's illegal radio for transmission, Antonescu now asked for a personal cipher with which to communicate personally with General Wilson, Commander-in-Chief of Allied Forces in the Middle East. When this had been arranged, instead of making practical suggestions for the cessation of Romanian hostilities against the USSR, Antonescu sent Wilson a maudlin telegram begging 'a great and glorious soldier' not to 'ask an old man and honest soldier to end his days in humility'.* The bombing had temporarily broken Maniu's radio link with Cairo and when the telegram finally reached London it was a month out of date. Churchill and Eden, partly out of a sense of decency towards Antonescu, suppressed it and it was not, therefore, copied to Moscow.[14]

Finally, on 8 April Ambassador Novikov circulated the draft text of the armistice terms. Within four days and with few amendments it was cleared with London and Washington and despatched to Maniu and Antonescu. The Allied (Soviet) conditions as received from Cairo were briefly as follows.[15]

1. The Soviet Government's minimum conditions for an armistice were:
   (a) Romania will break with the Germans and carry out joint operations against them with the allied forces, including the Red Army, the object being to reestablish the independence and sovereignty of Romania.
   (b) The Romanian–Soviet frontier will be restored to conform with the agreement of 1940. [return to Russia of Bessarabia and Northern Bukovina]
   (c) Romania will pay reparations.
   (d) Romania will return all prisoners of war, Soviet and Allied.

These conditions can be modified to Romania's disadvantage if not accepted without delay.

2. Although the Soviet Government does not wish to occupy Romanian territory during the whole duration of the armistice, Soviet and allied troops must when necessary have unrestricted freedom of movement in the execution of the war.
3. The Soviet Government considers the Vienna Diktat to be unjust and is ready to carry out joint operations against the Hungarians and Germans with the object of returning all or the greater part of Transylvania to Romania.

Since he considered the free movement of Soviet troops to be tantamount to occupation, Antonescu did not even acknowledge Cairo's telegram. Without consulting King Michael he then called on Romanian troops to fight alongside

---

\* Col. de Chastelain and I who, from our prison in Gendarmerie Headquarters, enciphered and deciphered the telegrams passing between Marshal Antonescu and the British, were appalled at the tone of this telegram. De Chastelain told General Vasiliu, Inspector General of the Gendarmerie, that London must be heartily sick of requests for impossible guarantees against Russia. Vasiliu refused, however, to return it to the Marshal for redrafting.

the Germans to the last man, adding that the King, the country and their families expected it of them. 'It's really the limit,' Queen Helen noted on 11 April, 'after he swore last week to ask for an armistice.'[16]

The King felt that, with time running out for Romania, the Marshal's cavalier treatment of Cairo's armistice proposals had been foolhardy. On 20 April Maniu, Brătianu and Sănătescu (representing the King) drafted a telegram to Ştirbey saying that they were prepared to negotiate an armistice on the basis of the Cairo terms and of their own proposals which included Maniu's contention – which, unknown to him, was shared by London – that the transfer of territory would be more appropriately dealt with in a peace treaty.

This exchange exploded at the end of April when Lord Moyne, the British representative at the Cairo talks, sent telegrams to Antonescu and Maniu, which, though worded differently, were both in the nature of an ultimatum. Antonescu ignored his. Maniu was told that there would be no negotiation; he must accept or reject the Soviet terms as they were and let the Allies have immediately 'a final and definite statement of your attitude to, and your intentions for implementing them'.[17]

King Michael took Lord Moyne's telegram very seriously. On 17 April he had asked Sănătescu to consider urgently the composition of a post-*coup* administration. He had had in mind a military government with specialists for Foreign Affairs, Finance and Agriculture. Now, on the evening of 30 April 1944, Maniu and Brătianu were brought clandestinely to the Palace for their first direct talk with him. He first persuaded them that nothing could be gained by reviving the Crown Council; on the contrary it might alert the Germans. They then discussed the *coup*. Unless Antonescu agreed to an armistice or resigned in favour of someone who would, he must be arrested. The Marshal had a guards regiment at his command, he himself only a battalion. Of the army commanders two – Niculescu and Racoviţa – could be trusted. General Korne was pro-German, others undecided. Romanian front-line troops were mixed in with German troops and the Germans had a powerful all-German force in reserve. The Marshal's arrest and the anti-German volte-face to follow would, therefore, be high-risk, interdependent operations. After this frank discussion the two political leaders promised to send the King a letter undertaking, first, to support a military government which, after concluding an armistice would assume power and, second, to accept the risks that such a radical change of government and policy would involve. He received the letter eight days later.

At that meeting the King and the political leaders must also have discussed the formation of a National Democratic Bloc which would present a united political front to Antonescu and to Nazi Germany. Maniu and Brătianu had already united but were now being pressed by the Western Allies to expand the bloc to include the Social Democrat Party led by Titel Petrescu and, in particular, the minuscule Communist Party.

Following the dissolution of the Comintern in May 1943, the Romanian Communist Party had sought legitimacy through collaboration with the two main bourgeois parties, the National Peasants and the Liberals. Lucrețiu Pătrășcanu, a Moldavian landowner and lawyer, was chosen to undertake this liaison. He was a 'National Communist' – a communist but still with some commitment to Romanian interests – and was seen by Bodnăraș, Gheorghiu-Dej, Luca, Ana Pauker – the hard-liners who had been trained in Moscow or by communist cells while in Romanian prison – as dispensable. Maniu at first repulsed Pătrășcanu's approaches but the King knew that a united front of anti-Nazi elements in Romania was essential if the *coup* were to have the backing of all three Allies – and without that it could achieve nothing. On the evening of 8 May, after his first meeting with Lucrețiu Pătrășcanu, General Sănătescu noted 'a dynamic man, a man of spirit and am convinced that he will be of great help to us'.[18] When the National Democratic Bloc was formed on 20 June it therefore consisted of the National Peasant Party, the National Liberal Party, the Communist Party and the Social Democratic Party.

Despite Lord Moyne's ultimatum, Juliu Maniu was still convinced that, if handled properly, the Western Allies would understand 'the political and legal problems on which Romania's future depended'. He insisted, therefore, on sending out Vișoianu, his first choice, whose plan to join Știrbey had been postponed after the press leak of 14 March. He arrived in Cairo on 25 May. Maniu had instructed him to see the British delegation before anyone else but instead he found himself being wheeled straight into a meeting of all three delegations, after which he had to spend the evening with Novikov, the Russian ambassador. Next day he managed to see Christopher Steel of the British delegation alone, and plunged straight into the Bessarabian question. Maniu, he said, could not ask his countrymen to make sacrifices if he had already 'signed away their birthight'.

Steel was frank. Throughout the negotiations, he said, Maniu had shown himself to be out of touch with reality and here was another case. The Russians would take Bessarabia. That was certain. It was for Maniu to decide how best to present the situation to his countrymen; the truth might be best. 'Romania had gone or been led sadly astray and must face up to a painful sacrifice.' 'Should Maniu try to re-open the terms of the armistice, which had been agreed by all three allies, he would be overtaken by events before he had done anything to merit generosity.' When London learned of this conversation they instructed Lord Moyne to bring it immediately to Novikov's notice and to make it clear to Vişoianu that anything further he might wish to say in connection with his mission should be said in the presence of both Lord Moyne and Ambassador Novikov.[19]

By then the Allies had lost interest in a Romanian *coup d'état*. Owing to problems with the tide, the Normandy landings had been postponed for one month until 6 June, but when the Romanian *coup* had failed to meet even this deadline, the British delegation in Cairo were instructed to leave all further initiatives regarding Romania to their Russian colleague. Since Novikov was too frightened of Moscow to take any initiative, and the Americans always looked to the British for a lead on the Balkans, communication between Cairo and Bucharest simply dried up. Vişoianu sent Maniu a message assuring him that Ştirbey's reporting and advice over the last two months had been sound. After that there was silence.

The King could not know of Vişoianu's meeting with Christopher Steel, nor that three weeks before Vişoianu reached Cairo, Eden had begun a series of talks with the Soviet ambassador in London, which would lead to the conclusion of a so-called 'percentage agreement' between Churchill and Stalin, codifying their respective major interest in the Balkans – a predominant Soviet interest in Romania and a predominant British interest in Greece.

What the King did know was that Romania had become Hitler's most valued co-belligerent in Europe and that should it continue to fight the Führer's war to defeat, its credit at the peace settlement would be nil. A volte-face at this late stage could guarantee nothing. It would be a leap in the dark but one that he was convinced had to be taken if there was to be any hope at all of saving anything of pre-war Romania.

# SIX

## *The* Coup d'Etat

Almost fifty years later King Michael summed up his collaboration with Maniu and Brătianu in an interview with the Romanian journalist Mircea Ciobanu.

> We had first to put together the broad lines of a realistic plan of action and then work it out in detail. We had to be prudent and particularly careful not to compromise Antonescu's relations with the Germans. An important element in our operation was Maniu's radio link which enabled him to transmit news and information to the Allies in Ankara and Cairo. Our secret meetings became more frequent. Maniu and Brătianu came to the Palace from time to time to report anything of special interest from the Allies. The operation seemed to become more and more concrete though sometimes we felt that instead of getting closer we were moving away from our objective.[1]

By June 1944, planning, Queen Helen noted, had become 'more serious'.[2] On 21 June a telegram drafted by Sănătescu representing the King and Buzeşti representing Maniu was sent to Cairo proposing that:

> Following a change of government Romanian troops would be ordered to let the Russians through and to attack the Germans. Romanians would require (a) three airborne brigades with, if possible, an additional 2,000 parachute troops to coincide with the coup d'état. These could be either Anglo-American or Soviet. (b) heavy bombardment of Romania's communications with Hungary and Bulgaria.[3]

Lord Moyne commented to London that the Romanian plan seemed reasonable and acceptance of Soviet airborne troops 'a definite step forward'.[4] London was unimpressed. Ambassador McVeagh, the American, proposed a tripartite meeting to consider the Romanian proposal. The British delegation followed their standing instructions to leave initiatives on Romania to the Soviet representative and agreed with Novikov that a meeting would be premature. As a result the Bucharest telegram of 21 June remained unanswered.

Moscow had always been unwilling to deal with Maniu and after they had circulated their draft of the Armistice they had, unknown to their two allies, opened a unilateral negotiation with the Marshal. The American and British representatives in Cairo could not, therefore, understand a reference in the telegram of 21 June to terms offered exclusively to Marshal Antonescu, and it was Vişoianu, recently arrived from Bucharest, who put them in the picture. London and Washington decided that since nothing had come of Moscow's initiative they saw no reason to raise this embarrassing betrayal of Allied solidarity with the irascible Molotov.

The security precautions taken by the King's group were uncomplicated but effective. We have for instance Mircea Ionniţiu's account of the simple procedure which made it possible for the King to have safe meetings with the four political leaders.[5] Liaison with Maniu and Brătianu was effected through Niculescu Buzeşti, and with Pătrăşcanu and Titel Petrescu through the Royal Master of Ceremonies, a cousin of Pătrăşcanu's. Maniu and Brătianu would drive up to Prince Ştirbey's house on the Calea Victoriei. The Siguranţa,* who always tailed Maniu, would park in sight of the front door and remain there until they came out again some hours later. Maniu and Brătianu would walk through the house to the back door where Mircea Ionniţiu was waiting to drive them to the Palace and, after the meeting, the procedure was reversed. As for Pătrăşcanu and Titel Petrescu, they were picked up at a pre-arranged place in town by Ionel Styrcea.

Security was made easier at Casa Nouă by the modest way the King and his mother lived. The few servants they needed left the premises at 10 p.m. The meetings were held after 10 o'clock round the dining-room table. Buzeşti, Ioaniţiu, Sănătescu and Styrcea – who by now was spending more time in Bucharest than at the Săvârşin estate – would usually attend. Problems were analysed in detail, everyone making his point without protocol or formality. No record or notes were kept. Should an alert sound, the politicians would promptly leave the house, so avoiding any chance of, say, Pătrăşcanu and Maniu being spotted together in the palace shelter, which was open to the public. The secrecy of these meetings remained intact. There was much talk in Bucharest about projects to sign an armistice but the Germans seem only once to have seriously associated the King with them.

---

* The Siguranţa were the Romanian secret police headed by Eugen Cristescu.

On 15 July Ionel Styrcea was invited to dine at the SS headquarters with General von Gerstenberg, head of the Luftwaffe mission; General Friessner, newly appointed commander of Army Group South; Manfred von Killinger; and Karl Clodius, in charge of economic relations with Romania with direct access to both the Antonescus. This high-powered group tackled him about King Michael's true role. How could he dare go on to his roof during American raids: had he not some link with Washington? Was he not plotting? Styrcea flatly denied this. What, he asked, had the King or he to gain by siding with the Communists? 'What the hell!' He himself had a fortune of some $135 million and had no wish to lose it. To the Germans his arguments made sense. During the air raid they played ping-pong in the basement and next day von Killinger, who had walked back to the Palace with Styrcea – just for the exercise – almost certainly sent Berlin a reassuring message.[6]

The King's military planning was effectively in the hands of Generals Sănătescu, Aurel Aldea, Mihail (Chief of the General Staff in King Carol's time), and Colonel Dămăceanu (whose duty immediately after the *coup* would be to immobilise German troops in Bucharest). They were all in contact with commanding officers in the field including the commanders of the 4th Army and the 5th Army Corps, the commander of the 5th Territorial Corps in the important Ploieşti oil region and the military commander for the capital, who was Colonel Dămăceanu's general.

By early July detailed military planning had been completed. Friends of Mircea Ionniţiu, two telephone engineers, had identified German circuits which passed through the Romanian telephone exchange. At a word from the Palace these would be disconnected, thus isolating German barracks from their headquarters. This would be of immense value to Colonel Dămăceanu's operation.

Pătrăşcanu had introduced to the King a certain 'Engineer Ceaşu', a code name for Emil Bodnăraş, one of the ruling triumvirate of the Romanian Communist Party and responsible for the Party's defence policy. Bodnăraş joined Dămăceanu's sub-committee and, given the shortage of Romanian troops in Bucharest, undertook to recruit workers to defend such key buildings as the Post Office, the Telephone Exchange and the Broadcasting Station. A suggestion that with 2,000 armed men he could also arrest Antonescu and other prominent Nazi sympathisers met with such strong opposition from the army and Maniu that it was dropped.

Immediately after the *coup d'état* the army would be ordered to cease hostilities against the Russians and, to facilitate this, a Romanian officer would be attached to Soviet army headquarters. The proposal had come from

Cairo after Vişoianu's talk with the Russian ambassador on the evening of 25 May. General Aurel Aldea had volunteered for the mission but, since field commanders could find no secure place for him to cross the lines, the operation was postponed. On 3 August, less than three weeks before the *coup*, Sănătescu, Buzeşti and Maniu revived the plan. Aldea was provided with a mandate signed by the four signatories of the National Democratic Bloc.[7] Soviet clearance was sought on 21 August and granted two days later. The request for military help made in their telegram of 21 June to Cairo would clearly not be met. However, they decided to ask for Allied air support on the day of the *coup*.

Foişor was chosen for the site of the critical talk between the King and Antonescu because it would be easier to defend than the Casa Nouă. Royal guards were being moved discreetly from Bucharest to Sinaia. The Marshal, it was agreed, would be arrested only if he refused to negotiate for an armistice or to stand down in favour of somebody who would. This would be done in the presence of the four political leaders representing the Romanian people. The King asked the leaders of the political parties to draw up a list of the post-*coup* government. It was important that the country should be without a government for as short a time as possible. It was also agreed that the army should not be asked to act as policemen. Since the present police could not be trusted, Pătrăşcanu suggested that each of the four political parties should provide volunteers to be responsible for Antonescu's temporary custody and this was approved. Engineer Ceaşu, Pătrăşcanu said, could get together a group of workmen. Maniu offered some Transylvanian partisans. Brătianu for the Liberals and Titel Petrescu for the Social Democrats had no one to offer.

However, the group suffered a serious setback when in mid-July Maniu's wireless operator was arrested. In future they would have to rely on Buzeşti's far slower Foreign Ministry communications with Cairo and Ankara.

On 20 July an attempt was made on Hitler's life at his Rastenburg headquarters. This was followed by a period of extreme terror in Germany while Romania was pervaded by a false sense of calm. Antonescu even insisted that Michael should pay his annual visit to the graves of his ancestors at Curtea de Argeş though the King thought this ridiculous at such a time. When they returned, the Marshal left for the small watering town of Olăneşti for a cure.

On 5 August the Marshal was summoned to the Führer's headquarters. He returned the following afternoon, sooner than expected. He avoided contact with his government and drove straight from the airport to Sinaia, reporting to the King, and then retreated once more to Olănești. The previous night he had remarked to his entourage that the Germans were 'gangsters' and the Führer 'raving mad'. He had produced for Hitler firm intelligence that an early Red Army offensive on Romanian positions was being prepared. He therefore asked for the return of at least some of the Panzer divisions removed from Bessarabia during the previous few months. When Hitler refused, Antonescu proposed withdrawal to the Focșani–Nămăloasă–Braila (FNB) line, which could be held without armour. This line, closing the 80km gap between the Carpathian Mountains and the Danube delta, was one of the best natural fortifications in Europe. But again Hitler hesitated; since the attempt on his life he seemed incapable of any rational military decision. He was to decide to move back to the FNB line during the night of 21/22 August, by which time German and Romanian troops were retreating in disarray and controlled occupation and reinforcement of the line had become impossible. Later he turned down Ribbentrop's request for the tranfer of a Panzer division from Yugoslavia to Bucharest, a move which would have made the *coup d'état* impossible.

While Cairo's silence persisted and the inevitable Soviet offensive drew closer, the King seemed unwilling to pre-empt a reply to his telegram of 21 June. Finally, Știrbey and Vișoianu in Cairo got a message through to him; in their considered opinion the Russians would prefer to make a straightforward military conquest of Romania without any Romanian help. He should therefore go ahead with the *coup* without waiting for Allied approval. By then, however, the Soviet offensive was imminent.

The directive followed by Generals Malinovski and Tolbukhin 'envisaged an advance of 200 kms, which would breach the Carpathians–FNB–Danube line and reach Bucharest and Ploiești. Any further exploitation was expected to be contingent on securing Romania's capitulation.'[8]

An artillery barrage early on 20 August pulverised the Romanian 5th Infantry Division. The Soviet 52nd Army overwhelmed the Romanian 7th Infantry Division and advanced to Iași. As Antonescu had foreseen, the initial attack concentrated on Romanian defences and so compelled the more powerful German forces on their flanks to withdraw in order to avoid encirclement.

The King, who was in Sinaia, was first told of the Soviet offensive at lunchtime on 20 August. Over tea – the English tea Queen Helen rarely missed – they agreed that he must have more information before reaching a decision. So Ionnițiu warned Styrcea on an open telephone line that the King was coming to Bucharest to inspect a new military aircraft and, in coded language, that he should call a meeting of the group for that evening. Michael picked up General Mihail from his villa in Sinaia and drove him, Mircea Ionniţiu and his adjutant, Colonel Ionescu, down the mountain to Casa Nouă.

His meeting that evening was attended by Sănătescu, Styrcea, Buzeşti, Ionniţiu, Generals Mihail and Aldea and Colonel Dămăceanu. After summarising the situation on the Moldavian front Sănătescu said that he considered the Soviet attack to be the real thing – not, as did the Germans, diversionary. Some Romanian units might regroup; others were already destroyed. The King asked Dămăceanu how soon he would be ready to occupy strategic points in the city. Five days, the Colonel replied. The King then proposed that, subject to the agreement of the political leaders whom he would see the next evening, they should proceed as follows: on Saturday, the 26th, the Marshal, who would no longer be in Sinaia, and his deputy, Mihai Antonescu, would be invited to lunch here, at Casa Nouă – not at Foişor, as previously planned. During the audience that would follow he would raise with the Marshal the urgency of concluding an armistice. Should he refuse to undertake this or to give way to someone who would, the King would remove him from his post, arrest him and name a government on the basis of the list still to be drawn up by the political parties. The new government would ask the Germans to leave Romanian territory, would announce the cessation of hostilities with the USSR and would transmit to Romania's representatives in Cairo, Ştirbey and Vişoianu, the legal powers to sign the Cairo armistice terms. He would inform General Wilson, the Allied Commander Middle East, of these decisions. In the telegram to Wilson, which he would dictate himself, he would also ask for the following limited air support: at 1300 hr on the 26th a raid on German barracks to the west, north and north-west of the Baneasă airport (which would provide cover for Colonel Dămăceanu's operation), also the Otopeni aerodrome 8km north of Baneasă, and specific Hungarian railway centres. As from the 27th he would ask for frequent and heavy bombardment of railway centres on Romania's frontiers with Bulgaria, Hungary and Yugoslavia so as to deter the entry of German reinforcements. All this was approved. After the meeting, Michael asked Mircea Ionniţiu to take a message to Queen Helen in Sinaia first thing next morning.[9]

Having spent much of the night helping to pin-point map references for the telegram to General Wilson, Mircea Ionniţiu left for Sinaia rather later than he had hoped. The King's message to his mother was to prepare to leave with her entourage at short notice. Were Antonescu to be arrested and the Germans to intervene, the Sinaia–Bucharest road would probably be unusable. Should contact be broken her convoy should go westwards to Craiova where General Manafu, commandant of the region, would direct her to wherever Michael and his party had taken refuge. The General had been instructed to choose the most easily defended locality and to disclose it only to the King or Queen Mother in person on their arrival in Craiova.

That evening, 21 August, the four political leaders meeting at Casa Nouă approved the King's programme together with the draft telegrams addressed to Ştirbey and General Wilson. When Ionniţu arrived late from Sinaia they were already haggling about the composition of the new government, a discussion which the King cut short by asking Maniu and Pătrăşcanu to produce a government list by midday on the 23rd. Meanwhile he and his military advisers would take what measures they could to ensure army cooperation. It was also agreed that until the 26th the political leaders should be careful not to draw attention to themselves.

After the meeting Ionel Styrcea took the telegrams to the Foreign Ministry communications centre in the woods near Lake Snagov. Piki Pogoneanu, who was on duty, told him that they would be despatched by the 1900 hr schedule to Ankara next day. They then settled down to the cumbersome task of ciphering, and since it was already dawn on the 22nd when they had finished, Styrcea decided to have a swim before returning to Bucharest. Some days before, the King's doctor in Sinaia had warned Styrcea that the Marshal was getting ready to move his present headquarters to a more secure site in Transylvania – news which the doctor had overheard when a captain of Antonescu's guard, quartered in his house, had answered a telephone call from Bucharest. Antonescu had not told the King of his plan and it was only now at Snagov that Styrcea obtained confirmation and precise details. On the lake he saw the Secretary General of the Foreign Ministry, who, after a night's work, was taking a little exercise in a rowing boat. While Ionel trod water, Davidescu told him that Antonescu, who was at the front, would arrive in Bucharest that evening, return to the front the following day, the 23rd, and from there go straight to his new headquarters in Transylvania.[10]

The news was devastating. In less than 36 hours the *coup* would have been bypassed. The King was flying with Udriski that morning. On returning to Casa Nouă and hearing from Styrcea that Antonescu would not be in Bucharest on the 26th, he called an immediate meeting to reassess their plan. There was no time to consult the political leaders so King Michael took full responsibility for the drastic modifications that had now to be made. As Mircea Ionniţiu has pointed out, 'he never hesitated'. 'He understood that the time for discussion had passed and that only action could save whatever was left to save.'[11] The chances of carrying out their plan with Antonescu at large and pursuing his present policy were nil. The audience, the King said, must, therefore, be brought forward to the 23rd – the following day – before Antonescu left for the front. This was agreed. Maniu and Brătianu were found later that afternoon and promised to despatch delegates to Antonescu, who would try to persuade him not to return to the front without first briefing the King on the situation.[12]

Meanwhile Mihai Antonescu had, unwittingly, created a diversion by asking the Turkish prime minister, in the name of the King, the Opposition and the Marshal, to act as intermediary between Romania and the Allies. The King had not been consulted, nor probably the Marshal. Ica's indiscretion may, however, have provided a useful smokescreen for King Michael's activities.

When the Marshal flew in that evening, Mihalache and Gheorghe Brătianu had independent meetings with him and urged him to brief the King before returning to the front. Antonescu at this time seemed ready to consider any Opposition proposal for an armistice and Brătianu undertook to let him have their thinking the following morning.

Unknown to the King's group, Antonescu was already considering the suicidal course of confiding to the Germans his inclination to accept an armistice. When later that evening he met Clodius, he tried to convince him that unless Hitler gave him immediate assistance he would be forced to withdraw from the war. Yet, according to Clodius's report to Berlin, Antonescu had undertaken to throw all his reserves into the battle, and only if that failed, to feel free to seek an armistice.[13] Clodius, believing that the Marshal's reference to an armistice was not pressing, sent Berlin a non-priority telegram which reached them on the 24th. By then Antonescu was under arrest.

Early next morning, Wednesday the 23rd, the day of the *coup d'état*, Ica and Madame Antonescu tried hard to talk the Marshal into seeing the King and agreeing to an armistice. 'Why continue to take all the responsibility yourself?' his wife pleaded.[14] Although Antonescu was still non-committal, Ica telephoned the Casa Nouă, woke Ionnițiu who, since Sunday, had been sleeping in the King's office, and asked for an audience for himself at three o'clock and one for the Marshal later. Ionnițiu was sufficiently excited by the news to wake King Michael, who said he would see them both at three. He then went to examine the new Air Force plane – his ostensible reason for being in Bucharest.

At ten that morning, the Marshal made a fighting speech to his inner Cabinet.

During a working cold lunch the King again went over the plan with Aldea, Sănătescu, Buzeşti, Styrcea and Ionniţiu. The fact that Antonescu wished to see the King meant, they hoped, that he had decided either to conclude an armistice or to resign. His arrest might still be avoided. Maniu had let them know that he could not possibly get his Transylvanians to Bucharest by that afternoon, so the Antonescus would have to be retained by Ceaşu's men only. Pătrăşcanu had undertaken that the prisoners would be treated with respect but nobody was entirely happy with the arrangement.

Over lunch it was agreed that, as originally planned for the 26th, the political leaders, as representatives of the Romanian people, should be asked to attend the audience with Antonescu that afternoon. Colonel Dămăceanu must also be told of the change of plan, which could seriously jeopardise his operation. Also, should the Marshal be arrested, so then must his escort, and those of his collaborators powerful enough to scupper the *coup* even after the arrest of the Marshal and his Deputy.

After lunch Buzeşti could not locate Maniu but expected to meet him later in the afternoon at Prince Ştirbey's house. Dinu Brătianu had already left for the country. Styrcea spoke to Pătrăşcanu's cousin, who told him that Pătrăşcanu and Titel Petrescu would come to the Palace but only after dark – which meant around eight o'clock at that time of year, well after the crucial meeting. The absence of all the political leaders from the Casa Nouă that afternoon and their failure to produce a government list left the whole responsibility to the young king – a mark of unforgivable cowardice.

The King brought his adjutant Colonel Ionescu and Captain Anton Dumitrescu of the royal military household up to date and discussed with them arrangements for the possible arrest of the Antonescus. So many soldiers had been moved to Foişor under the earlier plan that only about eighty were now available for the defence of the Palace. Ionniţiu warned his friends at the telephone company to be ready to disconnect German lines.

By then the afternoon was at its hottest. Offices were closed and most people taking a siesta. King Michael waited for Buzeşti to return with news of Antonescu's intentions, preparing himself for what might well be his last interview with the Marshal.

During the last two years he had found in himself qualities which would prove to be of even greater value than the royal prerogatives lost at his father's abdication. While preparing for the *coup* he had shown a determination, a clear-headedness and a power of concentration and grasp of detail without which he could not have mastered the complexities of the operation. Although, at 22, the youngest of his group, the least experienced and probably the most modest, his was a natural leadership which gave them all, himself included, the confidence to win. Looking back on the next 48 hours, the King later remarked, 'We were tense, but at the same time clear-headed. There are difficult moments in life when your judgement becomes clearer rather than befuddled. I don't know how, as if you were a different person. As for fear, there was no question of it. Excitement, yes – but not fear.'[15]

At ten that morning Maniu, driven by his young colleague, Corneliu Coposu, who after the collapse of the Soviet Union in 1989 was to emerge from prison as head of a mere shadow of the National Peasant Party Maniu led in 1943, had gone to Dinu Brătianu's house for a meeting of the four party leaders.[16] Petrescu, who arrived half an hour later, warned them that Pătrăşcanu would probably avoid this house because of the Siguranţa car standing outside. He would expect to see them at the more discreet flat of his friend Manuila.

Meanwhile they waited for Gheorghe Brătianu. He had driven to Snagov, extracted Marshal Antonescu from his Cabinet meeting and assured him that, should he be prepared to conclude an armistice, Juliu Maniu and Dinu Brătianu would stand solidly behind him. The Marshal asked for this assurance formally in writing. The timing of the armistice, he said, would be for him to decide. It would not, in any case, be until the Russians had been held at the FNB line long enough to be softened up. He also needed time, he said, to convince the Germans with 'unassailable arguments' that Romania must withdraw from the hostilities.

Maniu, Brătianu and Petrescu were appalled when they heard this. The armistice must be concluded immediately and on no account should the Germans be forewarned. Gheorghe Brătianu returned to Snagov with this further message and was told that the Marshal would put up with no more mixing in matters which lay exclusively with him. Brătianu later told his uncle that the Marshal showed no intention of seeing the King and would probably leave immediately either for the front or for his new headquarters in Transylvania. Dinu Brătianu telephoned this disastrous news to Maniu, who was by then with Pătrăşcanu at Manuila's flat. He then left for the country.

When Maniu reached the Ştirbey house where Buzeşti was anxiously waiting, he warned him that Antonescu was determined to discuss the situation with the Germans. It would be a *gaffe* that would imperil the whole country. Hitler would use the most brutal methods to prevent an armistice. Buzeşti agreed. Maniu also confirmed that he would not lead the post-*coup* government, which should be entirely military with the sole purpose of signing an armistice. Nor would he be present at the audience that afternoon with Antonescu. Buzeşti ascertained where he could be contacted and drove back to Casa Nouă.

By 3 o'clock the King's office was thick with cigarette smoke. When Mihai Antonescu arrived, escorted from the Palace by Colonel Ionescu, the King and Sănătescu received him in the drawing room. Aldea, Buzeşti, Styrcea and Ionniţiu remained in the office. Mihai Antonescu apologised for the Marshal's delay. Since to be late was one of Antonescu's habitual discourtesies, the King was not particularly bothered as long as he turned up eventually. After a while the King returned to the office while Ica and Sănătescu walked over to the main Palace to await the Marshal. Shortly afterwards the Marshal, Ica, Sănătescu and Colonel Ionescu were seen coming down the path. The King joined Sănătescu and the Antonescus in the drawing room. The others remained where they were. Colonel Ionescu and Captain Dumitrescu took up positions at the foot of the stairs and three NCOs stood in the corridor alongside the stairs.

Sănătescu was in civilian clothes, Ica in a morning suit, the Marshal in cavalry uniform, the King in grey flannels.

When the four men were seated at the round table, the King asked: 'What is the situation, Mr Marshal?'

'Desperate, Majesty. The fronts are pierced in both Moldavia and Bessarabia.'[17]

For a while they discussed the situation at the front and then, as was his habit, the Marshal went on to the attack, holding the army responsible because they had lost their appetite for the fight, holding the political leaders responsible for weakening the army's morale by their propaganda, implying that the King and Sănătescu must take part of the blame. He himself was, of course, blameless.

The King waited patiently, and when there was a pause, asked him: 'What should we do? Don't you think that the moment has come to conclude an armistice either by you or by another government?'[18] The Marshal replied that he had made certain contacts but that he would not enter into any armistice discussion until he had warned the Germans of what he was about to do and until he had had guarantees from the Allies that the country would not be occupied and that all Romania's frontiers would be settled only at the peace conference.[19]

For the King and Sănătescu this reply, with its complete disregard for the reality of the situation, was frightening. When the King suggested that the time had passed for haggling, Antonescu replied that without these guarantees he would contiue to fight alongside the Germans. His attitude seemed to have hardened since his last talk with Gheorghe Brătianu, and Ica, sensing the consternation felt by the King and Sănătescu, interjected, 'Perhaps we should ask for an armistice, but let us wait a couple of days to see what reply we have from Ankara.'[20]

'Mr Vice-President', Sănătescu asked, 'don't you think that by waiting two more days we run the risk that the present conditions for an armistice will be withdrawn and we shall find ourselves faced by an unconditional capitulation? I have a feeling that things are moving fast and that it is a matter of hours, not days'.[21]

When the King asked Antonescu whether he would not give way to someone who was prepared to conclude an armistice he replied 'Never'. Then, turning towards Sănătescu, he added, 'How could I go and leave the country in the hands of a child?' and King Michael realised, with a shock, that the Marshal's attitude to him had not changed at all over the years: he still saw him as the boy he had met when he had first come to his father's palace.[22] At that point, he said later, the struggle became personal between himself and the dictator. 'What do you intend to do?' the King asked him.

'We shall try to hold the fortified line of Focşani–Oancea–Bolgrad', Antonescu replied.

'With what?' Sănătescu asked. 'The defensive equipment is not ready and the German and Romanian forces withdrawing from the front will be in no state to occupy the position – they are withdrawing in such disorder.'

'With battalions of recruits which I have posted there and with others, troops from within the country. As a matter of fact, should we fail to hold the enemy on this line we will withdraw to the mountains and will try to hold them there. We cannot abandon the Germans.'[23]

Faced with this categorical reply the King told Antonescu, in his level, quiet voice, that he no longer enjoyed his confidence and was dismissed. 'If that's how things are, then there's nothing more for us to do.' He stood up and Sănătescu and the two Antonescus, who were also on their feet, were locked in silence.

The King's last sentence had contained a key phrase. Captain Dumitrescu and the three NCOs entered, saluted, and went up to Antonescu. The captain, King Michael records, told the Marshal to follow him and put his hand on his arm. Antonescu became immediately rigid, turned to Sănătescu and asked him, 'What does this mean?' Sănătescu then had a moment of hesitation and wanted to take Dumitrescu's hand away from the Marshal's arm. The King records:

When I saw that I left. I had had enough misunderstandings with Antonescu but it gave me no pleasure at all to be at his arrest. Realising that this moment of confusion could get out of hand and finally compromise the whole operation, my adjutant, Emilian Ionescu, who was watching everything from the doorway, shouted, 'Carry out your orders'. To this man who did not lose his presence of mind we owe much. Those three took hold of him and started for the door. When they were climbing the stairs Antonscu turned to them and said, 'tomorow you will all be executed'. And he spat into the officer's face. They took him up to the first floor – we were in Casa Nouă behind the Palace – and locked him in the strong room where my father used to keep his stamp collection. The collection had been taken so now the room was available.[24]

# SEVEN

## Romanian Army Drives out the Germans: Soviet Army 'Liberates' Bucharest

Measures had to be taken during the next 24 hours which would require the full authority of the state. A government was required and, more immediately, a prime minister – a man who could act on the King's authority. The reluctant General Sănătescu was appointed on the spot. Ionniţiu typed the necessary decree, the King signed it, and Sănătescu set out with it for Army headquarters.

Antonescu's Chief of Staff, General Şteflea, was on tour and when his deputy, a Maniu man, saw the decree he readily collaborated. He and Sănătescu despatched signals in the King's name ordering Romanian troops to cease hostilities against the Soviet army and in some cases to concentrate urgently in the Bucharest–Ploieşti region. Troops in particularly difficult situations – the encircled 3rd Army, for instance – could not lay down their arms immediately but not a single unit defected in favour of Antonescu. Even the pro-German Generals Şteflea, Dumitrescu and Korne, when told by General Friessner of the *coup*, were surprised, but firm in their loyalty to the King. Mark Axworthy has noted, 'King Michael's role in taking personal responsibility for arresting Antonescu in the absence of the politicians, and the binding nature of the officer corps' oath of allegiance to the Crown, made him indispensable to the success of the coup and ensured that Romania's break with Germany was unanimous and total.'[1]

Back in the Palace, it had become urgent to arrest first Antonescu's bodyguard, then his close collaborators.

Colonel Negulescu, Colonel of the King's Guard, undertook the first of these delicate operations. The Marshal's escort of officers, drivers and orderlies was parked in the courtyard alongside the busy Calea Victoriei. They could be seen by Eugen Cristescu's Siguranţa men from the Ministry of the Interior and were less than a hundred metres from the Gestapo headquarters.

An officer of the royal guard casually invited them to wait inside where it would be cooler. Most accepted, were arrested in the ADC's waiting room, and put under guard at the palace barracks. A little later half a dozen guardsmen marched out of a side door, eyes forward, apparently about to relieve the sentries. Instead, they formed up between the cars and the street and when the officer said quietly, 'Drop your weapons and get out,' the remainder of the Marshal's men, taken completely by surprise, obeyed, were escorted inside and the cars driven into an underground garage.

The King, walking across from Casa Nouă to the better-equipped offices of the military household in the main building, saw the remnants of Antonescu's escort being led away. Negulescu had done an excellent job and Sănătescu had telephoned to say that everything was under control at army headquarters. Nevertheless the *coup* still hung in the balance.

At first the arrest of the Marshal's key ministers also went smoothly. Colonel Ionescu telephoned Generals Vasiliu and Pantazi – the Ministers of Interior and War – to say that the Marshal wished to consult them at the Palace. They came and were arrested. So was the Prefect of Bucharest. General Tobescu, head of the Gendarmerie, agreed to come but changed his mind. Only Eugen Cristescu, who knew from his agents that the Marshal's cars had been put into the palace garage – an unusual procedure – insisted on speaking to the Marshal personally and, when Antonescu failed to come to the telephone, drove to the German Legation to alert von Killinger. Fortunately the German Minister was dining that evening with his secretary at her villa in Saftica and took over an hour to drive back to Bucharest.

Maniu and Pătrăşcanu had failed to produce the governmental list but the formation of a government could no longer be postponed. Appointments had to be made impromptu. General Mihail was appointed Chief of the General Staff and despatched to army headquarters to relieve Sănătescu. General Aldea became Minister of the Interior, Niculescu Buzeşti, Foreign Minister. When General Dumbrovski, a popular mayor of Bucharest in King Carol's time, walked into the room unwittingly, Michael, by then in high spirits, told him he was surprised to see the Mayor of Bucharest who was also Prefect of Police wasting his time at Court. The King then put Dumbrovski in the picture and asked him to take on both jobs for the time being.

Most ministers were military men well known to Sănătescu, who also refreshed his memory from the *Army Year Book* on his desk. In quick succession senior army officers were appointed to Health, Education and Aviation. Prudence had to give way to speed and it is not surprising that the Minister of Economy and Finance was appointed before anyone remembered that he had been a signatory to the declaration of war against Russia. A less excusable *gaffe* was Aldea's failure to cross the lines and liaise with the Soviet military commanders as arranged.

# Romanian Army Drives out the Germans

The King knew that a purely military government risked being accused of lacking popular support. To meet this point Maniu had proposed the appointment of Secretaries of State from each of the four political parties. The King now went further and appointed the four party leaders as Ministers without Portfolio and, since they were absent, this was done without their agreement.

Dumitriu Negel, who was made Minister of Justice, descibes what he saw from the doorway when he returned unexpectedly from a tour of inspection in Moldavia.

> Feverish confusion with people coming and going in an unbroken stream. At a desk sat Sănătescu, masses of papers before him, people all round him, his voice sometimes rising above the general hubbub. At another was a Signal Corps colonel with a battery of telephones, passing orders in the King's name to army commanders, civil governors, the police. At side tables clerks clattered at typewriters. People moved around talking clamorously, smoking incessantly and in the midst of it all stood the King.[2]

Despite this impression of informality, security that night was tight. All but one door of the Palace were locked and this was guarded by an officer and soldiers armed with automatic rifles and hand grenades. Visitors, who, after identifying themselves and explaining their business were allowed to enter, had then to pass through a second checkpoint inside.

Their first visitor was the German Minister, Manfred von Killinger, accompanied by his political counsellor. He was immediately seen by the King with Sănătescu, Niculescu Buzeşti and Styrcea in attendance.

Given the imbalance of forces in the Bucharest area, King Michael knew that he must avoid armed conflict for as long as possible. When the Minister, wearing his black diplomatic uniform with silver facings, asked in his usual bullying way what had happened to Antonescu, he answered him mildly. Antonescu, he said, was unharmed but in view of the country's dreadful situation he had resigned. A new government had been formed with Sănătescu as Prime Minister and Niculescu Buzeşti as Foreign Minister, and since Germany had not been able to fulfil her obligations to Romania, this government would take Romania out of the war. If German troops were withdrawn immediately there need be no armed conflict.

When von Killinger protested loudly against the formation of a government unacceptable to Berlin, he was reminded by the new Foreign Minister that he was accredited to King Michael, not the head of the previous government.

When he demanded to know whether they had considered the grave consequences of their step – the fact that without German help the Russians could overrun the country in a matter of days – he was assured by the King that they had, indeed, considered this point very carefully. For a moment von Killinger, who had repeatedly assured Ribbentrop and the Führer that Romanians would never have the nerve to break with the Axis, seemed baffled. Then, remembering his dinner with Styrcea at the SS club only a few weeks before, he turned to him, spat out 'Vorträter' and left.[3]

Since the German Legation was now in the picture, discretion was no longer necessary. German telephone circuits were disconnected at the Central Exchange and engineers were soon on the streets finishing the job. Germans still had their radio links with Berlin but not the Bucharest telephone network on which they relied for communication between headquarters and barracks, and most of their Bucharest troops were consequently without orders, immobilised. Dămăceanu's superior officer, General Teodorescu, commander of all Bucharest forces, had already been to the Palace to receive further instructions from the King personally.

Shortly after von Killinger's visit, Lucreţiu Pătrăşcanu arrived with a draft of the King's proclamation to the nation. He also brought for the King's signature two decrees approved by the four political leaders on 17 August – one granting an amnesty to political prisoners, the other abolishing concentration camps. Pătrăşcanu was behaving as a Minister of Justice and, although he must have known of Negel's appointment, he now pressed the King to let him have that portfolio. The King, with neither Maniu nor Brătianu there to be consulted, compromised by appointing him Minister of Justice *ad interim*. Negel now became Minister of Agriculture. In terms of the Communist hierarchy Pătrăşcanu's appointment had little or no significance but it was to prove of useful nuisance value to the Party. Maniu was undoubtedly unhappy about it, but since he had failed to support the King that afternoon or to appear at the Palace he was in no position to criticise.

Michael was for the first time exercising the full prerogatives of a head of state. In the turmoil of that evening he appears to have been the only one to remember other miscellaneous matters. The prisoners in Casa Nouă should be given refreshment and taken out of the strong room under guard from time to time, the American air force prisoners in Sinaia should be brought to Bucharest where they would be safer, the SOE prisoners at Gendarmerie headquarters should be brought to the Palace before the Germans kidnapped them. At about six o'clock, he had sent Colonel Negulescu to Sinaia to tell his mother what had happened and stand by to escort her either to Bucharest or to Craiova.

Three hours later, Negulescu used the radio telephone from Foişor to inform him that the Queen's party had packed and were ready to leave for Bucharest. The King hesitated. The road to Bucharest could become a battlefield. He spoke to his mother direct and asked her to remain in Sinaia until the situation became clearer.

The head of the broadcasting company brought his equipment to the Palace and Michael registered the proclamation on a wax disk to be broadcast after the 10 o'clock news. His mother heard it in Sinaia and felt a mixture of anxiety and pride. Rica Georgescu, who had organised Maniu's radio links with Cairo from his Siguranţa prison, heard it while in a delicatessen buying supplies for a prison celebration. At Văcăreşti prison, where the young Ceauşescu had recently spent some time, a doctor shouted, 'You are free, an armistice has been concluded. Your Pătrăşcanu is at Justice.' Following an aeroplane accident Vergotti was in Bucharest and when he heard the proclamation he rushed to the Palace to congratulate King Michael and then to arrange for palace transport to be standing by in case the King had to leave Bucharest urgently. The BBC monitoring service heard it and within half an hour had made it world news. The SOE prisoners in the Gendarmerie heard it, were surprised that the *coup* had been carried out by King Michael rather than Maniu, and were deeply moved and excited by what he said:

> Romanians, in this most difficult hour of our history I have decided, in full understanding with my people, that there is only one way to save the country from total catastrophe; our withdrawal from the alliance with the Axis powers and the immediate cessation of the war with the United Nations.*
>
> A new government of national unity has been formed charged with fulfilling the resolute wish of the people to conclude peace with the United Nations. Romania has accepted the armistice offered by the Soviet Union, Great Britain and the United States of America. From this moment the fighting and any hostile act against the Soviet armies ceases, as does also the state of war with Great Britain and the United States . . .
>
> Dictatorship has ended and with it all oppression. The new government marks the beginning of a new era, in which the rights and liberties of all citizens of the country are guaranteed and will be respected.[4]

---

\* At that time Britain, the USA and the USSR were known as The United Nations.

Half an hour later the SOE prisoners were called to the Palace. The great Square was by then crowded with people cheering their King for breaking with the Axis. The Palace was ablaze with light marking the end of a three-year black-out and, when people recognised their English uniforms, the embarrassed prisoners were carried shoulder high to the palace gates.

The communication centre at Snagov, where the night before Styrcea had taken telegrams to be despatched, was now in a military zone and could not be used. Michael was not even certain that his telegram to General Wilson had arrived and when Colonel de Chastelain offered to fly out to Turkey, confirm the King's requirement for air support, and restore communications between Bucharest and Cairo, he readily agreed.

The King was then given some of the most heartening news of the evening. The vital Ploieşti road into Bucharest was to be defended at the Baneasă bridge by the King's Guards Regiment under Colonel Olteanu. General Teodorescu, the City Commander, now informed him that Marshal Antonescu's own guards regiment had obeyed with no hesitation his order to join Olteanu's troops. If men who had sworn personal allegiance to Antonescu were prepared to fight the Germans, then, Michael felt, he might well have the whole Romanian army behind him.

General Hansen, the chief German military representative in Bucharest, and General von Gerstenberg, Head of the German Air Force Mission, being unable to telephone, arrived at the Palace unexpectedly and King Michael asked the Prime Minister to see them. Sănătescu, accompanied by Niculescu Buzeşti, explained the situation to Hansen and requested him to disperse concentrations of German troops in the Ploieşti area known to be approaching Bucharest. At this point von Gerstenberg intervened. The German Command, he said, had lost contact with their forces, but if he could have a pass to get him through the Romanian lines he would himself give them the necessary order to retire. To Buzeşti's dismay, the Prime Minister not only offered him a pass but also a Romanian colonel to escort him. Von Gerstenberg, he argued later, was a cavalry officer like himself and a man of honour. Sănătescu's colleagues had far less confidence in von Gerstenberg's word.

Suspicion about German intentions served to strengthen a growing feeling that the King and his mother should go into temporary hiding. The military could not be sure of holding the Germans until front-line troops had reached Bucharest. Should either the King or the Queen be captured, Hitler's hand would be immensely strengthened. His advisers were unanimous. He had taken the critical step of removing Romania from the Axis. His duty now was to stay out of German hands.

At about 3 a.m. on the 24th, a convoy of four cars – the King driving his own Lincoln – left by the private gate and took the Alexandra road. Among the passengers was his dog Azo, who went everywhere with him. There was little traffic at that time of the morning but at Bragadiru, not far from Bucharest, they met a column of cheerful, excited Romanian troops on their way to the capital. To avoid the Germans at Turnu Măgurele they took the Roşiori de Vede road to Craiova and at about 10 o'clock, when Michael for one had been at the wheel for over seven hours and petrol was running low, they pulled into a lane just short of the town.

Colonel Ionescu took a car to obtain fuel and to speak to General Manafu, the garrison commander, who had been warned to prepare a secure refuge for the King and Queen Helen. Michael and his companions parked their cars behind haystacks and, waiting in the field two hundred yards from the road, felt reasonably secure until a German convoy travelling towards Craiova was stopped by a lorry at the end of their lane and soldiers jumped down, talking excitedly. From behind a hedge the King watched the convoy through binoculars, very much afraid that their cars would be spotted. When Ionescu reappeared he stopped right alongside the convoy. His driver got out, opened the boot as if to check something, and then stayed gossiping with the soldiers until they all climbed back into their trucks and headed for the town. 'They know about the *coup*,' he told the King, ' so we'd better keep off the main road.'

They took a minor road into Craiova and by 1 o'clock were parked in a secluded square away from the centre. Bucharest, General Manafu told them, was being bombed. He had no news of Queen Helen. He directed them to Tîrgu Jiu and from there they were sent on to Bumbeşti Jiu in the foothills of the western massif. They reached it at about 4 o'clock. The King was by now extremely worried about his mother. There was nothing he could do but telephone the garrison commander at Craiova.

At 3.30 that morning, Styrcea had telephoned Sinaia to say that the Queen Mother and her party should now leave for Craiova. Although she was able to have a quick bath and be ready within the hour, it took until nearly 6 o'clock to assemble and brief the escort of fifty guardsmen. They made quite a column of cars and trucks rolling slowly out of the grounds and heading for Tîrgoveşti. They were to dive for the floor in case of attack. The Germans might try to hold the bridges, might even have mined the roads. Yet in Tîrgoveşti they saw only a few German officers 'with hang-dog expressions', and so it was all the way – a risky and exhausting 14-hour drive which at any point could have gone badly wrong. At Craiova the General would tell them nothing about the King, not even whether he had passed through the town. They were to go to

Tîrgu Jiu. At Tîrgu Jiu they were told to go on to Bumbeşti Jiu, and there they saw King Michael in their headlights waving them down and 'Oh what joy to see Sweetie again, and, of all people, Jacques.'[5]

In the summer of 1943 Albert Speer had forecast that the war would end ten months after the Balkans were lost to Germany. He proved right. Within weeks of King Michael's *coup* Hitler had lost all Balkan oil, bauxite, chrome, territorial space and mountain defences and the war in Europe ended nine months later. According to General Rundstedt, the *coup* had brought Allied victory six months closer.

For Stalin the military benefits of the *coup* were substantial. By 23 August the Red Army had occupied Moldavia. But after the *coup* the Romanian rather than the Soviet army became the front line in the Allied advance westwards through Romania, and logistics rather than enemy resistance now governed the speed of Soviet troops. They reached Bulgaria on 8 September and within weeks were at the frontiers of Greece and Yugoslavia. Their directive for the offensive beginning on 20 August had foreseen the eventual capitulation of Romania, but to find themselves at the gates of Bucharest within ten days was an unexpected windfall.

However, the Red Army, which had been fighting the Romanians for three years, did not treat them as allies after the volte-face of 23 August 1944, and it is difficult to say with any certainty how much this was due to General Aldea's absence from Soviet military headquarters. The great majority of men missing from the 3rd and 4th Romanian armies had been captured and despatched to the USSR after 23 August.[6] Of the reinforcements ordered to Bucharest on the evening of 23 August, only 1,000 men and 120 vehicles reached the capital – the rest had been captured by Soviet forces on 25 August when Romania had been at war with the Reich for 24 hours.

Yet Soviet disregard for the anti-German resistance of East European countries had not the disastrous effect in Romania that it had during the Warsaw uprising. Nor had they succeeded in turning Romania into a battlefield, which would have helped them to eliminate Romania's democratic parties during an ensuing 'purge of fascists'. When on 31 August General Kravchenko entered a German-free Bucharest with flags flying and bands playing and with a directive to eliminate Romanian nationalists and to forestall Anglo-American intervention, the King had already set up a government hell bent on preparing for free elections. It would take Stalin over three years to make Romania part of the post-war cordon of satellite countries he had described to a sympathetic Eden in 1941.[7]

When he first heard of the *coup* at about 9 o'clock on the evening of 23 August, Hitler ordered his people in Bucharest to crush the uprising, arrest King Michael, destroy his Palace and restore a pro-German *régime* within 48 hours. It was the way the SS would have normally proceeded. Yet thanks to the careful preparation of the *coup* and the new hope that the young King's audacity had inspired in Romanians, it was apparently they, not the German Special Forces, who seemed to be taking the initiatives during the early vulnerable stages of the revolt. Hansen, von Gerstenberg and von Killinger jointly informed Berlin that they had sufficient evidence of solid support for the King to doubt whether the Führer's orders could be carried out.

Von Gerstenberg must have anticipated Hitler's reaction before going to the Palace, for he had already ordered a Ploieşti force of 2,000 men with AA guns to advance towards Bucharest.[8] Once he had crossed the Romanian lines he arrested his Romanian escort, ordered the air bombardment of Bucharest to begin, and the Ploieşti force, which had already secured the military airfield at Otopeni, to be ready to advance on the capital. When Michael began his journey to Craiova, Romania was already, in effect, at war with Germany.

Von Gerstenberg's advance on Bucharest was stopped by Colonel Olteanu's forces at the Baneasă bridge and by the 25th his flanks were being squeezed by reinforcements from Constanţa and Tîrgoveşti. On the 26th German troops inside the city surrendered and at 1300 hr that day, the hour originally fixed for the *coup*, the Allied planes King Michael had requested carried out a massive raid on German positions in the Baneasă woods. Colonel Olteanu's troops then moved in and surrounded them. Following a courageous initiative by his Romanian escort, von Gerstenberg, together with General Stahel – the man responsible for suppressing the Warsaw uprising and now sent to Romania to replace von Gerstenberg – were among the seven generals and 7,000 other German military personnel to surrender to the Romanian army in the Bucharest area. On 2 September the Romanian High Command reported to Sănătescu that Romanian forces had cleared all Romanian territory of Germans\* and would now concentrate in Transylvania to await the Soviet armies for the campaign into Hungary.

Stalin recognised the importance of eliminating from Western public opinion any idea that Romania had demonstrated her anti-Nazi credentials and her value as a co-belligerent. The line he took was that Romanians had played no

---

\* That is, those Romanian territories still occupied by the Germans at the time of the *coup*.

part in liberating their country and were so riddled with Nazis and Nazi sympathisers that in order to protect their lines of communication it was essential for the Red Army to continue to occupy the country. Stalin rightly assumed that, once convinced of his determination to communise Romania, Western opposition would collapse into a series of diplomatic gestures intended mainly to pacify their own public opinion. The Red Army, with the acquiescence of London and Washington, remained in Romania for many years after the war ended – in fact until King Michael had been removed and the last vestiges of institutional democracy had been destroyed.

On 24 August 1944, King Michael and his mother sat up late in the stuffy little sitting room of the house lent to them by the military director of the Bumbeşti explosives factory. Jacques Vergotti was happy to be back with the family and said very little. Colonel Negulescu was relieved that the journey was over. Had Queen Helen been recognised, had there been a skirmish and she had been captured, there was no knowing how Hitler would have behaved.

On the 25th they had news of the destruction of Casa Nouă and most of the Palace, '18 poor little soldiers of our guard killed,' Queen Helen noted. 'Lots wounded'.[9] The King knew that until they could secure at least one adjacent airfield – Otopeni, for instance – the Romanian Air Force could not regain control of Bucharest airspace. As for the land battle, it seemed to be going quite well.

One thing, according to the government, was certain – since the Germans were searching for him, the King must keep on the move. At 7 o'clock that evening they therefore said goodbye to the factory director and set off for a small mountain village called Dobritza. Here they were put up by a charming general and his wife though their two-storey red brick house perched on a hillside was far too small for the royal party. The King, his mother, Nelly Catargi and Mircea Ionniţiu slept upstairs. The three ADCs – Robert Bossy, Emilian Ionescu and Jacques Vergotti – slept in a little house in the garden. The chauffeurs slept in their cars, the servants on chairs and sofas in the sitting room. On the 27th Niculescu Buzeşti arrived with news of the US air raid on the Baneasă woods and of Olteanu's reoccupation of the airfield. The Romanian air force now had an operational base. Romanian troops had occupied Ploieşti and forestalled German sabotage of the oil installations. They had taken the important industrial towns of Sibiu and Reşiţa and had occupied the southern Carpathian passes, one of the few positions the Germans might have held with relatively few troops. Meanwhile the Red

Army was heading for the capital across territory which had already been cleared of German forces, and Buzeşti told the King that the previous day the Communist Party had issued a statement about the *coup d'état* which did not even mention him. The *coup*, they claimed, was theirs. In normal circumstances such a statement, coming from a party of under a thousand members and in whom 99 per cent of the people had not the slightest interest, would have been dismissed as ludicrous. Now, with the Red Army showing every sign of occupying the entire country, it had become a serious threat.

On Monday the 28th, Ionel Styrcea brought news of the Marshal. While in the strongroom he had made his will and written to his wife and, much later, at about four in the morning, some time after the King had left, Bodnăraş and his men had taken him and the other prisoners to the Luminoasa district of Bucharest where the Germans would not find them. That evening Queen Helen wrote in her diary: 'Oh why did he always treat us like enemies and why didn't he retire while the going was good. What misery he would have spared himself and the country.'[10]

According to Styrcea, all their servants – except for old Madame Kopkov – were on a list of people supposedly reporting to the Siguranţa. Given the great pressure they must have been under from the secret police, King Michael was inclined to forgive them but he had to agree with Styrcea that he could not lay himself open to the charge of protecting people who were known to have been German agents. His mother, however, was far too upset to be rational about the fate of her servants and was never to forgive Ionel Styrcea for their imprisonment.

The camouflaged Junker stood by for a quick get-away to Turkey if this became necessary. Udriski, who had made himself responsible for the King's security, was convinced that the Luftwaffe would eventually locate them. Time after time they had to scramble into cars in their night clothes and drive off in a cloud of dust – which Queen Helen loathed – to some flea-ridden cottage away from the village. Queen Helen suffered more than the others from the general grubbiness.

On 24 August the US Secretary of State had referred to Romanians 'abandoning their inglorious war at Hitler's side', without a word of encouragement about the *coup*.[11] Moreover, the King was growing sick of hearing the BBC announce that Soviet forces had 'liberated' yet another Romanian town which he knew had already been cleared of Germans by his own army. On 31 August, the day the Soviet army marched into Bucharest, Marshal Antonescu and his collaborators, despite Sănătescu's protest that they were Romania's prisoners, had been despatched to Russia. Senior German officers who had surrendered to the Romanians, and even German diplomats whom Maniu had intended to trade for Romanian diplomats, were also in Soviet hands. Only von Killinger had escaped this. He had shot himself and his secretary.

On 4 September Ionniţiu brought for the King's signature the royal decree re-establishing the 1923 constitution. Up to now the government had urged him not to return to the capital, but they now began to feel that the Russians would find it more difficult to take them prisoner in Bucharest than where he was. On 8 September Soviet troops were reported to be only 16 kilometres from Tîrgu Jiu and, driving back from Bumbeşti with his mother that morning, Michael had seen two Mongolian horsemen with thin drooping moustaches watching the car. Soviet troops were advancing along the road to Craiova; German aircraft had unexpectedly reappeared in Romanian airspace. The King decided that if it could be arranged they would leave with the trans-European train next evening.

Princess Ştirbey and her daughter Katherine with her two children had taken refuge with them; also Princess Elisabeta with the Scanavi family. The guests took the 3 o'clock train next afternoon. Ionniţiu flew back with Udriski. The King and the rest of his party left at six o'clock from the nearest station.

They were given two small unlit coaches with wooden seats on the little puffing-billy train which could negotiate the sharp curves to Filiaşi on the main trans-continental line and they cheerfully ate bread, chicken and ham as they chugged down the mountain in the dark. Just before they reached Filiaşi their mood changed for it was here, Queen Helen later told Lee, that they felt for the first time the full impact of the Red Army.

> As the sun set and darkness approached, we saw that all round the horizon of the plain through which we were now passing was a ring of strange red flares. Shortly afterwards we realised what they were – beacon fires for the Red Army moving towards where we had just come from. Soon the roads and tracks on either side of us were filled with Russian troops, carried in every form of transport, not only military lorries but looted buses and private cars of all kinds, even peasant carts. I remember what an impression it made on me to see two Russian officers sitting in an ordinary two-horse carriage, they seemed so incongruous in all that mêlée. We could see them plainly in the headlights of the cars, in columns all across the plain, the lights winding away into the distance, with the dust rising everywhere like a mist.[12]

When they changed trains, his mother and Nelly Catargi seemed delighted with the comparative comfort of a sleeping car. But the attendant was in tears. The Russians had broken into the carriage the night before and had stolen his money, his wedding ring, all his clothes except for those he stood up in. Robert Bossy told the attendant about his wife who, after a visit by Soviet troops, had been left with nothing to wear but her nurse's uniform.

During the night Michael was wakened several times by the clanking of the train as it stopped to give way to military traffic. They reached Bucharest at 8 in the morning of 10 September and were met by Sănătescu and members of the Government. Maniu and Brătianu were not there.

# PART THREE

Soviet Occupation:
September 1944–3 January 1948

## EIGHT

## *Vyshinsky Imposes a Communist Government*

Despite what he had been told about the changes in Bucharest, King Michael was shocked. Casa Nouă was an empty shell; at night you could still hear bits of it tumbling down.[1] The bedrooms they were to use in the least damaged wing of the big Palace were pitted by bullets and shrapnel. His mother and Madame Kopkov searched through the ruins for furniture that could be repaired for servants who had lost everything in the bombing.

Palace Square was a wasteland where well-dressed Romanians taking an evening stroll had been replaced by jeeps piled high with Romanian carpets and lorry-loads of Soviet soldiers, some women, many drunk.[2] Peasants were too frightened to come into town so the markets were empty. They invited General Burenin, commander of the Bucharest garrison, to lunch. He did not reply. There would be not even a semblance of normality, he was told, until the Armistice was signed.

The Cairo meeting had moved to Moscow and was now under Molotov's chairmanship. Juliu Maniu had refused to lead the Bucharest delegation and had been replaced by Lucrețiu Pătrășcanu, who believed that, being a Communist, he could obtain better terms for his country. As a result he became one of the first post-*coup* Romanians to experience the cold douche of Soviet *realpolitik*.

Nothing had yet been heard from the delegation, not, as the King assumed, because of Soviet obstruction but because the British had objected to executive power being vested exclusively in the Soviet representative to the Allied

Control Commission which was to be set up in Bucharest. When, finally, the British gave way to Russian determination and American silence Molotov presented an agreed Soviet text to the Romanian delegation and the Armistice was signed by Molotov and Ştirbey within 48 hours. Pătrăşcanu was thrown by Molotov's rudeness, but other members of the Romanian delegation spoke well and achieved nothing. Romania, they were told, had still to work its way towards co-belligerency status; the *coup*, the King thought, might never have happened.

Yet, thanks to the *coup d'état*, much of Romania's economy had survived intact. If the massive Soviet requisitioning and economic obstruction eventually ceased and, as Molotov had promised in his April broadcast, Romania was allowed to conduct her affairs in her own way, the country would survive.

On 12 September the King and his mother moved to Princess Elisabeta's elegant villa behind the tree-lined Chaussée Kiselev. For his study the King chose a room on the ground floor looking on to an inside courtyard. Here he would meet his advisers and members of the Household who had their offices in what was left of the Palace. On the ground floor was also a dining room suitable for entertaining members of the Allied Control Commission, diplomats and Romanian ministers. They spent weekends at Sinaia, but for the three weeks that Princess Elisabeta stayed on in her house Queen Helen found the living quarters upstairs very cramped.

While preparations for a *coup d'état* against the Axis had bound the royal household together, the uncertainties of Soviet occupation seemed to be having the opposite effect. On 14 September when the Papal Nuncio, doyen of the diplomatic corps, was their first guest at the Kiselev house, Ionel Styrcea ranted against the Americans and British for 'betraying' Romania and then shocked the table by announcing that he had just cancelled an audience with the American General Eacher. After lunch the King reinstated the appointment and he had to agree with his mother that Styrcea's outbursts and off-hand treatment of government ministers were doing the monarchy no good.

Michael knew that his mother would never be really happy in his Aunt Elisabeta's house and was in any case under considerable strain. She had not forgiven Styrcea for refusing to help her Saxon servants. 'Those miserable servants', she noted, 'about 15 have been put out as spies with not a single proof against them in a way which makes me boil.'[3] She was now convinced that Ionel Styrcea was trying to replace her in her son's confidence.

On 22 September, nine days after signature of the Armistice, they had General Burenin and three Soviet officers to lunch. It seemed to go well. The young captain interpreter spoke perfect Romanian. One of the majors claimed to have known Queen Olga – Queen Helen's grandmother – in St Petersburg in 1913. 'At lunch the atmosphere so cordial that I thought we would end up by a kissing party . . . They swore they had come here as friends & allies.' She closed her diary that evening with 'Oh god help us, the gen. looked exactly like a german gen. If only relations become easier after this contact.'[4]

After his first press conference on the lawn in front of Elisabeta Palace, all Moscow newspapers reported Michael's reference to the common struggle against Germany which he described as a prelude to good neighbourly policy and mutual confidence between their two countries.

Yet every day it became clearer to the King that 'neighbourly policy' and 'mutual confidence' were not among the aims of the occupying power. On 18 September the Minister of Health told them that the Russians had requisitioned everything from hospitals down to boots. Two days later, when 400 Romanian wounded arrived from the Western front, there was no transport for them. On 28 September at his inauguration ceremony as Minister of Justice, Lucrețiu Pătrășcanu refused to take the oath either before a priest or to the King. Pătrășcanu, whom the King described as a communist who 'had some national feeling',[5] was the victim, he thought, of intimidation – in which case the outlook was bleak.[6]

As for the Communist Party, which at the time of the *coup d'état* had had less than one thousand members, it was now being allowed to recruit Iron Guard thugs to swell its ranks. The party carried out economic sabotage which the Allied (Soviet) Control Commission then blamed on 'reactionary' elements in the National Peasant and Liberal parties, thus giving them a pretext for calling out large street crowds to demonstrate against the economic incompetence of the Sănătescu government.

The Allied (Soviet) Control Commission (ACC) had also allowed Bodnăraș to form the 'Patriotic Guard', armed by the Russians and, more importantly, the only Romanian civilian body permitted to carry weapons. At a time when the ACC imposed disabling restrictions on the Romanian police and Gendarmerie the Patriotic Guard could ensure that any non-communist, post-*coup* government would be unable to maintain law and order.

In September, London appointed a diplomatic representative to Bucharest who, unlike Air Vice-Marshal Stevenson, the head of the British Military Mission which formed part of the Allied Control Commission, reported to the Foreign Office rather than the War Office and was not bound by Control Commission restrictions regarding access to the Romanian administration. Ian Le Rougetel arrived on 1 October and two months later was followed by Burton Berry, his US colleague. On 5 October, Le Rougetel, accompanied by his deputy, James Marjoribanks – a quiet Scot with a warm smile – lunched at the Elisabeta Palace. The other guest was Niculescu Buzeşti, the Foreign Minister.[7]

Conversation was a little stiff until Queen Helen, knowing how touchy the English were about their Russian ally, referred to Soviet behaviour in Bucharest without any hint of recrimination – even adding that it was only to be expected after the Romanian excesses in the USSR.

The King agreed with Le Rougetel that the Government would benefit from more competence and expertise; it had been cobbled together in a hurry on the night of the *coup* and had only been intended to conclude the Armistice and prepare for a general election. Still, this communist pressure on it for immediate agrarian reform was in his view no more than a disruptive populist appeal to the least educated of the peasants. He reminded Le Rougetel of the great agrarian reforms of the 1920s. Those had required carefully drafted legislation, as would this if it were to be effective. Also it should not take place until peasants at present fighting alongside the Soviet army at the Western front had returned to their villages.

He also questioned the Soviet decision to disband all Romanian divisions except for the twelve fighting at the front, a measure which would deprive the Romanian Government of any effective means of enforcing its authority inside the country.

Le Rougetel asked what progress was being made to purge pro-German Romanians. King Michael, who had personally arrested the chief Romanian war criminals on 23 August, realised that for London the purge of Romanians with German sympathies was a simple black-and-white issue. For him, instinctively against witch-hunts, it was rather more complex. He pointed out to Le Rougetel that the worst of the Nazi elements had already been absorbed into the Communist Party. The germanophile tradition in Romania had never been strong and though many Romanians had approved of Antonescu's attempt to recover the eastern provinces in 1941, they had had no interest in Hitler's ideological war. Le Rougetel found the King's analysis balanced and 'a refreshing contrast to the hidebound attitude of some party leaders I have met here lately'.[8]

On 6 October King Michael obtained the release of those servants who were proved to be innocent. The following day they had news that everything was still well with the house at Săvârşin. On the 13th Queen Helen noted 'Athens liberated. How lucky they are to have Eng & Ams.'[9] But there the good news ends and on 11 October she had noted in her diary 'Crisis growing daily'.

During the second week of October the Communist Party formed the National Democratic Front or NDF, an important step towards communisation of Romania. Except for Titel Petrescu's Social Democratic Party it consisted of three communist satellites of no independent political status. Yet within weeks the Government was being pressed to accept the National Democratic Front as a genuine coalition of independent political parties, each of which could claim a ministerial portfolio. Faced by these tactics Sănătescu was completely out of his depth. Bodnăraş provided the fire power, Ana Pauker called for a political crisis every ten days; it is not surprising that Sănătescu never got round to seriously planning for free and fair parliamentary elections.

Moreover, under the armistice agreement Romania had undertaken to dissolve all pro-Hitler organisations (of a fascist type) as well as other organisations conducting propaganda hostile to the United Nations, in particular to the Soviet Union. Since in Communist semantics any organisation opposed to Communism or the Soviet Union was 'of a fascist type', the two democratic parties were made the targets of this article.

On 13 October a small demonstration of the National Peasant Party was fired on by Communists. This was so routine that the Queen Mother did not mention it in her diary. Yet at 1.30 a.m. on 15 October 1944, Sănătescu was called from his bed to the Soviet Control Commission and shown a telegram from Moscow claiming that the National Peasant demonstration had been 'of a pro-fascist type' and 'directed against the United Nations, particularly the Soviet Union'. The demonstrators had shouted 'Down with the Red Army' and fired arms. The ACC, therefore, forbade another NPP demonstration planned for the 18th.

The King knew that although the Soviet accusations were false, the public association of Maniu's name with 'fascism' could be an important step towards suppressing the democratic parties. The Communist press in Moscow and Bucharest was by now systematically spreading the kind of confusion that was to bedevil every non-communist government the King appointed.

The Communist Party, with the support of the Allied Control Commission, now pressed for a government of the political parties to replace the military government appointed on the evening of the *coup*. They also demanded the same number of portfolios for their NDF satellites as would be normally given to the historical parties led by Maniu and Brătianu. For a time, therefore, Michael worked hard for a government of technicians, knowing that the NDF could provide little of the expertise the country so badly needed and, according to his mother, would come down to dinner at around ten o'clock, 'dead beat' after spending the day with the party leaders. Queen Helen saw no solution and wondered at what point the Russians would step in with military force. She began to fear for her son's safety. She spent much of her time trying to save hospital beds and medical supplies from Soviet requisitioning. She was also setting up a soup kitchen in the palace dining room. As the political situation worsened, she felt an urge to undertake with Vergotti and Madame Kopkov an inventory of generations of historical treasures that had accumulated in Peleş.

Apart from the deteriorating situation in Romania, one of their main worries concerned Michael's father. After his abdication King Carol had gone to live in Rio de Janeiro, but was now thinking of moving to Europe. Michael had heard rumours that he was already in touch with the Russians. He would have been surprised to know that Churchill saw no objection to King Carol's return and had accused his Foreign Office, which opposed it, of narrow-mindedness about the mistress and of having 'a prejudice against all kings'.

On 28 October Sir Alexander Cadogan, the Permanent Under-Secretary at the Foreign Office, wrote to Churchill:

> The internal situation in Roumania is precarious and the elder statesmen seem quite incapable of coming to grips with it. King Michael is the only person who may be able to pull the country through the coming months and save it from anarchy or communism. It is our policy, therefore, to give him the fullest support.[10]

In the same minute Cadogan assured the Prime Minister that the Foreign Office's anxiety to keep King Carol on the other side of the Atlantic had nothing at all to do with his mistress. During the last four years King Carol's son had matured

> to a most remarkable extent. He has an extremely good grasp of Romania's internal and external situation. His heart has always been in the right place and everyone is in agreement that it was he who took the initiative in dismissing the Antonescus from office and bringing about Romania's surrender . . . His father, however, is an inveterate intriguer. . . . By hook or by crook he would get back to Romania and that would be the end of the monarchy.

'OK but stick to the Boy', Churchill minuted back.

When, after three weeks' struggle, the King had to agree to a government of the parties, he was determined that it would be as representative as he could make it. When Sănătescu proposed to give the Interior to the Communists, who in spite of their Soviet backing had virtually no support within the country, he flatly refused. The post went to a National Peasant called Penescu but Teohari Georgescu, a leading Communist activist, was made Under-Secretary in the same ministry and Michael was not sure that Penescu could handle him.

In the middle of this crisis Air Vice-Marshal Stevenson, head of the British military mission, accepted, for the first time since his arrival, an invitation to lunch with them. During the audience that followed, the King, who had spent the previous night negotiating ministerial appointments, was tense and more outspoken about Soviet behaviour than he had been with Le Rougetel a month before.

In reply the Air Vice-Marshal said them that since Romania was 'a sovereign state under agreement with nations', he recommended a strong government in order to carry out its armistice responsibilities, one in which 'the Crown must perform its sovereign will without fear of outside pressure'.[11] In her diary that night Queen Helen wrote of Stevenson: 'I was delighted that he told Sweetie to go ahead, do what he thinks best, form a strong gov. & that allies support crown. Most encouraging.'[12]

She would have felt differently had she known that Eden had struck out the sentence in the Foreign Office telegram to Stevenson approving his language in conversation with the King and Queen Mother. Or that the Air Vice-Marshal, who had already obtained the authority of Marshal Malinovski, the Head of the Allied Control Commission, to accept lunch at the Palace, was now instructed to inform General Vinogradov, the Marshal's deputy, of what had transpired at the Palace.

For Michael, the rest of that afternoon was a nightmare. While he had been entertaining Stevenson, Sănătescu, under pressure from those who were determined to force the King's hand, had published the new governmental list without discussing final details with him. As a result Vişoianu replaced Buzeşti as Foreign Minister without being consulted. Ionel Styrcea then picked up the telephone, called Sănătescu an 'escroc' and handed in his resignation. The King now felt he must accept it. He replaced him with Negel, a pleasant easy-going man without Ionel Styrcea's convictions, brilliance, or outspokenness. Also, since he had once served in Antonescu's administration,[13] the new Marshal of the Royal Court would be vulnerable to Russian pressure.

This seemed to be a season for brainstorms. On 1 November Maniu suggested that he should visit London and Buzeşti and Mihalache Moscow in order to be briefed by the British and Russian governments about their plans for Romania. Even Le Rougetel must have seemed in London to be badly out of touch when he proposed that Churchill and Eden should visit Bucharest on their way home from their recent Moscow meeting since such a visit 'could greatly strengthen Britain's position in Romania'.

On 4 November 1944 Churchill minuted Eden that Le Rougetel evidently 'does not understand that we have only a 10 per cent interest in Romania and are little more than spectators'[14] and, three days later, 'here are a new batch of telegrams showing the zeal with which Le Rougetel, Stevenson and others [the whole diplomatic staff, had he but known it] are throwing themselves into the agonising turmoil at Bucharest'.[15] Le Rougetel and Stevenson were then informed that on 9 October Churchill and Stalin had agreed in Moscow that for the duration of the war they would recognise Britain's 90 per cent interest in Greece and the Soviet Union's 90 per cent interest in Romania. With the Red Army already installed in Romania, Churchill could do very little for that country, but should Stalin now withdraw the considerable assistance he was giving the Greek partisans, he had a reasonable chance of saving Greece. Churchill therefore considered the so-called Percentage Agreement to be something of a diplomatic *coup* and British representatives in Bucharest were asked to stay their hands.[16]

Very few British diplomats were told of the Moscow deal and some of those found it very difficult to swallow. Three weeks after being put in the picture we find Le Rougetel telegraphing London immediately after an audience with King Michael, who knew nothing of the agreement: 'With the greatest respect I submit that unless we can persuade the Russians to drop the project of communising Romania it will be too late to intervene, and the experiment may then be repeated on an increasing scale elsewhere.'[17]

The Percentage Agreement probably made no material difference to Romania. By the summer of 1945 Churchill was getting on top of the Greek situation and soon after the Labour Party came to power in July they decided that the agreement was now out of date and could be ignored. Although the Americans had had no part in the Percentage Agreement, which has been widely blamed in Romania for British inability to help their country, Washington's attempts to stand up to Stalin were no more effective than London's.

On 6 November 1944 the Queen's soup kitchen in the big palace became operational. Eighty-five children came that first morning. During the next three months 11,000 helpings would be served and, she notes, 'Red X ladies efficient and quick and cook practical and economic.'[18] On the 8th, Michael's name-day, a huge crowd gathered in Palace Square. 'He went on the balcony and I went out also for a moment at the end. Then we all went down to see our soup kitchen. I am so pleased with it.'[19] Michael admired the way she kept up with her social work during the following months of almost continual political crisis: attending the annual opening of the school for nurses run by her friend, Madame Pacioga, getting new baths for the military hospital and a new wing of 200 beds furnished, partly with things from the big palace and Cotroceni and, in spite of Russian obstruction, getting supplies into Moldavia during the typhus epidemic.

Less than a month after its formation the NDF had taken the vice-presidency of the Council of Ministers and six portfolios and had under-secretaries in three other key ministries. Buzeşti had been replaced as Foreign Minister by the less outspoken Vişoianu. Andrei Vyshinsky's arrival early in November could be taken, therefore, as a sign that the Romanian Communists had earned the backing of bigger Soviet guns.

Deputy Foreign Minister Vyshinsky, chief public prosecutor during the worst of the Soviet purges, lunched with the King and his mother on 11 November.

> I imagined [Queen Helen wrote in her diary] Vyshinsky would look cruel & gangsterish instead of which he was a small white-haired man with a very amiable smile. Looked a professor of any nationality. . . . Vinogradov brought me two dictionaries & wrote a dedication.[20]

Although Vyshinsky had come ostensibly to speed up execution of the armistice terms, his main purpose seems to have been provocation. So when at a lunch given for him on 14 November Vişoianu toasted Stalin, Vyshinsky replied that since signature of the Armistice was as important for Romania as the *coup d'état* he did not propose to toast King Michael.

On 29 November Vyshinsky urged a delegation of NDF demonstrators to take direct action against Nazi sympathisers rather than wait on the Government. Maniu and Brătianu called for Sănătescu's resignation, citing his weakness in the face of Communist and Soviet pressure. Sănătescu thankfully tendered it and was asked by the King to stay on until a new government could be formed.

King Michael ignored the NDF's call for Petru Groza, leader of one of the Communist Party's satellites, and turned to a man who, at Russian insistence, had replaced General Mihail as Chief of Staff. General Rădescu was 71 and without political experience, but he had shown his courage during the

Antonescu *régime* by publicly standing up to the German Minister, von Killinger. Vyshinsky told the King on 7 December that the Russians had no intention of imposing communism on Romania. Moscow seemed now ready to accept a prime minister whose democratic credentials were solid and who was nobody's stooge.

There followed a rare period of good news. Queen Helen noted that on 8 November, King Michael's name-day, the day Vyshinsky left, a large friendly crowd gathered outside the Palace. On 13 December they heard that his aunt Irene and her baby were alive, though prisoners of the Germans.[21] Relations with the Russians improved under Rădescu. An ACC demand for 30,000 horses – more than there were in the country – was reduced to 20,000.[22] Michael got in some shooting at Mănăstirea. He skied at Praedeal. He flew AVM Stevenson's plane but 'no cross country flights', the amiable Vinogradov warned; there were too many keen young Soviet fighter pilots around. The King had already been buzzed by one of them.

Meanwhile, however, preparations were being made in Moscow for the final sprint to a Communist-controlled government and in the third week of January 1945 Ana Pauker returned from Moscow with a new directive for the Romanian Communist Party. They should now work directly for a Communist-led government and the early destruction of Maniu and his party. To preserve stability during this process, King Michael should be retained and plans to nationalise banks and industry for the moment shelved. Once they were in power, matters for which the King had been pressing – Transylvania's return, recognition that Romania's was the fourth largest army fighting the Reich, the repatriation of Romanian POWs – all these would be granted to demonstrate the favourable treatment Romania would enjoy under a Communist administration.[23]

The King knew of the Pauker briefing within 48 hours of her arrival. An NDF manifesto issued on 28 January made no mention of nationalisation – previously one of its main policy planks. On 9 February Rădescu discovered that Groza was plotting with an under-secretary in the Minister of Interior to overthrow the Government. He sacked the under-secretary and Groza temporarily left the capital. In the second week of February there was a sudden influx of NKVD troops. Since only the Communists caused serious disturbances which might call for additional security, this latest measure seemed ominous to the King – a feeling that deepened when the usually friendly Vinogradov refused to discuss it with his British and American colleagues. London saw this concern as Bucharest scaremongering which, should it continue, might harm Anglo-Soviet relations. Le Rougetel was asked to break his leave in England and return to his post to keep an eye on things. He fell ill in Bari and was unable to reach Bucharest until the next, and this time critical, Romanian crisis was over.

King Michael believes that the first concrete warning of what was to occur was not the arrival of NKVD troops but news that General Vinogradov was to be replaced by General Susaikov, a known hard-liner who arrived with Vyshinsky on 27 February accompanied by Alexei Pavlov, his hawkish political adviser. Before their arrival Rădescu had been given due credit for his efforts to pull the country together and fulfil the terms of the Armistice. The Russians had already reduced the Bucharest police force to 700 men, the national Gendarmerie to 14,000 and the regular army inside the country to three divisions of 3,500 men each. With the arrival of Susaikov the police and Gendarmerie were to be further reduced and the Romanian authorities warned that should they ever use the army to suppress internal disorder (which would be created solely by the NDF), this would be treated as civil war calling for Soviet military intervention.[24]

Red Army occupation of Romania was essential to its communisation. King Michael has pointed out that the Soviet Union could not legally prolong the stay of Soviet troops on Romanian territory unless Romania had been formally recognised as a defeated country and that, since a large Romanian army was inflicting considerable losses on the German army in some of the most difficult sectors of the front and was winning the praise of the Western Allies, this was out of the question. The Russians and their Romanian representatives therefore provoked such political and social disorder inside the country that finally the Western Allies had to agree that only the continued presence of Soviet troops could secure the Red Army's line of communication with the front. At the end of the European war in May 1945 only a Communist-controlled government would welcome the retention of Soviet troops until such time as the communisation of the country had been stabilised. The establishment of such a government was, therefore, the object of Ana Pauker's brief and Vyshinsky's second visit.

Two events possibly accelerated the Soviet plan.

First, when on 19 February Rădescu announced that municipal elections would take place on 15 March, Moscow knew that if the Communist Party were to avoid an electoral disaster, Rădescu must be replaced by a Communist-controlled government within three weeks.

Second, on 15 February the workforce of the Malaxa armament factory – at the very heart of Romania's heavy industry – overthrew the self-appointed Communist-controlled Workers' Committee, elected a committee of the democratic parties by 3,750 votes to 270, discovered the Communist arms dump and defended themselves next morning against armed railway workers led by Gheorghiu-Dej.

The Romanian Communist Party had suffered a severe humiliation; the Russians threatened military intervention which the King knew must be avoided at all costs; and the Allied Control Commission authorised a large NDF demonstration for 24 February which chanted 'Down with Rădescu'. Marksmen opened fire on Rădescu's office and the Palace from flats in Palace Square. When attempts were made to break into the Ministry of the Interior, the guards, as instructed, fired into the air. Communist agents then fired at random with hand guns into the crowd and when the demonstration had dispersed, the two dead and eight wounded were found to include schoolboys, policemen, a stone mason, some chauffeurs, and the man who operated the projector at the Tivoli cinema. None of the bullets extracted from the bodies of the dead and wounded were of military calibre yet Rădescu was accused of 'murdering innocent workers while they were demonstrating for a democratic Romania'. That evening, when a group of students cheered the Prime Minister outside the Ministry of Interior, urging him not to give in, lorries of armed NDF shock troops drove up, killed two and wounded eleven.

These murders proved too much for Rădescu. He drove immediately to the radio station and, in a peak-time speech after the ten o'oclock news, denounced the three communist leaders, Ana Pauker, Lazlo Luca and Emil Bodnăraş by name. To a nation probably listening to the last criticism of the Romanian Communist Party they would hear from Radio Bucharest for the next half-century, he said that these three were responsible for the unrest which was destroying Romania and that the letters FND (the Romanian version of NDF) fitted them like a glove for they were *Fără de Neam şi Dumnezeu* – without Nation or God.

Rădescu was escorted to Soviet Headquarters and grilled for four and a half hours. When the Russian admiral in charge denied that his authorities were interfering in Romania's internal affairs, Rădescu asked him why, in that case, he had been instructed to cancel a National Peasant Party demonstration but to allow a minority Communist group to murder and terrorise the people – 'is not that interference?'

The Communist Party went into overdrive. Officially inspired telegrams asking the King to dismiss Rădescu poured in from all over the country. Workers' delegations came to the Palace. The printers' union refused to print Rădescu's speeches. In the newspapers of 27 February an open letter signed by a group of high-ranking army officers denounced Rădescu and called for his

*Above, left:* Three Generations: King Carol I, Crown Prince Ferdinand, Prince Carol.
*Above, right:* Elizabeth of Wied, Queen of Romania, in peasant dress. *(Both Private collection)*

*Below, left:* Queen Marie of Romania. *Below, right:* Prince Michael on the beach at Mamaia. After King Ferdinand's death the house was given to Princess Helen by Queen Marie with the agreement of the family. She later sold it to the government in order to buy Villa Sparta in Florence where she lived in exile. *(Both Private collection)*

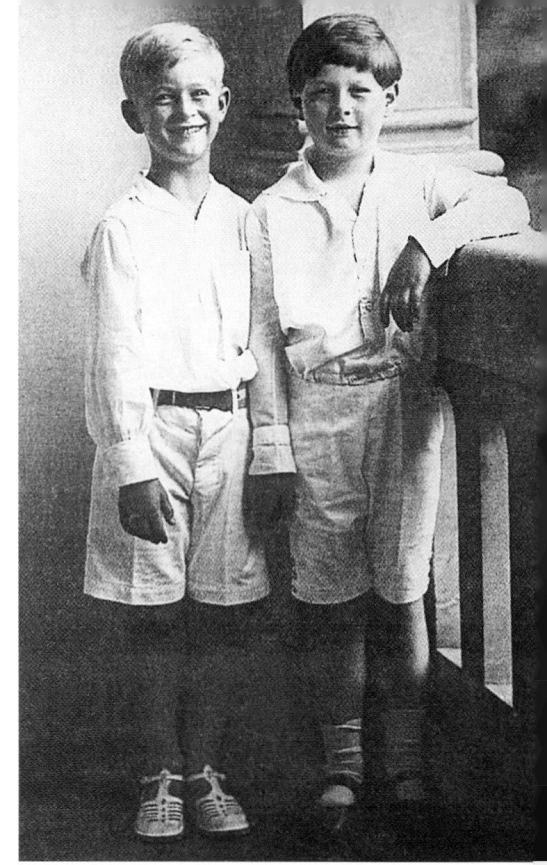

*Above, left:* Crown Prince Carol, Crown Princess Helen, Prince Michael and dog. *(Studioul Julietta) Above, right:* King Michael with his cousin Prince Philip of Greece (later Duke of Edinburgh) 1928. *(Private collection)*

*Below, left:* Princess Elisabeta, Queen of Greece. *(Studioul Julietta) Below, centre:* Princess Maria 'Mignon', Queen of Yugoslavia. *(Studioul Julietta) Below, right:* Princess Ileana, Archduchess of Austria. *(Studioul Julietta)*

*Above, left:* In July 1930, on the anniversary of King Ferdinand's death, the Royal Family attend a memorial service at Curtea de Argeş. In the front Queen Marie with King Carol, behind Princess Helen and Prince Nicholas, King Carol's brother. This was the first time that King Carol had appeared in public with his ex-wife, Princess Helen, since his return to Romania in June. *Above right:* Crown Prince Michael during the State Visit to London in November 1938. *Below:* Memorial service for Queen Marie at Curtea de Argeş, January 1939. King Carol followed by Crown Prince Michael, Princess Elisabeta and the Patriarch Miron Cristea. In the Orthodox Church a memorial service is held six months after the death. This had occurred in July 1938. *(All Private collections)*

Strained relations at the palace: King Michael, Queen Helen, Madame Antonescu – just shown standing behind the Marshal – Mihai Antonescu and Baron Ion Mocsoni-Styrcea trying to spot the photographer. The man saluting is, according to Baron Styrcea, the Marshal's chief spy in the King's Military Household.
*(Private collection)*

The house at Săvârşin in western Transylvania, which King Michael bought partly as a retreat away from government spies.
*(G. Valeanu)*

In front of King Michael's twin engined Fokker Wolf at Săvârşin in 1946. L-R Wing Commander Udriski, Prince George Sturdza, Princess Greta Sturdza, King Michael, Mrs Ioana Negroponte Boxshall, Major Jacques Vergotti, Mr Vanya Negroponte.
*(Private collection)*

The Royal Palace in Calea Victoriei with Casa Nouă in ruins after German bombing following the *coup d'état* of 23 August 1944. *(Private collection)*

On 22 September 1944 King Michael's first press conference after the *coup d'état*. Outside the Elisabeta Palace is the King, Ionel Styrcea with, among others, Sam Brewer the *New York Times*, Archie Gibson *The Times*, A.T. Cholerton the *Daily Telegraph*. *(Private collection)*

The Moscow Three Power Commission at Sinaia, 8 January 1946. Sir Archibald Clark-Kerr, UK Ambassador in Moscow, Deputy Soviet Foreign Minister Vyshinsky, the King, Queen Helen, Mr Averell Harriman, US Ambassador in Moscow, Mr Harriman's daughter. *(Private collection)*

Prime Minister Groza, King Michael and Marshal Tolbukhin. Date and occasion unknown. Possibly 19 July 1945 when the King was awarded the Soviet Order of Victory. *(Private collection)*

Princess Anne of Bourbon Parma saying goodbye to King Michael and Queen Helen as she leaves for Copenhagen from Lausanne station, 18 December 1947. *(The Star, 19 December 1947)*

**1.** Juliu Maniu head of the National Peasant Party and one of the prime movers of resistance to the Germans. **2.** Dinu Brătianu, leader of the Liberal Party who worked closely with Maniu. **3.** Marshal Antonescu, pro-German dictator of Romania after the abdication of King Carol II, during his trial in May 1946. **4.** Gheorghe Tătărescu, King Carol II's favourite prime minister who, after Vyshinsky's coup of March 1945, became Vice President and Foreign Minister in Groza's communist-controlled government. *(All Private collections)*

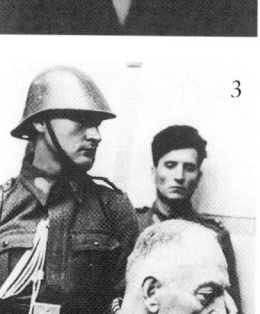

King Michael and Princess Anne at Athens airport on 7 June 1948, three days before their wedding. L-R Queen Helen, Queen Frederika of Greece, King Paul of Greece. *(Associated Press)*

Princess Margarita and Mr Radu Duda after their wedding ceremony on 21 September 1996. *(Reuters/Denis Balibouse)*

1. President Nicolae Ceaușescu. Appointed 1st Secretary of the Communist Party in 1965, became President in 1974. Executed with his wife Christmas Day 1989. *(Associated Press)* 2. President Ion Iliescu became president after the revolution of 1989. He lost the election of 1996 but was re-elected in 2000. *(Reuters/Bogdan Cristel)* 3. President-elect Emil Constantinescu photographed after he had defeated Ion Iliescu in the presidential election of November 1996. *(Associated Press)*

King Michael on 28 February 1997 on his first visit to Romania for seven years and only his second since his exile in January 1948. *(Richard Hollis: Daily Telegraph Syndication)*

removal. There was immediate disciplinary action and by evening the King had signed the decree authorising dismissal of this group.

The King felt that his hand had been strengthened by the summit meeting at Yalta between 4 and 11 February where the three Allied leaders had pledged their governments to help countries of liberated Europe form 'broadly representative interim administrations whose main purpose would be to prepare for free democratic elections reflecting the will of the people'. On 27 February he told his mother that the Americans had sent Molotov a strong note, backed by the British, insisting that Romania's coalition government should not be replaced by a minority government, that it should be allowed adequate means to maintain law and order and that there should be freedom of the press as guaranteed by Article 16 of the Armistice. It was up to him, therefore, to resist the dictatorship of a minority government for as long as he possibly could.

His mother was far less optimistic. By the end of February the Russians had arrested, tried and executed virtually the whole former government of Bulgaria, including Prince Cyril, one of the three regents acting for the boy King Simeon. In Romania King Michael's *coup d'état* had made such prompt Soviet action impossible but Michael and his mother knew that their eventual fate might be no different from Cyril's. On 16 February she wrote in her diary:

> God protect my Sweetie and Rădescu as those two alone are keeping the whole country's head above water and nobody else would be capable of preventing a disaster if – god forbid – anything were to happen to either of them.

Almost every entry in February contains the words, 'Oh God help us all.' She does not mention the Yalta Summit but on 25 February notes, 'Americans & English behaving au dessous de tout. They tremble before the Russians. Its disgusting to see.'

Vyshinsky, accompanied by the newly appointed Susaikov, had arrived on the 27th and immediately asked for an audience which was arranged for 9 o'clock that evening.[25] The Russian, reading from a typed statement, said, in the name of his Government, that demonstrations in the streets, disorder in factories and Romanian press attacks on the Prime Minister showed that Rădescu was no longer capable of ensuring the order that was essential in a territory close to the front line and on which there were Soviet bases, troops and provisions needed for the defeat of Germany. He therefore requested the King to dismiss him immediately and to call to power a government which would be 'truly representative of the democratic forces of the country'. One should listen to the voice of the people, he said, clearly referring to the demonstration of the 24th. King Michael said that he was anxious to see the formation of a government representative of all parties in accordance with their strength. When he referred to the Yalta Declaration Vyshinsky replied curtly that it made no mention of Rădescu. He would be in Bucharest for a few days and a solution was most urgent. The King said he would think over what had been discussed.

Next day Michael began consultation with the political leaders. At lunchtime Vyshinsky again asked for an audience and, although the King had very little new to tell him, it was arranged for half-past three. Vyshinsky now took on the role of prosecutor rather than diplomat. When the King told him that he had already seen General Rădescu and had started consultations about a successor, he shouted: 'This reply does not satisfy me. We consider General Rădescu and his government to be fascist or at least kept in power by fascists. I tell you officially that we cannot tolerate such a government. . . . 'You do not understand the gravity of the situation', he told Michael. 'Nor do the people around you. The government must be changed immediately. By six o'clock you must announce its resignation and by eight a new government must be formed.' When Vişoianu tried to intervene Vyshinsky told him to be quiet since this conversation was entirely between the King and himself. 'I must consult the chiefs of the political parties,' the King replied, whereupon Vyshinsky got up, hit the King's table with his fist and shouted, 'I want Your Majesty's reply right now!'

King Michael was not afraid. He listened attentively to what this man, whose coolness and self-discipline was proverbial, had to say. Clearly he was putting on an act, trying to exploit their differences of age just as Antonesu had done in the early days of the war. During the four years since he took his oath, the hardships his country had suffered had had a decisive effect on him. He had not only matured; he had aged. Vyshinsky might have been acting but Moscow's determination to force a Communist-controlled government on Romania was real and alone he could not stop it.

The King agreed to Vyshinsky's first request but said that a successor could not be designated at such short notice. When Vyshinsky demanded cancellation of the decree dismissing the ten army officers for mixing in politics – since it revealed an attitude hostile to the Soviet Union – the King felt obliged to agree though under protest.

'That is all', Vyshinsky said. 'I await news of General Rădescu's resignation.' He then left, slamming the door so violently that plaster fell off in the passage outside. According to Vergotti, who escorted him out, he was grinning to himself as he got into his car.

General Susaikov had now replaced the amiable General Vinogradov as Deputy Chairman of the ACC. Soviet tanks were deployed in the streets and King Michael felt that he had no alternative but to ask Rădescu to resign. The resignation was announced that evening. An hour later Vyshinsky asked again to see the King but when Negel was suggested instead he surprisingly agreed. Half an hour later Negel returned to say that he had been quite friendly but had insisted on the appointment of Groza as prime minister with Tătărescu as vice-premier. Groza, the ambitious provincial lawyer who led the Ploughman's Front, one of the satellite groups which made up the NDF, was described by the King as a man without personality. The Russians were offering him an identity which he could not resist. As for Tătărescu, the man for all seasons, he would support anyone – King Carol or Vyshinsky – who would further his career. Negel was for accepting, Vişoianu against. Berry had advised the King to try to give the Allies time to exert their influence in Moscow and the King now made a formal request for British and American advice.

At 4 o'clock on 1 March Vyshinsky again asked to see him and this time would not be put off with Negel. He gave the Palace just five minutes to let him have their reply and an audience was fixed for 10 o'clock.

Again Vyshinsky indulged in a threat which, given his body language, was hardly veiled: 'We have no need of your territory', he said. 'Russia is large. We are not short of men, we have a large population. We need only your friendship', meaning we want you to do what we want you to do. Then his language became almost biblical. 'A government in which Your Majesty has confidence, we, too, will have confidence in it. And if we have confidence, then Your Majesty, too, will have confidence.' Dr Groza, he added, was the person who had the confidence of the Soviet Union and could unite the sentiments of truly democratic elements in the country, while Tătărescu was a patriot and democrat who as vice-president would pursue a policy of friendship with the USSR.

The British advised King Michael 'not to take the irrevocable step of abdicating if he could possibly help it'. The State Department preferred to give him no advice until they knew the outcome of their representations in Moscow.

On the evening of 2 March the King asked Groza to form a representative government with the help of all political parties. Within a few hours Vyshinsky let him know that Moscow would not admit members of the National Peasant

Party since they were considered fascists and Hitlerites. 'Is it possible', wrote Queen Helen, no friend of Maniu's, 'when he was the one who opposed the Germans with all his might?'[26]

Next evening Groza reported failure and the King asked him to try again. Vyshinsky sent a message to say that to turn down Groza at this stage would be seen as an affront to Marshal Stalin.

On the 4th Groza told the King that unless he accepted the cabinet as it was he could not answer for what might happen during the big NDF demonstration on 6 March.

On the evening of the 5th Ionnițiu brought news from the American and British missions that London and Washington had not changed their opinion of events in Romania but, regretfully, were unable to help. With this Michael felt that he had come to the end of the road. Queen Helen, who expected to be arrested along with her son, made the following entry in her diary – the last for over four months. It is in the form of a prayer but, unlike other entries, it seems to be intended for others to read, an appeal to posterity to understand the depth of the tragedy now facing her son and the country.

> God help and bless us.
>
> I am entrusting my diary to Mr Berry, American representative in Bucharest. If something happens to us it will be a big blot on the pages of civilisation.
>
> Michael has behaved like a hero and not one person has been found to stand up for him. He has suffered martyrdom in the name of justice, honour and the good of his people. My heart aches and bleeds for him. May God give me the necessary courage to help encourage him to the last. Amen.

But by then Moscow had no use for further disruption; they had obtained all they wanted. Next day Soviet patrols escorted the demonstrators, and Soviet troops secured government buildings. At an NDF meeting that morning Laslo Luca, the NDF's Secretary General, told the speakers chosen to address the demonstration not to attack the King. His entourage was fair game but the country was not ready for a republic. 'However leftist we might be, the historical development of the last decade shows that a monarchy can be far more democratic than a fascist republic.'[27] The fifty thousand NDF demonstrators who gathered in Palace Square that afternoon were orderly and rather bored, and within a couple of hours they were on their way home.

The King summoned Maniu and Brătianu for five o'clock that evening but Maniu had had a fall and could not attend. He showed Brătianu two documents – one an instrument of abdication, the other a decree accepting the Groza Government – and asked him which he should sign. Brătianu replied that while abdication might solve the King's problems it would not in any way help the country as a whole. It would, in fact, hasten communisation. Since the King was the country's last hope, he could not advise him to abdicate.

Fourteen of the ministries in Petru Groza's Government went to the NDF, three to Tătărescu's dissident Liberals with himself as Deputy Prime Minister and Foreign Minister, and one to the recently formed dissident Peasant Party. The historic, democratic parties of Maniu and Brătianu were not on Groza's list. Groza took his oath on the Bible. Others took it on their conscience. 'Events in Romania', Moscow's evening broadcast announced, 'have once more proved that the alliance between the Big Three is perfect.'

Rădescu asked the British Mission for sanctuary and this was granted. The general remained there until 7 May, when it was considered safe for him to return to his house in Bucharest. The Mission was also authorised to give sanctuary to King Michael and Queen Helen should they request it. They did not.

In the year 1991 Mircea Ciobanu published verbatim what King Michael had told him during a series of interviews covering the first 25 years of his life. In it the King summarised Vyshinsky's visit and concluded:

> He was a messenger with a single-minded message which he was not allowed to deviate from or interpret. He had to freeze Soviet/Romanian relations at a point before the 23rd August 1944. He had to erase from history – but using a Romanian hand – the whole period between 23 August 1944 and 9 May 1945 [when the Wehrmacht capitulated]. Otherwise he had no psychological basis for treating us as a defeated people and – as representative of the victorious powers – for dictating the rules for our political existance... Yes, I did feel that the monarchy was threatened. But that in no way changed the nature of the problem. What I want to emphasise is that not one of Moscow's actions in Romania as from 1945 had any legal basis.[28]

# NINE

## King Michael Goes on Strike: the West Dithers

King Michael was tormented by the thought that Romanians would blame him for appointing Groza, and his anxiety deepened when in March, by acting on the advice of his Marshal of the Court, he committed a serious political *gaffe*.

As Ana Pauker had promised, soon after the new government came to power the administration of Transylvania was returned to Romania and to mark the event the Communists planned for 13 March a great ceremony in Cluj. The King was disinclined to go but when assured by Negel – who had been misled by Deputy Prime Minister Tătărescu – that the Western representatives would be present he changed his mind. Consequently he found himself in the freezing Cluj Square exposed to speeches by Vyshinsky and Groza and a march-past of clenched-fist saluting workers, aware that by his presence he was approving a ceremony which had not only been boycotted by the Western Powers and all Transylvanian leaders but, worse, had given virtually no recognition to the Transylvanian peasant, the backbone of the province.

Still, the people of Cluj had welcomed him enthusiastically, as had the country people at every little station they stopped at on the way home. Each time he returned to his carriage after thanking them for their kindness, he felt a little more confident, and after his trip to Cluj he saw that the new Government, who were finding it difficult enough to discipline the workers, could well meet with even greater resistance in the countryside.

The Groza Government soon began to make itself felt. In April the Agrarian Reform Bill became law amid great fanfare and since it had been drafted with ideological rather than economic interests in mind the annual grain production dropped by about one million tons and its export virtually ceased.[1]

The King was more successful with some other legislation. One decree would amend the 1923 constitution to permit both the death penalty and the confiscation of property. Another would set up People's Tribunals consisting of one magistrate and eight 'People's Judges' chosen to carry out Party instructions regardless of legal niceties. There was no appeal.[2]

These two decrees, taken together, would, the King knew, provide a machinery of terror capable of suppressing all individual liberty in Romania. He refused to sign them and the consequent constitutional crisis dragged on to the end of the year. But by then he had obtained substantial amendments. Appeal from a People's Court to a constitutional court was permitted. Since Moscow had already decided on Antonescu's execution, the death penalty as such could not be dropped but this part of the legislation was amended to apply only to war criminals.

None the less, press censorship became stricter. The armed forces were being indoctrinated, the People's Courts were kept busy trying 'war criminals', 'fascists' and other non-communists.

On VE day, which was celebrated on 9 May 1945, newspapers publishing photographs of the Western leaders and King Michael were confiscated. At the last minute the King, who was in Sinaia, was invited to review the parade and stood with Susaikov, Stevenson and Schyler (head of the US military mission), while two army battalions – one of NKVD infantry – marched by, followed, to his surprise, by a hundred thousand workers giving the clenched-fist salute.[3]

The following day, 10 May, was Independence Day, and since large parts of the country were still under Soviet occupation, King Michael refused to authorise a big official ceremony. For him Independence Day was the people's day and on that day in 1945 he felt more confident than at any time since Groza's appointment two months before. Any resentment Bucharestians may have felt about his apparent weakness over Groza's appointment had evaporated. The streets to and from the Patriarchate, where he was attending a *Te Deum*, were thronged with cheering crowds. Children climbed lamp-posts and telegraph poles. Respectable men and women hung on to the railings round the Palace. The King was called out to the balcony eleven times. The Queen was asked to come to the Palace and, entering by a side door, she joined him in front of the cheering crowd. 'It was a refreshing change', Le Rougetel reported, 'to hear various individual and entirely different cries instead of the staccato refrains to which the ear is now accustomed.'[4] There was a spontaneity about this demonstration which the government could never achieve, and clips of it were later inserted into news films of open-air speeches by Pauker, Groza and other government leaders.

That summer Burton Berry, Le Rongetal's US colleague, made extensive trips throughout Romania and reported that widespread enthusiasm for the King dwarfed that for any other personality. The people did not expect him to interfere in the normal processes of government, but when events reached a stage critical for the nation they expected him to assume leadership. He had done that on 23 August 1944 and they felt that he would do it again when necessary.

The King was afraid that his popularity would provoke a Soviet reaction, but at this time the Russian authorities were behaving in a remarkably friendly and hospitable way. In the first week of July Susaikov told him that in recognition of his bravery in 1944 his government wished to confer on him a high decoration. King Michael was not able to believe his ears at first and asked Susaikov to repeat the message.

The prestigious Order of Victory was, in fact, awarded to only five non-Russians, including King George VI and General Eisenhower, and its award to the king of a country due for communisation and satellite status naturally surprised many observers of Soviet strategy. Admittedly Vyshinsky's March *coup* had gone far to balance the political consequences of Michael's *coup* of August 1944 and Stalin knew that, while reassuring Romanians and the Western Allies, the award would pose no threat to his long-term domination of Romania. Nevertheless Soviet officials told members of the King's Household that the presentation had political importance since through the King the Soviet Union was recognising Romania's wartime role. For that reason they insisted that every member of the Romanian Government should be present at the ceremony. It seems just possible that Stalin also felt a genuine admiration for this young man who had given him so much trouble. When Groza confided to Michael 'Stalin likes you', perhaps there was a grain of truth in what the old buffoon was saying.

The palace throne and dining rooms had to be made ready at short notice – quite an achievement, given the state of the building since the German bombing of August 1944. On 19 July Queen Helen watched from the musicians' gallery while Marshal Tolbukhin\* performed the investiture. The citation, signed by President Kalinin and awarded by a decree of the Presidium of the Supreme Soviet of 6 July 1945, referred to King Michael's courageous action which took Romania into the war against Hitlerite Germany on the side of the Allies 'at a moment when the defeat of Germany could in no way be clearly foreseen'.

In his reply the King referred to the high distinction addressed

> to all those of my people who on 23rd August 1944, answered my call with their devotion, to my army which, following my orders without defection,

---

\* Marshal Tolbukhin had replaced Marshal Malinovski as Commander of the Soviet troops in South-Eastern Europe.

compelled the enemy to withdraw from the country and northern Transylvania . . . In this high acknowledgment of Romania's services, I see a new proof of the promise of a better understanding and friendly relations between the peoples of Romania and the Soviet Union.

Then followed a banquet for about a hundred people. Since the kitchens were still unusable, the food was provided by the Capşa restaurant over the way. Michael just had time to go to Chaussée Kiselev and get rid of his medals – all, that is, except the Order of Victory – before Tolbukhin called for him at 5 and they drove to the airport for the presentation of two Soviet trainer aircraft – a present from Marshal Stalin. After more speeches and a flying display there was another large meal which lasted until 7.30. The King, who lived a rather frugal life, was not used to all this eating and drinking, and with so many people on the verge of starvation, he always felt uneasy and embarrassed on such occasions. When they got home 'Sweetie', Queen Helen noted, 'was sober but exhausted but Negel completely squiffy, frightfully dignified and very sentimental. They drank liters [sic] of vodka and champagne, couldn't be avoided. The star is very pretty & beautifully made with lovely stones'.[5]

The King offered a reciprocal decoration to Marshal Stalin, who wrote to say that, although he did not accept decorations, he would appreciate it just as much if it were offered to Marshal Malinovski. Malinovski was, therefore, awarded the Order of Michael the Brave.

On 8 March 1945 Churchill telegraphed Roosevelt about the Vyshinsky *coup*: 'if we do not get things right now, it will soon be seen by the world that you and I by putting our signature to the Crimea settlement [Yalta] have underwritten a false prospectus'.[6] When the three Allied leaders met in Potsdam between 17 July and 2 August they announced that peace treaties with Bulgaria, Finland, Hungary and Romania would only be concluded with 'recognised democratic governments' and – more to the point in the absence of a definition of the word 'democratic' – each of the Allies would decide for itself when to resume diplomatic relations with these countries. London and Washington saw this clause as a powerful lever with countries whose future prosperity would inevitably depend on good relations with the West. Perhaps, in spite of Churchill's fears for the credibility of Yalta, Potsdam would authenticate it.

During the third week of July both Maniu and Brătianu had already called for a change of government but the King had decided he would never again risk a repeat of the March fiasco. He would take no step against Groza unless he was quite certain of Allied support. On 7 August 1945 he told Le Rougetel that although everyone saw the need for a change of government he was opposed to any ill-considered action which could prejudice the whole issue at the eleventh hour. He knew that during their period in power the Communists had built up an organisation which, in the absence of Allied intervention, could easily undermine any alternative government.[7]

To everyone's surprise during the Potsdam meeting, Churchill and Eden were replaced by the new Prime Minister, Clement Attlee, and his corpulent Foreign Secretary, Ernest Bevin. Hitler had been defeated; the danger of a separate Russo-German pact, which had tormented Churchill for much of the war, had evaporated. Roosevelt had died on 12 April and neither Truman nor Attlee felt themselves committed to get on with Stalin at any price. The foundations for a cold war were in place. On 7 August the USA dropped her first atomic bomb and was to become a superpower and the acknowledged leader of the Western democracies. American foreign policy began to reflect a new confidence. On 14 August Queen Helen noted in her diary, 'Thank God things seem to be moving the least tiny bit. Roy Melbourne sent word through Ioani he wanted to see Sweetie right away. So he came to lunch.'[8]

Washington had instructed Roy Melbourne, the US Chargé d'Affaires, to make it known in Bucharest that the US government hoped to see a more representative government established in Romania, either as a result of action by the Romanian people themselves or, if necessary, with the help of the Allied governments. The US Government looked forward to establishing relations with a government in which all important democratic parties were represented or which had issued from free elections.

When Melbourne explained Washington's thinking to him the King spoke much as he had to Le Rougetel the week before: he would proceed only on strictly constitutional lines. He did not, therefore, propose to take the initiative. Melbourne then saw Ştirbey, Maniu, Brătianu and Petrescu, all of whom agreed that the Groza Government was not a recognised 'democratic government' within the meaning of the Potsdam Declaration and must go. Given this unanimous support by the principal party leaders, the Americans believed that the King could now proceed constitutionally to require Groza's resignation.[9] After a word with Le Rougetel, Roy Melbourne decided to put his Soviet colleague in the picture. Otherwise, when Moscow complained about their intervention, they could also have accused them of deceit.

The Democratic leaders proposed various ways of bringing down the present government but the King decided to follow the normal constitutional practice.

He would invite the Prime Minister to the Palace on 19 August to discuss with him how Romania was to meet the Potsdam terms. He would then see Pătrăşcanu, Petrescu,* Maniu and Brătianu in that order, and since three of the four party leaders would advise that there must be a change of government he would then ask for Groza's resignation. This procedure was followed.

However, Groza was bullish, telling the King that he saw no reason to take the British or US attitudes to his administration seriously. When the King pointed out that peace treaties with London and Washington depended on Romania meeting the criteria agreed at Potsdam, Groza replied that neither America nor Britain counted for anything in Romania so long as his government had the full support of the Russians. He seemed genuinely surprised when the King said he would have to open consultations with the party leaders. 'What? About a thing like this?' And he shrugged.

The three non-communist leaders Maniu, Brătianu and Petrescu confirmed, as expected, that they considered the King right to take the American intervention seriously. The Communist Pătrăşcanu told him that the Americans were making no more than a gesture which would achieve nothing.

The Foreign Office informed Le Rougetel that they were reluctant to offer advice or encouragement to the King because they would be unable to protect him and his mother from the consequences of an attempt – even if constitutional – to overthrow the present government. 'Though the Americans are now intervening vigorously in Romanian internal affairs we still cannot assume this responsibility', and Le Rougetel should therefore give the Americans 'carefully worded' support.[10]

Next day the King asked Groza to help him by resigning and trying to form a broader government which would meet the terms laid down at Potsdam. 'I refuse to resign', Groza said, and the King rose to his feet. The audience had lasted only 15 minutes. King Michael knew at that moment that as soon as possible he would cut all links with the Groza Government. No law was legal without his signature, and by refusing to sign their decrees he would paralyse the Administration and force Groza to submit to a constitutional solution.

He prepared letters to the three Allied governments requesting their advice on the broadening of the government in the spirit of the Potsdam Declaration. He sent for Susaikov and Pavlov, who read his letter at first incredulously, then with consternation. When Susaikov protested, Michael replied that he, personally,

---

* Although Titel Petrescu, leader of the Social Democratic Party, had joined the National Democratic Front which at its creation he had seen as a moderate left-wing body, his thinking on broad political and constitutional issues was more like Maniu's than Pauker's.

was responsible and that he did not intend to work with Groza until his request to the three Powers had been met. The British and American representatives were not discouraging and later he was told unofficially by the Americans that if he stuck to his guns he would be supported. Susaikov called the vulnerable Negel to his house to tell him that should he persuade the King to withdraw his letters, he would be well rewarded. Otherwise he would be in serious trouble.

Susaikov received two letters from Moscow which he allowed the King to copy. The first was a mild rebuke, the second to say that they would not allow Groza to resign and demanding that the King stop interfering with him. The King told Susaikov that he was determined to give his country peace and democratic government.[11]

That occurred on the morning of 23 August, the first anniversary of King Michael's *coup d'état*. He had already decided to absent himself from the official celebration, which had been turned into an NDF demonstration in support of the Communist *régime*. He attended neither the religious service at the Patriarchate nor the parade that followed. His large empty box draped in red became the centre of interest among the crowds, who had noticed that the British and Americans were also absent. By leaving their places on the stand to greet the Prime Minister, Susaikov and Pavlov made it clear that the Soviet Union supported Groza against the King. The Romanian crowd were awed and became sullen.

'I went on strike', the King said later and on 23 August Le Rougetel wrote to the Permanent Under-Secretary of the Foreign Office, 'Whatever the final verdict on recent events here may be there can, I think, be no doubt about the courage, insight and restraint which the King has shown. . . . I should be less than human if I did not hope that it will not have been in vain.'[12]

The King himself felt that on this occasion his timing had been right. He had resisted pressure from Maniu and Brătianu to take steps to remove Groza until it seemed safe to count on the effective support of the Western governments. If as a result a reasonably representative government replaced Groza's, and should a peace treaty be followed by withdrawal of Soviet troops and the holding of free elections, then his decision in March to give way to Vyshinsky rather than to abdicate would have been justified and his people would be back on the path he had intended his *coup d'état* to open up for them.

After spending an uncomfortable six weeks of isolation at the Kiselev Palace – too small to house the ADCs properly – the King and his mother outwitted the police pickets one afternoon and drove up to Sinaia. Here they had more space and the park to walk in. But the King had no official duties and his mother was cut off from her hospital work. He played the piano, listened to the radio, read and waited in vain for news that the Western Powers were pressing Moscow to accept a more representative Romanian government.

Meanwhile Moscow boosted Groza with praise and cosmetic aid. They invited him with a large delegation to Moscow to discuss the Romanian situation before Molotov left to attend a three-power Foreign Ministers' conference in London. On 9 September the Romanian press carried an article published by *Izvestia* which claimed that King Michael had never had any objection to the Groza government but had been forced by the US and British representatives in Bucharest to take steps to get rid of him.

When Groza returned to Bucharest two groups of naïve young anti-Communists known as The Free Youth and the 'T' Organisation were charged with having had contact with the British and US missions. The president of the court – notorious in Antonescu's time for the punitive sentences he had passed on communists – had been retired immediately after the King's *coup d'état* and was still on the Russian list of war criminals. Now, however, just two days before the trial began, he was reinstated and on 11 September passed harsh sentences on the young prisoners under a law promulgated by Antonescu and abrogated by King Michael on 2 September 1944.[13]

The King saw this trial as pure Soviet provocation. He could do nothing to help these young people, and London and Washington appeared not to react to the trial. A word of encouragement from his cousin King George VI would have greatly helped his morale, but until a peace treaty had been concluded he was officially the king of England's enemy. Soon after the Vyshinsky *coup* King George had written to his mother:

Poor Michael and his mother Zitta [sic] in Romania have been having a very worrying time from the Russians and again we can do nothing to help them for the moment. I feel so differently towards them than the attitude taken up by the Government. The latter say Romania was an enemy and is now in the Russian sphere.[14]

On 4 October Berry noted

Above all this the King continues to display great resolve and patience while waiting for a reply to his letter. He has indicated that he will maintain this attitude until the reply is forthcoming. But his position may become increasingly difficult if the Groza Government indulges in provocative acts or if the Soviet Government increases its pressure.[15]

Then on 8 October 1945, after two months of silence, the US Secretary of State James Byrnes announced that he was sending his special representative, Mark Etheridge, a newspaper publisher from Louisville, Kentucky, to investigate conditions in Bulgaria and Romania. For the King, this was reason for hope.[16] For the Communist press, however, it was proof that Washington was now ready to reconsider its position.

Silence from the West descended once more. While on a personal level the Russians were affable throughout the strike – on the King's birthday Susaikov sent him a present of vodka, caviar, a case of his favourite wine and scent for his mother – the Americans and British ignored him so pointedly that in moments of depression it was impossible for him to exclude the possibility of their abandoning him. Tension grew in the King's Household and, as legislation piled up for the King's signature, in the government too. In the country the great majority of people supported the King but felt powerless. The explosion finally occurred on the King's name-day, 8 November 1945.

In Sinaia that morning students brought him flowers and congratulations and told him of their admiration and gratitude.

In Bucharest the government had prepared as for an enemy attack. No trains were permitted into or out of the capital. Checkpoints on the roads were manned by gendarmes and detachments of armed Communists. Romanian soldiers were confined to barracks, officers ordered to take no part in demonstrations for the sovereign. Military cordons barred roads leading to Calea Victoriei and the Palace, and a body of special police was stationed in the middle of Palace Square – all this to prevent any manifestation of loyalty to the King.

It failed. During the morning some thousand people gathered in Palace Square. A group of thirty or forty disabled war veterans led by an army lieutenant advanced to the statue of King Carol I, produced a Romanian flag and sang the National Anthem. Other people were attracted to the square – workers, students, civil servants, school children, professional people and, in spite of their orders, a large number of officers and their wives – and they all joined in the singing which eventually turned into 'Long Live the King'. Kaftaradze, the new Soviet ambassador, was unable to reach the Palace to sign the book. Le Rougetel, who was also there, saw 'a spontaneous demonstration of the people's affection for their sovereign', but the Romanian authorities treated it as a threat to the state meriting brutal suppression. Lorries belonging to the State Railways drove in line through the crowd of by now some 10,000 people, shock troops leaning out and hitting people with their bars. The crowd became angry. A man leapt up, dragged down the man who had just hit his friend and beat him severely. The crowd overturned two trucks which burst into flames. The other trucks withdrew. Then there were cries of 'Down with Dictatorship', 'Down with Groza', 'Down with Terror', 'Down with the Government'.

A man ran out of the Ministry of Interior, knelt and opened fire into the crowd. Demonstrators rushed him and he was badly mauled before escaping back into the building. The crowd, though unarmed, then attacked the double doors and ten minutes later had forced them open with their flagpoles. They were now being shot at continuously and Le Rougetel commented, 'The behaviour of these spontaneous demonstrators contrasted remarkably with the conduct of the regimented National Democratic Front massed here last February, who broke up in disorder as soon as the Romanian guards fired into the air.'[16] Communist agents and police left the shelter of the Ministry to make arrests, concentrating on isolated groups who could offer little resistance. Around a hundred were taken at random in this way and beaten up.

An American soldier had to watch while a group of people carrying photographs of the King were shot down when they approached a cordon of the Tudor Vladimirescu regiment.* Eventually a three-star Russian general arrived – almost certainly Susaikov – and by his gestures ordered the firing to stop. By midnight the casualties – most of them workers and students – were 93 wounded and 13 dead, not including those who had been beaten up inside the Ministry of Interior.[17]

On 10 November 1945 the arrests started in earnest and up to 300 people were taken in for questioning. Next day *Scânteia* published a list of over a hundred names and addresses, including prominent members of the Liberal and National Peasant parties, ordered to report to the Public Prosecutor's office. Among those questioned by a court martial in the third week of November was Corneliu Coposu – the man who had accompanied Iuliu Maniu to meetings with Dinu Brătianu, Pătrăşcanu, Petrescu and Buzeşti on the day of the King's *coup d'état*. Coposu made a courageous statement to the court. The King's name-day, he said, had always been a public holiday to allow Romanians to meet and cheer their king. It was not a day for party-political demonstrations, and both the National Peasant Party and the Liberal Party had gone out of their way to inform the Minister of Interior personally that while there would be an orderly demonstration of loyalty to the King, there would be no political speeches. The people who gathered in Palace Square on 8 November had

---

* The Tudor Vladimirescu regiment consisted of Romanian ex-prisoners-of-war who had transferred their allegiance to the USSR.

represented no political party. But on 6 November the Union of Patriots had been ordered under circular no. 3279 to concentrate powerful forces in Palace Square 'to impede a possible demonstration of reactionaries for the King'. When their lorries appeared – and not until then, Coposu said – did any incident occur.[18]

On 19 November 1945 Byrnes's emissary arrived for a ten-day visit and was among the few people to meet the King during his 'strike'. His Majesty told him that he had resented the failure of the Powers to respond to his appeal almost as much as he had resented Groza's refusal to resign. Throughout his visit Etheridge was careful to show no bias whatsoever. He listened poker-face while the King explained why he had gone on strike but he later told Le Rougetel that he had been very favourably impressed.

On 26 November, after a week in Romania, Etheridge sent an interim report by ciphered telegram to Secretary Byrnes in which he commented on the King's popularity with his people and his enhanced prestige following his resistance to the Groza Government. Soviet exploitation of the country, he said, without regard to the armistice terms, had resulted in a degree of Soviet control beyond anything he had found in Bulgaria. Unless Washington could take firm and effective action in Romania, it would soon be too late.

For the King, perhaps the most unpleasant aspect of the strike was the fact that his aunts, the only members of his father's family still in Romania, continued to associate with his enemies. Princess Ileana was a good friend of Emil Bodnăraş, Moscow's most powerful agent in Romania. Princess Elisabeta hobnobbed with the Deputy Premier and Foreign Secretary, Gheorghe Tătărescu. On 6 December, Princess Elisabeta brought two letters to Sinaia – one from General Vasiliu-Răşcanu, the Minister of War, who held the King responsible for the demoralisation of the army; the other, an unsigned memorandum from Tătărescu, placing all responsibility for the present economic and financial crisis on the King and warning him that he could soon expect to share the fate of other monarchs who had counted on British support. Tătărescu was already canvassing candidates for a council of regency to include the Patriarch, the President of the Court of Appeal and Princess Elisabeta herself. The King thought of sending a further appeal to the three Powers, but was persuaded by Berry to wait until the Etheridge report had been studied. Berry told Le Rougetel, however, that he was convinced that pressure on the King would soon become overwhelming 'unless some action is taken on our side to relieve it'.[19]

When, finally, the three Foreign Ministers met in Moscow on 16 December 1945 to consider preparation for peace treaties with Italy, Romania, Bulgaria,

Hungary and Finland, they also discussed the advice to be given to King Michael in reply to his letter of 21 August. They had before them the Etheridge report, which had found the Romanian and Bulgarian governments unrepresentative and undemocratic.

London believed that insistence on a complete change of policy towards Romania and Bulgaria would in effect do nothing to help these countries but could well contribute to the deterioration of Britain's relations with the Soviet Union. Only when the Red Army had withdrawn from Bulgaria, and later from Romania and Hungary, could there realistically be hope for representative government in these countries. Meanwhile Moscow might, in exchange for British agreement to sign a peace treaty with Romania and Bulgaria, agree to admission into the government of one or two members of the Opposition so long as they were sure that these people would have no effect on government policy.[20] This line of thinking, which must have been shared by Washington, made an agreement with Molotov possible and was reflected in the conclusions signed in Moscow on 25 December, which read:

> The three Governments are prepared to give King Michael the advice which he requested in his letter of 21st August, 1945, concerning the broadening of the Roumanian Government. The King should be advised that one or two representatives, loyal to the present Government and not at present members of it, of the groups of the National Peasant and Liberal Parties should be included in the Roumanian Government (not including Maniu, Brătianu, Lupu).
>
> The three Governments note that the Roumanian Government, thus reorganised, will declare that as soon as possible free and unhampered elections will be held on the basis of general and secret suffrage. All democratic and anti-Fascist parties must have the right to take part in these elections and put forward candidates. The reorganised Government must give assurances concerning the grant of the freedom of the press, of speech, of religion and of assembly.
>
> M. Vyshinsky, Mr Harriman and Sir A. Clark Kerr are authorised as a commission to proceed immediately to Bucharest for consultations with King Michael and members of the present Government, with a view to the execution of the tasks indicated above.
>
> As soon as these tasks are resolved and the guarantees demanded have been received, the Government of Roumania, with whom the Soviet Government has diplomatic relations, will be recognised by the Government of the United States and the Government of the United Kingdom.[21]

To the King, who had hoped for a change of prime minister and, if possible, a roughly representative interim government as provided for in the Yalta Declaration, the Moscow solution was a dreadful disappointment. It excluded any democrat of political weight from the Groza Government. Worse, it made no provision for safeguards against government duplicity. In effect the Western Powers had neutralised the key clause in the Potsdam Agreement by undertaking to recognise the present government the moment it gave an assurance regarding free elections and the democratic freedoms, an assurance which on past form could be discounted. Moreover, the leader of the commission to visit Bucharest and arrange for the execution of the Moscow decision would be Vyshinsky, the man who had blackmailed and bullied King Michael into appointing the Groza government in the first place. In his new year message to the Romanian people King Michael did not even mention the Moscow Agreement.

When the commission of three saw him on 1 January 1946, Vyshinsky explained that their purpose in Moscow had been to reach a solution which would permit the US and UK governments to recognise the Romanian Government. King Michael, who showed great self-control during the interview, had supposed that the purpose of the Moscow meeting had been to provide Romania with a government sufficiently representative and democratic to meet the Potsdam and Yalta requirements and so permit peace treaties to be concluded with London and Washington.

Having sensed the King's concern about the absence of any safeguards, the two Western ambassadors assured him of the importance their governments attached to the guarantee of free elections and of their determination to satisfy themselves that the Romanian Government's assurances were being carried out before they would recognise it. Vyshinsky added icing to this cynicism by asserting that the Moscow decisions had put a serious moral responsibility on the three Powers as well as on the Romanian government to guarantee genuine elections and the democratic freedoms. They must, he said, be faithfully carried out. After repeating to Maniu and Brătianu next day what he had told the King, Clark-Kerr reported to London: 'I did not fully convince them, nor did I, I confess, fully convince myself.'[22]

The National Peasant and Liberal parties showed their disdain for the whole process by offering Vyshinsky not individuals but lists from which he could choose. The Russian, quite unruffled, selected a university professor to represent the National Peasants and a banker to represent the Liberals. On 3 January 1946 Ambassador Harriman asked in a telegram to Washington whether he could assume that recognition of the present government did not necessarily imply recognition of the Government resulting from the election unless Washington was reasonably satisfied with the conduct of the election. It was a carefully worded request which nevertheless proved to be asking too much.

On 3 January Princess Elisabeta flaunted her disloyalty by attending a large official lunch at Tătărescu's home given for the Commission and members of the Government. Queen Helen squirmed when she heard this but recovered her good humour in Sinaia when 'Dear old Archie came to tea. Talked for two hours. It was delightful.'[23]

As a young man, Archibald Clark-Kerr had known the Queen Mother in Athens when she was still Princess Helen. When writing to the Foreign Office he said that his visit to Sinaia had confirmed the good impression her son had made on him during his meeting with the Commission on 1 January. While the Moscow Decision had been something of a humiliation for him, he was nevertheless ready to respect it. The King doubted whether the elections would be free or the democratic freedoms faithfully observed. Except for members of the Government, not a single Romanian Clark-Kerr had met would disagree with him unless an independent body was set up to scrutinise implementation of the Government's assurances.

> The King 'who is obviously riper than his years' had much to say of the difficulties of his own position as a constitutional monarch. It had been his habit to follow the provisions of the Constitution with all scrupulousness. But his government was in open rebellion, prompted thereto by Moscow, whence it drew all its guidance. He was convinced that communisation was in no way the wish of the vast peasant population – the backbone of the country – and he would do all he could to resist it.[24]

Queen Helen was still able to see the funny side whenever she was given the chance. On Tuesday, 8 January the three Commissioners with Harriman's daughter had lunch at Foişor and she noted in her diary:

> After lunch such a funny scene. The three had to draw up a communiqué. Archie promptly sat on the floor and Vyshinsky immediately followed suit dying with laughter. Only Harriman remained standing. They told us it was the first time Vyshinsky admitted a communiqué without changing it and arguing every point. Sweetie photographed them and V was delighted.[25]

Before leaving for Sofia, Vyshinsky told Harriman and Clark-Kerr, who were staying on for a few more days, that any further conversations they might have with Romanian officials would be considered private. In other words they could be ignored by the Romanian Government. Nevertheless on the 9th, the evening he left, Harriman and Clark-Kerr had a session with Groza and, when Harriman left, Clark-Kerr stayed on for yet another meeting with Groza on the 11th at which he handed the Prime Minister an *aide-mémoire* of the discussion the three of them had had two days before.

Groza, whom Clark-Kerr considered 'a genial fool and a liar', and Tătărescu, 'steeped to the lips in deceit and treachery', had already let it be known that in Romania the Moscow Decision meant nothing at all. The Government would see to that.[26] Coming from the darkness of Moscow, where he was used to the better-disciplined lies of the Kremlin and had been inclined to give the Russians the benefit of the doubt, Clark-Kerr admitted that his visit to Bucharest had somewhat shaken him.

On 5 February the US and UK governments sent differently worded though in substance identical notes to the Romanian Minister of Foreign Affairs in effect accepting the Romanian Government's window-dressing and agreeing to recognise it without further ado.[27] Three days later Groza, in a victory speech to the Ploughman's Front, let it be known that the Opposition (implying also King Michael) had been foresaken by the West.[28] London then published Clark-Kerr's *aide-mémoire*, setting out Groza's assurances of the 9th, but before it could be read in Bucharest trucks had removed copies of any Romanian newspaper daring to print it.

On 26 February, when Le Rougetel, who was moving to another post, came to the Palace for his last audience, King Michael asked him – probably as a formality – whether the British Government would 'continue to keep under observation and to concern itself with the execution of the Moscow decision'.[29] During the audience he knew that in another room his mother would be pouring out her heart to Mrs Le Rougetel about her fears for the future. She wrote in her diary that evening, 'If only my faith were stronger. God help me to be brave and not flinch from my duty.'[30] It was Queen Helen's unwavering faith that saw her through the almost continual anxiety, the torture and sometimes near despair of her life in Romania.

The Moscow Agreement changed nothing for the better in Romania. Speeches by Byrnes and Truman continued to be censored. Opposition newspapers were suspended or suppressed. Le Rougetel sent to London a sample of the metal cosh railway workers were manufacturing for use at the elections. National Peasant Party headquarters at Arad were destroyed and one member killed. An attempt was made on Brătianu's life. By 10 March the Central Committee of the Social Democratic Party had been so successfully infiltrated that its vote went overwhelmingly in favour of collaboration with the Communists. Titel Petrescu and a few brave supporters walked out of the meeting and kept his party going for a while but in effect the independent Social Democratic Party of Romania founded in 1893 ceased to exist in March 1946.[31]

Michael felt that he had shot his bolt: his strike had failed and no operation as potentially effective as the 'strike' was now available to him. He would fight off his country's enemies by any means left to him but only a miracle, he felt, could now save it.

King Michael was worried about his mother. The collapse of the 'strike', the atmosphere of intrigue and mistrust, living in the house of Princess Elisabeta – a woman she loathed – it was all having its effect. A formal dinner with the Russians had become an ordeal. 'I can't bear these things any more,' she wrote in her diary. 'My knees were trembling all the time. Stupid.'[32]

She was afraid for Michael's life. Palace cars were no longer serviced properly and he was often exposed on the roadside while repairs were carried out. When a piece of timber, probably dislodged by the thaw, leapt down the mountain and hit their car she was so convinced it was an assassination attempt that Michael telephoned Stevenson to ask him to come over for a drink. Although the Air Vice-Marshal reassured his mother about the accident, the evening finished badly. She asked about Churchill's Fulton 'Iron Curtain' speech which she was afraid could lead to a war in which Romania would again be on the wrong side. She then put out a feeler about the security Britain could offer them should they have to escape. Stevenson knew that Le Rougetel had been refused authority to assure the King on this point at his final audience. So the Air Vice-Marshal hesitated, and his hesitation fuelled Queen Helen's anxiety.[33]

The Queen Mother's fears for Michael were well founded. In December 1945 a Russian colonel had called together twelve Romanian soldiers of the Tudor Vladimirescu division. After reminding them of the oath they had taken to the USSR, he ordered them to draw lots to decide who would be detailed to assassinate King Michael. The unlucky man was carefully briefed but when the time came he preferred to kill himself. He left a note for his family describing the events which led up to his suicide. On 17 January 1946 the Russians eliminated the Colonel, who had become a security risk. He was buried with military honours, and 'reactionaries' were blamed for his murder. Yet no one was brought to trial for this murder of a senior Soviet officer, which was so exceptional that the Americans carried out their own investigation. This confirmed what the King had told them.[34]

When discussing this plot with the King after Sunday lunch on 17 March 1946, General Schyler felt that he must, in all fairness, warn his hosts about the limitations put on American sanctuary. Under their standing instructions, unless a person's life was immediately threatened they were to refer all requests for asylum to the Allied Control Commission – that is, the Soviet authorities. That evening Queen Helen wrote in her diary:

> After all M. has done for them it is simply shameful and one can't even put it on paper. But God is just and He will help us if no one else will. Gen. Schyler is such a nice man and a real friend. I saw how upset he was to have to tell us such a low down thing. It's not his fault poor thing.[35]

Following the Moscow Agreement the Russians treated the King with less respect. After the Independence Day parade on 10 May 1946, a crowd picked up the royal car with them inside it, shouted 'Long live the King' and began to sing. In sheer revenge the Russians forced him to award Groza a high Romanian medal with a ludicrous citation extolling his great services to the country. If he had continued to refuse they were ready to arrest Maniu and Brătianu and destroy their political parties.

Another matter was weighing on King Michael: Antonescu, after spending almost two years in Russia, had been despatched to Bucharest for trial. At the time of his *coup d'état* the King had assumed that if Antonescu were tried it would be by an independent Romanian court drawing its authority from a democratically appointed constitution. Instead he was tried by a people's court. The sentence itself was straightforward; it had already been decided in Moscow. The main purpose of the trial was to build up a case against Maniu and Brătianu and, if possible, the King.

The trial opened on 6 May 1946 and ran for eleven days. Maniu was the chief witness and it was his clear and detailed evidence and the frank statements of Marshal Antonescu that together dominated the proceedings and even brought popular sympathy round to the side of the prisoners.

On 17 May all the prisoners were condemned to death. They were Marshal Ion Antonescu, Mihai (Ica) Antonescu, General Pantazi, General Piki Vasiliu, Eugen Cristescu, Radu Lecca (Commissioner for Jewish Questions) and Professor Gheorghe Alexianu (Governor of Transniestria). After the sentences the King appealed for commutation of all death sentences on the grounds that the Romanian constitution did not permit the death sentence in peacetime. When this failed he resorted to the prerogative which allowed him to commute a wartime death sentence on appeal. He argued that execution, taking place so long after the offence, would not be in accord with public sentiment. All the condemned men except Marshal Antonescu sought a royal pardon. Antonescu refused and the appeal was signed by his lawyer.

At this point the Russians stepped in to say that the King was only allowed to reprieve Pantazi, Cristescu and Lecca. Cristescu, a highly professional Intelligence officer with a prodigious knowledge of the Antonescu *régime*, was, in fact, released to collaborate with Bodnăraş.

When Maniu, on leaving the court, went over to the Marshal and shook hands with him, the President of the Court protested violently. Antonescu, Maniu explained, was an adversary, not an enemy. 'There is a difference', the King said later, 'between a clash of ideas in a society which recognises and respects the laws of debate and the cannibalism of the communist *régime*.' What, he asked, did the Communist authorities expect Maniu to do in the circumstances – hurl insults at him? turn his back on him, instead of walking over to him and saying goodbye?[36]

# TEN

## Royal Wedding in London: Royal Engagement in Switzerland

The elections were due to take place in November 1946 and, however fraudulent they might be, on past form the Western Allies could be expected to recognise the government they produced. Meanwhile King Michael would try to amend or, at least, delay the present government's decrees.

For six months he fought off the Armed Forces Bill, which would put some 10,000 non-communist officers and warrant officers on the reserve list and when, under the pressure of a Soviet ultimatum, he was in August 1946 forced to sign away much of his army's loyalty, the country knew why.

When the draft Electoral Law was published in the newspaper *Universul* on 30 May 1946, King Michael welcomed the articles lowering the age for electors and candidates and opening the candidature to women. He opposed the articles giving the government sole right to amend the constitution and the chamber sole right to dissolve itself, so legalising tyranny in perpetuity. He was successful on both counts.

When, in local elections held in three Oltanian villages which were considered to be a pointer for the country, the Communist Party came a poor fourth after the National Peasants, the Liberals and Petrescu's independent Social Democrats, the Government abandoned any pretence of holding democratic elections. They forbade the use of broadcasting facilities and poster publicity by the Opposition parties. They controlled the distribution of newsprint. They sacked magistrates who could not be trusted to toe the line. They selected the names to appear on the electoral rolls and anyone complaining had to obtain sixteen certificates from various ministries – virtually impossible even for those living in the capital. Workers not registered as government supporters were denied use of the factory canteen where they obtained their one decent meal of the day. Army officers were compelled to canvass troops on behalf of the Government. Young Communist workers were recruited into the police force for temporary duty during the elections. On 22 October 1946 the leaders of the three Opposition parties, Maniu, Brătianu and Titel Petrescu, declared that, since the Government had fulfilled not one of its obligations under the Moscow Declaration, and since their common belief in liberty far outweighed any ideological or political differences there might be between them, they had formed an electoral pact.[1]

The King and Opposition parties pressed London and Washington to appoint an international supervisory commission and for strongly worded notes from the Western Allies who should threaten to withhold recognition of any government brought to power by an irregular election. Neither was forthcoming. Foreign press coverage of the elections was pathetically small. When London and Washington protested about the Government's unscrupulous behaviour before the elections, the Ministry of Foreign Affairs replied that since the Moscow Agreement had been tripartite any protest concerning it must also be tripartite.

During the week before the elections the Romanian Government made a final attempt to discredit the Opposition,[2] and the King's name was involved. General Rădescu (*in absentia*), General Aldea and activists from the National Peasant and Liberal parties were charged with plotting to overthrow the Communist Government once the Red Army had been withdrawn. Had they been a credible resistance movement they would have had the overwhelming if unspoken support of the Romanian people. But they were, in fact, small amateurish organisations bearing such improbable names as The Voice of the Blood and The Black Coats, and posed no threat whatsoever to the authorities. If Bodnăraş infiltrated them with his agents it was for political rather than security reasons. Unfortunately General Aldea, without consulting the royal family, asked a Black Coat – undoubtedly a Bodnăraş agent – to look out for a hiding place in the mountains in case King Michael should ever require one.

The trial was a farce. The Communist authorities failed to brief defence lawyers who, therefore, interrogated government *agents provocateurs* among the accused so effectively that they broke down. The prosecuting attorney was thrown into confusion and next day many defending lawyers were debarred from the court room. The president of the court allowed defence lawyers in the closing session to make a courageous attack on the illegality of the trial and the complete absence of factual evidence. He then pronounced harsh predetermined sentences which bore no relation to the court's proceedings.[3]

Maniu asked King Michael to intercede for members of his party and the King, having no influence with the perpetrators of the trial, asked his aunt, Princess Ileana, to help. Her patron, Bodnăraş, was out of Bucharest but she was able to instruct the president of the court to acquit one prisoner and substantially reduce the sentences of others. For General Aldea she did nothing and he was sentenced to hard labour for life.

The elections took place on 19 November. To help maintain order at polling stations the Ministry of the Interior had the support of 2,777 army officers, 3,869 NCOs and 43,414 troops.[4] Some Opposition representatives were arrested. Many government supporters voted more than once, ballot boxes were filled with government voting slips before representatives of the Opposition parties were allowed into the polling station. Thugs in civilian clothes stopped anyone entering the National Peasant or Liberal party headquarters in Bucharest. Yet this extensive abuse did not prevent the Opposition winning 80 per cent of the vote. In spite of the political commissars, some 30 per cent of army officers voted against the Government. Worse for the Government, groups like the railway workers, who were seen as the hard core of their support, voted heavily for the Opposition. Even in Teohari Georgescu's Ministry of the Interior one in three civil servants dared to vote for Maniu, and Maniu had the majority of votes in Gheorghiu-Dej's Ministry of Communications. In the 1930s Bucharest radio had usually given the country a fair idea of an election result by about 2 a.m. In 1946 the Broadcasting Station fell silent after announcing the first few results and telephone communications with the provinces were cut to prevent Opposition headquarters hearing the regional results.

Romanian communists were appalled. However, the three Moscow stalwarts – Ana Pauker, Lazlo Luca and Emil Bodnăraş – sought Moscow's permission to falsify the results and this was given. For three days there was silence and then a resounding victory was announced for the government parties. The NDF were allotted 348 seats, the National Peasants 32, the National Liberals 3 and Petrescu's Social Democrats no seats. The two Opposition ministers appointed after the Moscow Agreement resigned. Government ministers who, while serving the occupying power, still felt some hankering for popular support, were bewildered by what had happened. However, the thick-skinned Groza simply shuffled his pre-election government and stayed on.

As the truth about the elections filtered through, Romanians saw it as a great moral victory for the Opposition and felt sure that when, after ratification of the Peace Treaty Soviet troops were withdrawn, they would return to power. Maniu retired to Sibiu to draw up a progressive social and economic programme for post-war Romania. His party even discussed measures to prevent excessive anti-communist demonstrations when the Russians left, since these might give them a pretext for returning.

The King was now faced by another difficult decision. Should he agree to open the new parliament? Constitutionally his duty was to open parliament whatever its political complexion, but never before had a Romanian parliament been so blatantly appointed against the will of the people.

As usual he was given conflicting advice. Maniu was opposed to his opening such a flawed parliament, arguing that each time he compromised on principle he made the ultimate communisation of the country and his own disappearance from the scene that much more likely. Negel urged him to open parliament rather than flout the authorities. Queen Helen, his most trustworthy adviser, who had previously urged her son to stand firm on principle, had been so disillusioned by the Moscow Agreement that she now permitted herself to care mostly about her son's safety.

King Michael had been told on good authority that should he not open this parliament, the Russians would remove him. Admittedly expulsion in these circumstances would be expulsion with honour and might even give international opinion a healthy shock, but in Romania it could lead to an uprising and Soviet military intervention, with considerable loss of Romanian lives. Bloodshed he would avoid at all costs. Nor would he ever again allow himself to be used by the Western Allies as a decoy for testing Moscow's determination.

He assumed that the Western Powers, after complaining about the Romanian Government's undemocratic behaviour before the election, would feel compelled after the election to send strongly worded notes condemning their conduct of the election itself. When these notes had been received he would seek an explanation from the Minister of Foreign Affairs, and when Tătărescu replied that the notes could be ignored since the Soviet Government were satisfied with the conduct of the elections he would force Susaikov to bring considerable Soviet pressure on him before agreeing to open parliament. In this way he could avoid the possibility of bloodshed, retain his people's respect and remain to slow down the process of communisation as best he could in the hope that after ratification of the peace treaty Soviet troops would be withdrawn.[5]

The King's tactic collapsed when London and Washington decided not to protest. Week followed week of silence from the West. An oral communication, the Foreign Office told Holman, supported by a statement in the House of Commons would make the Government's views on the election perfectly clear. To go further could encourage the King to refer the whole matter back to the signatories of the Moscow Agreement and the outcome would help neither him nor his country and would advertise the impotence of the Western Powers.[6] After his experience of the Moscow Agreement, the King had no intention of repeating his mistake and had given the Western Powers no reason to think that he would.[7] At the very last minute on 30 November, the day before parliament was due to be opened, Adrian Holman was indeed authorised to make a verbal complaint about the elections, but by then it was of so little consequence that Tătărescu could ignore it.

On 1 December 1946, when King Michael opened parliament, the Opposition, the UK and the USA were not represented. The government were still very shaken by the true election result and the speech Michael read out to the Assembly on their behalf was one of studied moderation.

He stood, his mother noted, 'in the same spot where he had stood when a little boy of five on his accession nearly twenty years before, when the Regents had taken the Oath on his behalf'. The present ceremony ended with shouts of 'Long Live Stalin' 'Long Live Michael' but, as his mother remarked, 'by now both Michael and I had learned how to cry with one eye and laugh with the other'.[8]

When Adrian Holman had tea with the King on 5 December he found him 'rather despondent'. The absence of any Western reaction to such a disgraceful election had, he said, embarrassed him with Romanians, but his popularity did not matter to him so much. He wanted above all to avoid civil war. Both he and the Queen Mother seemed to regard his departure from the country sooner or later as inevitable.[9]

Berry and Holman were so disillusioned by their government's inaction that they saw no further useful role at their present posts and both asked to be transferred.

When the Soviet draft text of the Peace Treaty was published in June 1946, what most concerned King Michael and the Opposition parties was the article providing for destruction of organisations 'of a fascist type' – which effectively annulled Article 3 guaranteeing the democratic freedoms – and the article stating that until an Austrian treaty was concluded Soviet troops would remain in Romania to protect lines of communication with their sector in Austria.

During negotiation of the Treaty Bevin had invited Tătărescu to a meeting where he had administered a severe dressing down. 'No effort', he told the Romanian, 'of any sort had been made to honour' the promises given to Sir Archibald Clark-Kerr in Bucharest and, as for the elections, he could see little difference between the methods used in Romania now and those used by the Nazis.[10] The thick-skinned Tătărescu could ignore this meeting since it was not, of course, publicised.

The Romanian Peace Treaty signed on 10 February 1947 gave Moscow all it wanted. Moreover, Molotov's delaying tactics were to prove so effective that the Austrian treaty negotiations and the concurrent Red Army occupation of Romania had a longer run than *South Pacific*, the longest-ever running American musical. The King's struggle to postpone the more destructive of Groza's decrees had come to little because much of the language used in them had now been incorporated into the Treaty and so had achieved international approval.

Among the most telling reflections on Romania's situation are the blank pages in Queen Helen's diary covering over eight months of 1946. For nearly ten years she had kept an account of events – personal and political – which must be among the most moving and perceptive records of her day. Yet after her entry for 12 April 1946 it ceases. There is no mention of Michael, the elections, the Treaty, no mention of her lunches or hospital work, her riding, her anguish over her sister Irene of whom she had still no news. Her silence is broken only twice during the rest of 1946. There is a bitter half-page comment on Independence Day and in September brief references to her 'lessons': she is learning to play golf.

After elections which had demonstrated Romanian opposition to communism at every level of society, the Peace Treaty was widely seen in Romania as international approval for continued occupation and communisation and of a government appointed and operating in flat contradiction to the will of the people. The feeling was not limited to Opposition politicians and intellectuals. During the so-called 'Treaty Week' railway and tram workers refused to parade for the continuance of Soviet occupation. They demonstrated instead against the fraudulent management of their factory cooperatives. Workmen blew up a furnace at the Reşiţa steel works which produced arms for the USSR, causing the Government to invent yet another 'fascist plot'. There was even talk of a popular uprising.

With the Government still on the defensive Maniu was pressing the King to get rid of Groza. London and Washington agreed with him. The King did not. The Peace Treaty had legitimised Soviet policy in Romania for an indefinite period. Then why, the King asked, should Moscow – which had in effect the support of the Western Powers – allow their puppet government to be removed? Why should they hesitate to crush any attempt to alter the *status quo*? Once, when Berry had said, 'We didn't want to give the impression of putting our spoon in your soup,' the King had replied, 'You may not have wanted to give the impression that you were putting your spoon in our soup but meanwhile the Russians have put theirs down my throat'.[11] The opportunity for resistance, he felt, had been in 1945 and 1946; 1947 was for holding on. While the Government's unpopularity was not in doubt, neither was the power of the bayonets behind it. Should the occupying forces leave before the local communists had obtained a stranglehold, there was still hope of saving the country. But should the Soviet authorities be provoked now, even this slight hope could disappear. The King could only wait, which he knew would be particularly difficult with economic and social conditions deteriorating so quickly.

At their Kiselev home they had water for three hours a day; electricity (which meant heating) was cut between 9 a.m. and 1.30 p.m. In January that meant a very cold house. His mother had sixty women making clothes for Moldavia in a large room over in the main Palace. Sometimes, as when she tasted the 'bread' Moldavians were trying to keep alive on, she felt acutely inadequate. But in spite of these periods of depression, she kept at it and when it became known that her supplies to Moldavia were getting through and not, as most Romanians had assumed, being side-tracked into the USSR, contributions began to pour in. Factories sent her cloth; the Jewish community, who were receiving American help, gave her 30,000 garments, 'all very good quality', and when with the help of a few soldiers they got the first wagon-load to Iaşi they were able to clothe two villages and feed 800 people.

On 5 January 1947, Queen Helen spoke, for the first time in three years on a very bad telephone line to her sister Irene in Lausanne. Although for some time now her husband had been working with the British in the south of Italy, the Duchess of Aosta had been stranded in Mussolini's republic in the north, then moved by the Germans with her son Amadeo first to a family castle near Turin, then to prison in Bavaria. After her release at the end of the war she was in very poor health and had gone to Switzerland. Queen Helen obtained permission to pay her a flying visit and travelled with Udriski and Bielle Styrcea in the two-engined Beechcraft they had recently bought from the British Mission. While there, she obtained a three-day extension to attend the funeral of her eldest brother, King George II of Greece, who had died on 1 April. King George was succeeded by his brother Paul, whose marriage to Princess Frederika of Hanover Michael had attended in 1938. Queen Helen returned to Romania on 8 April 1947, and later that month was allowed to fly again to Athens, this time to attend the marriage of her youngest sister Katherine to Major Richard Brandram.

During these two trips she realised how important it was for Michael to have a break from the Romanian nightmare. Into the last seven years had been crammed a lifetime's responsibility trying to defend his country from the two most powerful dictatorships of the century. Since the age of 19 he had matured far beyond his years but it had been a forced, not a natural, process.

Michael was by now almost as isolated as he had been during his strike. He had nothing to discuss with his government. Mircea Ionniţiu was mostly in

Bucharest studying for a law degree and, so as not to endanger them, Michael saw few Romanians outside the Household. While his mother was away he spent much of his time at Săvârşin with his friend Vanya Negroponte who, being genuinely apolitical, was less vulnerable to governmental intimidation. Vergotti says that Queen Helen was always friendly towards any young people Michael brought home, but she longed for him to settle down with someone suitable and one of her new year prayers for 1947 had been, 'May he find a sweet wife to love him as he deserves.'[12] There was little chance of this happening while he was isolated in Romania.

On 10 May 1947, Romanian Independence Day, King Michael was awarded the US Legion of Merit, Degree of Chief Commander, in recognition of his services to the Allied Powers in their struggle against Hitler. The presentation by General Schyler took place at the Bucharest Palace and, since the royal family were in mourning for the death of King George II of Greece, the ceremony was brief. President Truman's citation concluded with the words, 'By his superior judgement, his boldness of action and the high character of his personal leadership, King Michael I has made an outstanding contribution to the cause of freedom and democracy.'[13]

During the spring of 1947 the Soviet authorities put a stop to the unrest and low morale that had infected the Romanian Communist Party and Government since the election of November 1946. In March Gheorghiu-Dej returned from trade negotiations in Moscow with a new brief for the Party. They should give up the idea of ever being popular with the Romanian people and had nothing to lose by pushing ahead with rapid communisation.[14] Large-scale arrests of 'war criminals' and the catch-all phrase 'subversives' were now extended to take in ordinary people of no political leaning, and these were imprisoned in atrocious conditions without interrogation or trial. This mass intimidation succeeded. Even the independent-minded Transylvanian peasant refused now to talk politics with strangers. Tătărescu, in an uncharacteristic gesture of desperate courage, circulated a cabinet memorandum drawing attention to a drop in national production since 1939 of 48 per cent, protesting against illegal and widespread arrests and attacking a government which, having failed to introduce any real reforms, had nevertheless attracted the hatred of every class of society. It was his last attempt to hedge his bets should the Communists ever be removed from power and only a man with such a long history of the betrayal of Western democracy could have got away with it.

Soviet control was by now absolute. When the Romanian Government gladly accepted the aid offered to European countries under the Marshall Plan, an order from Moscow ensured an immediate U-turn. The Romanian Government had to learn that their historical friends were not only their future enemies but had always been so.

In the early days of their drive to take over the country the Romanian Communists attacked the structure on which the monarchy depended – the church, the army, the judiciary, the police, the civil service, the constitution, the democratic process – but the King and his mother were treated with respect. Even as late as 1946 in their election manifesto Groza's Ploughman's Front saw advantage in expressing their appreciation of the traditional institutions of which 'the first place is given to the Monarchy'.

However, by the autumn of 1947 the Peace Treaty was safely in the Soviet bag and it was time to make the King feel redundant. Attempts on the King's life, threats to certify him as mad, the treacherous behaviour of his aunts, the conviction by now that the Western democracies could do nothing to help had had their effect. Even the English newspapers that Holman sent to the Palace were not reaching him.

In all this there was one very practical matter which worried Queen Helen. What would they live on abroad? Whenever she had urged her son to transfer some of his private income he had always refused, saying that to do so would be unpatriotic. She told Holman that she was now considering whether to take the next opportunity to move some of their more valuable possessions abroad.

They lived in an atmosphere of fear, rumour, espionage and confusion, and the King longed for some fresh air outside the country. He had never been to a theatre, a restaurant or a night club. The staff served him poorly, and when the Holmans were invited to lunch nobody seemed to have warned the guards at the palace gates that they were coming. After lunch King Michael told the Holmans that if the Peace Treaty was in force he hoped to be invited to Princess Elizabeth's wedding. An invitation direct from the King would make it more difficult for the Romanian Government to prevent him from accepting.

> I realised [the British Minister reported to London] that life within the palace was gloomy and tense, but not until this visit did I understand its real significance. I have unbounded admiration for the way the King and his mother have managed to carry on under such trying conditions, but unfortunately, except in a very small way, there is little that can be done to improve their lot until the whole political situation takes a turn for the better.[15]

On 15 July the King flew his mother back from Săvârșin to be told on landing that Maniu had been arrested. Although he had warned Maniu that the Communists were laying traps for him, this was shattering news. Without Maniu the aged Brătianu and the ineffectual Petrescu could put up no real opposition. Juliu Maniu had tenaciously held on to the hope of restoring democracy to his country until it became too late for him to escape abroad. Sick in a sanatorium, having lost faith in the Western Allies, sometimes at odds with his sovereign, he could see no future for Romania, and when some of his henchmen, including Mihalache, had asked whether they should take the opportunity to flee, he had advised them to do so. On this occasion the *agent provocateur* provided by Bodnăraș had been the pilot. The newspapers carried a photograph of them all standing in front of a plane which was clearly too small to carry them and their luggage. Maniu had been promptly arrested.

On 29 July 1947 the Government dissolved the National Peasant Party and former members were either rounded up or fled to the mountains for temporary shelter and someday perhaps a chance to retaliate. There were signs of preparation for the King's removal. Police agents were trying to obtain evidence of a fictitious wireless transmitter which he was supposed to be using. The airstrip near Săvârșin was under observation. Funds for its repair, the repair of one of the King's aircraft and for aviation fuel were withheld.[16] During a lunch in Sinaia on 5 August one of the Russian interpreters had spent much of his time spitting on the floor and, after lunch, Susaikov had removed an ancient Chinese sword from the wall in Peleș and had broken it without a word of apology.[17] Stalin, it was clear, no longer loved King Michael.

On the eve of the third anniversary of his *coup d'état*, the King attended a festival at the Atheneum. Groza spoke of the *coup* without once mentioning him but announced that the Government would destroy fascist remnants whatever guise they might have adopted – a direct reference to the terms of the Peace Treaty which Romania would ratify the following day. As Groza spoke these words Ana Pauker was seen by the diplomats present to turn and stare pointedly at the King.[18]

'Although he is a lone figure without a National Peasant Party or any effective organised opposition at his back,' Adrian Holman wrote on 2 August, 'he is the last hope to which the people can turn for their salvation. Any act of voluntary desertion on his part now would never be forgiven.'[19]

Towards the end of October a secret meeting took place at Princess Elisabeta's Banloc estate near Timișoara and not far from Săvârșin, where King Michael was staying. It was attended by staff officers of the Czech, Yugoslav, Polish and Romanian armies, members of the Romanian Government including

Bodnăraş, Lazlo Luca, Gheorghiu-Dej and Groza and by Tito, the Yugoslav head of state. The King was not informed officially about this meeting, and when he heard of it he was disgusted by his aunt's behaviour. He also saw it as a clear pointer towards his removal.[20]

Just as the main object of the Antonescu trial had been to incriminate Maniu, the main object of Maniu's trial, which opened on 29 October, was to incriminate the Western Powers, particularly the Americans and, if possible, the King. Maniu's own fate had already been decided. The Government claimed to have evidence that members of the National Peasant Party had discussed with two American officers the possibility of armed resistance to overthrow the Government. Also – though far less dramatic – members of the Ministry of Foreign Affairs had passed confidential material to the British Legation (via the author).

The King's Household became jumpy. The Americans under a new minister were lying low in the hope that following these disclosures they would not be expelled. Adrian Holman, when authorised by London to pass a message to the King from three prominent Romanian exiles, telegraphed back that such an act of folly would be tantamount to offering his own and the King's head on a platter.[21] When later London asked him about passing a message of sympathy and encouragement from King George VI to King Michael, Holman warned that it should be purely formal and publishable and that any personal message accompanying the letter should be passed to King Michael orally by him.

Then something occurred which was to change King Michael's whole life. The Foreign Office suggested that since a peace treaty with Romania was now in force, King Michael should be invited to the wedding of Princess Elizabeth and Prince Philip and Buckingham Palace replied 'His Majesty has always intended to do this.'

When he was told privately of the forthcoming invitation, King Michael thought he would familiarise the Romanian Government with the idea of his making official visits abroad by expressing a desire to go to Moscow to meet Marshal Stalin. Taken aback, Groza said he would consult his colleagues and nothing more was heard of the suggestion. Meanwhile London was considering the political consequences of his leaving the country. King Carol's arrival in Europe and reliable information that he had already been in touch with Romanian Communist leaders weighed in favour of Queen Helen attending the wedding alone.[22] The possibility of the King going and his mother staying behind to hold the fort for him was abandoned on the grounds that London could not guarantee her safety. Finally, on 5 October, invitations were sent to them both.

King Michael replied that while the invitation gave him deep satisfaction he could not give a definite reply immediately. Yet when the Government finally reached a decision it was surprisingly positive. Both the King and the Queen Mother, Groza told him, should attend and, in keeping with the dignity of a head of state travelling abroad, should be accompanied by members of the Court. 'Otherwise people will think you are being held prisoner here.' London considered that, while the Government's reaction was suspicious, they were unlikely to stage a *coup* in the King's absence at a time when Molotov would be attending a meeting of foreign ministers in London.[23]

Groza told Vergotti to make sure that the King and his mother took with them everything they would need abroad – in particular anything the Queen might require for her villa in Florence. Udriski had been under arrest earlier that year but was now free to pilot the Beechcraft to London with Michael as co-pilot. They decided to fly to Lausanne on 12 November, pick up Princess Irene, the Duchess of Aosta, in Lausanne and proceed to London. At the last minute they were told that General Petre Lazăr who, after Antonescu's removal, had returned to the royal household and Mircea Ionnițiu (who spoke fluent English) did not have permission to go. Vergotti, who would now act as private secretary as well as equerry, drew 140,000 Swiss francs, 150,000 French francs and £50 at the Romanian National Bank to cover their expenses.

On the day of their departure Juliu Maniu was sentenced to solitary life imprisonment. The King and his mother were told of the sentence during lunch. Although they had not expected Maniu to be released, that a Romanian court could pass down such a punishment on a frail old man of 74 years who had devoted his early life to liberating the Romanians of Transylvania and his later life to defending Romania's fragile democracy from the assault of the two most powerful tyrannies of the twentieth century left them dumbfounded. It also brought home to them the fact that on his return from London the King would be the only obstacle to complete communisation of the country.

At the airport they found the whole Government waiting to see them off. Groza wore a black hat and black overcoat over his tennis gear and carried a racket. His ministers had dressed properly and were affable. Ana Pauker, who knew that at a meeting of Party cadres that morning a resolution had been adopted to abolish the monarchy, was particularly friendly.

They refuelled at Munich. At Geneva they were welcomed by members of the Swiss Confederation and by the Romanian acting Chargé d'Affaires. Vergotti opened a bank account for the King with the Union des Banques Suisses (UBS), and the two small El Grecos which, unknown to her son, the Queen had packed, he arranged to be put into her Zurich safe deposit.

He also fended off insistent telephone calls for the King from his father and Prince Nicholas.

On 15 November they flew to Heathrow. It was unusual for a King to pilot his own plane with his mother and aunt as passengers, and people took to the tall, well-built young man, taciturn and serious but with a warm smile. Few of them had any idea of his tragic childhood or the fact that this was the first time he had ever been in a country where he was not spied on. It was, he told people, like taking deep breaths of fresh air after living in a tiny cell for many years.

In London they stayed at Claridge's rather than Buckingham Palace so that they would be free to see as much as possible of their family and friends. 'On arriving at the hotel,' Queen Helen writes, 'I was very touched when Queen Mary, for whom I had always great respect and affection, suddenly paid us a visit and stayed for tea, asking us to tell her many details about the recent difficult years in Romania. Her words of praise were very heartening, and moved me deeply.'[24] That evening they had dinner at Buckingham Palace.

Next day the King and his mother went to Coppins at Iver in Buckinghamshire to visit her cousin Marina, the Duchess of Kent, sister of the Princess Olga of Yugoslavia, ('Cookie') who, with her two little boys, had visited them in Mamaia during the summers of 1928 and 1929. In the evening the Romanian Minister, Richard Franassovici, known by his colleagues as 'Trichard', came to the hotel to present the respectful good wishes of the Groza Government – a government which already seemed very remote to them in their sitting room in London.

King Michael met members of his mother's family he had not seen for ten years. At receptions he could talk to people without having to watch every word he used or be prepared for some sudden rudeness to him or his mother. The staff of the hotel could demonstrate about their pay without anyone being arrested and people on the street cheered the royal guests to the wedding without hooligans coming to beat them up with iron bars. After seven years of Antonescu and the Communist triumvirate it was like rediscovering a forgotten world.

The news from Romania was not good. Following Maniu's trial Tătărescu had resigned from the Government, Ana Pauker, who had replaced him at the Ministry of Foreign Affairs, had already set in motion a purge of the Foreign Service, Lazlo Luca had taken over the Ministry of Finance and it was rumoured that Bodnăraş, the third member of the ruling Communist triumvirate, would obtain a ministry before Christmas. During the King's absence Tito had paid a second visit to Romania, this time signing a treaty of friendship – another signal that the monarchy was being eased out.

## Royal Wedding in London: Royal Engagement in Switzerland

The Duchess of Kent and other members of the family and friends pressed them not to return to Romania. King George arranged for him to see the Foreign Secretary privately at Buckingham Palace and Bevin was very frank. For over an hour he asked questions, listened attentively to what the King and his mother told him and at the end said that he would not offer advice since he was a member of the British Government and 'in all honesty Britain is in no position to help or do anything'. The US Ambassador, too, told him on instructions from Washington that the question of his return to Romania was one for him to decide but that 'his continued presence in Romania would not serve any useful purpose'. Only when he saw Field Marshal Smuts and Churchill, the latter – no longer in government – told him straight that he had always taken the courageous course.

This was what King Michael wanted to hear. Very few of the men and women he met in London – knowing something of what he had been through in Romania – could have guessed at the strength of his feeling for the Romanian people.

Then, suddenly, he fell in love.

In 1946 his mother had invited Princess René of Bourbon Parma and her family of three sons and her daughter, Anne, to stay with them in Romania, but the political situation was so bad in early 1947 that the visit had to be cancelled. Michael had once caught a glimpse of Princess Anne in a news film they were watching in Sinaia and he had asked the operator to roll back the film and make a still photograph for him. He had already heard of her charm, her intelligence, her high spirits. On 19 November 1947 she arrived in London for the wedding.

On the collapse of France in 1940 Princess Anne of Bourbon Parma had left with her parents for the States. She worked in one of the large New York stores and was so good at window decoration that the store pressed her to stay on. But she was determined to follow her brothers into the army. Jacques was already a fighter pilot in the Norwegian air force and, when Michel became a parachutist, she asked her mother if she should not join the French army as a volunteer. Her mother simply replied 'Yes'. So she trained as a nurse and mechanic, learned to strip an engine, to march and live a barrack life and then joined a French ambulance unit, served in Casablanca, Algeria and Italy, landed at St Maxime in southern France a month after the French invasion and was with them as far as Stuttgart. In the spring of 1945 she was awarded the Croix de Guerre.

In 1946 she stayed in a small Paris *pension* with her Luxemburg cousins and studied art. When her parents received an invitation to the London wedding she decided that she was too busy with courses at the Louvre to go with them. It was her cousin, the hereditary Grand Duke of Luxemburg, who persuaded her to go. She took a plane to Croydon, a fellow passenger gave her a lift to London and she found her way to Claridge's. 'I shot upstairs to meet the family, and that's where I met the King for the first time. He was in uniform, the blue uniform of the airforce and instead of making a curtsey I clicked my heels. That was terrible. That I remember. Then I ran out and went off with my brothers.'

Next day Princess Anne watched the procession from a Buckingham Palace window with her old nanny and young cousins. In the evening she went to the Luxemburg party.

> And there we talked to him. I mean there was nothing doing. He was such a wonderful man. Yes, he talked about his country all the time. His life there. His worry about his country. He met a lot of people in London. We went to cinemas, that was with my brother and cousins, but always at the back of his mind was his country and also if something happened how to get his mother out. He said 'I can face what's happening until I am forced to go. But it's my mother. . . .' We used to say 'Don't worry. Just send her to us.'[25]

During the next few days they saw the wedding presents in St James's Palace, went shopping and sightseeing together, and Michael, who found it difficult to relax with most strangers, was completely at ease with her. Within a few days he had asked her to marry him. She felt that she could not give him an answer so soon but Michael was absolutely certain. She could take life as it came so much more easily than he could and yet was one of the few people he met in London who really understood what he felt about his Romania and the fate of his people. Although they had had such different lives and in many ways had such different characters, both were direct and without pretence.

The Scotland Yard detective had grown used to Michael's almost middle-aged gravity even when flying in the latest Fairey helicopter or trying out the latest Bentley. But now, quite suddenly, he was like everyone else of his age.

Once, when Michael, Anne, her brother Michel and, of course, the detective, left a cinema show ahead of the others they found themselves caught up in a crowd of enthusiastic sightseeers. For Michael to be jostled and carried along by a good-tempered crowd was something new and exciting and he too joined in the cheering outside the cinema as his mother, the Duchess of Aosta and other members of the party got into their cars and drove away.[26] Towards the end of the wedding week Massigli, the French ambassador in London, invited him on behalf of the President to visit France on his way back. Since he had already arranged to fly straight to Lausanne, he declined but said that he would very much like to visit France later, at a time which could be agreed. His decision was, of course, influenced by the fact that his mother had invited Princess Anne to join them in Switzerland. Vergotti gave up his seat to her on the Beechcraft and went by train.

Queen Helen was delighted. What she had prayed for two years earlier seemed now possible. Anne, she felt, was right for her son. Princess Anne, for her part, remembered that when she was little Queen Helen had sometimes visited her mother and that she was the lady who had made her feel so terribly sad because she had a son, Michael, whom she was hardly ever allowed to see.

Queen Helen had never known him to be so relaxed and happy. She knew too that if Anne married him she would do so with her eyes open, ready to face with him the risks of returning to Romania or the prospect of exile or worse.

The King and Princess Anne spent much of their time driving round the Swiss countryside while Queen Helen talked to her sister Irene and kept in touch with Princess Anne's family in Copenhagen. By then Danish newspapers were publishing photographs of the couple and, according to the Associated Press Agency of 2 December, an engagement would be announced within the month, 'though we have to wait for an announcement from the [Romanian] government'. When flying weather deteriorated, Negel telephoned Bucharest to say that he would arrive on 6 December and would return to Lausanne with the royal train. In Switzerland Anne gave Michael her reply and on the 6th they were unofficially engaged. The King, Princess Anne, her mother, Princess Margarethe of Denmark, who had arrived from Copenhagen the day before, Queen Helen and Jacques Vergotti had a celebratory lunch together.[27] Michael did not want the engagement to be made public until it had the Government's official blessing. When his father telephoned from Lisbon that afternoon King Michael did not mention the engagement. The CIA representative in Switzerland told Vergotti of unconfirmed information that the Communists planned to get rid of the King by the end of the year. Vergotti therefore asked his friend Bianu, a police inspector attached to the Palace, to come with Negel in order to brief the King on the present situation at home. On 8 December Michael took his dog Azo for a check-up at the vet's and next day he and Udriski made sure that the Beechcraft was properly garaged and serviced.

Negel returned on the 16th with mixed news. Although Groza had been affable he would require a little time before he could give a reply regarding the wedding. His provisional view was that the time was not opportune and that there might have to be a postponement. Madame Pauker had told Negel that, personally, she thought Romania could not afford such an expensive ceremony. On the 16th she refused to discuss the question of the monarchy with Holman, who speculated that early in the new year the Government would be ready to suggest constitutional changes.[28] Vergotti's friend, Bianu, had firm information that Romania would be declared a republic on 31 December and he considered that the King was running a great risk by returning. King Michael was not deterred. He loved Princess Anne, and wanted above all to make her his wife. Yet his responsibilities to his country would always come first.

Princess Anne and her mother left for Copenhagen on 18 December for what everyone pretended and hoped would be only a temporary parting. King Michael and his mother left for Bucharest a few hours later.

# ELEVEN

## *An Illegal Abdication*

The King and his mother arrived on 21 December and that evening Queen Helen wrote in her diary 'All Gov at station. Official flowers. Amiable but cold.' and then crossed out 'amiable'. Pătrăşcanu had pretended to be distracted by something behind him at the moment the King was offering him his hand; other ministers had been surly to the point of rudeness.[1]

The crunch for both the Communist Party and the King was now close. Now that his assumption that King Michael would not return from London had proved wrong, Gheorghiu-Dej, the Romanian Communist Party's Secretary General, was under considerable pressure to suppress the monarchy.

On the 22nd, after presenting the staffs of office to three Communist-appointed archbishops of the Romanian Orthodox Church, King Michael took Groza aside to complain about inroads into his authority during his absence. Groza as usual had a wordy explanation for everything, and then began to ruminate aloud about the changing face of Europe, about Romania's progress as a Communist state under Russian protection and the inevitable difficulties this was causing the monarchy. When the King pressed him to say what he really meant, he replied, 'Nothing, Your Majesty, nothing at all. I'm speaking entirely in generalities. Although I am a republican, I personally don't consider that Romania will be ripe for republican status for another ten or twenty, or even fifty years.'[2]

Bodnăraş, who had been appointed Minister of Defence in the King's absence, came next day, the 23rd, 'to take the oath' without priest or Bible and with no more than his personal word to the King. Vergotti noticed that he seemed particularly interested in the layout of the house and grounds and was escorted by a large number of guards from the Tudor Vladimirescu regiment.[3]

That afternoon the King and Queen Helen went to give Christmas greetings to the Household and servants at the Palace in Calea Victoriei, and next day went to Sinaia for the Christmas party there. That evening King Michael telephoned Princess Anne in Copenhagen to say that all was well.

They had a quiet Christmas Day. On the 26th Princess Ileana, her husband Anton and all their children came for lunch and Michael, who could not feel any warmth for his aunt, escaped to Predeal with his friend, Vanya Negroponte. He also worked on the new year speech he always delivered on the last day of the year.

On 29 December the Central Committee of the Communist Party finalised plans for the abdication scheduled to take place the following day. The audience with the King should be not later than 1200–1300 hr. Once news of the abdication had been released, the Ministries of the Interior and National Defence would be responsible for the security of VIPs and such strong points in the capital as the telephone and broadcasting buildings, railway centres, bridges and tunnels. The army would arrange demonstrations of enthusiasm for the new republic by all army ranks and for the new oath of allegiance to be taken without delay.[4]

That evening Groza telephoned Dimitriu Negel – who was in Bucharest with Mircea Ionniţiu – to request an audience for the following morning. The King should be at the Kiselev Palace by ten o'clock and since he wanted to discuss an 'intimate family matter' his mother should be there too.[5] Negel telephoned Sinaia, where they were having supper with friends in the cosy study at Foişor, and King Michael got up from the table to answer the telephone. When Negel gave him Groza's message the King took exception to the Prime Minister's peremptory manner and said he would drive down to Bucharest in the afternoon. Ten minutes later the telephone rang again and Negel told him that Groza insisted on seeing him in the morning. The King assumed that an 'intimate family matter' referred to the wedding and, since Groza was inclined to make heavy weather of any good news he had to communicate to the King, he said he would be in Bucharest by midday.

Early next morning Princess Anne sent Michael a telegram 'I am thinking of you. Love Nan'. It was not delivered.[6]

The King drove his mother, the duty ADC and Vergotti down to Bucharest. He noticed a long line of cars waiting at one of the familiar road-blocks but did not realise that no cars except his own were being allowed into town. Negel and Ionniţiu, who waited for them at the Kiselev villa, were worried. The telephone line to the big Palace was not working and they had noticed soldiers of the Tudor Vladimirescu division grouped near buildings in the Museum of Romanian Villages beyond the trees at the back of the house.

Negel telephoned Groza to say that the King was expecting him. Vergotti took the King's car to the palace garage in Calea Victoriei for its regular service and then walked to his office in the Palace. When told that the telephone line to the King's residence was not working he rushed back to the garage and drove in his own convertible sports car to the Kiselev villa. Tudor Vladimirescu guards stopped him in the drive leading from the boulevard to the entrance and while they were examining his identification card he saw a young man and what looked like his girlfriend disarming the sentries of the Royal Bodyguard. Bodnăraş's agents were operating in pairs, pretending to be innocent couples out for a walk and then producing pistols and taking the sentries, hampered with their heavy equipment, completely by surprise. Two young men jumped into Vergotti's car, which had the top down, and drove him to the Ministry of the Interior, where he was arrested.[7]

King Michael decided to receive the Prime Minister in the upstairs drawing room at the back of the house. This was entered through a small sitting room from the first-floor landing which also gave on to the stairs and the King's and Queen Mother's apartments. Queen Helen waited in her apartment while the King went downstairs to receive his guest.

When he saw that Groza was accompanied by Gheorghiu-Dej, the King knew that something was badly wrong. As Minister of Trade, Gheorghiu-Dej could have nothing to do with arrangements for the wedding. As Secretary General of the Communist Party, he could have much to do with the removal of the Romanian monarchy. He took them up to the sitting room and crossed the hall to fetch his mother. When she entered, both men came forward to kiss her hand – the bulky Groza, his close-cropped head bent and grinning like a genial buffoon, Gheorghiu-Dej, a slight man with black hair greying at the temples and of more natural dignity than Groza.

The Queen Mother, who was wearing a dark woollen dress, led the way to the drawing room. She and her son sat on the wooden seat fitted over the central heating radiator. Groza, carrying a red folder, took the sofa and Gheorghiu-Dej, in his dark blue suit, sat in the armchair to Groza's right and facing the King and Queen. To a casual onlooker, Queen Helen said later, they could have been a group of four people sitting in a corner for a quiet chat.[8] But Gheorghiu-Dej was tense, the King and his mother said nothing, just waited, and it was Groza, his usual breezy self, who opened the conversation with, 'Well, Your Majesty, the time has come to arrange an amicable divorce.' After a pause King Michael asked him, 'What divorce are you referring to?' The Prime Minister then spoke about the future of the monarchy but in more precise and urgent terms than he had used the week before at the archbishops' ceremony. The political situation, he said, was very serious, the Great Powers expected the monarchy to go, there was no longer any need for it and it was slowing down the democratisation and modernisation of the country.[9]

The King had expected the *coup*, should it come, to be at the end of a long political crisis – not to be tossed at him casually like this. For a while he was too shocked to say anything. Then he said slowly to Groza, 'It is not for you to tell me I must go. That is a question for the people to decide. You must know well enough how they regard me. I have always done my duty by them in the way I saw best.'

The Prime Minister agreed and then implied with an exaggerated gesture in the direction of Moscow that it was not the Romanian Government that were asking him to go. When the King pointed out that only the other day Groza had told him that Romania would not be ready to become a republic for many years, his prime minister seemed stuck for an answer and Gheorghiu-Dej intervened with a passionate diatribe. Michael knew that, despite all his ideological verbiage, Gheorghiu-Dej, not Groza, was the one to be taken seriously. Groza he never thought to be more than an actor in a piece written by others. ' I still think', he said in 1991, 'that he knew only a very small fragment of the play. The rest escaped him.'[10]

Through the shock of what they were proposing and the earnest yet passionate outpouring from Gheorghiu-Dej about the blessings the country would enjoy when they had achieved the status of a communist republic, it occurred to the King that if he had not followed the rules of constitutional democracy quite so meticulously they might not have been able to corner him in this way. It was he who had guaranteed the constitutional legality to which he was bound and which they, for their part, with the armed connivance of a foreign power, had felt themselves free to flout and exploit.

Groza seemed to consider Gheorghiu-Dej's lecture to be unrelated to the matter in hand; he interrupted the flow and took the conversation on to a different tack. Michael, he said, would have a much happier time abroad.

'But it is outrageous to ask me to leave,' Michael said. 'I was born in this country. I belong to it. I have spent all my life here. The people do not want me to go. We have been through much together – the *coup* and these last few years . . .'

Groza stuck to his point. Abroad, he pointed out, the King could marry, have children, buy a farm, start a business and, because of his share in the *coup* and because they wanted to settle things amicably, he would still have the revenues from his personal properties in Romania. Gheorghiu-Dej supported this. 'We promise to let you keep your personal estates. You shall have the full income and they won't be interfered with in any way. You will still be a Romanian citizen and when things are quiet you can come back and visit us whenever you want.'

Michael, who had never been particularly interested in his material welfare and at this moment thought it irrelevant to the problem he had to face, reminded them of his links with the Romanian people, of the oath he had taken seven years before. These things could not be set aside so lightly. The people and only the people had the right to decide the destiny of their monarchy. 'I swore an oath,' he said, 'to protect my people, and most of them do not accept communism and do not want it to be forced on them.' Gheorghiu-Dej interrupted him.

> Your Majesty gives the very reason why you must go. You are an unsettling influence and while you are here there will always be trouble. Every reactionary looks to your person as an inspiration for resistance. More than that, we know that you have been in touch with these people, plotting against us with the British and Americans. We shall tolerate this position no longer.[11]

The King, who had never been involved in any kind of anti-Communist subversion, replied 'This is not true. I plot with no one.' He was astonished by the accusation.

Then Gheorghiu-Dej said that, among the evidence taken against Maniu and 'other fascist traitors', many statements had incriminated the King. They had been suppressed up to now but should there be trouble, this would all have to come out and the law would then have to take its course. Michael saw no point in arguing. He knew as well as Gheorghiu-Dej that the so-called evidence must have been extracted by torture. It had no foundation.

He referred to the serious constitutional implications of what they were proposing and it was then that Groza, with some inane remark about their having thought of everything, opened his red file and handed him a sheet of paper. When the King saw that it was one of the official forms on which decrees were submitted for his signature he became even more angry. He would study it later, he informed Groza and, when Groza replied that they would not leave the house until it had been signed, it occurred to Michael, as stray thoughts sometimes do to someone in a crisis, that Moscow always expected their requests to be carried out immediately, without question or consideration.[12] In fact Gheorghiu-Dej himself was probably under considerable pressure. He remembered Vyshinsky two years before in the room downstairs hitting the table with his fist out of sheer frustration when he had questioned Moscow's analysis of the situation in Romania. When Michael now told Groza that he could not be expected to sign such a vital document without examining it properly and would require 48 eight hours, the Prime Minister said that their people were at that very moment waiting for news of the abdication: 'if we don't have your signature soon there will be trouble'.[13]

Then King Michael stood up and said he would read it alone. He crossed to the french window, went out on to the balcony, and round to his apartment. He called Negel and Ionniţiu, who were waiting in the hall downstairs. He handed the document to Negel and asked him to read it aloud for Ionniţiu's benefit.

> We, Michael the First, King of Romania, to all present and in the future, greetings! During recent years in the life of the Romanian State, deep political, economic and social changes have taken place which have created new relations between the components of government. These relations do not satisfy the present conditions of our State, as laid down by our constitution.
>
> The monarchical institution is a serious obstruction in the way of the development of our country. I have considered this situation, and in full agreement with responsible authority, I hereby abdicate in my name and in the name of my descendants, from all prerogatives which I have so far exercised as King of Romania.
>
> I leave to the Romanian people the freedom to choose their new form of State. Given in Bucharest, this day, 30th December, 1947.

The King noticed how cleverly it had been drafted, how it would sound to people who did not know the circumstances of the so-called abdication. He had resisted the bribes and blackmail of these men and still found it impossible to accept the idea that his link with the Romanian people could be severed by his signature on a false document. Only when he heard what Negel and Ionniţiu had to tell him did he know for certain that he was trapped. The telephone, they said, had been cut; he could not seek the advice of anyone outside the house. The royal guards were under arrest and had been replaced by soldiers from the Vladimirescu regiment, who now surrounded the house. He was isolated. As if this were not enough, the house was in the sights of an artillery unit which could be trusted to fire if ordered to. He reread the document. It was as false and yet as absolute as before, and now the others were telling him that if he signed it everyone would still know that his abdication had been obtained by naked intimidation, against his will and the will of the people. 'But if Your Majesty is arrested or killed, all hope will die in Romania.' He picked up the draft decree and left them.

Meanwhile, in the drawing room Gheorghiu-Dej was telling the Queen Mother that as Secretary General of the Communist Party he had been put in a very unpleasant situation. They should have realised, Groza added, that the facilities which the Government had given them for attending the royal wedding in London had been meant to indicate that they should not return.[14] When the whole government came to the airport to see them off it was also to say goodbye. 'Now', Gheorghiu-Dej added, 'they blame me for not making it clear to Your Majesties that you were to stay away from Romania. They say I'm too soft with the King, that I let him run me. If he refuses to sign', Groza added, 'I won't answer for his life.'

Later, King Michael wrote:

I returned to the drawing room. I tried to discuss the matter with those two in a rational way. There was no possibility of our reaching an understanding. In fact the Constitution which I invoked had long since ceased to have any influence on them. They had recourse to blackmail. They informed me that, should signature of the document be delayed, the people of Bucharest would realise that something special was happening here and that, in order to thwart any kind of opposition, members of the government, the communists that is, would be forced to execute about a thousand students who were already under arrest.[15]

These, the King knew, were the youth of the Opposition parties who had been arrested during a long series of anti-Communist demonstrations. Their threat to disclose his own so-called plotting carried very little weight with him. He knew that their 'evidence' was flimsy. Had they even falsified evidence that would stand up to public examination they would have already used it. But with their second piece of blackmail they had found his Achilles heel. He would never consciously, they knew, be responsible for the torture and murder of hundreds of young Romanians.

I had begun to understand the ferocity of these men. Nothing would stop a man like Dej, not even the murder of these students who were guilty of knowing that to sustain the Crown was their only way of avoiding the communist threat. There was no way out and if at this stage I thought there was, it was only because for a moment I had forgotten that we were surrounded. . . . The whole thing had taken an hour, perhaps an hour and a half.[16]

Turning to Groza, the King said slowly, 'The last thing I want is that people should suffer on my account. There has been enough slaughter in this country. I have no choice but to submit to your threat of violence.'

He got up and walked to the long Italian table by the wall between the two windows overlooking the trees at the back of the house, placed the document upon it, took out his fountain pen, signed it, crossed the room to Groza and handed it to him. He then joined his mother and waited for them to go.

But Groza could not resist one more act of buffoonery. He showed the Queen Mother the pistol he was carrying and said, 'Just so that the same thing did not happen to me as happened to Antonescu.'

Gheorghiu-Dej remained deadly serious. 'Remember, no more contacts with the British or Americans', he warned the King, 'or any foreign legations, whether direct or through go-betweens. Don't try to get in touch with any of your friends, or there will be trouble for them.'[17]

Finally, Groza asked the King whether he would not like to stay on in Romania.

> I realised immediately that to remain in the country would mean remaining as a complete prisoner in their hands. I said 'No.'
> When they had left Mama looked at me and I saw that she had been crying. In front of strangers she knew very well how to hide her feelings and I was surprised to see tears on her cheeks. . . . Afterwards we had lunch. But we did not get round to eating anything. Then we left for Sinaia to get ready to leave. We hurried because it gets dark early in Winter.[18]

Downstairs they found the servants in tears. Madame Catargi arrived during lunch, flustered and very angry. When the police had stopped her car she had tried to run for it, had been arrested and kept with Rosa under guard until the abdication had taken place. But where, they all wondered, was Jacques Vergotti?

After lunch they did not return immediately to Sinaia. Michael and his mother went up to the drawing room to tackle the future together. Queen Helen smoothed the cushions, eradicating, as it were, that dreadful meeting. They agreed that they must leave the country as soon as possible and discussed whom they might be allowed to take with them. After Gheorghiu-Dej's warning it would be unwise to contact friends. The servants had better go back to their villages; the further away from Bucharest they were, the safer they would be. Princess Anne was safe, but since Moscow had already broadcast news of the abdication, would be very worried. Weeks later they discovered that Princess Anne's parents, knowing that she would make a dash for Romania if she knew what had happened, kept the news from her for three whole days.

Finally they decided to go to Switzerland, where they could meet Anne and work out something together. Queen Helen was worried about what they would live on for she rightly had no faith in the Government's promise to transfer Michael's personal income to him. She would have the two small El Grecos and her villa in Florence, but her son had nothing abroad.

Bodnăraş had been instructed to get rid of King Michael with as little disruption as possible, and the statement in the abdication document to be signed by the King that 'the monarchical institution is a serious obstacle in the way of the development of the country' had been inserted with this in mind. It was repeatedly plugged by government propaganda to confuse and keep the people quiet. In his broadcast Groza assured Romanians that the King had abdicated of his own free will in order to be able to marry, the Government were giving him £750,000 and allowing him to keep his personal estates and the income from them, he could stay in Romania if he wished and 'come and go just as he pleased'. Even after the 1989 revolution these lies were still being used in anti-monarchist propaganda.

Republican status does not follow spontaneously from the abdication of a monarch, even when this is genuine. It requires a major amendment to the constitution, which, in Romania, could only be performed by a constituent assembly elected specifically for that purpose by an extraordinary meeting of the Lower House of Parliament. Such a meeting could not possibly – as the Government claimed – have been held that evening because parliamentarians during the Christmas recess were scattered in midwinter conditions over the whole of Romania. The meeting that took place at 7 p.m. probably included the deputies who happened to be in Bucharest but was then packed with non-parliamentarians whose names could not be recorded – hence the exceptional absence of a roll-call for that unique session.

Forty-five minutes was allowed for the whole proceeding, of which 20 minutes were devoted to ovations and applause. During the remaining 25 minutes two bills, it was claimed, were read out, debated and voted on – impossible even if we allow only five seconds per deputy per vote. 'Speed', the King remarked later, 'is an essential element in any rape.'[19] The whole process announced by Groza to be The Act of Birth of the Romanian Peoples' Republic was no more than a deception which was not to be challenged until Eleodor Focşeneanu published his *Constitutional History of Romania* in 1992.

Next morning, 31 December, the King and his mother said goodbye to the staff amidst a great deal of distress and despair. Negel and Ionniţiu stayed in Bucharest to liaise with the Government about the people they would be allowed to take with them and to obtain visas for Switzerland. To pay for the journey Negel sold wines from the King's personal estates.

On their way up to Sinaia they passed open lorries carrying the soldiers of the Royal Bodyguard, covered with snow and looking very miserable. The King pulled up, hoping to speak to them, but the lorries drove on. He heard later that the officers of the guard were insulted publicly and their swords taken from them.[20] It was snowing when they reached Sinaia at about 4.30 p.m. They said little to each other that evening and Queen Helen went early to her rooms, though not to sleep. 'We were suffering a kind of spiritual torture,' the King explained.[21]

The King's guards had been replaced by members of the Tudor Vladimirescu division with orders to treat the royal family with the minimum of civility and, on 30 December, even before the abdication had been signed, a commission had arrived to take an inventory of everything in Peleş, Pelişor, Foişor and the dependencies. These people ensured that the King and his mother took with them only 'things of immediate use'. 'They followed Mama's every step. They did not leave her for a single minute. Didn't let her take even an ash tray from the table. They rummaged through our baggage again just before we boarded the train. It was a nightmare.'[22] Lists, in the servants' handwriting under the commission's supervision, were made of every shirt or tie or suit or dress that the King and his mother packed to take with them.

When pressed later to say what he thought about during his last three days in Sinaia, King Michael replied that he and his mother were too involved with getting ready to think of much else. Once or twice it had crossed his mind that Romanians would see that what had happened was a highly illegal act and that his signature on that document represented neither their will nor his. But later he realised that the only reaction you could expect to the abdication document as drafted was one of stupor, and stupor, as he said, is never likely to give rise to coherent thought or coherent action. 'For some days I, too, lived in a curious kind of confusion. When you have suffered a great deal there comes a moment when you no longer feel any pain. I had been taken by a kind of numbness even before the 30 December.'[23]

Jacques Vergotti arrived on the evening of 3 January shortly before they left. He was accompanied by old Soare, the caretaker, who had just taken down the Hohenzollern-Sigmaringen flag for the last time. Vergotti had brought him along to say goodbye to the King.[24]

Vergotti had been stripped of his commission and given a one-way exit passport. His interrogators had asked about King Michael's finances abroad and when Vergotti replied that he had only what was left from the sum allowed for the London visit they had admitted to having no evidence of any transfer of funds abroad at any time except for official palace cars. He had been told to drive to Sinaia with Madame Kopkov and report to the head of the commission. When this man asked about the King's 'gold bed', Vergotti was stumped until Madame Kopkov remembered that Queen Marie had once furnished a bedroom with gilded wood in the Byzantine style. After the earthquake it had been put in store but this, she thought, probably accounted for the legend of the 'gold bed'.

When instructed to tell the assembled personnel of the two castles and Foişor that they should continue their duties under the management of the head of the commission Vergotti had taken the opportunity to inform them of Groza's promise that the King would retain his ownership of the entire domain of Sinaia, which had been left to him, personally, under the codicil to King Ferdinand's will.

Later the King said:

When we set off for the station I remember that two members of the commission got into the car instead of the ADC. The gate was closed, which had never happened before. Since we were only allowed 'things of immediate need', why did they let us take four cars, which could have been full of our belongings? I have never understood that.[25]

At the station the King went over to the Siguranţa escort car, shook hands with the policemen and the driver and said goodbye.

We did not expect the public to be on the platform. But instead of the public we saw officers drawn up in two ranks, their backs towards us, forming a corridor through which we passed feeling rather puzzled. The last thing I saw, my last image of Sinaia, was when one of the officers, I don't remember his rank, turned his head a little towards me and I saw that tears were running down his face. Then the door was shut, the blinds pulled down.[26]

Among those accompanying the King were Negel, Ionniţiu, Madame Catargi, Vergotti, Negroponte, his wife and little boy Sandy, General Lazăr, Colonel Emilian Ionescu, and Bianu, the gendarme director of security who had advised the King in Lausanne. There was Queen Helen's maid, Rosa, and three other servants.

Troops checked every compartment for stowaways, pushed their bayoneted rifles under the beds, searched luggage for jewels and currency. Some people were subjected to a body search. Even the bread and fruit on Queen Helen's table was cut open.

The doors were locked. A guard stood at each end of the coach. The Soviet officer in charge asked Vergotti to let him have his pistol. The Romanian conductor gave Vergotti the train schedule which showed their destination to be Lausanne. The atmosphere was leaden. Michael and his mother were silent, but when they were on the outskirts of Braşov and some workmen shouted 'Long Live the Republic', the King, who rarely showed his emotions, suddenly said 'May God help my country.'[27]

They travelled through Transylvania that night and at Braşov and Fagaraş they heard the national anthem being sung by people who had braved not only the icy night but the brutality of the station guards.[28] Early next morning they stopped at Săvârşin, and Bibi Popescu, the administrator of the estate, got down with the King's aged and sick dog Azo. No one else was allowed to leave the train, but Vergotti saw Mircea at the other end of the coach, helping aboard his fiancée, Rodica Haţiegan. About half an hour later the guards left at Curtici, the last station before the Hungarian frontier. When they stopped in the Soviet sector of Vienna their papers were checked and the Russian officer who had removed Vergotti's hand gun at Sinaia left the train without returning it.

The train then moved forward into a no-man's land between the Soviet and American zones where they waited on a bridge for so long that King Michael began to wonder if there had been a hitch. Throughout the journey, he says, his mother did not say much, 'though the way she looked at me said much more about our and the country's situation than any amount of conversation'.[29] After what seemed hours, they moved forward again and stopped at a station. Then he heard the sound of a car approaching:

> A few minutes after it stopped – it was a jeep – the carriage door opened noisily and into our room came an American captain who stood at attention, saluted and said in English 'Sire, now you are free'.[30]

Next day they reached Lausanne and were surprised to hear some Swiss in the station shouting 'Vive le Roi. Vive la Liberté.'

For the King, what the American officer had said had not been over-dramatic, for

we now knew for certain that we had not been handed over to Moscow. Neither when we left nor at any time had anyone ever given us the assurance that what was happening to the country would not happen to us . . .

Yes, in a sense I was leaving a hell, a communal hell which affected everyone, in order to enter one reserved for me alone. In exile I suffered mostly from isolation, and this grew worse as I realised that people could not believe me when I spoke of the longing I felt for the country and my need to live together with Romanians . . . But that is another story.[31]

# PART FOUR

Exile:
January 1948–December 1989

## TWELVE

## The Wedding of King Michael and Princess Anne of Bourbon Parma

After Antonescu's arrest in August 1944 his guards were posted to other duties. After King Michael's forced abdication in December 1947 his were treated as traitors and their military careers destroyed.

The army, which, after the monarchy, was considered the main obstruction to communisation, had suffered multiple purges at all ranks. The USSR's unofficial arms embargo which had starved it of spare parts had destroyed its armoured divisions, and its soldiers were subsequently treated by Soviet commanders as infantry fodder.[1] However, Romania's forces were not easily intimidated. On 9 January 1948 a senior political commissar reported from the Iași region that the NCOs, half the younger officers and the majority of troops had shown no enthusiasm for the Romanian Popular Republic.

The abdication left civilians in a state of shock. Almost everyone – even government agents whose job it was to cheer for the republic – stayed indoors during the celebrations. 'To the people of Romania' the British Chargé d'Affaires wrote to the Foreign Office, 'or such of them who have expressed opinions to myself or my friends, there is but one comfort in the present situation and that is that their King has escaped with his life'.[2]

Few people believed the Government's version of the abdication; a man who had stood up to Hitler and Stalin for so long would not voluntarily abdicate in order to promote a Moscow-type dictatorship. Only they wanted to hear this confirmed over the BBC from the King himself. They could have no idea that he was unwilling to embarrass the Swiss authorities who had given him refuge by making a public statement about the abdication while on Swiss territory.

Communist propaganda did its utmost to denigrate the King and eventually obliterate him from Romanian minds. Few people knew that the decision to destroy the monarchy had been taken in Moscow before King Michael had even met Princess Anne, and when Bucharest spread the idea that the King had abdicated because his fiancée did not want to live in Romania some Western newspapers seized on the story. Had not his father given up the throne for a woman in 1925? Had not King Edward VIII of England done so in 1936? So as not to add fuel to this rumour, King Michael decided that for a little while he should not see his fiancée; Anne would stay in Copenhagen, he in Lausanne. Princess Anne agreed; although she had plenty of her mother's independent spirit she would always defer to Michael on matters concerning Romania.

Many Romanians felt that with the King gone they had lost their last link with the West. London and Washington, they thought, would now wash their hands of Romania – not of the Republican Government with whom they would do business but of the Romanian people. Before King Michael and his mother had even finished packing, the US and British governments had decided, correctly, that there were no formal grounds for non-recognition of the Romanian Republic. Washington, it is true, suggested that the new accreditation of their representative in Bucharest be carried out as unobtrusively as possible, and on 17 January when King George VI gave his formal assent to British recognition he asked the Foreign Office to ascertain from King Michael himself what had really happened. On the day, therefore, that His Majesty's Government recognised the new Romanian People's Republic King Michael gave the British envoy to Switzerland a detailed account of the meeting of 30 December with Groza and Gheorghiu-Dej, adding that in his view the USSR (not having the atomic bomb) would be unable to resist a firm US challenge and that the longer this challenge was put off the more dangerous the position would become for Western Europe.[3]

Although he had no doubt that in Bucharest all legal and constitutional restraints to the country's communisation would now be removed, Michael was not aware that laws and decrees had been issued in his name while he had been in London. After he went into exile, an eighty-page addendum was printed – page 299 *bis* – backdated to 29 December 1947 and inserted between pages 299 and 300 of the relevant *Monitor Oficial*. Thus nineteen laws and fifty-four decrees, which the King had never seen, were promulgated under the royal seal.[4]

King Michael did not respond to pressure from his father to meet in Lisbon. He knew that they differed so much that nothing constructive could come of it. During the December crisis Carol had advised him to send all the great pictures in the royal collection to an exhibition abroad and the royal yacht to be repaired in Istanbul so that he could recover them if he were exiled.[5] His advice had been almost entirely concerned with preparing for Michael's material comfort in exile – that same self-centred attitude to a major national crisis that Gheorghiu-Dej and Groza had been disappointed not to find in Carol's son during the abdication meeting of 30 December.

King Carol wrote to his ex-wife complaining that his failure to meet his son was causing talk and intrigue. 'All that I want', he insisted, 'is his good; with my fatherly love and, with my experience, who can give him better advice than me?'[6]

The day after his talk with the British Minister, Michael, his mother, Princess Irene and Jacques Vergotti left for Davos. Princess Anne with her mother and brothers would be there too and at that altitude they hoped not to run into gossip-page journalists. For twelve days King Michael and Princess Anne ski'd and drove around in the jeep, and he pointed out views that reminded him of the Carpathian Mountains. They saw part of the Olympic games in St Moritz. So long as they were together everything seemed better. He caught a glimpse of a life in which even the traumas of his childhood might matter less. They talked about jobs in that ordinary world which she knew and he did not. He would make a good constitutional king, she said, given the chance, but he could also make a good engineer, mechanic, pilot or photographer. 'If you can't be the first,' she told him, 'then we'll try one of the others.'[7]

Michael knew that whatever job he might take must allow him time to carry out his duties to Romania as a king in exile. He had devoted his adult life to trying to save his country from first Nazi then Communist dictatorship. Now he had been forcibly removed from the turmoil in Romania but there were still things he could do for his people. He would travel – first to France, England and the USA and convey to their leaders and other influential citizens his experience of Soviet strategy as the head of state of an East European country. He would take the opportunity to tell the international press and the people at home what were the true circumstances of his so-called abdication. He could also help to set up a Romanian national committee which would work with the Western Powers for the eventual liberation of his country.

In Davos King Michael had his first taste of exile politics. The Western Powers could not permit on their territory a Romanian exile government with policies diametrically opposed to those of the government they had recognised, but a national committee without governmental status representing the democratic parties destroyed in 1947 was acceptable.

At the Derby Hotel in Davos King Michael met Niculescu Buzeşti who, before leaving Romania, had been asked by Maniu to represent the National Peasant Party, the National Liberal Party and Titel Petrescu's Social Democratic Party. One of his first acts on arrival in Western Europe had therefore been to create the Council of National Political Parties which on 1 August 1948 would begin to publish its news sheet, *La Nation Roumaine*. In audience with the King, Buzeşti advised that a Romanian National Committee should consist of three members of the National Peasant Party, one Liberal and one Social Democrat, and that, should membership be extended beyond these parties, anyone chosen should have worked actively against the Nazis and Communists; otherwise they could not effectively represent the Romanian people of today. The King listened carefully but before reaching a decision he felt that he should consult General Rădescu, who had headed Romania's last constitutional government, which was also the last one to include the three traditional parties.

King Michael favoured the inclusion of representatives of the three suppressed democratic parties which, when the time came to return home, would provide a political link with pre-Communist Romania. General Rădescu, who was now in the States, was, however, planning a new Independent Resistance movement open to any Romanian exile of consequence and the King knew that he must tread carefully in this political minefield. Finally, he asked Rădescu to form a committee of ten people representative of both party and non-party exiles and he let it be known that he would like to announce its formation during his forthcoming visit to the United States. General Rădescu did not meet this deadline.

On 16 February King Michael and Queen Helen returned to Lausanne, and Princess Anne with her mother, Princess Margarethe, to Copenhagen. Princess Margarethe's parents were the Protestant Prince Waldemar of Denmark and the Roman Catholic Princess Marie of France. When they married it had been agreed that their sons would be brought up Protestants and their daughters Catholics. Princess Margarethe was therefore Catholic but all her brothers were Protestant. She had married Prince René, son of Robert I, Duke of Parma. His eldest brother Xavier, a priest, was now head of the Bourbon Parma family. Princess Anne's Aunt Zita had been the last Empress of Austria. Felix, another uncle on her father's side, had married into the Luxemburg family and his son, Jean, was often to have Queen Anne and her husband to stay when later he became the Grand Duke.

Since Prince René had been unable to obtain a dispensation for his daughter to marry someone of the Greek Orthodox faith, Queen Helen and Princess Margarethe decided on a joint personal appeal to Pope Pius XII. Their intervention was not well received.

Before leaving for Great Britain and the USA the King suffered another rebuff. He proposed to take up Massigli's earlier invitation to pay an official visit to France and asked whether it would be convenient for him to do so on his way to the USA. Paris, with a powerful communist party of its own to cope with, regretted that, as the situation had changed since November 1947, an official visit was no longer possible. They also asked him to make no political statement while passing through their territory.

Unlike his mother, the King had not yet realised just how hard up he was going to be. It was by now clear that Groza had reneged on his promise to send him the income from his private property in Romania. He therefore had no income abroad and in the bank only what was left of the money drawn for the London wedding. He loved driving and had been allowed to bring several cars, a jeep and a motorcycle with him. It took a little time for Jacques Vergotti and the Swiss bank manager to persuade him that most of these and eventually the Beechcraft plane he had garaged in Geneva after the trip to London would have to be sold. His Household had to be reduced almost immediately. He would no longer need a Marshal of the Court and General Lazăr would stay on as his principal adviser and Private Secretary. Mircea and Rodica Ionnițiu had married in the Greek Orthodox church at Lausanne and he had promised to take them to the States where they had friends who would help find Mircea a job. Jacques Vergotti had relatives in the USA where he hoped to live permanently, but until his American papers came through he would continue to help the royal family with their administrative problems.

On 27 February Queen Helen left for Paris and within hours Prince Frederick of Hohenzollern-Sigmaringen and Michael's uncle, Prince Nicholas, called on him without any warning to discuss, of all things, the order of succession to the throne. Little came of the talk and Michael only had confirmation later that the man behind this odd behaviour was his own father. In an interview published in the French newspaper *Le Figaro*, Urdăreanu, now King Carol's spokesman, expressed strong support for Prince Frederick and asserted that Michael would never return to his throne.[8]

Two days later he and Vergotti drove to Paris, where he stayed with his mother at her favourite Hotel Vendôme and spent a happy four days with Princess Anne and her family. On 4 March the royal party, which included Madame Nelly Catargi, General Lazăr, Major Vergotti and Mr and Mrs Ionniţiu, left for England. King Michael and his mother were met at Victoria by the Lord Chamberlain and driven straight to Claridge's, where the King made the following statement to the press, the first since leaving Romania:

> In the morning of December 30th, 1947, Mr Petru Groza and Gheorghiu-Dej, members of the Romanian Cabinet, presented to me the text of the act of abdication, urging me to sign it at once. Both of them came to the Royal Palace after it had been surrounded by armed detachments, informing me that they would hold me responsible for the bloodshed which would follow as a consequence of the instructions already issued by them in case I should not sign within the time limit.
>
> This act was imposed on me by force, by a Government installed and maintained in power by a foreign country, a Government utterly unrepresentative of the will of the Romanian people.
>
> This Government had violated international pledges binding them to respect the political freedoms of the Romanian people, had falsified the elections and annihilated the democratic political leaders who enjoyed the confidence of the country.
>
> The removal of the monarchy constitutes a new act of violence in the policy for the enslavement of Romania. In these conditions I do not consider myself bound, in any way, by this act imposed upon me.
>
> With unshaken faith in our future, animated by the same devotion and will to work, I will continue to serve the Romanian people with which my destiny is inexorably bound.[9]

At lunch with the King and Queen were Princess Elizabeth, the Duke of Edinburgh and the Duchess of Kent, a cousin of Queen Helen. Michael and his mother expanded on what King George already knew about the abdication. They also spoke about his forthcoming marriage, and Michael explained his difficulties with the Vatican. King George felt that the Pope was being unduly rigid and, later, the British Minister to the Holy City was asked to reinforce the arguments in favour of a dispensation. King George also arranged for a personal message to Clark-Kerr (now Lord Inverchapel, British Ambassador to Washington) asking him to do anything possible to smooth King Michael's arrival and to keep a generally helpful eye on him. King George, who liked and admired his young cousin, was surprised to discover that he 'was apparently completely without any means'.[10]

After lunch they took the boat train to Southampton. The crossing was rough and Lazăr and Vergotti spent much of it on their bunks reading the recently published *I Chose Freedom* by the KGB defector, Kravchenko. On 10 March the ship eased past the Statue of Liberty. Two tug-loads of journalists came aboard, mainly to interview Jews arriving for the UN meeting which would recognise Israel as an independent state. Some journalists, however, concentrated on King Michael. He had never experienced anything like this before.

According to the report published in next morning's *New York Times*, he said that while he hoped to return to his throne, he doubted the feasibility of liberating Romania by peaceful means. He would marry Princess Anne though the date was not yet fixed. His mother's visit to the Vatican had been purely a courtesy call (not quite true). He denied ever having considered the idea of a government in exile (absolutely true). When asked whether Ana Pauker was cruel, he replied: 'Look at her photograph.'

He was asked 'When Petru Groza, now Premier, insisted on the abdication did King Michael leave Romania voluntarily, or was he forced out?'

Michael thought for a minute and a broad sidewise grin spread over his face. Then he replied:

'They didn't say it, but it felt like that.'[11]

General Rădescu with other Romanian exiles came on board and – a pleasant surprise – the Rabbi Şafran, who had not forgotten what the King and his mother had done for the Romanian Jewish community during the war. During his twelve-day visit, the King met many people ranging from Sgt Eddie Hoffman in a New York lift to President Truman at the White House. At the National Press Club in Washington he had an opportunity to address a well-informed audience and to answer their questions. Lord Inverchapel gave a large reception for him at the British Embassy. He was the guest of Mr Harriman, Secretary of Commerce, at a lunch attended by the Secretary of State and other cabinet ministers. He discussed prospects for a Romanian National Committee with members of the State Department who told him of their concern that the Romanian exile community seemed so divided by petty political differences; King Michael shared their concern.

On 22 March he saw President Truman at the White House. The President was very friendly. Michael, he said, had well deserved America's highest decoration for what he had done during the war. He showed interest in details of the abdication and 'deplored the Soviet mentality'. He suggested that the

King stay on in Washington and Mrs Truman told Queen Helen that if they did so, Blair House* would be at their disposal.

Instead he went on an extensive visit of major industrial centres in the Mid-West, including General Motors, Ford, and Willis Overland, where he caused amusement by saying that until a few months before he was still driving the jeep Vergotti had captured at Stalingrad. He piloted a Beach Bonanza aircraft from Toledo to Cleveland and Detroit, where half a million Americans of Romanian origin lived. At a large dinner for the Romanian community he spoke in both Romanian and English.[12] He also spent a few days at a ranch near the Mexican border – a brief spell of Texan hospitality away from politics.

Back in New York the King attended the Armed Forces Day military parade and a large reception was given in his honour by General Maxwell Taylor, head of the West Point Academy. By now he had been away for over a month without news from Princess Anne and he was anxious to get back. With his mother and Vergotti, he flew to Europe on 8 April 1948. In London they stayed at Windsor Castle and then, before continuing on to Geneva, a few days with the Duchess of Kent at Coppins.

Princess Anne had sent no telegram because from the Vatican there was nothing but bad news. Back in Lausanne the King withdrew into his shell, would take long, lonely drives into the mountains or discuss with Lazar the pile of correspondence which had been awaiting his return.

Lord Inverchapel had reported to the Foreign Office that during dinner with him King Michael had given an impression of disappointment with the US Government.[13] As the only East European head of state with three years' personal experience of Soviet political warfare King Michael, it is true, had hoped – somewhat unrealistically given the restrictions on what the President could say – for more than an exchange of generalities with President Truman. Years later the King remarked that, when the President had expressed the hope that the situation would quickly change in Romania, it was only done out of politeness.[14]

To avoid a possible rebuff to King George personally, the British Minister at the Vatican had approached not the Pope himself but cardinals in close touch with His Holiness. It soon became clear that Princess Anne could possibly obtain a papal dispensation for her marriage to a member of the Greek Orthodox Church if an undertaking were given that their children would be

---

* Blair House, opposite the White House, was sometimes offered to VIPs visiting Washington.

brought up in the Catholic faith.* But under the Romanian constitution such an arrangement would exclude their children from accession to the Romanian throne and even to save his wife from the anguish of excommunication King Michael would not break the Romanian constitution, nor his oath to the Romanian people when he had sworn to defend the Orthodox Church. Princess Anne knew that unless she had the courage to break the ruling of her own church there would be no marriage. Her love for Michael was tested at the very start of their relationship, and her decision meant that henceforth she too would be bound up with Romania, its constitution and its people.

On 23 April Princess Anne took the train to Geneva. They had only three days together, much of it spent driving in the Swiss mountains. She was his passenger when he clocked up 430 hours of flying time and wrote 'Nan' in the log book he had kept for the last five years. They attended the Greek Orthodox Mass in Lausanne, after which the priest, Vergotti notes, gave them his good wishes. They never even considered marriage outside the Church. They wanted a real wedding and since Michael could not be married in a Catholic church Princess Anne was prepared to marry according to the Orthodox rite.

'If that's the position,' King Paul of Greece said, 'come here. I shall marry you.'[15] King Paul, tall, always radiating warmth and within the family full of jokes and teasing, knew that this gesture of kindness could lead to trouble with the Vatican and more particularly with his own government; he therefore assumed full personal responsibility. King Paul, who had seen his father's sufferings in exile, went out of his way to respect Michael's rank. When the Romanian Government complained that in Greece Michael was treated as if he were still a reigning monarch, King Paul instructed the Marshal of the Royal Court to inform the Romanians that 'that was how it was and would remain'.[16] King Paul, King Michael commented many years later, was a straight talker and one of the few monarchs to show him such friendship during his exile.

There was a strong possibility that Princess Anne's parents would not feel able to attend the wedding. On 12 May Queen Helen and her sister, Princess Irene, drove to Paris, convinced that they would persuade the Bourbon Parma family to relent. Cardinal Roncalli (later Pope John XXIII), Apostolic Nuncio in Paris and a great admirer of the Queen for what she had done for the Jews

---

\* Even this was not certain. King Boris of Bulgaria had promised when marrying Princess Giovenna of Italy that their children would be brought up as Catholics. He had broken his promise, something the Vatican could not forget when considering King Michael's case.

in Romania, would surely help. They stayed again at the Vendôme. The chestnut trees were in blossom. French and English flags were out, for Princess Elizabeth was staying at the British Embassy a little further up the rue St Honoré.

But when they left Paris on 16 May they had failed with the Bourbon Parmas and two weeks later Anne telephoned Lausanne to say that her mother would come herself to explain why they would be unable to attend the service.

Princess Margarethe of Denmark, with no sisters and four brothers, was something of a tomboy and a bit of a rebel. She was a tough-minded lady with an infectious smile who would do all she could for her daughter's happiness, but in her own way. During her visit with Queen Helen to the Pope she had at one moment banged her fist on his table. The Pope had said 'eee' and that, said Queen Anne later, 'was the end of the conversation'.[17] The *gaffe* made no difference to the Vatican decision and the two mothers would continue to pull together long after their children were married.

On the question of dogma Princess Margarethe had done no better with her husband's family than had Queen Helen and her sister. Prince Xavier had laid down the law about the wedding of his niece and it was he rather than the Vatican who forbade the attendance of Anne's parents. 'Princess Anne', King Michael commented later, 'accepted the provisions of the Romanian constitution. The price of this acceptance was quite considerable: her family had no right to come to the wedding, neither her father, nor her mother, nor her brothers.'[18] This was the message that Princess Margarethe brought to her cousin Queen Helen. Anne, she said, would be given away by her uncle Prince Erik of Denmark – a Protestant and the only member of the family she would have with her at her wedding.

King Michael, who respected all religions and in his own country encouraged the oecumenical spirit, never asked his wife to become an Orthodox. 'Our orthodox marriage', she said 'I received in all faith and all my being and I don't believe that in doing so I betrayed my religion.'[19] Nor did she believe that her family would have done so by attending the Athens wedding though she understood their reserve.

Michael and Anne travelled to Athens as regular air passengers with Queen Helen, Petru Lazăr and Jacques Vergotti, but when the plane landed they were invited to get off first and were greeted by a band and a guard of honour.

The wedding, which was private, took place on 10 June in the throne room of the Royal Palace in Athens and was conducted by Archbishop

## The Wedding of King Michael and Princess Anne

Damaskinos, who had been Regent of Greece until King George's return in September 1946. King Paul, who had suceeded his brother George in April 1947, was their *kumbaros* – the Orthodox combination of godfather and best man. Princess Anne was given away by Prince Erik and among her attendants were King Michael's Greek cousins – Crown Prince Constantine, Princess Sophie and Princess Irene. Her dress was by Lanvin with a long train, which was to serve her daughters in their turn. As Princess Margarita said at her own wedding in September 1996, whenever the bodice had to be modified the train simply became shorter. The bridegroom wore his Air Force uniform. Vergotti, a Roman Catholic, held the gold crowns over the heads of the bride and bridegroom and wore, for the last time, the uniform of an ADC and major of the Romanian army, from which he had been expelled on the first day of that year.[20]

The wedding breakfast was given by King Paul and Queen Frederika and, apart from the bride and bridegroom, Queen Helen and her sister Princess Irene, Greek dignitaries and members of both courts, there were present Princess Paul of Yugoslavia, the widowed Princess Nicholas her mother, Princess Andrew,* and the Prince and Princess George of Hanover.† Queen Helen had written to King Carol about the wedding but he was not invited.[21]

King Michael and his bride spent a few days at King Paul's summer palace in Tatoi and then flew to Geneva and on to a hotel in Locarno. They were invited to spend part of their honeymoon in the States but decided that the trip would be too expensive. Queen Helen returned to the Villa Sparta on 4 July to make sure that everything was ready for them. In early August they joined her there, glad to escape the curiosity of visitors and the press in Locarno.

On 20 February 1948 the Romanian Government had stripped King Michael and 34 relatives and collaborators of their Romanian citizenship.[22] Since it was based on two very dubious pieces of legislation, Pătrășcanu hotly opposed the decision and by doing so he hammered yet another nail into his own coffin.

On 17 May the *Monitor Oficial* published a decree nationalising the property in Romania belonging to King Michael or to other members of the royal family. The effective date was 6 March 1945, the day that Vyshinsky had blackmailed the King into appointing Romania's first Communist-controlled government.

---

* Prince Andrew of Greece, father of Prince Philip, had died in 1944.
† The Prince of Hanover was Queen Frederika's brother. His wife was Prince Philip's sister, Sophie.

Though Groza and Gheorghiu-Dej had assured Michael that the income from his personal estates in Romania would be transferred to him in Switzerland, this did not happen. Vergotti and Monsieur Lang of the Union des Banques Suisses were greatly concerned about the King's financial position and strongly advised him to settle down in the Villa Sparta.

When King Michael and his new wife arrived from Locarno, Queen Helen took 'Regina Mică', as the Household now called Queen Anne, to introduce her to her favourite picture galleries and shops in the old town of Florence. Meanwhile in the study Lazăr brought the King up to date about exile politics.

In spite of his disappointment in Washington, the King hoped that the West would not continue for long a policy which seemed dangerously like appeasement. He could not foresee at that time an exile lasting for decades, a cold war freezing over for half a century, the economic gap between Western and Eastern Europe becoming an abyss, or a new breed of Soviet and US professionals communicating in coded language across the Iron Curtain so as to maintain a balance of nuclear power and thus one of the longest periods of peace that Europe has experienced.

In the King's view, therefore, the main political objective of a Romanian National Committee should be to persuade Western governments not to accept the *status quo* in their country and, until the Romanian people could again speak for themselves, to continue to distinguish between the people and the *régime* in power. To this end the Committee should provide Western governments with sound information about economic and social conditions in Romania, much of which might not be available to their Legations. But the King must have known that as the Communist Party tightened its hold on the Romanian people, the Committee's reliable independent sources would dry up. Should the Allies fail to take effective steps to liberate the peoples of Eastern Europe reasonably soon, their National Committees would become irrelevant.

As yet no Romanian Committee was in sight. Buzeşti's formula for a committee of people with whom he had worked closely in Romania would give him virtual control. Rădescu countered by inviting sixteen prominent non-party émigrés to join him and, before seeking the King's approval, cleared this with the State Department. On 5 August Lazăr wrote to Rădescu repeating that a committee of ten of the most qualified delegates would be an acceptable group for King Michael to recommend to the State Department. Rădescu replied that he could not obtain agreement on a committee of such limited membership and planned to come in person to see the King.[23]

The US authorities found General Rădescu arrogant and difficult to deal with. They also knew that having no money abroad he was dependent on

Malaxa, the industrialist, whose close relations with Nazi Germany and Soviet Russia were well known to them.[24] The King, who agreed with Rădescu about many things, 'did not understand why he should think that a non-party person would serve Romania better then a party man. Most refugees belonged to one or other of the three parties and had we followed Rădescu's idea we would have produced an empty space between the Committee and them.'[25]

Since Rădescu on his way to see the King had had talks in Paris with a group of 'reformed' Legionaries and then with pro-Antonescu officers who wanted to set up an exile association independent of the King's, it is not surprising that his reception was rather cool. To make matters worse the General accused Petre Lazăr of being in the pay of Cretzianu and Vișoianu.[26] Dashed was any hope the King might have had of including in his first new year message from exile the news that a National Committee had now been formed.

Exiled Romanians seemed incapable of a united front. 'They told me', King Michael remarked years later, 'that they praised my moral stand, to which I replied that "If my moral stand does not inspire action, it is of no use to anyone but me". To get them together I made appeals, sent messages, asked for unity. Beautiful! Bravo! But no unity.'[27]

There was, however, good news in Sparta which had nothing to do with exile politics. The Regina Mică was pregnant. She decided to have her baby in Lausanne at Dr Rochat's Clinique Montchoisie. Vergotti went ahead to make arrangements with Dr Rochat and to find a suitable house for them to rent. But they spent most of the second half of 1948 at Villa Sparta.

Princess Anne's brothers Michel and André came to congratulate them and brought Princess Anne a Pekinese puppy which she called Whimpy. Some time later her father came to see her and their relations became normal again. That autumn she met members of her husband's family – Princess Elisabeta, Prince Nicholas and Queen Maria of Yugoslavia. She was never to meet King Carol. He wrote to her exhorting her to be an exemplary wife, to love and be a moral support to her husband and she wrote back saying that she would try to be a better partner in marriage than he had been to the Queen Mother.

Princess Margarethe invited Michael and Anne to spend part of the winter with her at her villa in Villefranche. The Villa Idris was built at the foot of a cliff which had been excavated to make guest houses. Queen Helen, when she arrived for Christmas, was intrigued by the multi-terraced rock gardens and the underground swimming pool – so different from Sparta. Queen Anne's brothers Jacques, Michel and André got on well with Michael. Her mother was easy, her father less so. It was a nice party, Queen Anne said later, with a tree and plum pudding. She had hoped to give her husband something he had never had, some ordinary family life.[28] But this was King Michael's first Christmas since his expulsion from Romania and, try as she might, she could not prevent him feeling – more particularly during the Christmas festivities – the deep unhappiness of his exile. On 31 December 1948, he read his first new year message in exile to the Romanian people from the steps of the Orthodox church in Nice but only a handful of journalists turned up to report it.[29]

The young King drove up to Lausanne from Villefranche on 2 February and his wife followed by air next day. Vergotti had found them a small house above the lake – La Petite Grangette de la Conversion – together with Mademoiselle Albertine, the housekeeper.

Michael and Anne enjoyed La Petite Grangette, waiting for their baby, walking down to the lake, seeing Dr Rochat from time to time. By the time her mother and Queen Helen arrived on 16 March Queen Anne was becoming impatient and nine days later on the eve of the birth was still driving around with Michael. Their daughter was born at 1.30 a.m. on 26 March 1949.

King Michael was overjoyed and four days later Queen Helen noted, 'Nan looking so pretty again.'[30] Queen Anne left the clinic on 11 April. On the 15th Princess Margarita was baptised at home by the Greek Orthodox Archimandrite Valliadis. 'Very primitive', Queen Helen noted. 'So different to what it ought to have been . . . in their tiny house. God bless them. Oh dear my heart is heavy sometimes.'[31] But King Michael and Queen Anne were quite happy to be alone together in their little house with their new baby, whom they called 'Bunny'.

# THIRTEEN

## *Searching for an Identity, Working for Romania, Making a Living*

At the beginning [Queen Anne wrote later] we failed to establish ourselves definitely anywhere. We were looking for ourselves, we were looking for a place, an identity and the obvious place was closed to us. It took the King about ten years to find himself again. Even when he had adopted a certain well-structured attitude towards exile he did everything he could to be alongside the country, with the country, for the country. During the first three years everything was confused, harrowing, difficult to bear. Our first three daughters grew up with a kind, just, loving father who was also a very silent, serious and sad one.[1]

He kept up to date with Romanian affairs through General Lazăr – a soldier and an academic. On matters of policy his advice to the King was invariably sound. Sometimes he seemed absurdly independent – once even refusing the present of a hot water bottle from Queen Anne.[2] He was often abrupt and tactless, not popular with either the Romanian exile community or the US administration. But he was a conscientious, thoroughly honest man and devoted to the King.

The fact that the Czechs formed a National Committee put pressure on General Rădescu to accept the King's Committee of ten members representing both the three democratic parties suppressed in 1947 and non-party émigrés. The Committee met for the first time on 3 May 1949 and had as representatives of the democratic parties Niculescu Buzeşti and two other members of the National Peasant Party, one Liberal, Mihail Fărcăşanu and one Social Democrat, Iancu Zissu. The non-party men were Rădescu (in the chair) Vişoianu and Cretzianu plus Caranfil, an engineer and founder of a very succssful refugee organisation, and Gafencu, Romania's last pro-Allied Foreign Minister before it was overtaken by the Second World War.

On Independence Day, 10 May, the King announced the formation of the Romanian Committee, 'which will devote all its efforts to the struggle for the liberation of the country'.[3] The State Department were pleased to have, as they thought, a body with which they could now do business.

King Michael and Queen Anne with their baby spent the summer of 1949 at her mother's house in Copenhagen. They mowed the lawn and weeded the rock garden. Most of the day Michael read books ranging from engineering, flying and politics to Perry Mason thrillers. His wife's family and their friends arranged duck shooting or deer stalking for him. Sometimes Anne and he rented a boat with an outboard motor, sometimes they went to see Danish castles, once to the Tivoli and they were in and out of relatives' houses all the time. He particularly liked Anne's uncle, Prince Axel, who lived two houses away. Virtually a professional deep-sea fisherman, in July he took them to his place on a Norwegian fjord where they could experience the real north.

Yet for all their kindness he had no peace of mind. He remained a stranger among strangers. He felt uprooted. Sometimes when he went out to a dinner he would suddenly find that he could not breathe but that, said the doctor, was a normal physical reaction after many years of great tension.

In October 1949, the King and his family returned to the Villa Sparta. Since his aunt, Princess Irene, was already staying there with her boy Amadeo, they lived in the guest house. He had the use of the main drawing room and library during working hours.

During the summer of 1949 it had become clear that the Romanian National Committee in Washington was not operating. Relations between the Buzeşti and Rădescu factions worsened. Without consulting the Committee the autocratic General Rădescu had suggested to the American CIA that Romanian Resistance fighters be brought out for specialist training and later even took it upon himself to offer Romanian recruits for the US army. These were delicate matters which should have been discussed in committee and with the King. Although the death from leukaemia of Niculescu Buzeşti on 4 October slightly eased the situation, not once had the Committee met as an entity, and in November it had demonstrated its incompetence publicly.

On the 16th of the month in the UN Political First Committee, Ambassador Warren Austin, the US representative, accused Vyshinsky of having in March 1945 forced King Michael to make Groza prime minister of Romania by threatening military intervention. Vyshinsky challenged Austin to produce witnesses to substantiate this 'fairy tale'. For nine days no member of the Committee – nor therefore the King – was aware of this exchange. On the 25th General Rădescu, without referring to the Committee, informed the UN Secretary General that he was ready to testify. Without the King's knowledge he also told the press that he would invite King Michael to give evidence. When finally Vişoianu heard what was happening and sent a telegram to Warren Austin offering his services, as the Foreign Minister who had attended all Vyshinsky's meetings with the King, replied that this was no longer possible since the dossier had been closed and the work of the First Committee had moved into plenary session.[4]

King Michael's patience was running low. He informed Rădescu of his deep regret that a matter of such national interest had not been discussed in the Committee and suggested that correspondence to and from the Committee should in future be handled by the Secretariat and despatched under two signatures, one of which should be that of Cretzianu, the Secretary General.[5] On New Year's Eve, when he made his first BBC broadcast to Romania, the King did not mention the National Committee.

In the new year of 1950 Princess Irene was able to move into her own villa and Michael and his family moved out of the guest house to the Villa Sparta proper. However, they still seemed unable to settle down and Vergotti* was still concerned about the cost of so much travelling. In January 1950, they went for three weeks to stay with Queen Anne's mother in Villefranche. They were back in Florence for Princess Irene's birthday on 13 February and then visited King Paul and Queen Frederika in Athens. On 10 March they returned to Sparta and by the end of the month were in Lausanne to see Dr Rochat again. They had lost La Petite Grangette and now rented a house next door to Queen Ena of Spain, not far from the clinic.

Michael and his wife spent September in Denmark and Sweden but were back in Lausanne by mid-October. Their second child was born at 6.30 a.m. on 15 November 1950, a baby girl who would be christened Elena. Their enlarged family arrived at Sparta on Christmas Eve, Michael by car, Anne, Margarita, the baby and her nanny by train. The weather was so bad that King Michael barely made it in time for the Christmas tree ceremony.

By now news of the National Committee had improved. On 14 September 1950 Rădescu, Gafencu, Caranfil and Fărcăşanu had left to set up their own Association of Free Romanians. King Michael had appointed Vişoianu chairman of a committee of only six members – Vişoianu, Cretzianu, three members of the National Peasant Party, and one Social Democrat. It was hardly representative of Romanian exiles but was at least a coherent and competent body with which the King could work.

---

* It was about now that Vergotti left for the States and was greatly missed by the royal family and his old friend Petre Lazăr.

In Romania the Government carried out its programme now undeterred by the King. In January 1948 industry, banking, insurance, mining and transport had been nationalised. At the elections on 28 March they organised a 92 per cent victory. By August instruction in Marxist-Leninism became compulsory, texts were rewritten, chunks of Romanian history disappeared altogether.

In January 1949, the Gendarmerie were replaced by a miliţia whose declared purpose was to protect the rights of working people. Two months later the state expropriated all agricultural property of over 50 hectares and villagers found themselves in pitched battles with this same miliţia.

After the Vyshinsky *coup* of 6 March 1945 the Siguranţa had begun to target Romania's political and social structure and the will and dignity of its citizens. Arrest for acts 'considered to be a danger to society' hung over everyone's head. 'Animated conversation gave way to furtive whispers or parables, suggestion replaced open discussion and the simplest of messages was wrapped in a code'.[6] In August 1948 this updated Siguranţa was replaced by the infamous Securitate under the Soviet agent Pantelium Bodnorenko (renamed Gheorghe Pintilie) with ten subordinate directorates each under a Russian. Judges would in future be assisted by party appointees known as People's Assessors, a step which King Michael had firmly resisted while he was in office. Also, private legal practice would now be forbidden.[7] As part of their re-education process, the Securitate experimented with a practice which is probably unique among Soviet satellites: when a political prisoner's morale had been completely broken after a period of torture, to save their lives he or she would willingly torture or execute another prisoner, sometimes their best friend.[8]

On the night of 25 October 1950, soon after they had returned to Lausanne, they found that their home had been broken into. Nothing – including Queen Anne's jewels – was taken. The King and the Swiss authorities presumed that the operation was carried out by Soviet or Romanian Intelligence agents looking for confidential papers. Although they left empty-handed, the operation was a reminder that in the unsettled Europe of 1950 King Michael was vulnerable and a prime target.

Many exiled Romanians felt that the continent of Europe was no place for their King and his family. Soviet pressure on Berlin, and through the powerful post-war communist parties of Europe, was still seen as a major threat and on 10 August 1950 the King's representative in London had left with the Foreign Office a memorandum underlining 'the absolute necessity that King Michael should be in England, the United States or North Africa at the moment a future war should break out'. However, King Michael's financial situation and his determination to remain free of political strings had also to be taken into account. While he could afford to live in Villa Sparta he could probably not have afforded to buy a suitable house in either England or America.

It was during the first half of 1951 that two unexpected events helped him to decide on a place where they could settle.

On Friday, 2 February two Romanians arrived from America – Mircea Ionniţiu, until recently the King's Private Secretary, and Rica Georgescu, an oil executive who had played a critical part in Maniu's wartime Resistance. They had brought a message from Frank Wisner, a senior member of the CIA who had served in Romania immediately after the war. To his envoys Wisner's message to the King seemed almost too good to be true. President Truman wished to offer King Michael an annual income of $60,000 and an estate of 300 acres with a house and servants. The invitation was extended to the King and his family and did not include General Lazăr. The CIA, Wisner explained, had been used as a go-between to make it easier for the King to turn down the offer if he so wished. It would at a stroke solve the King's financial and security problems, and the envoys were astounded when he did not accept it. They stayed on for eleven days but failed to change his mind.

Exclusion of Lazăr the King took as a personal slight, but this was by no means his reason for refusing. When told that he would fly to the States under a cover commonly used by the CIA, Michael rightly suspected that the initiative for this generous offer had been taken not by the White House but by the CIA. Strings would be attached. Should he accept, Romanians at home might well believe that he had sold his independence in exchange for a comfortable life. It was a risk he would not take.

The King did not know of Philby's activities on behalf of the Soviet Union, but he did know of the failed attempts, sometimes with total loss of life, to parachute freedom fighters into Albania, Yugoslavia and Romania. He would not lend the weight of his name and reputation to more of this slaughter.[9] In 1951 King Michael still hoped that a sustained and effective policy to remove Soviet occupation of his country would eventually replace these inconsequential operations and the rousing broadcasts from Radio Free Europe.

Vişoianu sought the advice of Burton Berry, now responsible for Asian affairs in the State Department but who still took a close interest in Romania. Speaking personally to Vişoianu, he emphasised 'the enormous capital Romanians had in their king'. This should not be frittered away on minor political activities. Although the King and his family would always be welcome to visit the States, he should come to live there permanently only when he had a crucial political role to play, at which time he would be invaluable. Vişoianu reported this conversation to Lazăr in a letter of 16 February 1951, and on 22 February Lazăr sent Vişoianu the following carefully drafted letter setting out the King's final position on this sensitive matter. The King:

1. Does not wish to come to the USA in order to perform any special and public activity, but he could ask for shelter and protection in the USA, it being understood that he would respect punctiliously all the rules of hospitality.
2. Will continue to serve the national interest through the Romanian National Committee – set up in accordance with the Romanian constitution – giving his full support to the committee whose activities will continue to develop so far as possible along the lines of US policy.
3. Will continue to accept no material help from anyone, not even the Romanian National Committee,* and will in future as in the past be careful to live as modestly as possible.[10]

In a separate personal note to Vişoianu Lazăr added that the offer of a house for the King was attractive but it did not seem wise for him to act as an agent for an 'underground liberation force'. He therefore postponed his next visit to the USA *sine die*.

The second event in 1951 that would influence King Michael's future was the visit in April of Prince Philip and Princess Elizabeth to Italy, which included a call on Queen Helen. At one point during their stay they suggested that their cousins might like to live in England. They liked the idea and Queen Helen, who knew that they would never really settle down at Villa Sparta, urged them to accept. It was time, she said, for them to strike out together.

By 14 May that year, 1951, they were in London staying with Queen Helen's old friend Madame Devaux (also known as Miss Thun or Mistun) house-hunting for something suitable in the country. It was finally Lord Brocket, a businessman and active member of the Upper House, who offered to rent them a furnished wing in one of his country houses – Bramshill Hall at Hartley Wintney near Reading.

In the autumn of 1948 King Michael had had the idea of establishing in Paris a cultural centre of university status which would ensure that young Romanians brought up under Gheorghiu-Dej would return to their country with an unshakeable belief in democratic government. It became one of the

---

* When, in the new year of 1952, the Committee sent King Michael food parcels, he thanked them but insisted on paying.

Committee's most successful enterprises until decade after decade of Communist rule in Romania and lack of Western interest in a democratic Romania made the object of the exercise irrelevant.

The King opened the Foundation on 11 June 1951 and then drove with Queen Anne to Florence to pack up their belongings. The children and their new nanny stayed behind with Queen Helen but on 21 June King Michael, Queen Anne and General Petre-Lazăr set off for England in two cars loaded with luggage. General Lazăr moved into the small Shellbourne Hotel in Kensington, from where he was to devote the rest of his life to King Michael's work with the Romanian Committee.

Bramshill Hall, Queen Anne says, was built of old heavy red brick, the colour of oak. Princess Margarita once described their new home as 'a huge wing of a haunted house' and Queen Anne has since described their psychic experiences while living there.[11] The King and Queen had a workshop where they made furniture. Once a week he went to London to see Lazăr and deal with the National Committee's affairs and the large number of individual letters he received. His only distraction apart from reading and music seems to have been shooting rabbits.

When they had settled in, Margarita and Helen joined them. Queen Helen came for Christmas and noted in her diary:

Very quiet here. One is in the back of beyond. Hears nothing, sees nobody, no radio and only a daily paper. Chr. tree. George Denmark* & wife. very nice. Nan arranged it all very well. . . . They are very kind. We all went to church which I loved.[12]

The affection that King Michael and Queen Anne had always felt for the British royal family was clearly a reason for their decision to settle in England. When Queen Anne was a little girl in St Cloud, she and Prince Philip had often played together. 'A terror he was,' she says, 'climbing on the roofs and all that.'[13] King George VI had been a good friend to King Michael ever since he put in a word for him with King Carol when Michael was still in his teens. Subsequently, King George had given him advice which, King Michael told Sir John Wheeler-Bennett, 'I have always tried to follow both as a King and a man.'[14] He had happy memories of visits to Buckingham Palace and his mother never failed to have at least one meal with her cousins whenever she visited

---

* Prince George of Denmark, son of Queen Anne's uncle Prince Axel of Denmark. His wife was Lady Anne Bowes-Lyon, a cousin of Queen Elizabeth.

London. When, therefore, King George died on 6 February 1952 the news came as a great personal blow.

The young Queen Elizabeth was to show Michael and his family the same kindness as had her father. They were quite often invited to Sandringham and Balmoral. Queen Anne remembers in particular the day when the Queen lent her her own gun and ghillie. Sometimes they took Margarita and Helen with them and the Queen's children – Charles and Anne – would also come to Bramshill for the day and play with their daughters, who were about the same age.

King Michael enjoyed shooting at Balmoral and Sandringham but there, too, he would meet people who seemed to have no interest in what was happening in the other half of Europe. One day, after a talk about Romania, a guest said to him something like: 'Well, I quite see why you should want your throne back. But you have to think of the people too; since they have chosen communism you should accept their wishes . . .'[15] In spite of what King Michael had told him, this man felt more comfortable with the thought that under Communist rule Romanians had still been given a choice.

When, in July 1952, Lord Brocket decided to sell Bramshill Hall, he leased them Ayot House in the village of Ayot St Lawrence, an unfurnished square house with a two-columned porch. 'Looks awful', Queen Helen wrote in her diary, 'will take year to arrange, completely empty.'[16] She gave her son £1,000, which she could ill afford, for furniture and linen.

The large kitchen garden and Mr Hobbs the gardener probably interested Michael and his wife more than the house itself. They were soon selling vegetables and flowers – particularly their roses and chrysanthemums – to neighbours and, as their production increased, to local markets and flower shops.

Encouraged by friends, they later attempted a poultry farm. Lord Brocket agreed to their using the barns and the disused tennis court so long as they eventually left the property as they had found it. They bought wire netting second hand, built hen houses partly from disused railway sleepers, and farmers let them collect unwanted bales of hay. As a child Queen Anne had had some experience of her mother's chickens, and it was Princess Margarethe who started them off with six chickens for their new enterprise. They ended up with 800.[17]

At first they sold their eggs and cockerels locally; later the Egg Board collected the eggs twice a week. They had geese, too. They did almost everything themselves – preparing the feed, collecting, cleaning and packing the eggs, checking in the middle of a stormy night that the hens were all right. For the first time since going into exile they were paying their way. And for a time they were happy there.

With hens, chicks, ducks, the dogs, bales of straw to build houses with and wild flowers everywhere, the children loved it. Their favourite toy was a fluffy squirrel and Margarita's favourite stories were from Beatrix Potter. When she had time Queen Anne made jig-saw puzzles for them.

Princess Margarita remembers going into the village to feed the birds on the lawn of what had been Bernard Shaw's house where he had died two years before.

'That was nice working together', the King said. 'There was even a small aero club there. I used to fly once in a while. We were near de Havilland and could hear the Comet engines being tested.'[18]

King Michael went weekly to see General Lazăr in his London hotel. The National Committee was running more smoothly under Vişoianu and the image of a fragmented exile community was beginning to fade.

In Romania Gheorghiu-Dej was suppressing potential rivals. Pătrăşcanu, a possible Titoist, was executed in 1952 – an act that estranged many left-wing Romanian intellectuals. The death sentence on Lazlo Luca was commuted to life imprisonment, but he died soon afterwards. Ana Pauker, a friend of Stalin and Molotov, was removed from power but never brought to trial. By the end of 1952 Gheorghiu-Dej had become Prime Minister and First Secretary of the Party, so controlling both the administrative and policy-making sides of government – in a position to impose Stalinism on the country without fear of effective opposition.

Her father, Princess Margarita says, seemed always to be worried about what was happening to Romania, but Ayot House

> was, I think, a therapeutic time – close to nature, dealing with animals. And he was happy with her. They had a very strong marriage, you know. She put a lot of joie de vivre into it.
>
> One day my mother sat me down, when I was about 4, and said to me 'look Papa's had a sad life and when you won't speak to him and run away he gets more sad.' So then I went and picked a bunch of flowers and gave it to him.[19]

To have her third child, Queen Anne went again to Dr Rochat's Lausanne clinic where Princess Irina was born on 28 February 1953. Having no house in

Lausanne, they stayed at the Beau Rivage Hotel. It was there, on the night of 3 April 1953, that Michael received a telephone call from King Carol's ADC to say that his father had died of a heart attack and to ask whether the King would be attending the funeral.

Although he knew his absence would be criticised, he did not go. His mother would have been hurt if he had and he had no wish to face Madame Lupescu and Urdăreanu again. He had not seen his father since 1940. The break had been clean; he had grown used to it.[20]

It soon became clear that King Carol's will, together with all his business correspondence, had disappeared. That King Carol should not have made a will seemed inconceivable, and the value of the money he had transferred abroad and of the pictures and stamp collection he had taken with him when he abdicated in 1940 was enormous. King Michael brought a case against Madame Lupescu and Monsieur Urdăreanu in the Portuguese courts but, although General Lazăr and his lawyers spent almost ten years trying to trace what was left of the fortune, without King Carol's papers this proved impossible. The couple who had dominated King Carol for two decades won the case.

The National Committee, the King once remarked, could never have fulfilled Romanian expectations, yet what it was able to do on its limited resources was in many ways outstanding. For instance, committee members reported regularly anything they had learned about conditions in Romania from newly arrived refugees and in 1950 they produced a brochure of 163 pages, *The Suppression of Romanian Human Rights*, which caused quite a stir. It was read in the UN and Western Foreign Ministries, by members of the US Senate and Congress and referred to in the *New York Times*.[21]

In 1952 Caranfil and Zissu had written a Committee paper on the massive deportations taking place in early 1950, when thousands of Romanians were sent to slave labour camps for work on such projects as the Danube–Black Sea canal. There were believed to be some 180,000 in these camps.[22] After the 1989 revolution, Corneliu Coposu put the total number of those arrested after 1947 at roughly 282,000, of which some 190,000 died in detention.[23] In May 1952 a Romanian delegation made up of members of the National Committee and others briefed President Truman on the size and nature of the canal operation and his subsequent public condemnation infuriated – even if it did not deter – the Romanian authorities. A criminal, the King commented, hates to be shown up so that the whole world and not just his victim knows what he is.[24]

Yet King Michael knew how dependent East European exiles were on their host governments. Any interest the Americans or British showed in the plight of their country raised their hopes unrealistically. Reticence had the opposite effect, and both were amplified. 'Without roots abroad,' the King said, 'we were as it were fighting the wind but if you took root you were no longer of your country.'[25]

Eisenhower undertook to denounce every agreement with the USSR that had failed to define such critical words as 'democracy'. Hopes were raised and National Committees held their breath, waiting for Congress to ratify the President's undertaking. But in March 1953 Congress ducked the issue, refused to describe as 'unsound' agreements signed by Western governments with the USSR, which, following the adept use by Moscow of communist semantics, had forced millions of East Europeans into a communist straitjacket. For a National Committee working with the Western democracies to return to democratic government was, the King once remarked, like riding on a rollercoaster. One was not even sure that the President had not made his proposal knowing that it would be rejected by Congress.

There followed a series of national and personal disappointments which by the summer of 1955 had left the King in a state bordering on despair.

In the Autumn of 1950 Vișoianu and other East European exiled statesmen had proposed that the Americans set up a commission to inquire into the Central and Eastern European activities of the Soviet Union. Four years later – tragically late, in the King's opinion – a congressional committee began to take evidence. The King was invited to meet them on the morning of 15 June 1954 in London, and his characteristically frank and informed answers to their questions seem to have made a good impression. When asked what the Romanian people wanted of the Western Powers, he replied that while his contacts were indirect and not necessarily up to date he could say that Romanians wanted to hear no more empty words. They wanted the West to liberate them. They wanted to become free people again, decent human beings. When asked if the King could see a solution other than war he replied, 'I'm afraid not.' When asked whether he was convinced that Romanians would shake off the communist yoke should a war make this possible, he replied 'Yes.' The Russians, he added, had already benefited greatly from the Western policy of appeasement.[26] When it became clear that nothing would come of the congressional inquiry he remarked: 'After a war it is usual for the victor's interests to take precedence over the reestablishment of the truth.'[27]

At the end of 1954 the Americans set up the Assembly of Captive Nations in New York, which weakened the ethnic character of national committees. The

Romanians moved their committee from Washington to New York where most of its members then took an additional job either with the new Assembly or with the Free Europe Committee, both of which could afford to pay salaries.

In June 1954 Ioana Lambrino's son, Mircea had claimed in the Portuguese courts to be the legitimate child of the late King Carol II by his first marriage. Although he had been born more than a year after this marriage had been dissolved by a Romanian court, King Michael must have known by mid-January 1955 that under the liberal Portuguese interpretation of legitimacy he would lose the case. He did, and in May Lambrino claimed in the Paris courts that, as the legitimate eldest son of King Carol, he should inherit his father's property in France. The French courts too were to find in favour of Lambrino.[28]

The King says that during the year 1954 and most of 1955 something happened to him. He became sullen – which was quite unlike him. He lost a little each day of the happiness of being alive.

> It was as if I would never see the end of my troubles. Though many people think that not to be allowed back into your country is easier to bear than not to be allowed out of it, this is not true. The feeling of powerlessness and loss of liberty is associated with both. What made my suffering almost insupportable was the fact that whatever I said about Romania was greeted with total disinterest.

Even if people realised that his concern was all for his country rather than himself, that the Romanian Government was from every point of view illegal, they wanted to be left in peace: 'It is natural to recoil from unpleasant thoughts or contacts.'[29] The King's prolonged, acute concern for his country appeared to verge on the unnatural. People who cared not a damn for Romania must have found him a bore. As the years went by his disillusionment was driven more and more into himself. In a letter to his mother during the winter of 1954, he blames the English weather and the damp cold house with furnaces they could not afford to switch on.[30] But his tension went far deeper than that.

His faith, which is less to do with ritual than a way of life, certainly strengthened him, and provided, as he puts it, a shield against his trouble. It has given him the ability to meditate as well as to pray. It protects him from any idea of racialism, or contempt of others, or the law of the strongest. It gives him the power to contain his problems, to ward off cynicism, to make him a gentle and naturally fair person. But it cannot prevent his sadness or his withdrawal.

During the third weekend of January 1955 Queen Anne had to cope with three nannyless children, a very depressed husband, her mother-in-law and, on the Sunday, photographers who had come to take pictures of the children. Princess Margarita tells how for the photographers King Michael had to get down on his hands and knees, 'and we sat on his back. And that was quite fun because he'd never done that before.'

2 photographers [Queen Helen noted in her diary] came and spent all morning taking babies, even at lunch. Terribly foggy and dark, such a pity sweetie couldn't be happy in this country I love so much. . . . if only I could help them, poor darlings.[31]

In July 1954 King Paul and Queen Frederika invited them with over a hundred other members of the royal families of Europe to make a tour of the Greek Islands. It was possibly this glimpse of other lives and people they might otherwise never have met helped them decide to give up the chicken farm and tour Europe looking for permanent and more congenial work. It turned out to be another disheartening business. When they found themselves all together in Switzerland in August 1955, Queen Helen, who knew that her offers of advice were not always welcome, invited a rather sceptical daughter-in-law to have lunch with her at Caux, where the Moral Re-armament movement* had its centre. She knew that they would meet people there who would at least understand the human side of Romania's problem and genuinely share their concern for what was happening. Queen Helen had kept in touch with the MRA's founder, the American Frank Buchman, ever since his therapeutic visit to Queen Marie and her family during the constitutional crisis in 1925 when Prince Carol had eloped with Madame Lupescu. Over the years Michael had, therefore, met 'Uncle Frank' several times.

At lunch at the big table Queen Helen and Queen Anne found themselves next to the American comedian Olson who, when he heard that Queen Anne's husband was a keen pilot, said that he must meet his son-in-law William Lear, the aviation man who would be in Florence in September. So while they were staying with Queen Helen that autumn, King Michael had lunch with Lear, who invited him to fly his plane. The King noted later:

After a few hours of talking and flying he revealed that he was soon going to set up 'a small operation' as Americans say at the Geneva airport, a little

---

* An influential evangelical movement founded by the American Frank Buchman.

European Lear firm with a kind of 'station service' as we call it for fitting and repairing aeroplane instruments. He asked me if I would like to work with him and I replied 'Sure'.[32]

The mood at Sparta changed overnight. Everything seemed to fall into place. Queen Anne returned in good spirits from seeing her mother in Paris, and two days later even found a wrist watch that Marina, Duchess of Kent, had lost in the woods near Pratalino.* A wonderful new nanny arrived after a very bleak period on that front.

The King's happiness was marred when on 12 October a message from Vişoianu informed him that in an interview with the *New York Times* Tătărescu had made public the death in prison of the heads of the National Peasant and National Liberal parties – Juliu Maniu in 1952, Dinu Brătianu in 1950. The King was outraged that Tătărescu – a man despised by these two great leaders of the historical parties – should have been detailed to make the announcement so casually. In a message broadcast to Romania by the BBC and Radio Free Europe, the King paid his respects to two men who 'had lived and died for the Liberty, Unity and Prosperity of the Romanian people and for Romania's Independence'.[33]

That autumn they gave notice to Lord Brocket, sold the chickens and performed the daunting task of restoring the barns and tennis court to their original state. Young MRA friends rallied round and helped them. The furniture they had bought for Ayot House they despatched to Geneva and some is in their Versoix house today.

They explained the situation to Queen Elizabeth who had offered them a grace and favour house. Had it not been for the Lear job which Michael, feeling that it could be the beginning of a real career, could not turn down, they would perhaps have lived permanently in Hampton Court and their life, as Queen Anne later commented, would have been very different.

They all spent Christmas at the Villa Sparta but on 2 January 1956 King Michael and his wife drove to Versoix, leaving the children with their grandmother. Michael was already on the Lear payroll. Lear, who was then about 60, had done considerable innovative work on the electronic side of flying – improved radio communication and automatic piloting – and had developed the instrumentation for blind flying. Michael was to make demonstration and test flights to check that the instruments they had fitted into a client's aircraft were working properly. He would also deliver planes all over

---

* The home of Prince Paul of Yugoslavia and his wife Olga, a sister of the Duchess of Kent.

Europe. First, however, Lear wanted him to take a four-month course in advanced piloting at his establishment in Santa Monica.

Michael left for the States on 13 May and a week later Anne picked up the children from Villa Sparta and took them to their new home. 'Fantasia', by the lake in Versoix, was not particularly handsome, with small rooms invaded by lake damp, but it had three bathrooms, which was rare, and it was not expensive. The children cycled on a path running down to the lake, played football with their neighbour's children and sometimes went out in their neighbour's rowing boat. While Michael was away Queen Anne worked on the house and it was much cosier when he returned. They were to live there for twenty-one years.

In Santa Monica King Michael enjoyed the advanced flying course and was able to take a few days off to visit the Romanian Committee. He returned to Switzerland on 6 October 1956 with the US licence of a professional pilot. Two weeks later he was made a director of the Geneva enterprise. Lear was very correct, expecting a lot from his colleagues but never beyond their capacity. He and King Michael got on well. His son, William Lear, junior, who worked in the Geneva office and was more flexible than his father, was in charge of administration. King Michael was responsible for the flying side of the operation.

Every weekday morning Queen Anne and her husband left the house at 7.30, he to drive to his work near the airport, she to get the children to school before 8 o'clock. At first she picked them up at 12.30, gave them lunch and took them back for the afternoon lessons. 'An endurance test', she said. 'You could never be late.' Later they had lunch at school and she had more time to do other things. They spoke French at school, English at home and always had an English nanny.[34] That was the age for them to have learnt Romanian too. Yet it would have been unnatural for their father to chat to them in a language no one else in the house understood, and Romania meant so little to his daughters at the time that they might have put up considerable resistance. As it was, Princess Margarita learned to speak Romanian fluently when it became necessary.

When Michael arrived at Lear's in the morning he first looked into the offices to see whether a client was expected that day, then went to the workshops where the mechanics and electricians worked and the hangar where the equipment was mounted. Normally, he made one or two test flights a day to check the new instrumentation. Often he got home not much before midnight. He had only one near accident when a tyre burst on landing and he just managed to avoid the night beacons, which could have damaged the plane quite badly. Once, when flying the president of the Lear organisation to Bremen, they ran into bad weather and had to land through the lowest bank of cloud he had ever experienced. With only 60 metres of altitude they had emerged from the cloud with the runway just ahead of them. He was a first-rate pilot and engineer, a naturally modest man, knew his job, and got on well with his colleagues. The Swiss called him Monsieur Michel, the Americans King Michael. Lear agreed to his having time off to deal with the problems arising out of the National Committee's work.

It was the ideal job for the King. He could not know that within two years Lear would have sold all the advanced aircraft instrumentation the European market could absorb. He was desperately afraid of being without paid work.

In July 1957, Queen Helen and Madame Catargi spent a day in Geneva on their way to London. Queen Anne was in Villefranche. On the 19th Michael dropped them off at the airport and went to his office for a meeting with the manager of Lear's US works. When he rejoined them in the VIP lounge he told them that in September the Geneva branch would close. 'It was a great shock to me', Queen Helen wrote, 'and am afraid to Sweety too but he didn't show it. I hated leaving him but luckily Nan returns tomorrow.'[35]

After the demise of the Lear enterprise King Michael with two Swiss colleagues planned to invest in a factory making electronic equipment for industrial use and, in particular, automation – the black boxes that work barriers at railway crossings and toll stations. This was still innovative and the Swiss, who did not seem to appreciate its potential commercial value, did not help. Michael spent the whole of 1958 searching elsewhere for finance.

Queen Helen could no longer help. By the summer of 1956 her Swiss account was empty and she had not much left in England. Her lawyer, and a business friend, were pressing her hard to sell the villa, and to move into a small house in the grounds.

Since there was no piano in Villa Fantasia King Michael collected records – mainly of classical music – which later he put on tape. The King's messages to Romania broadcast by Radio Free Europe were all taped at home by Queen Anne on the heavy equipment of the time. Their hobbies were photography and home-made films. They supported each other, gave each other confidence in the future, which was sometimes difficult to do. The children heard them talking into the night and knew it was about their money problems. King Paul had taken to sending his private plane for them when they went on holiday to Tatoi. Since the Swiss could not agree to their children born in Switzerland taking the title of Prince or Princess of Romania, Queen Frederika suggested to Queen

Anne that she have her next child in Greece. So Dr Louros, whose father had helped bring Michael into the world, officiated on 29 October 1957 when Queen Anne's baby was born in Tatoi, to be christened Sophie. They must have been worried by then because under the Salic clause of the Romanian constitution none of their children to date, being girls, could succeed their father.

On 14 January 1958 King Michael finally lunched in Geneva with a businessman who agreed to finance his project. Again the possibility of a worthwhile career was in sight.

They now felt able to send Margarita to boarding school in England which, once she had got over her home-sickness, she enjoyed. If Queen Helen were in London when she broke up for her summer holiday she would stay with her for a few days visiting the zoo, Marks and Spencer and Agatha Christie's *The Mousetrap*. Once when her grandmother was staying with her cousin she was invited to lunch at Windsor Castle and a palace car deposited her back at school on the dot of 6.30.

Easter 1960 was particularly exciting for the children. *The Guns of Navarone*, with Gregory Peck, Anthony Quayle, Anthony Quinn and David Niven, was being shot not far from Tatoi. For King Michael, however, their holidays were for a time clouded by a tension that had built up between his mother and Queen Frederika. Queen Helen was not the only member of the family who found her sister-in-law too outspoken and, being such a good administrator, somewhat bossy. For her part, Queen Frederika thought Queen Helen dated and too possessive of her brother Paul. For a time Queen Helen even stopped going to Tatoi and was touched when Michael and Anne came to stay with her for a few days on their way there.

In May 1962 King Michael and Queen Anne attended the wedding of Princess Sophie of Greece and Prince Juan Carlos of Spain who, unlike them, could be married with double ceremonies at the Catholic and Orthodox cathedrals in Athens. Through Queen Helen they met and later became good friends with Prince Rainier and Princess Grace of Monaco, and it was they who advised them to approach Pope John XXIII for permission to remarry in a Catholic church.

That summer Queen Anne lost her father. She was his only daughter and very close to him.

Prince René was born in Austria in 1894. During the First World War he had worked with his brother Xavier in the Red Cross. When the Soviet Union invaded Finland in November 1939 he became a volunteer in the Finnish army. Later he joined the Free French forces and occasionally Queen Anne had run into him during the war in Europe.

Like the rest of the family, Prince René lived mostly between France and the Scandinavian countries but, unlike them, he would never, one feels, have been entirely at home outside the culture of his birth in Central Europe. In July 1962 Queen Anne had an operation for appendicitis at the Hallerup Hospital on the outskirts of Copenhagen and was recovering in Versoix when she heard and rushed back to the same hospital to spend his last few days with her father.

By now it was again becoming urgent for King Michael to find another source of income. His firm, Metravel S.A., was doing well but could not pay him enough to meet his rising school fees and maintain the invaluable General Lazăr in London. Also it was becoming clear that the huge German and Japanese electronic industries would eventually swamp his little enterprise.

Their finances had become so desperate by March 1963 that they felt obliged to decline an invitation to the Jubilee celebration of the centenary of the Greek dynasty. 'All most upsetting, confusing', Queen Helen commented on her son's absence.[36]

Queen Frederika decided to seek advice on Michael's behalf of two of the great Greek shipping magnates who, after much prodding, proposed that Michael became a broker on the New York Stock Exchange. They would then give him their brokerage business on Wall Street.

Brokerage, however, was not King Michael's thing. The financial world did not interest him. He had loved his work with Lear and had tried hard to find another job in the world of flying or engineering; he had spent all the previous July looking for something in England. To become a broker would only be justified if it solved his money problems and still left him with time to fulfil his duties as King. This would depend on the good will of a group of hard-headed ship owners whom he hardly knew. Not surprisingly, he took time to decide. Queen Helen notes in her diary a 'violent discussion' she had with him on New Year's Eve:

> Obstinate as a mule and for such idiotic trivial things. Am very unhappy about it. What is their situation going to be in a short time and now this new burden if one can call it that.[37]

At the end of 1963 Princess Margarita was taken away from her boarding school and went for the next five years to the Maria Thérèse day school in Versoix where she missed being treated 'almost like an adult'.[38]

The year 1964 was a terrible one for them all, for the Greek and Danish as well as the Romanian family.

When Queen Helen flew into Athens on 14 January, for the first time ever King Paul, supposedly suffering from a bad attack of sciatica, failed to meet her. On the 22nd he was taken to hospital, Helen and his eldest son, Constantine, driving behind the ambulance. A crushed disk was diagnosed. When he complained of pain in his stomach, an X-ray showed nothing abnormal. Queen Frederica, who was in Washington to receive an honorary degree from Columbia University and had telephoned every day, returned two days earlier than planned. She pressed Queen Helen to stay on. Finally, on 21 February King Paul had the operation which confirmed cancer. King Paul of Greece died on 6 March and was buried on the 12th. A shattered Queen Helen left Athens on the 13th. She had lost a brother she loved greatly and Michael perhaps the best friend he would ever have.

On 8 July another close friend, Prince Axel of Denmark, died. Queen Anne was to suffer a more unexpected, more shocking loss than that of her father or uncle. Her eldest brother Jacques was killed by a truck driving in the wrong direction down a Danish motorway on 6 November of that same dreadful year, 1964.

In May 1964 King Michael joined the Droulia stockbrokers' company in New York and began a three-month crash course. In his classes he was known as Mr Michael King. He worked extremely hard and could not return to Copenhagen for the baptism of his youngest daughter Maria. In August he passed his exam with a grade A mark. He became broker no. 16 and in future if anyone bought shares on the New York Stock Exchange through the Droulia company, care of no. 16, the commission would go automatically to him.

Unfortunately the shipping magnates did not keep their word. For the Droulia company it was a severe blow; for Michael it was disastrous. He had too much National Committee work to spend his time chasing clients and had to agree with Droulia that he should take a commission only when he brought the firm a new client. 'I had two or three clients during the next eight years', he said, 'and the income from these commissions was quite good.'[39] It was not, however, anything like enough. In September 1964 Queen Helen wrote a rather desperate letter about her son's financial situation to the sympathetic General Schyler, but there was nothing he could do to help.[40] Despite the difficulties, he stayed at Droulia for nine years, but when he eventually lost the last of his clients in 1973 Michael was too old, at 52, to start again the kind of work he liked best.

They were saved by their friends the Marinescus. Milica Marinescu was an engineer and pilot, a man after Michael's heart, representing Olkon of New York and Buhrle and Co. of Switzerland. They were very well off and out of a genuine friendship for the King and Queen they contributed to the education of their five daughters and helped with General Lazăr's expenses. Petru Lazăr lived modestly and Jacques Vergotti recalls a depressing but pleasant evening spent with him and Marinescu in the General's small hotel room. This was in 1978 and since the Ceauşescus were staying less than a mile away at Buckingham Palace they avoided politics and talked instead about the Romanian poet, Eminescu, and his work.

Gheorghiu-Dej's commitment to Stalinism was unshaken by the dictator's death in March 1953 and Khrushchev's subsequent criticism of his policies. Thanks to its oil, Romania was the only satellite to have hard currency, and this, together with the withdrawal of Soviet troops in 1958, eleven years after ratification of the Peace Treaty, gave him the independence he needed to pursue his Stalinist policies in spite of Moscow's disapproval.

Gheorghiu-Dej died on 19 March 1965 and was replaced as First Secretary of the Romanian Communist Party by Nicolae Ceauşescu, a man also committed to his country's Stalinisation. He would always be a dull public speaker, rarely getting beyond a string of party clichés. Yet he prepared for committee meetings conscientiously and had risen steadily in the party hierarchy.

During his early days in power Ceauşescu distanced himself from Gheorghiu-Dej. He rehabilitated Communists executed in the 1940s and 1950s. He put a new emphasis on consumer goods, improved the supply of food, increased wages, gave more freedom to intellectuals and writers. In 1968 he was the only member of the Warsaw Pact to support Dubček and to condemn the invasion of Czechoslovakia. For a time he became a hero both in his own country and abroad. Later, Romanians realised that his so-called 'reforms' had been no more than a tactic to win him popularity before he reverted to a long-term agenda. While neighbouring countries were trying to remedy the defects of a command economy, he ploughed blindly on promoting heavy industry, undermining the agriculture that was Romania's greatest potential asset, building up a refinery capacity far in excess of Romania's oil production, and reducing his country to penury.

Yet in the West he was still seen as a kind of Dubček or Tito. In 1971 he visited North Korea, witnessed with his wife the absolute homage paid to Kim-il Sung and suffered what one Romanian ambassador later described as 'the rupture inside his head'.[41] In 1974 he became President and henceforth he maintained this position by oppression rather than the manipulation which before had served him so well and, with his wife Elena, ran for a decade and a half one of the most irrational and tyrannical *régime*s Europe has known.

By 1970 four of the princesses were at school either in England or Versoix and Princess Margarita was studying liberal sciences, sociology and international law as a freshman at Edinburgh University. The Marinescus were paying her fees. Her parents made her an allowance for food and essential extras like telephones, notebooks and newspapers and so on; she was anxious that they should not know that she had also written to Queen Helen, whose friend, Madame Boissevin, offered to help her buy the books she needed and to join one or two university societies.[42] Her parents had explained to all their daughters that they must have training for some kind of job. It was, they said, in the family tradition. King Carol I had been a specialist in forestry, King Ferdinand a botanist of repute, Queen Marie a successful writer. Their father was a good engineer. Margarita specialised in sociology and until 1989 worked with the United Nations and the Food and Agriculture Organization. Helen went to a school for hostesses, Irina to a secretarial college, Sophie studied graphics at the university until they could no longer afford the fees, and Maria, their youngest daughter, still only six, had a passion for children and later took a course in paediatrics.

# FOURTEEN

## *The Romanian Uprising of 1989*

In 1978, when President Carter invited him to Washington, Ceauşescu was no longer seen in Romania as the heroic figure of the 1960s; his opposition to the Soviet invasion of Czechoslovakia had not led to a more liberal Romania, and the machinery of terror set up in 1948 was still in place. However, Romanian disillusionment with Ceauşescu was not shared by Western governments, and, that same year, on the advice of her ministers, Queen Elizabeth agreed to a state visit by the Ceauşescus to Britain. They stayed at Buckingham Palace and he was awarded the Order of the Bath. It marked the peak of his career as the maverick of Eastern Europe. King Michael was later told that one reason for the invitation to London had been to boost the order books of the British aircraft industry. He also heard indirectly that his cousin had found the visit extremely distasteful and had made it clear to her advisers that there was no question of her paying a return visit to Bucharest.

The defection to the USA in 1978 of the exceptionally well-informed Securitate general, Ion Mihai Pacepa, not only enlightened Western governments about Romania's Intelligence activities, but also destroyed the Securitate's overseas network. When this was rebuilt its principal duty became the promotion of Ceauşescu's personality cult. And, as the megalomania grew, so did the harshness used against Romanians living in the West who had dared to criticise the dictator or his wife. Moreover, the revenge was quite often ordered by Ceauşescu personally. In July 1982 President Mitterand cancelled a visit to Bucharest when he was told by his Intelligence that the Romanian Securitate planned to murder two Romanian writers living in France.[1]

The children might not have as much pocket money as their school friends, but they were never short of their parents' love or the certainty that their mother and father loved and entirely trusted each other. They had the best education their parents could manage. Like the man in their parents' one-act play,* they were brought up to believe that real happiness lay in acceptance of the Christian way of life, so that it became as natural to them as having breakfast or riding their bicycles. What they sometimes missed was a little fun.

We never went out, Princess Margarita said, never, ever, ever, ever. Never went to a cinema, never went to a theatre, never went to a museum. My father was closed in. He was doing his own thing about Romania. He had a huge correspondence. He was trying his best, telling people about his country all over the world, keeping in touch with the Romanian community. But not anything frivolous ever. Which is, well you know, admirable but . . . a very good family life but every so often you want to go out.[2]

Yet theirs was a happy house. The parents would suddenly pile children, sandwiches and coffee into their two cars and drive non-stop, whatever the weather, to wherever they were going. They visited Queen Helen at least twice a year. Sitting in their kitchen watching her daughter-in-law and her granddaughters cooking 'good wholesome food'; Queen Helen noticed 'they have all become so pretty'.[3]

Michael and Anne tried to get away alone together at least once a year, sometimes to St Tropez, sometimes to shoot with their cousins in Luxemburg, but Lazăr always had their address and timetable in case anything urgent occurred on the Romanian front.

Princess Margarita had taken a year off in Florence before going to university. There she learned Italian, went with her grandmother to see Renaissance buildings and pictures, explored villages together, met Harold Acton and other interesting people, both Florentine and foreign, spent time with her cousin Amadeo and his wife Claude,[†] went to parties at the British Consul's flat and made her own friends.

Princess Margarita seems to have had closer relations with Queen Helen than with her maternal grandmother. In some ways Princess Margarethe of Denmark, with chickens in her sitting room and cherry trees on the balcony, could not have been less like King Michael's mother. Whereas Queen Helen took her grandchildren to museums, Princess Margarethe took them to the casino. Her mother's family, Princess Margarita once said, 'had always been a

---

[*] *The Choice*, presented at Caux on 30 July 1960 before an audience which included senators and parliamentarians from eight countries, German coal miners and President Adenauer's representative.

[†] Princess Claude, fifth daughter of the Comte de Paris. Her marriage to Amadeo, Duke of Aosta, was annulled in 1986.

bit anarchical, had never lived a court life as you might say'.[4] Yet Princess Margarethe had passed her life in one of the most secure and settled constitutional monarchies in the world. She was related to virtually every European royal family. But when the princesses were in their late teens and should have been seeing a lot of the sons and daughters of other royal families, Princess Margerethe was already in her seventies, still going on photographic safaris, but, at home, living very simply with relations and friends of her own generation.

Vişoianu, who had replaced Rădescu as chairman of the National Committee, not only had political vision; he had been ready to handle practical refugee problems. Under his chairmanship the Committee had worked effectively and on good terms with the King. In 1955 it had been expanded and Raoul Bossy and Mircea Ionniţiu were among its new members. But by the 1970s many Romanians in exile felt that it was time to follow the example of the Western Powers and consider collaborating with the Ceauşescu Government. Though the tougher ones stood fast, mistrust spread and the King remarked, 'When you destroy a man's faith in men, which is a kind of binding material or mortar for any society, I don't know how you go about putting the fragments together again.'[5] Although Romanian refugees poured into the West in even greater numbers, most of them had never heard of the present members of the National Committee, which was becoming dated and irrelevant. By 1972 it was down to four members. In 1974 Vişoianu resigned and a year later the funds that, for two decades, had kept the National Committee and King Michael's University Foundation in Paris going, dried up.

As it became clear that King Michael was the most senior person – certainly among Romanians – to resist the growing tendency to compromise with the Romanian dictatorship, the Securitate mounted a personal campaign against him. By the 1980s they were even circulating a rumour that the King had accepted an invitation from Ceauşescu to visit his country. Had it been true, it would have damaged the King irreparably. Even if such a visit had been kept secret – hardly the Securitate's objective – it would still, in King Michael's words, 'have condoned the insult to my person and the disparagement of the title I hold.'[6]

At the University of Edinburgh Princess Margarita became a good friend of Gordon Brown and through him discovered socialism. At home they had talked only about communism. She found that, just as you could be right-wing without being a Nazi, you could be left-wing without being a communist. It was a revelation that did not impress her father, who could not forget the betrayal in the 1940s by a substantial part of Titel Petrescu's socialists. So, in Princess Margarita's words, they had 'terrible arguments'.

> But the positive side was that, instead of just making black and white statements he would actually explain things, I could draw out of him what had happened to him, how it had happened, what the Communists did, what they stood for.[7]

King Michael and his eldest daughter trusted each other. If he understood why she wanted to explore socialism, she, too, understood the pain he had suffered from communism – not the kind of communism that West Europeans played with within a secure democratic framework, but the real thing with absolute power.

> His experience of the left wing is the most dreadful you can imagine. It was not normal. It's a miracle that he's not bitter, it's a miracle that he's not sick in spirit. It's extraordinary, his humanity.[8]

They lost some of their closest relations and friends in the 1970s. In 1972 King Frederick of Denmark died, followed in April 1974 by Michael's aunt, Princess Irene, after years of treatment for cancer of the throat. He had loved her ever since the days when, as a boy, he had been allowed to visit his exiled mother in Florence.

By the mid-1970s the family was also concerned about Queen Helen, now in her seventies, who was finding it hard to make ends meet. King Gustav of Sweden had, during the last five years of his life, become a close friend of Queen Helen. He was an archeologist of repute and they had a common interest in Italian buildings and pictures. They were both keen gardeners and would spend hours 'cleaning' his roses, or sitting on a bench talking and eating raspberries. He was one of the kindest and straightest people she had known. One evening, when King Gustav was spending a few days with her in Florence, she noted 'a touching conversation after dinner' and the following day, 'What a strange thing life is to think I should reach the age of 74 & a thing like this shld happen to me.'[9] But, although she had often longed for a good husband with whom she could share her problems and anxieties, she did not, if that was the meaning of her entry, wish to marry again.

In 1972 Sotheby's failed to sell a small Del Sarto painting for her, and by the beginning of 1973, having failed also to find a buyer for the villa, she mortgaged it. She now knew that her only way of surviving was to sell the two small El Grecos she had brought with her when they had gone to the London wedding. When she told King Gustav about the state of her finances he explained her position to a close friend, Baron de Geer, who, he thought, might be able to help. Largely, one feels, out of his friendship for the King, de Geer did all he could for Queen Helen long after King Gustav's death in September 1973. In 1976, with his help she finally sold her pictures.

Michael had taken little interest in the El Grecos; they were, he felt, his mother's concern. It was she, therefore, who had arranged for her old friend Vermehren – a fine-arts expert – to check their condition from time to time and, when they were transferred from Zurich to Berne in December 1966, had gone to Zurich to formally identify them before they were moved.

Although they were private property and Michael was certainly under no obligation to hand them over to Ceauşescu, in different circumstances he would probably have put up a much stiffer resistance to their sale out of the family. As it was, it allowed his mother to stay on in the Villa Sparta until she became too frail. In 1979 she moved into a flat in Lausanne where she lived rather unhappily without the independence that space and a very beautiful house of her creation had given her. Madame Catargi was still with her; she had friends in Lausanne and Michael and his family were only three-quarters of an hour's drive away. After a life of great courage, of devotion to her son, to wounded Romanian soldiers, to the thousands of Romanian Jews she had saved during the war, Queen Helen died towards the end of 1982, only two years after leaving Florence. At the close of his new year message King Michael spoke of a personal sadness, which many of his older listeners would share. 'My mind turns also to the memory of my beloved mother, who has been a priceless support at times of deep distress for the country and whom I had the pain of losing last month.'[10] Her funeral was conducted by the Metropolitan Damaskinos and she is buried in a simple grave in the cemetery at Lausanne.

For the last year she had lived at Versoix with her son and his family in their new home. It was her money, derived from the sale of the pictures in 1976, that enabled her son to pay off outstanding debts, and with help from Queen Anne's brother, Prince Michel, allowed them to make the down-payment on the house. Situated about a kilometre above the lake mists, it was a modern, well-built villa with a good-sized courtyard, a garden, a convenient arrangement of kitchen, pantry and dining room, and a handsome drawing room. It was altogether more spacious than their previous house and in 1980 Queen Anne's mother, who was 85 and too old, they felt, to be alone, came to live with them. The King had a small study off the entrance hall. There were garages and a workshop where he could put on overalls and relax. In the motoring world he is known less for being a king than for his skill with jeeps. He corresponded with and visited other jeep collectors in Switzerland, France, Italy, Australia and the USA and often, when the spare part he needed was not to be found, he made it at his bench.

For about seventeen years of his exile, until the West settled into a policy that accepted the *status quo* in Eastern Europe, King Michael could broadcast new year messages to his people via the BBC or Radio Free Europe. After that his voice was not heard in Romania for over a decade. He was, however, among the first people to recognise the early warnings of a possibly 'decisive' change in Eastern Europe, and in 1979 he sent Romanians a special message urging them to close ranks and prepare once more for the liberation of their country.[11]

By 1986 he was again broadcasting to his people and when asked during his first interview with Radio Free Europe whether, should the present *régime* collapse, he would return to the throne he replied, 'Yes, that is my duty, and if I did my duty in very difficult circumstances on 23 August 1944 when I was only 22 I shall not hesitate now that I am 64.'[12]

In July 1989, a team from the Hungarian *Panorama* programme interviewed the King in Versoix and, since this was his first opportunity to address Romanians in their own language on television, he tackled the question of monarchy head on. He compared Romania as it had been under a constitutional monarchy with Romania today,

> an absolute monarchy, in which every person belongs to the State. It has a dynasty which does not rule successively, one after the other, but all together, impoverishing the wealth of the country, trying to realise megalomaniacal projects and satisfying some wild goose chase. Indeed, would a constitutional monarchy be all that bad?[13]

Ceauşescu accused the Hungarian government of making 'a Fascist type attack on the independence and sovereignty of Romania', but the Hungarians replied coolly that 'the Hungarian media were free to report at their own discretion without state interference'[14] clearly reflecting the new Gorbachev reforms which Ceauşescu had never allowed to touch Romania.

At the annual meeting of the Warsaw Pact that same July, Gorbachev encouraged member governments to solve their national problems in their own way; there was no universal model of socialism. In other words, should they wish to reform their political or economic system, the Brezhnev doctrine would not be enforced – there would be no Soviet intervention. By late October large demonstrations in Eastern Germany were demanding the dismissal of the Communist *régime*. The Berlin Wall came down in November. On 10 December President Gustav Husak of Czechoslovakia resigned and was replaced by the playwright Resistance leader, Václav Havel.

Nothing like this was happening in Romania. Although King Michael had been one of the first to recognise the early signs of a weakening of the Communist hold on Eastern Europe, Romania was the last to act. Whereas Hungary and other neighbours had during the second half of 1989 freed themselves with the minimum loss of life, Romania got rid of Ceauşescu only after a bloody revolution towards the end of December. Just as Ceauşescu's treatment of his people had at last damaged his reputation in the West, his erratic policies and transparent obsession with personal and family interests isolated him from the USSR, neighbouring communist countries and ultimately from his own party. He had introduced economic and social measures which reduced his people – including the favoured workers who were at the core of his support – to abject misery. From 1982, he decreed, Romania would begin to pay off her foreign debts and by so doing would achieve true independence for the first time in her history. The scheme was mainly financed by the export of energy and food, affecting everyone, however poor. Domestic gas and electricity consumption was for seven years reduced to the point of impoverishment and most of the country's agricultural produce was sent straight into warehouses for export.

Ceauşescu used similarly brutal methods to increase the country's falling population. In a speech to the Great Britain–East European Centre on 7 February 1990 Dr (later Professor) Dennis Deletant pointed out that while health care was a major casualty of Ceauşescu's demonic drive for industrialisation and payment of foreign debts, under his anti-abortion legislation not only abortion but all methods of birth control were strictly forbidden. Married couples with fewer than four children were penalised. By the end of 1989 a quarter of the population were under the age of 14, many of them under 3. Parents living in one or two freezing rooms through the Romanian winter, without enough to eat, unable to find baby foods or medicines, their morale broken, saw children's homes as their only answer. Institutions which had been adequate in the 1940s were by 1989 damp, run-down old buildings, too long starved of funds for maintenance, or even laundries, blankets, food, medicine, syringes or specialised nurses. One could only admire the women who in such conditions were doing their exhausted best for the tiny jetsam of the Communist system.[15]

Before the December revolution, the King told Alan Hamilton of *The Times*:

> If the Romanians do not express themselves freely like their neighbours, it is because they cannot. They are exhausted, hungry and cold. The endless quest for food, the freezing winters with no heating, the physical and moral torture, all make the search for survival their only concern . . . The extent of police repression and terror goes far beyond that ever experienced in other countries, even in Eastern Germany. Dissidents have been eliminated.[16]

Another effective way of destroying the spirit of the people was Ceauşescu's policy of 'Systemisation'. In 1984 twenty-six of Bucharest's most beautiful little churches, along with hundreds of poor homes, had been destroyed to make way for an avenue worthy of Ceauşescu's massive House of the People. But it was rural systemisation which provoked a notable reaction in the West. Ceauşescu's overt reason for destroying villages and herding their inhabitants into blocks of collective flats was to release more land for exploitation. His covert reason was to break the rural tradition, to suppress what private life remained to the peasant and to homogenise and destroy regional cultures. In a broadcast to Romania in September 1989, the King said: 'The dictator in Romania, like his Pol Pot counterpart in Cambodia, is destroying the whole people, its spiritual, moral, cultural and physical life.'[17]

At the end of 1988 Romanian villages were adopted by villages in Belgium, France, Switzerland, Hungary, West Germany and Britain, and tens of thousands of letters sent to the mayors of Romanian villages and to President Ceauşescu undertaking 'to do everything in my power to assist in their preservation'.[18] In Britain the Prince of Wales condemned the systemisation programme in a speech delivered on 27 April 1989 and Şerban Cantacuzino, Secretary of the Royal Fine Art Commission, wrote a powerful letter to *The Times* and gave a series of illustrated lectures on the beautiful regions of Romania under threat.

Control by deprivation and terror was supplemented in the 1980s by the revival or introduction of specific additional restrictions to a citizen's life. A decree requiring the registration of typewriters with the police was revived in April 1983. So was a provision first introduced by Gheorghiu-Dej in 1958 which made failure to report any conversation with a foreigner (presumably including East Europeans) a criminal offence. The use of the few photocopiers available in public libraries was strictly controlled. Even wedding receptions and parties in restaurants were forbidden lest people took the opportunity to discuss the situation.

In Romania there was no independent trade union or Church as in Poland or Hungary, no civil society or *samizdat* clubs* as in Czechoslovakia and Soviet Russia. There were a number of courageous Romanian dissidents – among others Corneliu Coposu, Doina Cornea, Marian Celac and Ana Blăndiana – who spoke out for a change to democratic government but they were on their own, either in prison or under house arrest, or being shadowed for 24 hours a day. They had the respect and moral support of their peers in the West and through Radio Free Europe and the BBC could occasionally make themselves heard in Romania. But to the millions of average Communist Party members they were oddities or, worse, traitors.

Revolt by the workers was, as in other East European countries, potentially one of the biggest threats to the *régime*. If the strike of 40,000 Jiu valley coal miners in July 1977 had not been promptly suppressed, it could have had serious consequences for the administration. On 15 November 1987 the workers in two Braşov factories producing trucks and tractors, who had been paid no wages that month, invaded the Communist Party headquarters and shouted 'down with dictatorship' and 'we want bread'. Again the outbreak was quickly put down, and would have been smothered as effectively as the Jiu valley revolt had not Professor Brucan, a leading member of the Communist Party, in a statement issued to Western journalists, attributed the Braşov rising directly to Ceauşescu's harsh economic policy and warned him that 'a period of crisis had opened up between the Romanian Communist Party and the working class'. To crush the workers in these circumstances could lead to Romania's isolation by the East as well as the West.[19] The statement was transmitted in Romanian to Romania by the BBC, Radio Free Europe and the Voice of America. It was one of a series of events that confirmed Ceauşescu's growing isolation. In June 1986 *The Times* had quoted a Romanian as commenting that 'this must be the only country in Europe who would actually welcome a Soviet invasion'.[20] It was Gorbachev and Romania's neighbours – not the West – who finally isolated the corrupt *régime* of Ceauşescu and his family.

When Ceauşescu addressed the XIV Party Congress on 20 November 1989, his only foreign guest was Yasser Arafat. The communist governments of Poland, Hungary and East Germany had fallen, as would those of

---

* A group in the Soviet Union or its satellites which irregularly published and circulated articles and books not otherwise available in their country.

Czechoslovakia and Bulgaria by the end of November. His only friends were in Cuba, North Korea and China – too far away to help.

There had also been dissidents within the Communist Party, men who had been demoted or had some other personal grudge against Ceauşescu. However, their objective had been limited to replacing their leader, not destroying a system under which their careers had formerly prospered, or adopting a democracy with which they were, with rare exceptions, wholly unfamiliar and which they instinctively mistrusted.

After the 1989 revolution information came to light of such a group,[21] which was to have considerable influence on Romania's post-revolutionary history. In 1984 it had planned a *coup d'état* while the Ceauşescus were on a state visit to Western Germany. However, these once-senior party members had by then so little authority that they could not obtain the Intelligence and small arms required for their operation and had to abandon it. Some kept in touch through the next five years though, as Silviu Brucan,* who had links with them, admitted in *Romînia Liberă* of 17 July 1990, 'but for the December rising the plotters would have still been talking about how to get rid of Ceauşescu'.

Ion Iliescu, leader of this group, had in the 1960s been a favourite of Ceauşescu, a friend of the family. He had been made Secretary of the Union of Communist Youth in 1967 and a year later was promoted to full membership of the Central Committee. However, in 1971, following a clash with Ceauşescu over the latter's adoption of the North Korean model of communism, Iliescu had been removed from national politics.

The revolution began in Timişoara, capital of the Banat, about three hundred miles west of Bucharest, on the frontiers with Hungary and Yugoslavia. Timişoara was an unusual Romanian city where Romanians, Hungarians, Saxons, Serbs, Czechs and Bulgarians lived comfortably together. After the revolution it was to declare itself a European city which other Romanians should visit to learn tolerance.

On 16 December 1989 the local Communist Party had decided to enforce an expulsion order against the dissident Hungarian pastor Laszlo Tökes. Tökes barricaded his house. When the militia arrived to arrest him a small hostile

---

* Professor Silviu Brucan had edited *Scînteia*, the Communist Party's official newspaper. He was Romanian ambassador to the United States from 1956 to 1959 and to the United Nations from 1959 to 1962. His six years in the USA had given him direct experience of the West, which was rare among senior members of the Party.

crowd gathered and this grew into a spontaneous uprising which next day was joined by students and workers shouting for free elections and democracy.

On the afternoon of 17 December, before leaving for a two-day official visit to Iran, Ceauşescu gave orders for the army to open fire on the Timişoara demonstrators but, in his absence, General Milea, the Minister of Defence, refused to authorise the use of live ammunition. When he had been overruled, 97 civilians were killed and 210 wounded, and Gorbachev publically condemned the slaughter. Meanwhile there were uprisings in the Transylvanian cities of Cluj, Arad and Sibiu.

When he returned from Iran, Ceauşescu decided to defy Gorbachev by calling on Romanian workers to support his treatment of the Timişoara 'hooligans'. Trusted men from selected cadres assembled for the speech but were sent home when it was postponed. At noon next day, when Ceauşescu finally addressed his meeting from a balcony of the Central Committee building in Bucharest, he did not know that his audience now consisted of a mixed bag of workmen hurriedly brought together. He was heckled. He could hardly believe his ears. He faltered. He looked round for guidance, for assurance which was not there. The militia failed to control or disperse the crowd, which was now calling for Ceauşescu's resignation and an end to all communism.

Ninety minutes later regiments of the 1st Armoured Division were ordered to block all roads leading to the Central Committee building. By nine o'clock next morning, 22 December, a large column of well-organised workers had converged on the city centre, urging the troops not to suppress anti-Ceauşescu demonstrations. What, however, decided the army was news at about 11 o'clock that 'the traitor', General Milea, had committed suicide. They quite rightly took this to mean that the General had been murdered on Ceauşescu's orders and they promptly returned to barracks. Subsequent orders to take up their positions in front of the Central Committee building were ignored by divisional commanders. The Ceauşescus fled by helicopter from the undefended building and the demonstrators entered it.

By 1 p.m. those of the 1984 plotters, including Ion Iliescu, who had converged on the Central Committee building knew that without any help from them the uprising was well on its way to succeeding. They also knew that the replacement of Ceauşescu – the object of the the 1984 plot – would not satisfy the thousands of men and women now out on the streets of Bucharest calling for the overthrow of communism itself.

Since Romania had no democratic organisation to take control, the television station had been occupied by enthusiastic writers and artists who had no political programme.[22] When at lunchtime three senior officers arrived and took in the scene, they made it quite clear that they were only prepared to back the uprising on condition that 'serious politicians' took over, and not a bunch of 'crazy poets and intellectuals'.

When Iliescu, with Militaru, another member of the 1984 group, visited the TV station, he sympathised with the army's position and prepared to take over himself. According to Jeremy Bransten he invited a small group of authors, artists and army personnel to help him draw up his *communiqué* to the Romanian people.[23]

He then returned to the TV station, which was under attack by anonymous snipers and, according to Brucan,[24] he was lying down under a hail of bullets while broadcasting an assurance that the whole Communist power structure – the Presidency of the Republic, the Workers' Council, the Securitate, everything but the army – had been dissolved and would remain dissolved.

That evening the core members of the 1984 plot, including Iliescu, Brucan and Militaru, together with Petre Roman, son of Ionel Roman, a one-time member of the Communist Party's Central Committee and Iliescu's close friend, met in the Central Committee building to discuss the structure and, in very general terms, the future of their group, which they named the National Salvation Front. Petre Roman was made provisional Prime Minister and Militaru provisional Minister of Defence. But the most difficult decision remained the fate of the Ceauşescus.

Their helicopter had stopped briefly at their Snagov villa and then proceeded towards Piteşti, where a jet was waiting to take them out of the country. On the way the pilot had faked engine trouble and landed. The Ceauşescus were arrested and imprisoned at a military base in Tîrgoveşti.

The snipers who had erupted on 22 December had attacked not only the TV station; they were active throughout central Bucharest and in provincial cities. No one was certain who they were – probably Ministry of the Interior troops loyal to Ceauşescu. These so-called 'terrorists' were highly competent and the National Salvation Front was afraid that they would take the military base at Tîrgoveşti and release the prisoners. The Ceauşescus were therefore given a summary trial and executed on 25 December.

# PART FIVE

Romania Trapped in its Communist Past:
After 1989

## FIFTEEN

## *A Government of Reluctant Democrats*

When the Romanian authorities fired on the crowd at Timișoara King Michael knew that the end was in sight. King Baudouin of the Belgians was the first to telephone him. Later, people of all kinds and ages flocked to Versoix, letters poured in. He had to keep abreast of a rapidly changing political scene in Bucharest and to answer a mass of press and individual enquiries. It was clear that the King, who usually coped alone with a portable typewriter, now had far more work than he could handle. While Princess Margarita and Princess Sophie were home for Christmas the family decided to turn the old basement playroom into an office. The Queen collected and classified the papers accumulated during 45 years of exile and turned part of the room into a reference library. Princess Margarita gave up her job with the FAO to take charge of the new secretariat. Princess Sophie joined her. Friends helped out with equipment. Very soon the secretariat became the hub of the house.

King Michael's new year message opened, 'Let us all help to rebuild the country after the moral and material disaster the Communists reduced it to', and closed with the guarded assurance that 'We, all Romanians, have taken note that the new provisional government has promised free elections. We shall, everyone of us, watch that they are fulfilled.'[1]

Many Romanians ask why King Michael did not immediately return to Bucharest to show his support for the revolution. A decade later Queen Anne wrote that, after the frustration of an unlawful exile lasting for four decades, others 'would have taken the first train, truck or aeroplane. I myself would have been ready to do that from the start.'[2] Not the King, because he was legitimate he had the greatness, she said, to wait.

The 1989 revolution was not a monarchist rising. After three generations of communist myth about the monarchy, people would need time to learn the truth. 'The young', King Michael said, 'had not given their lives last December for me. Time must be allowed for some semblance of collective thinking to emerge as the political parties take shape again.' He would await a request by a democratically elected government.[3]

It has been suggested that the King lacked the courage to plunge into the maelstrom of Bucharest between 22 and 25 December but that makes no sense. Once they had thought it their duty to do something, neither the King nor Queen Anne had ever been influenced by physical danger or hardship. The King is thoughtful rather than demonstrative. One of the most courageous acts of the Second World War – his *coup d'état* of 1944 – succeeded very largely because of the meticulous care with which he had prepared it.

To change attitudes, the King knew, would be more difficult than to set up machinery for a free market or a pluralistic political system. The King hoped that Romanian intellectuals would help, men and women 'who loved their country rather than looking for an opportunity to get rich'.[4] After four decades of isolation and humiliation Romanians should be allowed to recover a sense of their worth, to learn that before the war Romania had had an economy almost as strong as Belgium's, and had contributed to Europe men and women of great quality. They might then no longer feel the need to claim that their country was always such a special case. They might overcome their obsessional suspicion of their neighbours. They might see a return to traditional values as a progressive rather than a retrograde step. And once they began to choose leaders they did not fear, in whom they had genuine confidence, they would begin to recover not only their own self-respect but the respect of other countries.

According to a Gallup poll taken at the end of 1989 there was more opposition in Romania to a sharp reduction of the role of the state in the country's economy than in any other country in the region.[5] After the experience of Ceauşescu's wild economic projects, it is not surprising that, once he had gone, they would instinctively hold on to what security the state could offer them. They were too exhausted for change, too easily made hopeless.

A growing number of Romanians had already begun to look askance at the National Salvation Front (NSF), which had appeared from nowhere to take over the revolution. The NSF Council, where power ostensibly resided, had been decorated with prominent dissidents appointed, without their agreement, solely to help win over the Romanian people. But the Executive, which had the real power, was controlled by *apparatchiks* of the old *régime*. And the Government, apart from Andrei Pleşu, Minister of Culture and Mihai Sora, Minister of Education, was solidly Communist. The people could only put their trust in the NSF assurance that theirs was a provisional government whose sole object was to prepare for the election of a constituent assembly which would then draft the new constitution. Meanwhile it would issue only such *ad hoc* laws as were strictly necessary.

On 23 January, the National Salvation Front made a U-turn: it announced its intention to present candidates at the April elections. Romanian democrats were appalled. Outside the Banat the Opposition parties had little natural support. Their political structures were fragile. Their leaders had spent most of the last half-century in prison, house arrest, or exile and were out of touch, particularly with the rural community. They had little chance of defeating a party which controlled the sole Romanian TV station, had the support of the *nomenklatura* and an electorate which they had brainwashed for 42 years. The dissidents Doina Cornea and Ana Blăndiana resigned from the NSF Council.

That spring the NSF began to show its colours.

Meetings in central Bucharest were now banned and when, on 28 January, some 20,000 people gathered in University Square to demand the provisional government's resignation, coal miners from the Jiu valley were brought in to break them up and to attack Opposition Party headquarters. Mihai Lupoi, the Minister of Transport, was sacked for criticising the Government's bullying tactics. Professor Brucan resigned from the NSF Executive.

On 19 and 20 March 1990 the extreme nationalist organisation Vatra Romînească, in cooperation with local mayors and officials, brought bus-loads of Romanians from neighbouring villages and, after arming and inciting them, let them loose on the Hungarian citizens of the Transylvanian city of Tîrgu Mureş. They left 3 killed and 269 injured. When commenting on this incident, Salvation Front leaders were careful not to accuse the popular Vatra Romînească by name. Petre Roman even had the effrontery to blame the Hungarians.[6]

Next month the National Salvation Front, without waiting for the elections which had now been postponed until 20 May, set up a new Romanian Intelligence Service (RIS). It was headed by Professor Virgil Măgureanu, one of the 1984 plotters who nevertheless by 1989 had become a Securitate colonel. Măgureanu chose his senior staff from his old firm, and when they moved over to the new organisation they brought their Securitate files. Henceforth, many of the Securitate staff who had worked for Ceauşescu would enjoy a certain immunity whereas members of the public, who had at one time or another done some small service under pressure for the Securitate, would be subject to blackmail. The King had declared himself against witch-hunts but in this case the witches became the hunters. The inertia Michael feared was already setting in. Eight years later Securitate files would still be withheld from parliamentary committees* and the Senate would still be debating whether to privatise state farms.[7]

After 42 years of exile, King Michael planned to spend the Easter of 1990 in Romania. He wished to worship in a Romanian Orthodox church in his own country and to pay homage to those who had died to bring democracy to Romania. He meant to arrive on 12 April and to stay about ten days. It would be a kind of pilgrimage, entirely private and non-political, an opportunity too for his wife to pay her first visit to Romania. Having no Romanian passport, he requested, and was granted, a visa on his British passport and was expected by everyone to spend Easter at home.

Princess Margarita and her sister Sophie had been welcomed enthusiastically when they visited Bucharest in January and at first the King's proposal seemed entirely acceptable. He was recognised as a 'Romanian citizen like any other'.[8] He was offered a villa, an escort from the Foreign Ministry and security arrangements, though he declined the first two in order to preserve the private nature of his visit.

Then, the day before he was scheduled to go, ROMPRES† issued a statement referring to a 'strong reaction by political forces' to the King's visit, claiming that it would 'bring unwanted elements to the election campaign, fire new passions, and violence may occur'. It also referred to 'obscure manipulations that may affect his dignity and cast a shadow on the Family'.[9] The King was asked to postpone the visit until after the May election. Members of the King's entourage, who were already in Bucharest, recognised, as did the King, the clichés of communist thinking and, knowing that his sole purpose was to celebrate the most important festival of the Christian calendar at home, thanked the provisional government for their advice and said that nevertheless the King had decided not to postpone his visit.

On 12 April, just when the King was due to leave, ROMPRES announced that his visa had been withdrawn and appropriate instructions sent to points of

---

* On 18 June 1998, A.P. (Web) reported that Securitate files were leaked that week with the object of exposing three politicians of the ruling Democratic Convention, including a minister who had to resign.

† ROMPRES was the Romanian state news agency.

entry throughout the country. Swissair were warned by the Romanian Embassy in Berne that if they carried King Michael to Romania they would be violating international regulations. The King cancelled his visit and told journalists at Geneva airport, 'I am a Romanian citizen who wants to return to his country. My whole purpose was not to get involved in political questions.'[10] He worshipped that Easter at the Romanian Orthodox church in Paris.

Meanwhile an election campaign of sorts was under way. The National Peasant Party was led by Corneliu Coposu, by far the most distinguished of the Opposition leaders. As Juliu Maniu's secretary in the 1940s, Coposu had been involved in planning for the *coup d'état* of 23 August 1944. He became Secretary General of the National Peasant Party in 1947 but after King Michael's abdication at the end of that year he and his wife were arrested and subsequently served seventeen years' forced labour. They were released in 1964. She died almost immediately. He had been in solitary confinement for eight years and had nearly forgotten how to speak. For the next 25 years continual police surveillance made any political activity impossible. Another leading National Peasant was Ion Rațiu, who had worked untiringly in London against Romania's dictatorial governments but who had not set foot in the country for fifty years.

The National Liberal Party was led by Radu Câmpeanu, who had also suffered a period of communist imprisonment and a long exile in France. The small recreated Social Democratic Party, under the leadership of Sergiu Canescu, now aimed to restore social democracy and a free trade union movement. The Hungarian Democratic Union of Romania (HDUR) set up by Geza Domokos had at first worked closely with the NSF. After the March event in Tîrgu Mureş they decided to stand on an independent ticket advocating rights for all minorities.

With their built-in electoral advantage the NSF won the elections hands down. The National Peasant Party (which in the 1940s had had 70–80 per cent support) obtained 2.6 per cent of the vote. Iliescu, running against Câmpeanu and Rațiu for president, won 85.07 per cent.[11] Of the combined total of 515 deputies and senators who would make up the Constituent Assembly, the NSF held 354 seats plus representatives of satellite and supporting parties. Nevertheless, students, workers and members of the Opposition parties continued to demonstrate in University Square for the exclusion from office of all ex-Communist officials – in effect the whole NSF administration. As in the 1940s, paramilitary workers wielding heavy metal bars from lorries failed to dissuade them and finally the President decided to put a stop to this 'hooliganism'.

First a rumour was circulated that the demonstrations were the work of the Iron Guard. Then, on 13 June, President Iliescu appealed for help to 'save democracy'. The subsequent miners' assault on the capital was far more vicious than that of January. Under the leadership of Măgureanu's RIS officers they arrested government opponents, beat up innocent civilians whom passers-by assumed to be members of the Iron Guard, destroyed Opposition Party Headquarters and anti-NSF newspaper offices, were thanked formally by the President and – without a single miner being arrested – left behind them some 20 dead and 650 injured.[12] Sora, the Education Minister, resigned. The NSF leaders were taken aback by the fierce criticism from the Western media.

Although the events of 13–16 June 1990 were followed by an exodus of young Romanians, Ion Iliescu still had the peasants' support. Rations had improved, systemisation had stopped. Iliescu had promised them land and seemed 'sound' about the Hungarians – which, according to the television, democratic leaders were not.

Meanwhile tensions were building between Iliescu and Roman: Iliescu had been educated in Moscow; Roman had taken his doctorate in Toulouse and had reformist ideas. In the long run it would split the National Salvation Front but for the time being the more conservative supporters of President Iliescu were dominant. When in the autumn of 1990 a proposal was made in parliament that civil servants should in future be appointed on the basis of competence, it was easily defeated.[13]

Many Romanians understood Iliescu's concern about the social effects of rapid economic reform yet felt that the country was getting nowhere and showing signs of perpetuating the inbred corruption which had characterised the previous *régime*. King Michael summed up their feelings when he told a Belgian audience in mid-1990, 'If Romania does need a long period of convalescence, I fear what will happen during that period.'[14]

Meanwhile the Opposition showed no sign of becoming a united democratic bloc with a clear purpose. The two principal parties – the National Peasants and the Liberals – were torn by internal discord. Many looked for a scapegoat for their inability to make any real impression on the electorate. In the summer of 1990 young Liberals were already leaving Câmpeanu, the first sign that the great historical party of the Brătianu times would not be restored. When in August 1990 a group of optimists tried to form an umbrella organisation under which all Opposition political parties could join in working to prevent the restoration of a communist state, they soon gave up the struggle.

In those early days the impetus for a united Opposition came rather from non-party sources. Soon after the revolution the Romanian army had set up the

Committee of Action to Democratise the Army (CADA) and had given it such powers that within months the Minister of Defence had been dismissed for his communist sympathies and the Minister of the Interior for his implication in the bloodshed of 21 December. CADA was dissolved in July 1990 for carrying out its brief too effectively but many army officers who were cashiered for not recognising its dissolution offered their support to other Opposition groups. The citizens of Timişoara fiercely criticised those who had 'kidnapped' their revolution. To promote the rule of law and, in particular, to keep an eye on the National Salvation Front, Bucharest intellectuals set up the Group for Social Dialogue, whose commentaries were published in the journal 22. In the autumn of 1990 they inspired the formation of the Civic Alliance, which was to provide a broad cover for all non-party opposition concerned for Romanian human rights.

Against this background the King, addressing foreign audiences, at first refrained from direct criticism of the Romanian Government. During his visit to Brussels in June 1990, he discussed the Romanian situation in the broader context of the last half-century. He did not agree with the West's over-emphasis on economic development, particularly when the people concerned were just emerging from such moral and spiritual deprivation. The distinction between economic and human rights he considered false. Without democracy there would be no long-lasting economic development and without a decent standard of living, democracy would remain fragile. The two concepts were inseparable.[15]

When invited to deliver a lecture at the Royal United Services Institute in London, King Michael addressed the transition problems of East European countries as a whole. He insisted that the basis of recovery was their moral and spiritual rejuvenation, a recognition that democracy was a way of life rather than an administrative process. In Eastern Europe, he said, ethnic problems had been festering under the name of 'workers' solidarity' ever since the war. While Western Europe had had the benefit of a Marshall Plan, Eastern Europe 'is today precisely where you left it in 1945'.

Ever since the May elections, King Michael had been waiting for an invitation to visit his country and in November he sounded out the Government about the possibility of a private visit over Christmas. He hoped in particular to visit the tombs of his ancestors in the ancient city of Curtea de Argeş. Friends offered to lease an aircraft and to make the travel arrangements. The flight path and permission to land were cleared with the Romanian aviation authorities and since, according to Otopeni airport, no passenger list was required, King Michael's name did not appear in the documentation.

Nevertheless the Romanian authorities were told repeatedly of his intention and on 24 December, Princess Margarita, who had had no problems visiting Romania and had a flat in Bucharest, told the Prime Minister that the King intended to arrive on 25 December and to stay for three days. Petre Roman, without either welcoming or forbidding the visit, advised her that the King should not proceed with his plan. Princess Margarita reported this conversation to her father and when he telephoned late that evening it was to say that, while he still wished to proceed, he would cut the visit from three days to one in order not to create problems. Next morning, Christmas Day, she was unable to contact either the Prime Minister, his deputies, or any other member of the Government but left messages marked 'urgent' at the Prime Minister's office and home informing him that King Michael and his party would arrive for 24 hours only, at 1800 hr that day.[16]

At Otopeni airport, the King, accompanied by Queen Anne, Princess Sophie and a small entourage, was met by Princess Margarita. They were given entry visas. The King was then escorted to the VIP lounge and, while their luggage was being cleared, he had an amiable conversation with airport officials. Although he avoided journalists, King Michael displayed the entry visa for the cameras. Princess Margarita told them that 'the visit was private, that the King intended to go to the monastery at Curtea de Argeş where his ancestors were buried, and that he planned to leave Romania the following afternoon'. She added that the King had delayed his visit until after the 22 December, the anniversary of the overthrow of Ceauşescu, in order 'to keep the visit strictly non-political'.[17] For the same reason the King had dropped Bucharest from his schedule.[18]

Only when they were ready to go did the chief passport officer ask for their passports again, allegedly in order to make a technical entry, which would take about twenty minutes. It was dark by then and, with a longish drive ahead, King Michael decided to leave, asking two members of his party to deal with this formality and bring the passports along later.

They had travelled about sixty miles when they were stopped and surrounded by police threatening them with automatic weapons and plain-clothes Securitate officers, who were studiedly insolent to the King. Princess Margarita later described those two hours as like something 'out of Nazi Germany with soldiers, Securitate, and men that I can only describe as yobs'.[19] Then they were forced to return under a ridiculously heavy police escort to the airport. The King contested this treatment and after hours of disagreeable negotiation was issued with an ultimatum to leave the country forthwith on a Romanian military aircraft. He was given no authentic reason for his treatment, just bullying and blatant lies such as that the two Swiss pilots were 'incapacitated by drink'. To avoid possible violence he finally left with his party at 5.40 a.m. on the 26th. They landed at Zurich instead of Geneva as had been promised, and they made their way home to Versoix from there. Margarita drove back to her Bucharest flat in a state of shock, appalled that Romanians whom he loved so much could have done this to him.

The Romanian Government issued a statement accusing the King of using a fictitious name to enter the country fraudulently and without visas. 'It was a cheap trick . . . He came like a thief, lying and physically forcing his way through the border crossing despite the pleas of the check-point workers . . . We can only see it as a sign of the continuing contempt this family has always shown towards our people whom this family has never respected and whom it does not respect to this day.'

Such a violent official reaction could only be explained by an obsessive hatred of royalty felt by NSF leaders. Entry visas, said the Romanian authorities, could not be issued at the airport on Danish diplomatic passports. 'A nonsense', Princess Margarita told a British journalist in Bucharest, 'I'm here now on a Danish diplomatic passport and I've never had any trouble getting a visa at Otopeni.'[20] On the 27th the King issued a detailed account of what had happened though by then the Romanian and foreign press had made full use of the NSF's own lurid version of the event.

When Princess Margarita had first seen conditions in Romanian hospitals, orphanages, old people's homes and what was left of systemised villages, 'a hole dug in front of each house, the house bulldozed into it', she had decided to offer her training in the social sciences and her experience of working for the FAO to the country. The King agreed and the Princess Margarita of Romania Foundation was set up with headquarters in the Versoix house and branches in Romania, Britain, Belgium, France and the USA.

The Foundation worked with other non-governmental organisations. In the educational field it has, among other things, equipped Romanian art schools, sponsored studies abroad for promising young artists and financed prizes for the best young playwright of the year. But health care is its most pressing concern, in particular the dreadful condition of old people and the thousands of young children in Romanian hospitals and orphanages. It has financed the provision of medical and legal advice for the aged, has organised an annual symposium on AIDS and has helped with a programme to fight tuberculosis. It has completely re-equipped the community centre at Braneşti, about 20 km east of Bucharest, which had ceased to provide even primary care for the region. It has provided medical equipment, proper nutrition, better nursing and a bright and stimulating environment for the children in Bucharest's Colentina hospital, many of whom are HIV positive through the use of unsterilised needles. The dying bodies of the little children one had seen so often on Western television became individuals living with a serious disease. These pilot projects at Braneşti and the Colentina hospital became models for the rejuvenation of health care throughout the country as and when this should become economically possible.

The King had told his audience at the Royal United Services Institute in London that only reformed economic and social policies could bring about a permanent improvement of East European health care; the long-term objective of the Foundation was, in Princess Margarita's words, 'to help revive and celebrate the rich cultural legacy and breathtaking environment that creates the Romanian spirit'. Meanwhile, however, charities like the Foundation could do much to alleviate the intense suffering inherited from the previous *régime*. Princess Margarita had many devoted fund-raisers and friends and her family gave her their full support, while the interest of the Prince of Wales was an enormous help. Her parents attended several Foundation events including the French Foundation gala at the Champs Elysées Theatre where Yehudi Menuhin conducted the National Orchestra of France; the orchestra interrupted a strike to raise money for the Romanian children. Yehudi Menuhin was a wonderful friend, always ready to conduct or to give recitals to raise funds for Princess Margarita and the native land of the composer Enescu – his teacher and the principal inspiration of his musical life.

According to Ana Blăndiana, the dominant NSF press directed its venom mainly against minority groups – Hungarians, Gypsies, students and dissidents. Those who had inspired the revolution had become pariahs.[21] In September 1990 the newspaper *Azi* described Doina Cornea as 'senile' and a 'crazed psychopath'. When she defended herself on television the Deputy Prime Minister called for her arrest a few days later amidst loud parliamentary applause.[22]

The weakness of the Opposition in the early 1990s and the Government's ambiguous attitude towards racism and human rights left a gap for the extremists to fill. Although Corneliu Tudor would not form his Greater Romania Party until just before the 1992 elections, his weekly newspaper of the same name was already in full cry against the 17,000 elderly Jews left in Romania. The fact that such campaigns were run by people like Tudor, who had previously composed songs of praise to Nicolae Ceauşescu, 'speaks volumes', the King remarked, 'about the true state of Romanian society today'.[23] When Yad Vashem declared Queen Helen a 'righteous gentile' for what she had done during the war to protect Romanian Jews, the extreme right took this opportunity to inform neo-fascist sympathisers that the royal family were 'jew lovers'.

Economically Romanians were having the worst of both worlds, enjoying neither the job stability of a command economy nor the benefits of private enterprise. The 'privatised' sector was entrusted to men with state control experience while genuine private enterprise was mostly limited to shops and small firms which would never influence the national economy. Collective farms were renamed 'cooperatives', their management unchanged, and considerable pressure was exerted on any farmer wishing to leave his cooperative. Since only half Romania's productive capacity was being worked, a drop of 5 per cent in living standards was foreseen for 1991 alone.

Feeling by September 1991 that their loyalty to the Government had failed to protect them from the effects of the economic slump, the miners of the Jiu valley went on strike. On the 23rd about ten thousand miners commandeered trains for Bucharest, but not this time to support Iliescu. They were welcomed in University Square by the student leader, Marian Munteanu. They attacked government buildings, parliament and TV headquarters. By the 27th they were calling for Iliescu as well as Roman to go, and even attempted to storm the presidential residence at Cotroceni. That evening, when they left, three people had been killed and about five hundred injured.[24]

President Iliescu siezed the opportunity to sack Petre Roman and promised the people a government of 'broad national opening'. He appointed as Premier Theodor Stolojan who had been Minister of Finance under Roman and had a reputation as an economic liberal.[25] The Liberal Party leadership now broke faith with Coposu and provided three ministers for the Stolojan Government, which helped to give it the appearance of this 'broad national opening'. The President had not only defied the miners, got rid of Roman and reappointed an NSF-controlled government; he had also seriously breached the Opposition.

On 10 July a draft constitution had been published which ignored Romanian constitutional tradition: not a single article was taken from the 1923 constitution.[26] It drew heavily, however, on the French constitution of 1958*

---

\* The French constitution of September 1958 concentrated power in the presidency to the detriment of the assembly and so anticipated General de Gaulle's Fifth Republic.

and was inspired, especially on presidential prerogatives, by the constitution of the Romanian Socialist Republic of 21 August 1965.[27] Article 1, which declared Romania to be a republic, was excluded from the usual process of revision, thus preventing future generations from expressing their wishes. The constitution was approved by 414 votes to 91 on 21 November 1991 and became law on 8 December 1991.[28] So, after fifty years of republican dictatorship the form of government the Romanian people were to have in perpetuity – that is, a republic – had been written into their draft constitution. In Italy, Bulgaria and Greece the normal legal procedure had been followed – a special referendum had been held with the exclusive purpose of allowing the people to choose for themselves their system of government. According to the constitutional lawyer Eleodor Focşeneanu, had Romania followed this procedure it would now have a legitimate form of government (whether republic or monarchy) rather than one which, in law, is provisional.[29]

On 27 January of that same year, King Michael with his wife and Princess Margarita attended a memorial service for Princess Ileana at the Romanian Orthodox cathedral in London. Princess Ileana had founded a religious order in the United States and she and King Michael had been reconciled in 1984 when the King had invited her to the wedding of his daughter Irina. Shortly before the uprising of 1989 they had begun to correspond regularly and in September 1990 Princess Ileana had returned to Romania in the company of the Princesses Margarita and Sophie. While in England the King also addressed a meeting of the British/Romanian Association and delivered a lecture at London University.

In April, again with Queen Anne and Princess Margarita, he made an extensive visit to the United States. He was warmly welcomed by the Romanian communities at Chicago, Washington and New York and, while there, addressed some of America's most prestigious audiences. In September he visited France, primarily with a view to strengthening relations with its large Romanian community. The monarchy as such played a relatively small part in the talks he gave during his travels. Constitutional monarchy, he said, was certainly not a universal panacea but it was under a monarchy that Romania had become a modern, comparatively prosperous, independent state with compulsory education, radical agrarian and electoral reform and an active system of parliamentary government – where, incidentally, a senator could criticise the royal family with impunity.

Unlike most East European countries, Romania, he said, had not experienced de-Stalinisation after Stalin's death nor any attempt by their Communist leaders to repair the effects of obsessional industrialisation or to reach an accommodation with their people. No civil society had been created, there was no kind of community structure to act as a buffer between the individual and the ruler. A dissident was isolated. As a result, after the 1989 revolution Iliescu not only became leader by default but then redefined the objectives of the revolution.

Romanians, he told one American audience, were living in a world of half-truths, neither dictatorship nor democracy. They were still afraid of their rulers, mistrusting them not only because of their policies but often because of who they were and what they had done in their communist past.

> The present government will not set up norms of decency. It sets Romanian against Romanian, Romanian against Hungarian and Gypsy, worker against intellectual, young against old. The revolution might have been expected to release a wave of genuine nationalism but the so-called nationalism of the Iliescu régime is still in the hands of rabble-rousers employing it for narrow political ends.'[30]

Had Romania at the end of 1989, he said, been able to return to a tradition based on the values associated with Maniu, Dinu Brătianu, Titulescu, rather than Groza, Gheorghiu-Dej and Ceauşescu, it would have had a much better basis for the regeneration required – a regeneration going far deeper than the adoption of a new economic mechanism. A consumer society would, in itself, not teach people the personal responsibility that goes with true freedom and which might one day make them the masters of their situation. 'The transition to a post-totalitarian society is an act of moral regeneration and a process of catharsis that cannot be achieved without a total break with the mendacity of the past and with its perpetrators.'[31]

King Michael's audiences were almost entirely foreign; he had few opportunities to talk to Romanians, even by radio. Given the clarity of his thinking, his historical sense and his undoubted love for his people, it is hardly surprising that the leadership of the National Salvation Front took extraordinary measures to keep him away from them.

# SIXTEEN

## *The Easter Visit*

Parliamentary and presidential elections were required within twelve months of the constitution coming into force. These were held on 27 November 1992 and were preceded on 9 February by municipal elections. The result was a flurry of political parties, some with impossible names, most sharing the responsibility for Romania's sluggish development towards genuine democracy during the next four years. Iliescu's National Salvation Front was expected to remain the dominant party. The Opposition, consisting of the National Peasant Party and Christian Democratic Party (NPP–CD),* the National Liberal Party (NLP), the Social Democratic Party (SDP), the Hungarian Democratic Federation of Romania (HDFR) and the new Civic Alliance Party (CAP), had formed an electoral coalition known as the Democratic Convention (DC) and this was expected to do well in urban areas. The political wing of Vatra Românească had been created during the Tîrgu Mureş atrocities of March 1990 and named the Party of Romanian National Unity (PRNU). The PRNU was to launch the extreme nationalist Gheorghe Funar on a career that would embarrass Ion Iliescu during his second presidency.

After the local elections the National Salvation Front finally split. The majority became Iliescu's new Democratic National Salvation Front (DNSF). Most of the others joined Petre Roman's new party – the Democratic Party–National Salvation Front (DP–NSF) – though about a dozen went over to the Greater Romania Party headed by Corneliu Tudor, the only politician overtly supporting the rehabilitation of Nicolae Ceauşescu. Like Gheorghe Funar, Tudor would play a sometimes critical part in Romanian politics during the next four years. The Romanian Communist Party had been reconstructed as the third extremist party under the name of the Socialist Labour Party.

---

\* After Coposu attended the British Conservative Party's conference in 1990 where he heard speeches reminiscent of the chauvinism he was fighting at home, he decided to associate his party with Chancellor Kohl's Christian Democrats.

The presidential election of 27 November was contested by Iliescu, Funar and for the Democratic Convention a new candidate, Professor Emil Constantinescu, a biologist and Rector of Bucharest University. Iliescu won with 61.43 per cent of the votes to Constantinescu's 38.57 per cent.

The parliamentary elections gave Iliescu's Democratic National Salvation Front 27.71 per cent, the Democratic Convention 20.16 per cent and Roman's Democratic Party–National Salvation Front 10.18 per cent. More important perhaps, the three extremist parties of both right and left had won seats for the first time ever in a freely elected Romanian parliament.

When in the spring of 1992 President Iliescu had announced that King Michael would always be accepted in Romania if he came as a private citizen, he may have thought that the King would not accept such a condition. Michael, in fact, had already said in private that the 'kingly side' meant less to him than being with Romanians again. When Archbishop Pimen of Moldavia invited King Michael to take part in the Easter services at Putna monastery and to be present at the canonisation of Steven the Great, the fifteenth-century king of Moldavia, buried there,* King Michael accepted the invitation and added that he would come in a purely private capacity.

On 21 April, when the visas were ready, Michael announced that on Saturday 25 April he would attend the Resurrection Mass at Putna monastery. On Sunday he would attend the Easter Mass at the church of Saint Gheorghiu in Bucharest. On the third day he would visit Curtea de Argeş to pay his respects to his forefathers (as he had tried to do in December 1990) and would return that same evening to Geneva.

Under the Salic law incorporated in all Romania's previous constitutions, women were excluded from succession to the throne and, therefore, the male descendant of a daughter of the King was also excluded. This meant that neither Princess Margarita – the King's eldest daughter – nor the 7-year-old Nicholas, son of Princess Helen and Dr Robin Medforth-Mills, a lecturer in history at Durham University, could succeed King Michael. The family decided that, nevertheless, this would be a good opportunity to present Nicholas to the Romanian people, and so in the car driving the royal family from Suceava airport to Putna monastery on the morning of 25 April were the King, the Archbishop, the Queen, Princess Helen and her son – who enjoyed the trip immensely and was a great success.

---

* Under Romanian Orthodox Church law canonisation can only take place in the presence of the King.

The clergy and the royal party entered the church and stood by the tomb of Stefan cel Mare.[1] First the Archbishop said a few words to welcome King Michael home. He had been anointed king and in the eyes of God and the Church he was king for ever. Then he and the King knelt in front of the tomb and the canonisation ceremony was completed. The Archbishop again recognised Michael as king by taking his arm and leading him to the door in the Iconostasis, thus following a procedure dating back to Byzantium which permitted only priests and the sovereign to pass through this door. According to the same tradition the King should have then administered communion to himself but he asked the Archbishop to do so.

After a late, relaxed lunch of cabbage and *fasole batută*,* they walked to the rock which had once sheltered a famous local hermit, and then on to the Putna museum.

The King was by now surrounded by journalists. Although he had not undertaken to refrain from saying anything political, he felt that on a private visit he should follow this rule. This was not always easy. Whenever asked what his ambitions were, he replied that the interests of the Romanian people, not the throne, concerned him most. When asked if Romania was not seen as the most undemocratic country in Eastern Europe, he replied, 'Again a matter of politics which I do not wish to speak about for the moment. Sadly though it is true that in the West Romania has a very bad reputation.' But Michael's discretion did not prevent the Archbishop from saying, 'We carry you all in our hearts. You are scions of this land. Let Your Majesties' steps be blessed by God'.

*Romînia Liberă* issued a daily bulletin on the visit. Romanian state television at first ignored it but, by Sunday, the extensive foreign coverage forced them to reverse their policy and even to speak of 'Michael the First, former sovereign of Romania', instead of 'ex-King Michael'.

All day people had been arriving from as far away as Timişoara, Bucharest, Cluj and Bessarabia and by evening some 7,000 people shouting 'Stay with us, King Michael. We love you, we love you', had gathered round the small monastery while Midnight Mass was being celebrated. Princess Helen sang the Resurrection hymn.

Since the church could not begin to hold so many, the clergy emerged in their vestments with their tall candles, and the royal family joined them on the steps. They lit their candles from the Archbishop's candle and the ritual of lighting one candle from another began. The King, moving slowly among the

---

* *Fasole batută* are white beans softened and crushed with garlic and a little oil.

people, lighting their candles, having a few words with them, looked happier than he had for years. The Queen had already disappeared with her candle into the crowd. The Archbishop, fearing that someone might be crushed in the narrow confines round the church, directed that the candle procession round the church be performed only by the clergy. When they returned to the main door he suggested that King Michael remain outside with the people for the rest of the service. Michael said a few words. Without a microphone it was difficult to hear but, whenever he called out 'Christos a înviat' (Christ has risen), the crowd roared back three times 'Adevărat a înviat' (Truly, He has risen). And whenever they shouted 'Down with Iliescu', the King replied 'Christos a înviat' to remind them that this was a religious, not a political, occasion.

During breakfast next morning two professors from Chisinau in Moldavia arrived just in time to see the King. They spoke gravely about the nature of the monarchy, using old Romanian words with a soft Russian accent. They brought an invitation from the Union of Moldavian Women written in most beautiful Romanian and the King asked them to convey his assurance that although he could not go now, he certainly would meet them and very soon.

The royal party left for Suceava airport at 9 o'clock. On landing at Otopeni at 11.30 they were met by city dignatories and a small group of about 500 people. The King was astounded, therefore, to find at the Arc de Triomphe such a large friendly crowd that they could not proceed until the chain had been removed to allow them to drive under the arch – something he had never done before. People waved to them all along the Chaussée Kiselev, where he and his parents had lived when he was little.

Half-way down Calea Victoriei they were again stopped and this time by such a weight of good-humoured people that gendarmes had to link arms to allow him to proceed at all. They numbered several hundred thousand and it took two hours for the King and Queen to drive from the airport to Saint Gheorghiu.

The noon service, which had already been postponed for an hour, finally started at 1.30 p.m. after the King and his party had been escorted by police to a side door. The Easter *Te Deum*, requiring a male and a female choir to sing the *Christos a înviat* and the response, men and women echoing each other, could not be spoiled even by this crush of people.

When afterwards the King spoke through a microphone to the crowd outside, he was greeted with 'Regele Mihai' over and over again; 'Don't leave Romania, Your Majesty, this is your home'; 'There will not be another 10 May without King Michael';* 'We love you'. Fortunately there was no 'Down with Iliescu' as at Putna, but plenty of 'Out with the Communists'. Later, from the balcony of his rooms at the Continental Hotel, he told the people what it meant to him to be back after 45 years. He had never forgotten them, he said, had always loved them and they roared back 'We love you.' He hoped that the Resurrection of our Lord would also mean the resurrection of the country. This was not farewell for he hoped to see them again very soon. He added 'so help me God', but this last phrase was drowned by shouts of 'We want you back at Cotroceni Palace.'

At the hotel the King gave a number of audiences to Romanian politicians, historians and writers. Coposu had been with him for most of the visit. The Patriarch Teoctist sent an emissary to say that he, too, would like to see the King. Although Easter was a time for reconciliation, Michael was afraid that the Patriarch was so hated for his collaboration with Ceaușescu's *régime* that he would be booed, or worse, if he came to the hotel. On the other hand, it would be difficult to arrange with the authorities for a car and escort to take the King to the Patriarchate through such a multitude of people. When this had been explained to the Patriarch's messenger, the King added, 'You know that there is another minor matter that has to be considered, God.' The priest caught his gaze and said no more.

Next morning they took the old road to Curtea de Argeș, so that Michael could see places he had known as a young man. There were over 12,000 people to greet him, calling out and mobbing his car. Outside the chapel he was so moved that for a few moments he could not speak and Queen Anne, seeing this, touched his arm which he said later almost made it worse.[2] 'We love you' the crowd called and he waved back and stammered, 'I love you with all my heart'. But it was a brief stay, just long enough for them to attend the church service and have something to eat before taking the fast road back to Otopeni.

This was Queen Anne's first visit, her introduction to the Romanian people. At Otopeni airport just before they left, the shouts of 'Regele Mihai' were at times drowned by shouts of 'Regina Ana', and then the King stopped waving to the crowds and allowed his wife centre stage.[3]

---

* Prince Carol I had arrived in Bucharest on 10 May 1866. Annually, 10 May was Romania's National Day until the Communists changed it to 23 August, the date of the 1944 *coup d'état* which they claimed as their own. After the 1989 revolution, 1 December, the day that in 1918 the Transylvanian deputies decided to unite with the Old Kingdom, was chosen.

The evening before, members of the King's party had suggested that, since they had been given visas for a five-day visit, they should stay on a little longer and perhaps go to Timişoara. The King turned down the idea. He had undertaken a three-day programme and after the extraordinary way the people had responded to him, he would give the authorities no pretext for refusing to let him come back. *Le Figaro* commented: 'In other circumstances the visit could have been interpreted as a royal plebiscite but King Michael was wise enough not to press things in a country where the history of the monarchy has long been obscured by Ceauşescu's propaganda.'[4]

All further invitations for the King to visit Romania were blocked by the Government and a campaign started to demonise him again. The communist myth about the monarchy was, in the King's words, a two-edged sword used against both the monarchy and the democratic opposition. If the latter tried to show the absurdity of the myth they were accused of monarchist leanings, and of being in favour of the feudal tyranny the myth described. The Opposition, stricken with the fear of losing votes by being dubbed monarchists, were continually on the defensive. The Easter visit had built up an enormous political capital which, in the King's view, the Opposition did not know how to handle.[5] Had they had the courage to tell the electorate that the election had nothing to do with the future of the country's constitutional structure, they might have done better. As it was they had to fight off well-established anti-monarchical prejudices at a time when they should have been concentrating on one thing only – getting rid of the existing *régime*, not because it was anti-monarchist but because of the harm it was doing.

Nevertheless, Gabriel Liiceanu used this confusion to make a telling point. Forty-five years ago, he wrote, outer-space invaders exiled the man who was fighting for our freedom and then threw us into a dark cave. For forty-five years they filled us with lies. 'The terrible thing now is that, when given a choice between this same man and the representatives of our conquerors, we have, in full view of the whole world, blindly chosen the latter; we have freely chosen to live on in our dark cave.'[6]

The 1992 elections had failed to produce the stability most voters had hitherto associated with Ion Iliescu. Having lost Roman's support, his new Democratic National Salvation Front did not have an overall parliamentary majority. In future he would often have to rely on the extremist parties – Tudor's Greater Romania Party with its nostalgia for the Ceauşescu *régime*, Funar's Vatra Românească, which would welcome a return to Ceauşescu's policy of ethnic assimilation, and the rehabilitated Communist Party, which had adopted the name Socialist Labour Party (PSM). All three parties had supported Ion Iliescu in his presidential contest with Emil Constantinescu. Though not the natural allies of his own party – which in March 1993 was again to rename itself, this time as the Party of Social Democracy of Romania (PSDR) – President Iliescu would often have to rely on their parliamentary support while trying to control their influence on government policy.

Nicolae Văcăroiu, who was Prime Minister during the whole of Ion Iliescu's second presidency, had had a successful career in state planning and proved to be an effective brake on any move to reform the command economy. EU aid was used to keep outdated state industries going. Foreign investment was hamstrung by bureaucratic regulations dating back to Ceauşescu's day. According to economic analysts, privatisation at the 1993 rate would take until 2035. Liviu Maior, the Minister of Education, whose portfolio covered the delicate matter of education in Hungarian schools, was known to be a member of Vatra Românească and in close contact with Gheorghe Funar. Paul Everac, known for his anti-Semitic and anti-Western views, was appointed head of Romania's state television, the only channel at the time and with more influence on public opinion than the whole of the relatively free press.

The extremist parties did not hesitate to attack the President publicly. When, in April 1993, he attended a Holocaust ceremony in Bucharest and the opening of the Holocaust Museum in Washington, the leaders of the Greater Romania Party and the ex-Communist Socialist Labour Party accused him of having been brought to power and kept there by the Jewish community. Funar's PRNU chose this moment to demand and obtain representation in government.

In June 1993 Petre Roman's Democratic Party-National Salvation Front – which had been a joker in the political pack since the elections – concluded an uneasy alliance with the Democratic Convention. This could give the Opposition about 47 per cent of parliamentary seats but it also forced the governing party into even more dependence on the three extremist parties.

One thing the government and extremist parties could agree on was the need to make King Michael's life as difficult as possible.

When Viorel Oancea, the mayor of Timişoara, invited the King for Christmas of 1992, the Government warned him that very stringent conditions would be imposed on the visit and that, should these be broken in the slightest way, even by a minor traffic infringement, he would be summarily expelled. Aircraft would stand by at Bucharest and Timişoara to carry this out. Moreover, neither his security, nor the security or freedom of the people wishing to see him, would be guaranteed.

King Michael cancelled the visit and on 22 December 1992 his office issued one of his strongest denunciations of the Iliescu *régime*. After describing the conditions attached to the King's visit the statement continued:

> He had no intention of making any deals with authorities who have shown persistent disregard and contempt for both the rule of law and elementary truth. . . . He will receive no lessons in patriotism from people who learnt their trade at party academies in Moscow and who have incited violence and discord amongst Romanians for years.[7]

The Romanian Government also revived a case against King Michael which in the mid-1980s Ceaușescu had already fought and lost in the New York courts. They claimed that the King was in possession of forty-two pictures belonging to the Romanian state. Their case was based on the argument that at the time of the abdication the Romanian Government had inherited all his property, including the pictures he was accused of holding. King Michael's lawyers pointed out that since the so-called abdication had been carried out by force and was therefore nul and void, even if the King had removed the forty-two pictures – which he had not – the Romanian Government would have no case.* The government referred their case simultaneously to the Swiss and American courts and failed in both. The King saw their move as a diversion to take public interest away from the gross corruption being practised in Bucharest.† One Romanian newspaper wrote under the headline 'Thieves Point And Shout Thief', 'It is not the first time that a government formed by the communists has attacked the King . . . with the sole objective of discrediting the Sovereign.'[8]

The pretensions of the Lambrino family provided another opportunity to harass King Michael. After King Carol II died a rich man in 1953 – and not until then – Mircea Grigore Lambrino took legal measures to establish his legitimacy. He won his case in the Portuguese and French courts and on 3 April 1991 granted his son, Paul, a power of attorney to seek recognition of the

---

* Romanian Royal Property fell into three categories: (a) state property was owned by the state for the King's official use – e.g. the royal palace in Bucharest; (b) crown property was state-owned land – for instance vineyards – administered by the Royal Household, the produce sold to supplement the civil list; (c) private property included property bought by the King eg his house at Săvârșin or inherited by him personally, e.g. the Sinaia estates and their contents.
† The sale, for example, under the cover of 'privatisation' of Romania's principal shipping company to a little-known Greek company at a knock-down price.

Portuguese decision in the Romanian courts. Iliescu made Paul Lambrino welcome in Romania. The case, he knew, would be grist for his anti-monarchical campaign while – unlike King Michael – Mr Lambrino offered no threat whatsoever to Romania's republic. He was encouraged to muddy the waters as much as he wanted. One of the many rumours asserted that, should the Lambrinos win, Romania's chances of joining European organisations would be improved. 'Naive and insolent', commented Eleodor Focşeneanu, one of the King's legal advisers. Nevertheless, as expected, the Romanian court found in favour of the Lambrinos.[9]

Although it had served to harass King Michael with unwanted publicity and legal costs, in the context of succession to the Romanian throne the court's finding was irrelevant. This was a matter of dynastic, not civil, law. King Michael, legitimate son of a marriage which had had the consent of King Ferdinand and of his government, was recognised as King of Romania both by the head of the house of Hohenzollern and, until his marriage to a Roman Catholic, he was on the list of succession to the British throne. The King's daughters are on this list.

Sir Yehudi Menuhin has left us a postscript on the lighter side of President Iliescu's anti-monarchism. When he agreed to take the Royal Philharmonic Orchestra to Bucharest to open the Enesco festival, Menuhin's condition was that he be accompanied by Princess Margarita, to whose charity he intended to contribute his fee.

> During the interval, the Festival Director, a distinguished elderly man, begged me (almost in tears) not to ask Princess Margarita to join me on the stage where I planned to present her with my cheque.

Yehudi Menuhin spoke to the audience of his meeting with King Michael in 1945 and of the good work his daughter was doing, and the audience applauded. Princess Margarita stood up in the stalls to take the envelope which was handed back to her from row to row.

Then followed a lavish party hosted by President Iliescu 'in the same monstrous edifice [The House of the People] . . . the conductor's dressing and receiving room . . . nearly the size of the Wigmore Hall!'

> I stood hand-in-hand with Princess Margarita and when it was suggested that I should withdraw my contribution to her charities and give it instead to a music school I replied, 'The music school is your responsibility. I have come to help Princess Margarita'.

We were introduced to a false Pretender to the Throne (Mr Paul Lambrino) with his Detroit girlfriend, both lavishly maintained by the Romanian state to discredit the King and monarchy altogether.[10]

Of the various forms of pressure and harassment practised on King Michael during the second Iliescu Presidency, the ban on his return to Romania was the cruellest.

In March 1993, three months after the Government had in effect banned the Timişoara visit, Queen Anne visited Romania on her own. Before leaving she told *Romînia Liberă*, 'I am making a short journey in order to know the Romanian people better, to help Romania recover its prestige and its appropriate place in the countries of the world.'[11] As it became clear that he would not himself be allowed back in Iliescu's time, his wife's visits to Romania meant more and more to King Michael. On this, the first, she avoided such key cities as Timişoara, which she felt Michael himself should visit before she did. But wherever she went her natural enjoyment, her gift of communicating with people in her far from perfect Romanian, won her friends.

The 75th anniversary of the day that Transylvanian delegates meeting in Alba Julia in 1918 had declared their union with the Old Kingdom fell on 1 December 1993. President Iliescu at first expressed the hope that the ceremony would be one of national reconciliation and agreed that the King (whose ancestors had contributed so much to making the union possible) should be invited to attend as a simple citizen. However, on 27 October the Presidency announced that 'ex-King Michael of Romania' should first ask for the recovery of his Romanian citizenship.'[12] Since this would be tantamount to recognising the validity of the Communist decree of 22 March 1948,* it was something King Michael could never do.

When by 22 November there was still no visa for King Michael, the Democratic Convention announced that if in two days' time a visa had not been granted they would not attend the Alba Julia ceremony.[13] The President was in a difficult position. Not to issue a visa would increase sympathy for the King and without the Democratic Convention the Alba Julia ceremony would become a farce. Yet should he issue a visa and the King come as an ordinary citizen, then Citizen Michael down among the people would become the

---

* The decree under which the Government of 1948 pretended to withdraw King Michael's citizenship.

central figure. Under considerable pressure from the extremist parties, he continued to refuse the visa.

On 1 December, the day of the anniversary, the Democratic Convention held a large demonstration in Bucharest's snow-covered Revolutionary Square. It was addressed by Emil Constantinescu, President of the Democratic Convention, and by the leaders of the Peasant, Liberal and Social Democratic parties. A leading political prisoner who had survived the communist era shouted from the crowd, 'The roots of evil in this country are to be found in the Cotroceni Palace,' and the crowd chanted back 'Iliescu is Ceauşescu. Resign, Resign.' Meanwhile, at Alba Julia, Petre Roman refused a place on the platform and instead mingled with the crowd where monarchists were selling the King's picture and the royal family's calendar. No greater dissension or lack of national unity could have been demonstrated to the world by this split in the commemoration of one of the high points of Romanian history.

# SEVENTEEN

## *President Iliescu Loses an Election*

In 1993 Romania had joined the Council of Europe. By 1994 she had set her sights on NATO – she was the first country to join the Partnership for Peace agreement – and, eventually perhaps, the European Union. But all these organisations required a presentable record on human rights and a genuine desire to live and work with their neighbours. Ceauşescu had left behind a large element which would not easily overcome their nostalgia for legal racism and dictatorial methods. Certain members of the administration together with such populists as Tudor and Funar would do their best to block any foreign policy that contemplated a future with Western Europe.

In May 1994 a newly elected Hungarian government had opened up a rare prospect of détente but, within a month, Liviu Maior, Romanian Minister of Education, had with Funar's support and in spite of President Iliescu's intervention, steered a racist Education Bill though Parliament which blatantly discriminated against the Hungarian minority of Transylvania.

As if this were not enough, Funar tried to use an archaeological dig in Cluj as a pretext for removing the statue of the fifteenth-century King Mathias, commissioned almost a century before to mark the millennium of the arrival in Europe of the Magyars. The Hungarian Prime Minister protested to Văcăroiu. The Bucharest Institute of Archaeology denounced 'this attempt to use archaeological research for political and nationalist ends'.[1] Yet, because Ion Iliescu first needed the parliamentary support of the extremist parties to defeat an Opposition motion of no confidence, only at the very last minute could Bucharest issue the order which prevented a set battle in the streets of Cluj.

Far greater damage to Romania's image in the West had already been done by the combination of neo-fascist Romanians and the many who, disillusioned with the outcome of the 1989 revolution, looked for a martyr. On 1 June 1991, the 45th anniversary of Marshal Antonescu's execution, Parliament had stood for a minute's silence.[2] Some 200,000 people – of whom the core were military or supporters of Tudor's Greater Romania Party – signed a petition calling for his posthumous retrial and acquittal of all war crimes. On 1 July 1991 Iaşi commemorated the 50th anniversary of the 1941 pogrom. Seven days later the

US Senate and House of Representatives condemned both the revival of anti-Semitism in Romania and the rehabilitation of Marshal Antonescu and asked the Romanian Government to demonstrate a more positive position on these issues.

The worship of Ion Antonescu continued for several years. Romania's relations, particularly with the USA, were damaged. Yet the Romanian administration had not sufficient urge or authority to suppress it. It was also used, with a nod from the President, to portray King Michael as a traitor whose *coup d'état* had opened the gates to Soviet occupation.

On the 50th anniversary of the *coup d'état* of 23 August 1944, both the US Senate and House of Congress paid their respects to King Michael for his contribution to the Allied victory.[3] Since the Romanian Government still held that the *coup d'état* of 1944 had been a purely Communist achievement, no such official recognition took place in Bucharest. Moreover, the King was not even allowed to attend the unofficial ceremony, a symposium to be held in Bucharest University on 8 and 9 October, although some of Romania's most distinguished citizens, representing the foundations and associations which had arranged the symposium, spent two weeks negotiating with the administration for the King's visa.

Their meeting with Theodor Meleşcanu, the Minister for Foreign Affairs, on 2 September 1994 gives us a glimpse of what many enlightened Romanians must have been thinking. They stressed the need, even at this late stage, to establish in the public mind the important co-belligerent role played by Romania during the last stages of the war. If Romanians were seen to unite in celebrating the 50th anniversary of their sovereign's decision to break with the Axis, the country's image, which had suffered from the prolonged campaign to rehabilitate Ion Antonescu and more recently by the appointment of ministers belonging to the PRNU, would be greatly improved.[4] Senior members of the administration were not unsympathetic to the group's reasoning but assured them that, since all decisions regarding the King were made at the Presidency, the response to any request for his visa would inevitably be 'no'.

To make it clear to all Europe that Iliescu meant to stop him entering his country, King Michael decided to fly with the Queen to Bucharest on the day before the symposium opened. 'I go as a Romanian,' he told journalists at the airport, 'not to contest the present constitutional order.'[5]

Although it seems that there had not been a single security incident when hundreds of thousands of Romanians had welcomed the King in April 1992, the Goverment now deployed large contingents of the Secret Service, police,

Gendarmerie and army troops in Bucharest, at Otopeni airport and the Television building. The situation, it was announced in all seriousness, was 'under control'. Romanian journalists were not allowed in the airport and had to rely on their French colleagues to tell them what was happening.

On landing, the King was told that visas were not issued at the airport on a Friday. While other passengers obtained theirs in the normal way at the terminal building, the royal party waited on the tarmac until the aircraft was ready to return. They then left.

Towards the end of 1994, Corneliu Tudor, who treated the Western democracies and all their post-war international organisations as enemies, insisted on more political influence. In January 1995 the government signed an agreement with all three extremist parties on the condition, for what it was worth, that all parties to the agreement bound themselves not to manifest racism, anti-Semitism, extremism or totalitarianism.

The enmity of the leaders of all four parties towards the King made him a prime target for subversive operations initiated in Bucharest. The one that would probably have done King Michael most harm, had it succeeded, occurred in 1993 during a visit to London by Virgil Măgureanu, head of the Romanian Intelligence Service. Măgureanu contacted certain people who had access to the royal family and told them that he wished to see the King. He was upset, he said, with the way things were going in Romania. In the autumn he would stage a *coup* against Iliescu and, should it succeed, he would, he implied, be prepared to talk about bringing King Michael back.

Had the King agreed even to listen to Măgureanu, Bucharest could have charged him with plotting to overthrow the elected government of Romania, and his relations with the West, particularly his hosts, the Swiss, would have suffered. Fortunately King Michael heard in time of this classic if rather naive attack, and it was promptly blocked.

After the King, Princess Margarita was the main target. Virtually everything that would damage her reputation was tried. She could hardly be accused of being a communist agent, but others, who genuinely helped the royal family and had links with Romania, ran that risk.

During an interview with Nicholas Shakespeare for *Harpers & Queen*, Princess Margarita listed the things she had read about herself in the anti-monarchist press, almost all of them originating in Bucharest.

I've gone out with Ceauşescu's son, Valentin. I've had an affair with the Prime Minister. One of my helpers is my lesbian lover, another a Mossad agent. I've two illegitimate children, one of them conceived in a Paris hotel – but I'm refusing to let him speak Romanian and this angers my father.

This was Shakespeare's leading paragraph, immediately followed by one explaining the context in which it had been said. The article was in the September 1992 issue of *Harpers & Queen*,[6] which appeared in mid-August. On 19 August Londoner's Diary of the *Evening Standard* quoted the first paragraph of Shakespeare's article, omitted the second and left their readers with the impression that this was Princess Margarita coming clean about herself – all in the spirit of the tabloid campaign being waged against the British royal family at the time. Next day the *Evening Standard* published a full and sincere apology, but for the enemies of King Michael and his family it had been an unexpected windfall.

In 1995 the British were to be hosts for the 50th anniversary of VE Day. The heads of state and of government of the Allied countries and countries associated with them would be invited to attend a thanksgiving service at St Paul's Cathedral on 7 May and on the following day a Guildhall reception and banquet hosted by the Queen and the Prime Minister.

In January worried Romanians telephoned Versoix to say that according to the Bucharest press the British Government had 'refused the King a visa'. Princess Margarita traced the story to a letter by Donald Forman, Secretary General of the Monarchist League, published in the *Daily Telegraph* of 16 January. Forman had not mentioned a visa; he had pointed out that although King Michael was the only surviving wartime head of state and had played a major role in the conflict, he was not, he understood, to be invited to the London ceremonies.

Other people had noticed Forman's brief letter and British ministers, MPs and officials began to receive telephone calls and letters. It was hardly a lobby; rather people who felt it their duty to make sure that those who were taking this decision were aware of the facts about King Michael. Even residents of Ayot St Lawrence, who remembered King Michael and his family, wrote to their MP and to their local paper.

The Romanian Government informed London that in their view an invitation to ex-King Michael would be inappropriate. Misinformation was set to work, that, for instance, King Michael had been responsible for the massive wartime deportation of Romanian Jews. Such lies were easily disproved and in February 1995 the British ambassador in Berne wrote to Versoix to say that, should the King wish to attend the thanksgiving service at St Paul's Cathedral on 7 May, he would forward to him an invitation from the Dean and Chapter. The King accepted 'on behalf of himself and of all those Romanians who had fought for the Allied cause.'[7]

Nevertheless a section of British public opinion felt that the King should also be invited to the official dinner. 'It is a strange way to treat a man who, fifty years ago, carried out one of the most extraordinary acts of political bravery of the war', wrote Noel Malcolm in the *Sunday Telegraph* of 19 March, and in the *Welwyn and Hatfield Times* of 26 April a letter made much the same point. 'What has happened to our once loud proclamation of a sense of fair play? Well, on this occasion it's pretty obvious, it's been dumped.'

When the list of guests to be invited to the Guildhall reception and banquet was finally approved, it included King Michael of 'Roumania' – spelt in the way it had been spelt when Michael was on the throne – while President Iliescu and his party appeared under the separate heading of 'Romania'. It was a neat solution to the problem of protocol. President Iliescu at one moment threatened not to attend but was nevertheless among the heads of state who watched the Queen enter the Guildhall with her family and greet her cousin, Michael, who had been placed with other royal guests near to the door.

This recognition by Western countries of 'the special contribution made by Romania and its heroes to the war'[8] inspired more thoughtful Romanian commentators to return to the theme which was at the heart of all the King's thinking. So we find Eugen Şerbanescu writing in *Romînia Liberă* that regardless of whether they are monarchies or republics, certain countries flourish 'mainly because their people have a system of values in which they believe, grafted onto a tradition and a history which is authentic, that is to say which they have made themselves, not one that has been imposed on them by others'.[9]

Relations between Tudor and the PSDR deteriorated during the autumn of 1995 and on 10 November 1995 the PRM withdrew its support from Văcăriou's Government, which then no longer had a parliamentary majority.

Corneliu Coposu died on 11 November 1995 aged 79. After the 1989 revolution he had failed to revive the spirit of the National Peasant Party of the 1940s. He was the only political leader to admit that neither he nor any of his political allies could give the country the inspiration and reassurance of legitimacy it needed to overcome its post-revolutionary inertia. At a press conference on 30 May he had said that 'the only solution for Romania at present' was to restore the constitutional monarchy and that, once he had obtained a parliamentary majority, he would modify the constitution to allow for the return of King Michael. On 6 June Coposu said he was sure that Emil Constantinescu would 'gladly participate'. Constantinescu did not respond. Since hardly 30 per cent of the population was in favour of a return to constitutional monarchy, Coposu's was a courageous political act, but other members of the Democratic Convention, though in favour of the King's return as a private citizen, were not ready to jeopardise their political careers by supporting the restoration of the monarchy. On his deathbed Coposu begged that King Michael be allowed to attend his funeral but the wish was not granted. Queen Anne and Princess Margarita did attend and were received by other mourners with great affection.

In April 1996 the Government committed a *gaffe* which, although the loss of Bessarabia had always meant less to Romanians than the loss of Transylvania, nevertheless must have cost them votes in the forthcoming general election. After visiting Romania on 8 April 1996 the Russian Deputy Foreign Minister, Krilov, in an interview with *Izvestia*, announced that the Russo–Romanian treaty which had been in draft for the last four years was now ready for initialling, and that the Romanians had agreed not to interpret any part of the treaty as a condemnation of the Ribbentrop–Molotov pact of August 1939, which had given Stalin the green light to invade Bessarabia. The Russian Foreign Minister Primakov would now go to Bucharest to receive this undertaking and then to finalise the treaty.

The Romanian Government had failed to take the Opposition into their confidence and the first they or the public heard of this new policy was when the newspaper *Adevărul* gave front-page coverage to Krilov's statement. Romanians were staggered by the news. Seven years after the Molotov–Ribbentrop pact had been universally condemned, the Romanian Government was still prepared to give an undertaking to the Russians which contradicted both world opinion and basic Romanian interests. On 25 April the Presidency wavered, spoke of 'transparency' and of their refusal to conclude the treaty on the conditions agreed by its Foreign Minister.

Foreign Minister Primakov arrived in Bucharest on 27 April but, according to Russian sources,[10] the Romanians had changed their minds. Primakov saw President Iliescu for quarter of an hour, then, having failed to conclude the treaty, angrily left the country.[11]

In the early 1990s, when NATO expansion had been no more than a passing thought, the NSF would have run little risk of an international scandal by omitting to consult the 'troublemakers' of the Opposition about an important treaty with the Soviet Union. By 1996, however, when the race was on among East European countries to join NATO, the direct consequences of failing to consider an Opposition to be integral to the governing process should have been forseen.

A few weeks later King Michael, for the first time, made his annual 10 May message a political statement directed to the Western Powers. He warned NATO and the EU not to isolate his country when planning for future expansion. He referred to the faster pace of Romanian privatisation and economic reform. He praised such PSDR achievements as reform of the armed forces and in particular Romania's role in Partnership for Peace. He also emphasised that since 1995 relations with Hungary had improved.

Romanians were surprised that the King should support a party which had behaved so appallingly to him. It was, in fact, a last-minute attempt to remind Western governments, if only implicitly, that the forthcoming elections could replace the present *régime* with one that was more in tune with Western thinking and, quite explicitly, that Romania was of major geo-political importance and 'cannot be left out of these structures without causing disaster for the whole of Europe'.[12]

In June 1996 Princess Margarita became engaged. Princess Helen had married Robin Medforth-Mills of Durham University in 1983 and had had two children, Nicholas and Karina. They divorced in 1991. In 1983 Princess Irina married John Kruger, who breeds horses and cattle in Oregon and has also had two children, Michael and Angelica. Princess Sophie was as yet unmarried. In 1995, Princess Maria, the youngest, married Casimir Wieslaw Mystkowski in New York. Princess Margarita's fiancé was one of Romania's most distinguished actors and a lecturer on drama, who was also becoming known in the rest of Europe.[13] She first met Mr Radu Duda, the son of a professor of medicine, in a Romanian hospital where he was helping to rehabilitate children through drama therapy. She liked him for his extraordinary understanding and kindness towards the small patients who through him were experiencing a little of a child's self-assurance and dignity and even a little *joie de vivre*. It was their work to ease some of the misery and sickness Ceaușescu had left behind that first brought them together.

Radu Duda is tall – even taller than his father-in-law – with an open face that reflects a genuine interest in people. He has none of the egotistic mannerisms associated with politicians, actors or other professions in the public view. When interpreting Kafka in a thirteenth-century courtyard or Luca's *l'Inventeur de l'Amour* at La Petite Molière in Paris he worked alone, face to face with the group of people who were witnessing his experience, using the absolute minimum of professional props.

Queen Anne and Princess Margarita had no problem about visiting Romania as tourists or for charity work, and in July 1996 Queen Anne paid a twelve-day visit, accompanied by her daughter and her daughter's fiancé. They were ignored by Romanian state television but covered by the national and local press and by the independent television stations which now existed. Most of their time was spent in central and western Romania and included Bucharest, Cluj, Oradea, Arad, Timişoara and, on the last day, Tîrgoveşti, where, according to the newspaper *Ziua*, the Patriarch Teoctist received the two royal visitors with ceremonies 'reserved for reigning monarchs'. But Timişoara in the Banat, which Queen Anne had hoped her husband would have been able to visit by now, gave them their most rousing reception. A special meeting of the county and city assemblies was called and while this was in session large numbers of Timişoara citizens gathered outside the town hall shouted pro-monarchist and anti-presidential slogans.[14]

President Iliescu, already upset by the PSDR's poor showing in the June local elections, was naturally infuriated. While Queen Anne was telling the crowd at the airport 'It's been a wonderful visit', President Iliescu was assuring the press that 'Romania, which is a presidential state, has no queen. I don't know any Queen Anne.'[15] The Government reserved the right to impose sanctions on those municipal officers whose behaviour had been incompatible with the constitution and with their status as local government officials of a republic. However, there seems to be no record of any such sanction and, even more humiliating for the Government, many of these 'traitors' had been newly elected in the local elections only the month before.

On 21 September 1996, H.R.H. the Princess Margarita of Romania and Mr Radu Duda were married in the tiny Greek Orthodox Church of St Gherassimos in Lausanne. The marriage service was celebrated by the Metropolitan Damaskinos of Switzerland.

Radu Duda's family was naturally outnumbered at the wedding by Princess Margarita's extended family. King Constantine of Greece, the Duke of Aosta, Prince Alexander of Yugoslavia and Mr Duda's younger brother, Dan, were among the witnesses who took it in turns to hold the crowns over the heads of the bride and bridegroom. Among the many royal guests were Queen Sophia of Spain and the Empress Farah of Iran, who sat between the bridegroom's parents and the heir to the Grand Duke of Luxemburg. The service was conducted alternately in Romanian and Greek, and printed in Romanian,

French and English. The Lord's Prayer was spoken aloud by everyone present in all four languages.

The reception and lunch were at the Mies Polo club near Versoix. Thanks largely to the bride's sister, Princess Sophie, who had looked after every detail of the day's events, it was altogether a happy and memorable day. Small children ran around and the King looked relaxed and young. Next day the newly married couple left for a two-week honeymoon as guests of the Crown Prince (now King) Hassan of Jordan.*

Wide use of TV gave the 1996 electoral campaign a more Western flavour than those of either 1990 or 1992. Images replaced ideologies. Iliescu was filmed playing billiards; Roman attending weddings. All were accompanied by rousing music, all their faces 'carried expressions of great concern for the country' and all were surrounded by cheering crowds.[16]

Văcăroiu's ineffective economic policy, the corruption, the association with the extremist parties, had probably damaged the PSDR irremediably. True, the last of the extremist allies, Funar's PRNU, had been dropped some time before the electoral campaign officially opened, but not soon enough.

At the party's conference in July Ion Iliescu had warned members that if they wanted his candidature they would have to clear out the 'corrupt elements'. During his campaign for the presidency he seemed to be dissociating himself from the PSDR.

The Democratic Convention offered the Romanian people a contract. If they had had enough of corruption, poverty and lies, the DC would undertake to give them a better life. If they wanted peace and good Christian people in power, they should vote for the DC. In 1992 the DC had failed to get their message across to the country people and workers. In 1996 an old peasant was shown on television determined this time to vote for the Democratic Convention.

While visiting the USA, Emil Constantinescu had remarked during an interview with the American *Micro Magazine* that King Michael 'should be able to take up residence in Romania like any other citizen'. This passed unnoticed in Romania until on 20 August, a fortnight before the campaign was due to open, Iliescu suddenly accused Constantinescu of endangering national security by publishing his monarchist sentiments. Constantinescu replied that as a candidate for the presidency he could not seriously be described as a

---

* On 5 February 1999, Mr Radu Duda received the title of Prince Radu of Hohenzollern-Veringen.

monarchist,[17] but the tactic gave Iliescu an excuse to revive the monarchical myth of the 1992 election. He warned voters that the DC's contract with Romania was in fact a contract with the monarchy: if they supported it they risked losing their homes and their land.[18] The PSDR video-clip showed Constantinescu's face morphing into that of King Michael although this demonising of King Michael had begun to wear a little thin, even in rural districts. The DC's video overlapped Iliescu's face with that of Ceauşescu, perhaps also a little outdated.

The parliamentary elections and the first round of the presidential elections were held on 3 November 1996. In the former, the Democratic Convention won 31 per cent of the votes, the governing PSDR 22 per cent and Roman's USD 13 per cent. Funar's PRNU and Tudor's PRM won 4.2 per cent and 4.5 per cent respectively. As soon as these results were known, the Democratic Convention and Roman's USD concluded a working agreement. They promised that, within six months, they would stop the deterioration of economic and social life and activate a foreign policy which would enable Romania to be in the first wave of East European countries to join NATO.[19]

The first round of the presidential elections was won by President Iliescu with 32 per cent. Constantinescu obtained 28.21 per cent, Roman 20.54 per cent and the HDUR candidate 6 per cent. Under the DC–USD electoral agreement Roman's supporters were asked to vote for Constantinescu in the second round, to be held on 17 November. Yet the outcome was still uncertain. Ion Iliescu was thought to have considerable support among older Romanians and in rural areas, which could be decisive. Constantinescu seems to have been saved by an unexpected swing in the countryside and among Orthodox Christians. During the final TV debate, instead of using the last thirty seconds to summarise his political position, Constantinescu said a brief prayer – a tactic which brilliantly differentiated him from his opponent.[20]

When on the night of 17/18 November 1996 the exit polls showed Constantinescu eight points ahead, President Iliescu accepted defeat.

Next day *Le Monde* published an editorial pointing out that Romania was the only East European country not to have experienced an alternative government since the fall of the Berlin Wall. 'It is up to the Europeans', the editorial continued, 'to throw their whole weight now into the balance to help Romania to bury once and for all Nicolae Ceauşescu.'[21]

# EIGHTEEN

## *King Michael Returns to Romania*

Victor Ciorbea, the popular mayor of Bucharest and now Prime Minister, promptly introduced a programme of economic shock therapy, the speed and scope of which OECD described as 'impressive even in comparison with other therapies in transition countries'.[1] On 12 May 1997 the president of the World Bank visited Romania for the first time in twenty years and made credits worth $600m available for the year 1997. Constantinescu's National Council of Action against Corruption and Organised Crime also promised to be effective, in May already reporting a significant decline in misappropriation of funds, smuggling and tax evasion. Romania's image at home and abroad improved miraculously. Romanians seemed overnight to have regained their dignity as a nation.

With the election of a centrist government under Constantinescu's presidency King Michael looked forward to visiting Romania and of even working alongside his people for the country's recovery. When in the third week of February 1997 the Government annulled the communist decree of 1948 and recognised his citizenship, he at once announced his intention to visit Romania for six days beginning on the 28th of the month. His eagerness, though it elicited a sharp reaction from anti-monarchists, was justified. At the beginning of February a government emissary had been sent to Versoix to ask for the King's help in persuading NATO governments to support Romania's membership. He had agreed and was now anxious to get started. To have any effect on the decision, which was to be taken at the Madrid summit in early July, he knew that lobbying must begin as soon as possible.

The new administration, while behaving correctly towards the King, were still on the defensive about 'the monarchy'. King Michael's visit, they announced, would be strictly private; the King had undertaken to make no public statements. President Constantinescu thought it necessary to go even further and assure Romanians in so many words that King Michael's return to his country was not a preliminary to constitutional monarchy.

The royal party arrived at Otopeni airport at about 1 o'clock on Friday, 28 February. They were met by Princess Margarita and her husband and in a private capacity by a number of government ministers led by Victor Ciorbea. They received the traditional bread and salt, but the planned ceremony was largely swept aside by the enthusiasm of a hundred or so people made up of war veterans, former political prisoners, teenagers, leaders of political parties, cultural leaders treading on each others' toes to get nearer to this man who himself showed signs of his deep emotion. Champagne was spilt. It was a shambles but a happy one. The King made no statement, but held up his new passport for the photographers to see.

At the Elisabeta Palace – their home during the visit – they were greeted by about two thousand people but the King only said, as he had at Easter in 1992, 'I love you all. Don't forget that.' When asked by a journalist whether they would now live in Bucharest, Queen Anne replied that she would be quite ready to but would want to make a number of changes at the Elisabeta Palace, which she found rather ostentatious. Later, during an interview with a British journalist, the King admitted that a return to constitutional monarchy could not be ruled out. However, his aim was to help Romania in the best possible way. 'There have', he said, 'been great changes here recently and things are getting better and better. Helping Romania to get into NATO and the European Community is something I can certainly do.'[2]

In University Square, where he laid a wreath at the memorial to the martyrs of the 1989 revolution, the crowd of about ten thousand was again far less than the massive, near-hysterical reception he had been given during the 1992 visit. At that time he had been seen as an outcast, a symbol of opposition to the neo-Communist *régime* in power. Now the welcome was less frantic but no less sincere, the King told me, and in a sense more solid. There was nothing like universal support for the monarchy among the peasantry and the general attitude of the urban population was probably summed up by a computer engineer in the cheering crowd, 'The King is very special to us – very modest, intelligent and religious. We would like him on the throne but we know it's impossible now. And we quite like the government.'[3]

On Saturday 1 March the King lunched with Victor Ciorbea, the Prime Minister, and discussed with his cabinet and members of parliament the Government's programme of economic and social reforms. When asked by the press afterwards what were the prospects for 1997, he replied, 'It is the beginning of normality in Romania. For that reason I shall return to Romania more often. I shall do everything in my power for Romania.'

If the service the royal family attended at the cathedral on Sunday was the most symbolic part of the King's visit, politically the most important occasion was a working dinner with President Constantinescu the evening before he left.

The King and Queen were accompanied by Princess Margarita and Mr Radu Duda, Gheorghe Antoniade, head of the King's Household, Jonathan Eyal, director of studies at the Royal United Services Institute and Ambassador George Berthon, honorary president of the European movement. The discussion lasted about one and a half hours, after which President Constantinescu made a statement to the press.

He praised Romanians for not being influenced by 'uncivilised propaganda' directed against the King. Their discussion, he said, had concentrated on the integration of Romania into European and European–Atlantic structures and how to present, in the short time available, the true image of today's Romania. He had invited King Michael to help not only because of his qualities and the connections that he had but also because he is a historical personality, one of the last great personalities of the Second World War.

King Michael replied briefly, 'I love my country too much not to accept this proposal and, as I stated on many occasions, I will do everything in my power to help Romania and at the same time to keep a collaboration with President Constantinescu so that we can carry through what we have in mind.'

The royal family spent Easter that year in Timişoara as the guests of the Metropolitan Nicolae of Transylvania. When Queen Anne had been there in July 1996 she had promised that next time she came she would bring the King with her. It was his first visit since his exile in 1948.

After the Midnight Mass, King Michael and the Metropolitan Nicolae circled the cathedral followed by thousands of people carrying their candles. Perhaps just as moving for the King was the lunch the Metropolitan arranged for him with the religious representatives of the Catholic, the Uniat, the Protestant, the Jewish, and the Moslem communities – a rare occasion where he saw his desire for harmony among all the faiths put into practice. The Metropolitan Nicolae, described by Queen Anne as 'a saintly and courageous man', had done a great deal for the poor and the old in his diocese. He had also been the first to return property to the Uniat church stolen under the Communist *régime*.

The King was to press Romania's case for inclusion in the first wave of new NATO entrants with seven members of the alliance – Belgium, Denmark, Luxemburg, the Netherlands, Norway, Spain and the United Kingdom. During his tour he spoke to heads of state but also to influential civil and military audiences, most of whom had never seen him before. He was no orator but spoke with modesty and conviction about the long-term advantages to European security of Romania's membership.

Three weeks after his meeting with Constantinescu he delivered a speech at the Royal United Services Institute in London. In 1997, four years before the war against terrorism was declared, most European countries still saw NATO as their sole guarantee against a revitalised Russia. So King Michael opened his speech by saying that Romanian security could only be guaranteed by the same structures that ensured stability in Western Europe. A truncated alliance would raise more problems than it would solve. The 1996 elections, he said, had demonstrated the effectiveness of Romanian democracy, but much was still needed to improve Romania's institutions. While there was undoubted civilian control of the armed forces, more effective democratic control of the internal security services was needed. He reminded his audience that in 1996 a treaty of friendship had been signed with Hungary. The Hungarian minority even had representatives in the present government. The issue of the Hungarian and Romanian minorities in their respective countries would always be there but, he argued, with both countries in the Alliance, it would be permanently diffused.

The King pointed to an important discrepancy between NATO thinking and NATO practice. Although it was generally agreed that the main security threats to Europe would come from the peripheries of the continent, the Alliance gave the impression of being only interested in the centre. Romania had good relations with both Greece and Turkey and, once anchored within NATO, could substantially increase the stability of the more vulnerable southern sector.

Throughout the speech King Michael stressed Romania's potential for making a considerable and permanent contribution to NATO. After Poland it was the largest state in the region both in population and military potential. It had been the last Central European democracy to collapse during the years leading up to the war. Once it had recovered its prosperity it would again become a powerhouse in that part of the world.

In February President Chirac had promised to support Romania's candidature and at the meeting of NATO Foreign Ministers a month before the summit led a group of nine – Belgium, Italy, Spain, Portugal, Luxemburg, Canada, Turkey and Greece – in a campaign to strengthen this southern sector. By the beginning of July the whole NATO membership except the USA and Britain was ready to accept Hungary, Poland and the Czech Republic plus Slovenia or plus Slovenia and Romania. Romania was recognised as having with Poland the only military punch in that part of the world and was already carrying out its peace-keeping duties competently. But its reform record was abysmal. Moreover, the average American or Englishman might have heard of the Prague Spring, the Hungarian revolution and 'Solidarity' in Poland but, thanks largely to Iliescu's prejudice against the King, not of the contribution to Allied victory made by King Michael's *coup d'état* of 23 August 1944.

However, US domestic considerations most probably had the last word. Twenty million Americans of Central European origin were concentrated in states whose vote could swing a presidential election.[4] Although at the last minute a few senators spoke up for Romania, President Clinton was advised that he could get the required two-thirds Senate majority for an enlargement of three countries only. The USA therefore announced in advance of the summit that it would support the candidature of the Czech Republic, Hungary and Poland, and this decision was reflected in the Summit *communiqué*.

President Clinton took immediate steps to reduce the damaging effect of his decision on Constantinescu's drive for reform. He sent the Romanian President a letter recognising the 'enormous progress that Romania has made since the new government took over last December'. He paid a flying visit to Bucharest and urged Romanians to stay on the course of reform, 'for this would open the door to NATO'.[5]

King Michael's message to the Romanians was:

We are disappointed.
  But we are not resigned because we managed what all the people thought impossible: in only seven months we made up for much of the time wasted in seven years.
  Thanks to your vote, to your endeavours, endurance and determination, those who spoke on our behalf could persuade almost all the NATO member countries that our country deserves to join them in the Atlantic Alliance, and that this would be a great advantage to them.
  From now on we have many friends who understand and respect us. The progress made in these past seven months gives me not only the hope, but the certainty that we will succeed.[6]

A possible consequence of the Madrid Decision could have been a return of what had been called 'Romania's deplorable fatalism': the Yalta syndrome, the assumption that decisions they could not influence would always decide their country's destiny.[7] This did not happen: Romania continued to work positively for acceptance by NATO. Yet some elements in the Constantinescu administration evidently insisted on a scapegoat, in the shape of their monarch. After the Madrid Decision the Romanian authorities were no longer prepared to discuss the possibility of his continuing to work for the integration of Romania into Europe – more especially the European Union. This was a deep disappointment for Michael. It would put him for the remainder of the Constantinescu administration on the sidelines, observing but without any means of directly influencing the destiny of his country.

On 28 August 1997 Constantinescu made a dramatic appeal to the Romanian people to support his drive against corruption.[8]

> We won the election in November 1996, but we did not win power because a great part of the economic power was and still is in the hands of a mafia-like system that has nothing to do with the national interest. We entered a jungle. Prominent 'private' corrupt persons had behind them prominent corrupt people from the state structures.

These mafia-like structures of Romanian corruption were still to be found in the army, the Intelligence services, in every ministry, in every governmental and non-governmental organisation, in private as well as state industries – together with the pervading influence of ex-Securitate agents. Whereas Constantinescu would fire a member of his staff at the first whiff of corruption, others in his administration, while opposing corruption as a concept, would always defend an offender who was a member of their own party. Most ministers preferred to come to terms with their bureaucracies so that reforms, after becoming law, were at serious risk of running into the sand before they could be applied. Should the Government ever dare to clean up a ministry from top to bottom they would be accused of carrying out a 'political purge'.

Constantinescu saw corruption as Romania's greatest handicap. But differing party policies within the coalition and the priority given by members of the Government to personal and party interests were also putting a severe brake on his drive for reform.

The truce which had united the Opposition coalition during the elections did not survive the test of government. Whereas the President at first had the authority of a leader fulfilling his mandate, a government of parties with different backgrounds and interests was from the start far less decisive. There was in-fighting both between and within the parties making up the administration. Consequently the Government was not coherent. The Democratic Party were particularly concerned about their image and would even on occasions vote with the PSDR. Government MPs lacked discipline and were often absent from crucial votes. Finally, in despair, the Prime Minister, who seemed unwilling to stand up to difficult ministers,[9] compromised the democratic process by circumventing the legislature and promulgating his reforms through government decrees. Thousands of honest Romanians had become entrepreneurs, taxpayers, small and medium investors. But the Government only began to shut down the large loss-making state firms in August 1997 and even then without the political and legal framework required for true reform. Embezzlement of state property followed and became the origin of new great fortunes similar to those of Iliescu's time. Meanwhile half of an average Romanian's income had to be spent on food; in the case of pensioners 60 per cent to 70 per cent, and even then their standard of nutrition was unacceptably low.[10]

The PSDR had at first been on the defensive, stupefied by the size of their electoral defeat. But at the first sign of popular dissatisfaction with the new administration they rallied and by August 1997 were smugly deploring the state of the country. By the end of the year they were already talking of a return to power. However, at a rally of all the Opposition parties held in October it was Tudor, leader of Romania's most extreme right-wing party, who out-manoeuvred and dominated the PSDR. It was the first hint that should a Democratic Coalition failure follow the failure of the PSDR, a collapse into the hands of Romania's extremists could not be excluded.

Under Constantinescu's *régime* Romanians probably saw less reason for constitutional change than they had before. In Iliescu's time opinion polls had asked the question and at least 15 per cent to 20 per cent had always been in favour of a return to constitutional monarchy. Paradoxically the electoral victory of the democrats (among whom there were many monarchists) had distanced the idea of the King's restoration. After Constantinescu's election a wave of optimism swept the country; Romanians who saw them sitting together on public occasions would think how lucky they were to have both a king and a president, and two such good men.

By now King Michael knew then that there was little likelihood of Romania changing to a constitutional monarchy in his time. Yet he had a duty to let it be known whom he wished to succeed him as head of the family. He announced this during a dinner he and Queen Anne gave at the Elisabeta Palace on 30 December 1997, the 50th anniversary of the *coup* which had forced him to abdicate. Their guests were leading figures of most political parties, prominent intellectuals and personal friends.

A monarchist group had recently issued a proposal for a return to the monarchy. The King immediately disassociated himself from it but a wave of anti-monarchist hostility could not be checked. 'Why', pleaded Roxana Iordache in Romînia Liberă, 'cannot we recognise constitutional monarchy as a form of state and recognise its contribution to our country's development? At least that, even if one cannot see what a great gift of God King Michael personifies.'[11] People like Iliescu and Roman, she said, can be expected to behave as they did but so-called democrats 'should have first condemned the action of 30 December 1947 and only then accused the signatories of the declaration of allegedly going too far'.

It was against this background that towards the end of his speech at the anniversary dinner the King introduced what was essentially a family and dynastic matter, one that would require amendments to the Family Statute and, should it ever be necessary, the annulment of provisions in the 1923 constitution flowing from Salic law. When the 1923 constitution was drafted, he said, women had few political rights. But times had changed and he had never felt that past traditions should be kept regardless of the present realities.

> In this spirit I wish to say that my desire is that my first-born daughter Margarita succeeds to all my rights and prerogatives when the Almighty decides that my time has come. I feel sure that Romanians will embrace my daughter with love in the same way as they embraced Queen Elizabeth, Marie and Helen and have shown so much affection to my wife and me.
>
> Conscious of my constitutional responsibilities I place her fate and mine as always in the hands of the Romanian people. In the end it is the people who will decide. But I think you will understand why I wished to share my point of view with you on this rather than any other day.[12]

This statement had been made after much consideration and in consultation with the President. Most guests enjoyed the occasion – some giving way to emotion and nostalgia – and saw no objection to the King's informing them of his decision. It was a warm and happy occasion. However, there was the usual reaction from the PSDR and extremist parties who accused Constantinescu of preparing to restore a constitutional monarchy.

Petre Roman, who was at the dinner, challenged the President to comment,[13] which Constantinescu did with some vigour. In his capacity as Romanian president, he declared, he would not during his tenure initiate or accept a change of the current form of government. He would, however, point out that the principal Opposition party (PSDR) and its leader, who now expressed such anxiety about the observance of the constitution, did not react when their former government ally* expressed anti-democratic views in Parliament and in the press, accused the head of state of being a foreign agent, and threatened the elected representatives of the people who opposed him with violence, summary trial and imprisonment. 'Since the 1996 elections,' he added, 'the PSDR had not once disassociated itself – much less protested against – anti-democratic actions and attitudes against the basic institutions of the Romanian state.'[14]

Two years later, on 19 December 1999, as part of the millennium celebrations, King Michael delivered a speech to the press in Bucharest which was probably his most outspoken public statement to date. It broke his rule not to raise the constitutional issue in public. After praising the press for its diversity of views – the essence of any democracy – he continued:

> I have a great deal of experience with the falsification of history and know that, ultimately, Carol I or Ferdinand will be remembered as better Romanians than Ana Pauker or Dej. . . .
>
> The past decade has been a mixture of excitement and disappointment, of hope and deception. . . . Of course we need better, more capable politicians, as does any democracy. But politicians have to rely on a structure which functions. One does not need to be a monarchist to realise that there is no sensible division of powers between the two houses of parliament, that it is virtually impossible to pass legislation without government emergency decrees, that ministers do not know what they are supposed to do and that a large part of the time is spent in perpetual personal fighting. Meanwhile privatisation stops and goes, foreign investors are afraid to come, inflation continues and the restitution of private property is still stuck. I do not doubt the government's good intentions. But I doubt the ability of the current political arrangement in the country to deliver the prosperity and stability which we all need.

King Michael had never believed that a republic was in itself any worse than a monarchy, but the so-called republicanism imposed on the Romanian people in the 1940s was of a different order.

---

* A reference to Tudor, leader of the extreme right-wing Greater Romania Party.

My criticism is directed against an entire system which was created in order to stifle democracy, and was imposed by people who believe that there is nothing we should preserve from the Romania we had before communism. I am also frankly disappointed by the entire political class which seems unable to grasp the simple fact that working within this structure is an exercise doomed to failure. We do not need a perpetual revolution. Marx and his associates believed in that. But we do need to complete the revolution of 1989.[15]

A year later President Constantinescu confirmed the King's words in a dramatic way. A few months before the presidential elections of November 2000 he admitted that the corrupt structures he had inherited had proved too much for him and he withdrew his candidature in favour of Mugur Isarescu, who had become Prime Minister on 16 December 1999. Isarescu was an honest, competent man whose main ambition was to return to his post as head of the National Bank. Not surprisingly in the general election Iliescu's PSDR won 37 per cent of votes, Tudor's PRM 21 per cent and the DC not a single seat. There was a real risk that in the run-up to the presidential election Corneliu Tudor could defeat Ion Iliescu. On 10 December 2000 the King intervened. Although, he told Romanians, they had the right to punish politicians who had failed them, 'if you choose to give your votes to politicians who encourage racial and ethnic hatred, who speak the language of violence, you will vote Romania out of Europe for decades to come'.[16]

Iliescu, who now represented moderation, defeated Tudor and returned to the presidency. His spell in opposition had given him time to reflect and he regretted, he said, having 'hounded' King Michael during the tensions of the early and mid-1990s. He felt that 'the moment had come to be rid of prejudices'.[17]

On 10 March 2001 the head of the presidential chancery, accompanied by a presidential counsellor, arrived in Versoix with an invitation for the King and Queen Anne to the opening of the Gallery of Modern Art. This was to take place in the National Museum of Romanian Art at the royal palace in Calea Victoriei on 24 March.* Owing to other commitments the King could not accept but said he hoped to visit the gallery soon. He sent a personal message to President Iliescu.

---

\* During the 1989 revolution the museum had been badly damaged. It had been reopened in 2000 in its new form, one of outstanding quality.

## King Michael Returns to Romania

On Friday 18 May 2001 the King and Queen accompanied by Princess Margarita and Prince Radu arrived at Otopeni airport for a three weeks' stay in Romania. They visited the exhibition and on the 19th had supper with President Iliescu. Ion Iliescu was waiting on the steps of Cotroceni Palace to shake hands with King Michael. They had never met. A few weeks later, when the President was in Switzerland for the Crans Montana Forum\* he visited King Michael at his house in Versoix.

It was the beginning of a normal relationship between the President and the King which, had the former been less obsessed by the threat of monarchy, could have been established eleven years before. King Michael had no wish to take part in his country's internal politics – had instantly turned down the idea when the Liberal Party had proposed it in 1992. He had repeatedly said that his duty as king was to no particular party or group but to the people as a whole.

The King has regained through the courts some of his private property, including Săvârşin, the house near Arad that he had bought in 1942. Under a law of 10 July 2001, which granted special rights to former heads of state, the King now has a pension and the right to a suitable house, bodyguards and a car. For the first time since his exile his status is, at least to this extent, recognised in Romania. He can now travel freely and play an active part in the civic life of the country without, as in President Constantinescu's time, feeling that he might embarrass the Government. However correctly President Iliescu might treat the King, he knew that, unlike his predecessor, he could always laugh off any charge of developing 'monarchist sympathies'.

On 21 October 2001 the King was 80, still very fit and ramrod straight. Apart from the more intimate celebrations of his birthday, Princess Margarita and her husband arranged a surprise party. On the evening of 22 October he went with Queen Anne to the Beau Rivage hotel in Geneva, expecting to meet his daughter and Prince Radu, and instead found a large group of friends and well-wishers waiting to greet him. At first he was startled; but as the evening proceeded he seemed to be enjoying himself.

In the summer of 2002 King Michael was active in the country's foreign policy, again campaigning for Romania's accession to NATO and this time success was more likely. Romania had halved the size of her bloated army and made it a professional force. It had competently handled its peace-keeping

---

\* One of the leading annual international conferences of decision makers 'committed to a more humane world'.

duties in Europe and anti-terrorist operations in Afghanistan. It had wholeheartedly supported Washington's post-9/11 anti-terrorist policy and the preparations for war against Iraq, offering the use of airspace, bases and Black Sea port facilities for the training and transport of US troops. Consequently, at the Prague Summit in November 2002 it was among the seven ex-Communist countries to be invited to join the Alliance. It became a member in March 2004.

During her interview with Nicholas Shakespeare in 1992 Princess Margarita had remarked 'I don't know if I'd be a good queen. But if it doesn't work out there is so much to be done in Romania.' No one could have worked harder since then, particularly for Romania's orphans and old people.

On 10 September 2002 Prince Radu was appointed Special Representative of the Government of Romania for Integration, Cooperation and Sustainable Development. He has the difficult and delicate brief of promoting, without political involvement, Romania's economic, commercial and business interests, foreign investment and membership of the European Union; its culture and history and the modernisation of education, particularly in the European context; and democratic values in Romanian public opinion. Prince Radu reports directly to the Prime Minister, and turns repeatedly for advice to his father-in-law. In his speeches Prince Radu has a talent for addressing Romania's difficult technical problems with conviction while on occasion evoking the physical beauty of his country and the talented, attractive and sometimes exasperating people who inhabit it.

Romania was among the most reluctant of the Soviet satellites to restore to their rightful owners property confiscated under communist rule. It was not until 21 October 2004, almost fifteen years after the Romanian rising of 1989 and execution of the Ceauşescus, that the Government approved a Bill (which had still not been approved by Parliament) under which King Michael would be paid compensation for the loss of the Peleş estate. Although the Peleş, Pelişor and Foişor castles would remain the patrimony of the State, the King would have the right to use them on special occasions. King Michael and his family would also have use of the Elisabeta Palace during his lifetime.

In a *communiqué* issued by the King's secretariat, His Majesty said that the object of the long negotiations had been to obtain a complete understanding which would reflect the inalienable right to private property and to rectifying the moral illegality committed by the communist dictatorship while, at the same time, taking into account the historical importance of the royal property to the country as a whole.[18]

Elections were due before the end of 2004 when Ion Iliescu would step down. He would remain head of the PDSR now known as the PSD (Social Democratic Party) and his Prime Minister, Adrian Nastase, was widely expected to replace him at the presidency.

The Parliamentary election of 28 November gave the PSD–PUR\* alliance a marginal victory over the Opposition – the Democratic Alliance consisting of the Liberal and Democratic parties – led by Traian Băsescu. In the Presidential election of the same date Nastase won 40 per cent of the votes, Băsescu 35 per cent and Tudor 11.6 per cent. However in the run off of 12 December Băsescu defeated Nastase by 51.23 per cent to 48.77 per cent and appointed as his prime minister Calin Popescu-Tăriceanu, leader of the Liberal Party. The government of the Democratic Alliance, which now included members of the Humanist Party and the Democratic Union of Hungarians and had the support of some of the smaller minorities, was approved by Parliament on 28 December 2004.

The charismatic, outspoken, determined Traian Băsescu, a sea captain for much of his life who became mayor of Bucharest and – after the fall of Constantinescu – leader of the Opposition, asked during a pre-election TV debate for this chance 'to pull Romania out of the hands of the Mafia'.[19] The European Commission's annual reports on Romania's record make depressing reading and Băsescu has much to do if it is to come anywhere near to meeting EU criteria by the deadline of 2007. As former mayor of Bucharest he is at least familiar with the tactics that will be used against him. He also knows that some influential member states are ready for their own reasons to turn a blind eye to EU standards but has, nonetheless, asked the West to support his reform programme.

Had there been a genuine attempt by all republican administrations of the 1990s to nurture Romania's fragile post-Ceaușescu democracy, the country would almost certainly be in better shape today. Return to a constitutional monarchy would have made an even more decisive break with the dictatorial past but, after forty years of vilification of the dynasty and virtual eradication of the middle class, a realistic opportunity for this did not occur.

As it is, the past still weighs heavily on Romanians. Although a new middle class is emerging they are still a country of the very rich and the very poor. Free elections and a free press are firmly established but so is systematic high-level corruption.

---

\* The Humanist Party.

The King and Queen Anne spend more time now in Romania, either at the Palatul Elisabeta with their daughter and son-in-law or at Săvârşin which after so many years of institutional service requires much restoration. After telling his wife what a lovely house it was, when they first walked in the only thing King Michael recognised was the staircase. In many ways things are easier for the King, less stressful. Yet there will always be a cloud over his life so long as Romanians – for all their talent, initiative, sophistication, generosity – still lag behind most other emerging East European states. At his age the disappointments show. But he has not given way to cynicism and his smile is as warm as ever.

King Michael will never hesitate to help his country in any way he can. The sixty-five years since he became king in 1940 have proved him to be, and he remains, the most reliable friend Romanians have.

# The Bourbon Parma Royal Family

```
Louis XIV    m.   Maria Theresa
King of           Infanta
France            of Spain
1638–1715         1638–83
              │
           Louis
      Dauphin of France
         1661–1711
              │
      ┌───────┴───────┐
  Louis XV         Philip V
King of France   King of Spain
  1710–74         1683–1764
     │               │───────────────────────────┐
     ▼               ▼                           │
Royal House    Royal House                    Philip
 of France      of Spain                  Duke of Parma
                    │                        1720–65
                    │                           ▼
         Juan Carlos  m.  Sophia of        Royal House
         King of Spain    Greece               of
            1938–         1938–           Bourbon Parma
                                               │
                                            Robert
                                        Duke of Parma
                                          1848–1907
```

| 20 other children | Xavier of Bourbon Parma 1889–1977 | Felix of Bourbon Parma 1893–1970 | m. | Charlotte Grand Duchess of Luxembourg 1896–1985 | René of Bourbon Parma 1894–1962 | m. | Margarethe of Denmark 1895–1990 |

```
                                    ▼                  ┌──────────────┬──────────┐
                              Royal House of       Anne of      m. Michael I      3
                               Luxembourg          Bourbon         King of      other
                                                   Parma           Romania     children
                                                   1923–           1921–
```

```
            Zita of           m.      Charles
        Bourbon Parma                 Emperor
          1892–1989                  of Austria
                                      1887–1922
```

# Romanian Royal Family – House of Hohenzollern

**KARL ANTON** Prince of Hohenzollern-Sigmaringen (1811–1885)

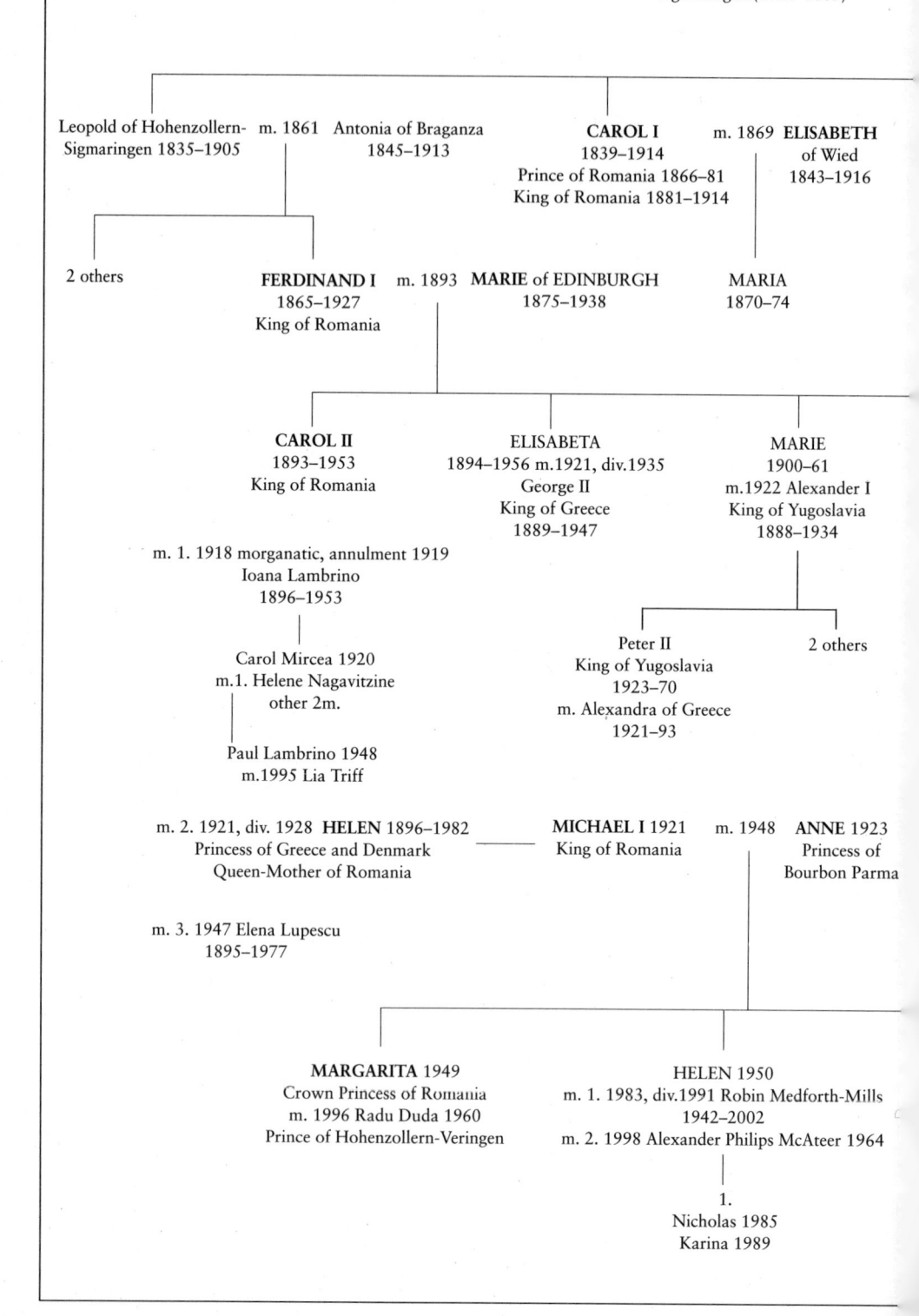

---

Leopold of Hohenzollern-Sigmaringen 1835–1905 — m. 1861 — Antonia of Braganza 1845–1913

**CAROL I** 1839–1914 Prince of Romania 1866–81 King of Romania 1881–1914 — m. 1869 — **ELISABETH** of Wied 1843–1916

2 others

**FERDINAND I** 1865–1927 King of Romania — m. 1893 — **MARIE of EDINBURGH** 1875–1938

MARIA 1870–74

**CAROL II** 1893–1953 King of Romania

**ELISABETA** 1894–1956 m.1921, div.1935 George II King of Greece 1889–1947

**MARIE** 1900–61 m.1922 Alexander I King of Yugoslavia 1888–1934

m. 1. 1918 morganatic, annulment 1919
Ioana Lambrino 1896–1953

Carol Mircea 1920
m.1. Helene Nagavitzine
other 2m.

Paul Lambrino 1948
m.1995 Lia Triff

Peter II King of Yugoslavia 1923–70 m. Alexandra of Greece 1921–93

2 others

m. 2. 1921, div. 1928 **HELEN** 1896–1982 Princess of Greece and Denmark Queen-Mother of Romania

**MICHAEL I** 1921 King of Romania — m. 1948 — **ANNE** 1923 Princess of Bourbon Parma

m. 3. 1947 Elena Lupescu 1895–1977

**MARGARITA** 1949
Crown Princess of Romania
m. 1996 Radu Duda 1960
Prince of Hohenzollern-Veringen

HELEN 1950
m. 1. 1983, div.1991 Robin Medforth-Mills 1942–2002
m. 2. 1998 Alexander Philips McAteer 1964

1.
Nicholas 1985
Karina 1989

m. 1834  JOSEPHINE OF BADEN
         1813–1900

Marie of Hohenzollern-   m. 1867   Philip of Flanders and         3 others
Sigmaringen 1845–1912              Saxe-Coburg
                                   1837–1909

                    Albert I Saxe-Coburg   m. 1900   Elisabeth of Bavaria
                         1875–1934                        1876–1965
                    King of the Belgians

NICHOLAS 1903–78                    ILEANA 1909–91                    MIRCEA
Co-Regent of Romania 1927–30        m. 1. 1931 Anton Archduke of      1913–16
m. 1. 1931 Ioana Dumitrescu         Austria, Habsburg-Toscana
           1909–63                  m. 2. 1954 Ştefan Issărescu
m. 2. 1967 Theresa Lisboa Figueira de Mello
           1913–97
                                              6 children

IRINA 1953                      SOPHIE 1957                    MARIA 1964
m. 1983 John Kruger 1945        m. 1998 Alain Biarneix of      m. 1995, Casimir Wieslaw
div. 2003                       Laufenbourg 1957               Mystkowski 1958
                                div. 2003                     officially separated 2000
                                                               div. 2003

Michael 1985                    Elisabeta-Maria
Angelica 1986                        1999
                                              Based on Genealogical Table in *Later
                                              Chapters of My Life* by Diana Mandache,
                                              (Sutton 2004)

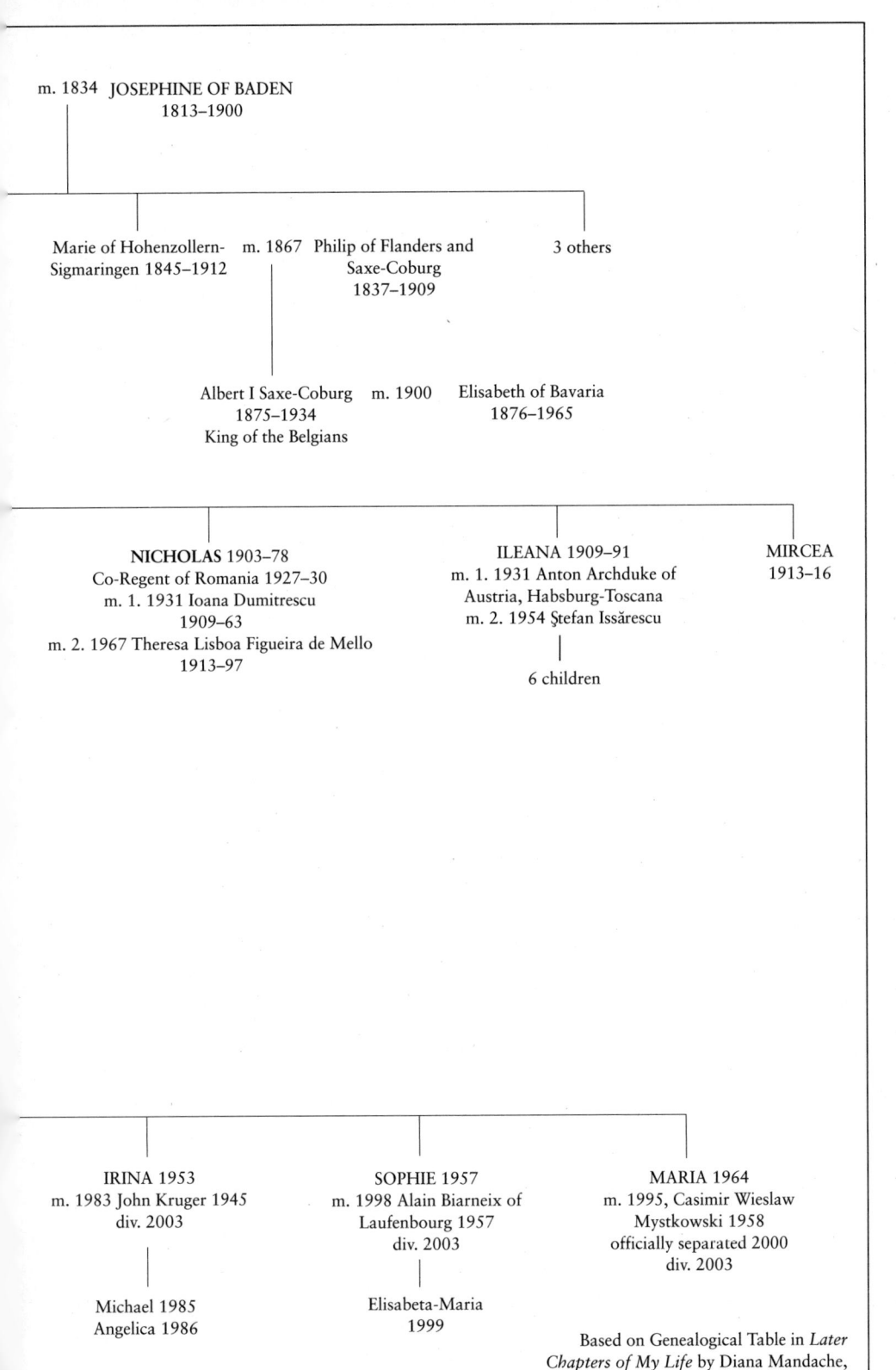

# The Greek and Danish Royal Families

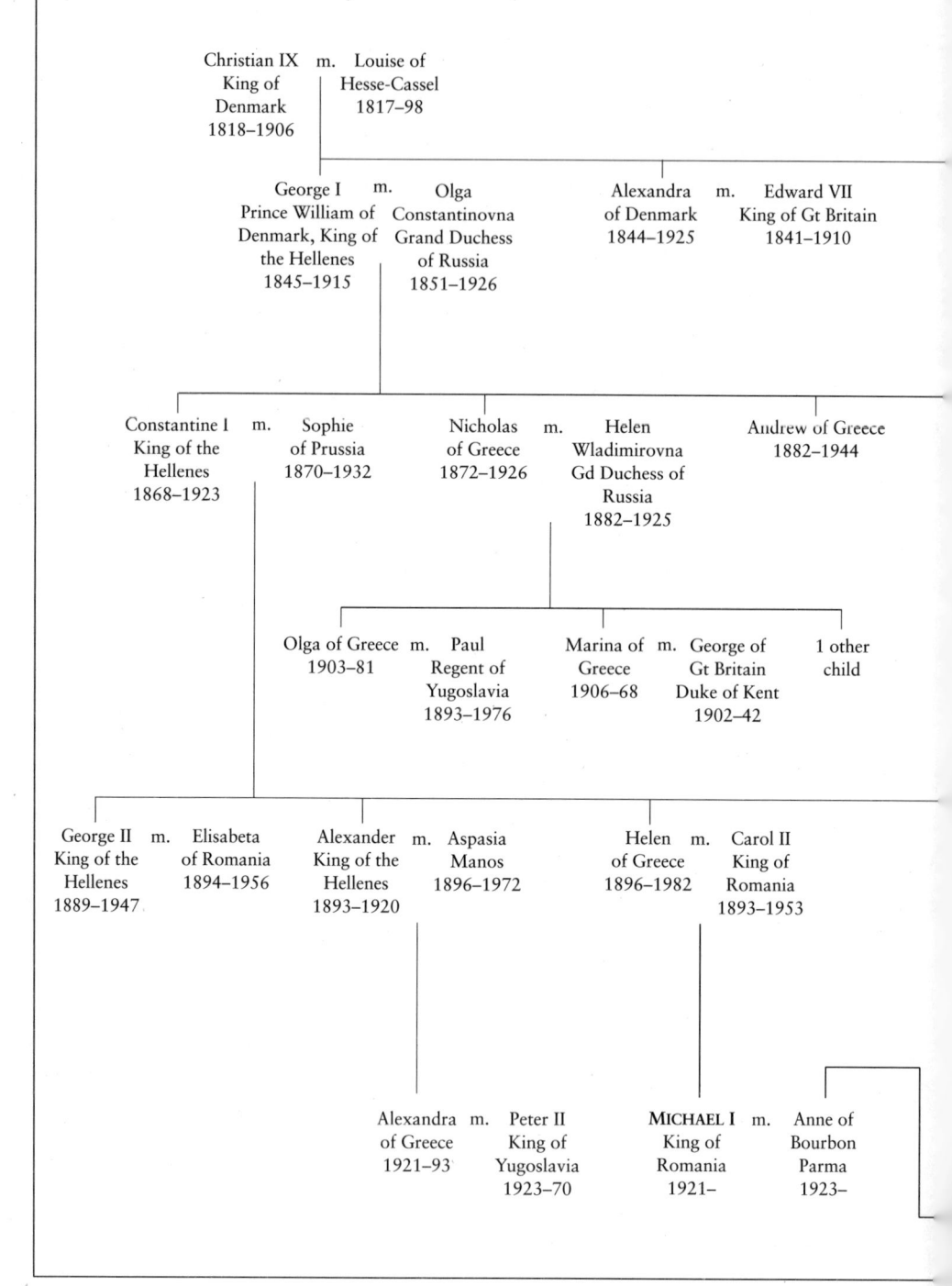

- Christian IX, King of Denmark, 1818–1906 m. Louise of Hesse-Cassel, 1817–98
  - George I, Prince William of Denmark, King of the Hellenes, 1845–1915 m. Olga Constantinovna, Grand Duchess of Russia, 1851–1926
    - Constantine I, King of the Hellenes, 1868–1923 m. Sophie of Prussia, 1870–1932
      - George II, King of the Hellenes, 1889–1947 m. Elisabeta of Romania, 1894–1956
      - Alexander, King of the Hellenes, 1893–1920 m. Aspasia Manos, 1896–1972
        - Alexandra of Greece, 1921–93 m. Peter II, King of Yugoslavia, 1923–70
      - Helen of Greece, 1896–1982 m. Carol II, King of Romania, 1893–1953
        - MICHAEL I, King of Romania, 1921– m. Anne of Bourbon Parma, 1923–
    - Nicholas of Greece, 1872–1926 m. Helen Wladimirovna, Gd Duchess of Russia, 1882–1925
      - Olga of Greece, 1903–81 m. Paul, Regent of Yugoslavia, 1893–1976
      - Marina of Greece, 1906–68 m. George of Gt Britain, Duke of Kent, 1902–42
      - 1 other child
    - Andrew of Greece, 1882–1944
  - Alexandra of Denmark, 1844–1925 m. Edward VII, King of Gt Britain, 1841–1910

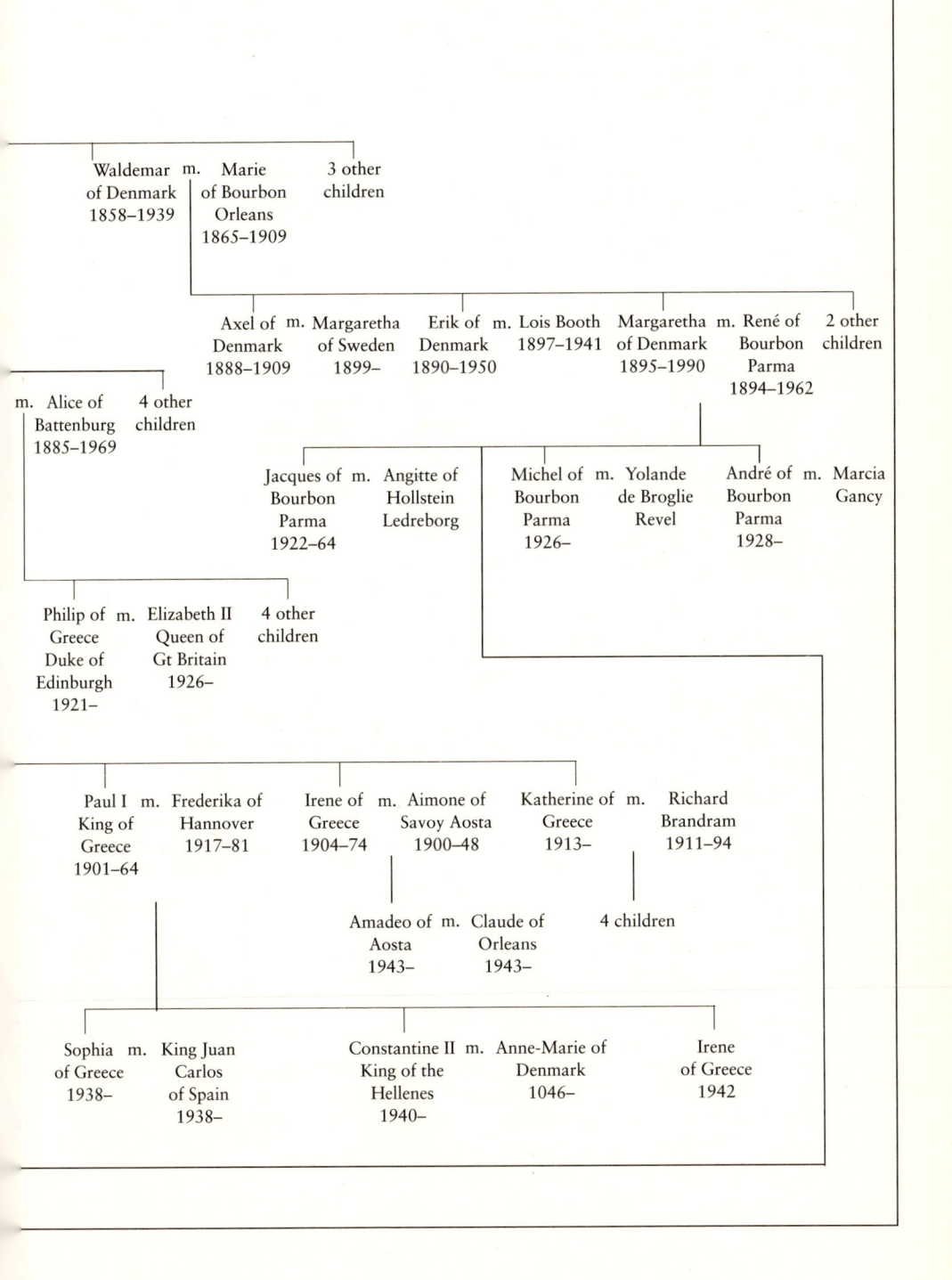

Waldemar m. Marie         3 other
of Denmark  of Bourbon    children
1858–1939   Orleans
            1865–1909

            Axel of   m. Margaretha   Erik of   m. Lois Booth   Margaretha  m. René of     2 other
            Denmark      of Sweden    Denmark      1897–1941    of Denmark     Bourbon     children
            1888–1909    1899–        1890–1950                 1895–1990      Parma
                                                                               1894–1962

m. Alice of      4 other
   Battenburg    children
   1885–1969
                          Jacques of  m. Angitte of           Michel of   m. Yolande      André of   m. Marcia
                          Bourbon        Hollstein            Bourbon        de Broglie   Bourbon       Gancy
                          Parma          Ledreborg            Parma          Revel        Parma
                          1922–64                             1926–                       1928–

Philip of   m. Elizabeth II   4 other
Greece         Queen of       children
Duke of        Gt Britain
Edinburgh      1926–
1921–

       Paul I    m. Frederika of   Irene of   m. Aimone of      Katherine of  m. Richard
       King of      Hannover       Greece        Savoy Aosta    Greece           Brandram
       Greece       1917–81        1904–74       1900–48        1913–            1911–94
       1901–64
                                         Amadeo of  m. Claude of     4 children
                                         Aosta         Orleans
                                         1943–         1943–

   Sophia   m. King Juan         Constantine II  m. Anne-Marie of        Irene
   of Greece   Carlos            King of the        Denmark              of Greece
   1938–       of Spain          Hellenes           1046–                1942
               1938–             1940–

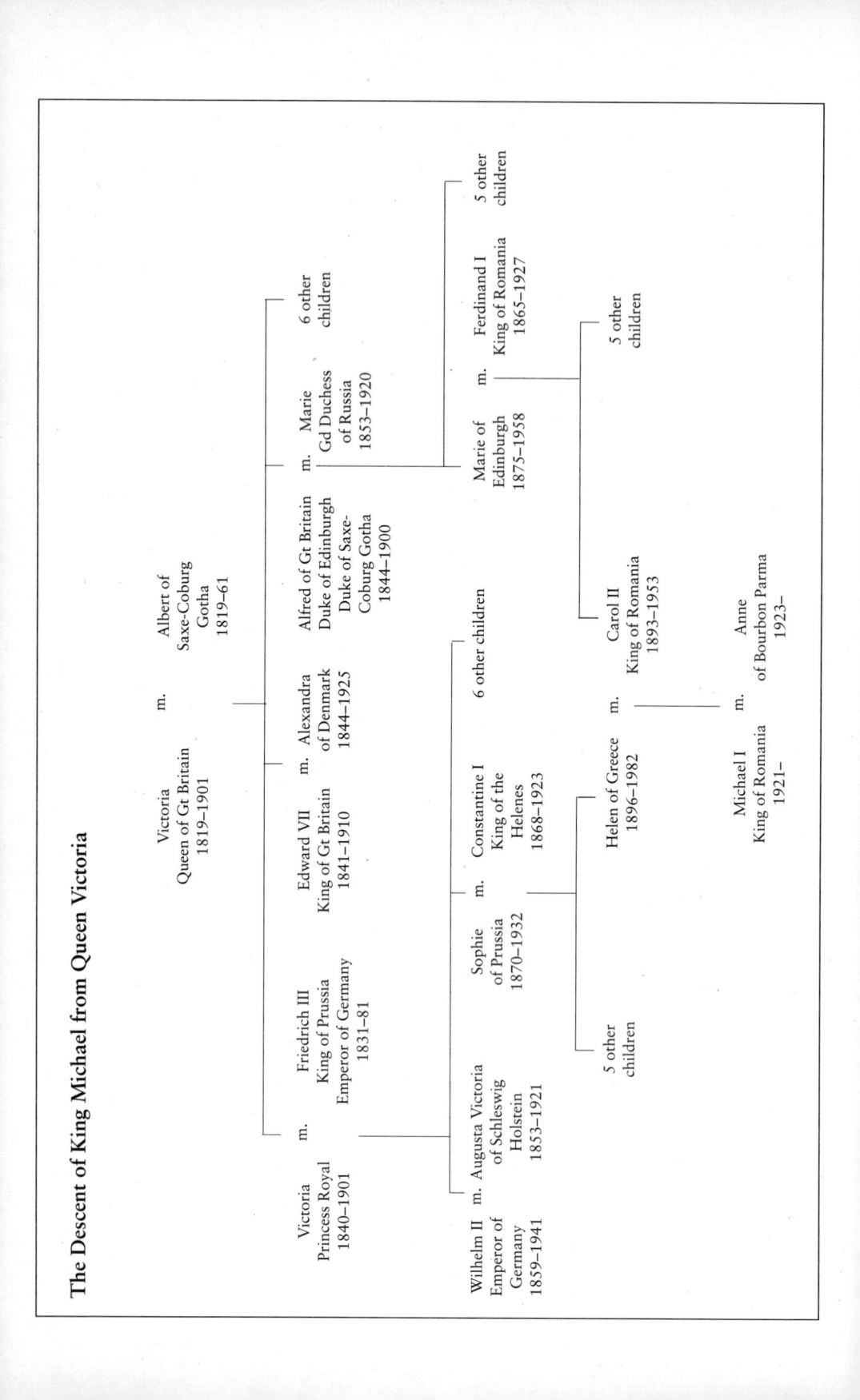

# The Descent of King Michael from Queen Victoria

Victoria Queen of Gt Britain 1819–1901 m. Albert of Saxe-Coburg Gotha 1819–61

- Victoria Princess Royal 1840–1901 m. Friedrich III King of Prussia Emperor of Germany 1831–81
  - Wilhelm II Emperor of Germany 1859–1941 m. Augusta Victoria of Schleswig Holstein 1853–1921
    - Sophie of Prussia 1870–1932 m. Constantine I King of the Helenes 1868–1923
    - 5 other children
- Edward VII King of Gt Britain 1841–1910 m. Alexandra of Denmark 1844–1925
  - 6 other children
- Alfred of Gt Britain Duke of Edinburgh Duke of Saxe-Coburg Gotha 1844–1900 m. Marie Gd Duchess of Russia 1853–1920
  - Marie of Edinburgh 1875–1958 m. Ferdinand I King of Romania 1865–1927
    - Carol II King of Romania 1893–1953 m. Helen of Greece 1896–1982
      - Michael I King of Romania 1921– m. Anne of Bourbon Parma 1923–
    - 5 other children
  - 6 other children
  - 5 other children

# Principal Romanians

Antonescu, Ion — Cavalry officer. Military Attaché in London during the 1920s. Put under house arrest for criticising King Carol II. Became pro-German dictator of Romania after Carol abdicated in 1940. Arrested during King Michael's *coup d'état* of 23 Aug. 1944. Executed on Moscow's orders 1946.

Antonescu, Mihai (Ica) — Distant relation of Ion Antonescu. Lawyer. Premier and Foreign Minister during the Antonescu dictatorship. Arrested during the King's *coup* and executed on Moscow's orders, 1946.

Averescu, General Alexander — Field Marshal. Hero of battle of Mărăşeşti at which the Romanian army defeated the Germans in Aug. 1917. Formed the People's Party. Prime Minister April 1920–Dec. 1921 and again March 1926–June 1927.

Băsescu, Troian — Born in 1951. Started life as a sailor. A rank and file communist but not associated with the Ceauşescu regime. Served as Minister of Transport in the 1990s. 2000 became very active mayor of Bucharest. Later led the Democratic Alliance and in Dec. 2004 defeated Adrian Nastase in the Presidential election.

Blăndiana, Ana — Distinguished dissident poet under Ceauşescu.

Bodnăraş, Emil — Influential member of the Romanian Communist Party concerned mainly with defence and Intelligence matters.

Bossy, Raoul — 28 July 1927–7 June 1930. Chef de Cabinet of the Regency Council. Minister at Helsinki, Budapest. Minister at Rome (Sept. 1939–Oct. 1940) – during which he took part in the Vienna Conference on Transylvania and Queen Helen's return to Romania. After serving at Berne and Berlin resigned from the Foreign Service in Aug. 1943. See Bibliography.

Boyle, Joseph — Gold prospector. Friend of Queen Marie.

Brătianu, Constantin (Dinu) — Engineer. Son of Ion Brătianu, brother of Ionel and Vintila. Succeeded Duca as leader of the Romanian Liberal Party in 1933. During the war worked closely with Maniu and the King in support of the Allies. Died in communist prison in 1950.

| | |
|---|---|
| Brătianu, Gheorghe | Professor of History. Leader of the Liberal Youth. Aroused his family's anger by collaborating with King Carol. A friend of Mihai Antonescu. Died in a communist prison. |
| Brătianu, Ion | 1821–1891. Student in Paris during 1848 revolution. Leader of the Liberal Party. In 1866 invited Prince Karl of Hohenzollern-Sigmaringen (later King Carol I) to be Prince of Wallachia and Moldavia. |
| Brătianu, Ionel | 1864–1927. Son of Ion Brătianu. Prime Minister during the First World War. Largely responsible for Romania's post-war agrarian and electoral reforms. |
| Brătianu, Vintila | 1867–1930. Engineer. Succeeded his brother Ionel as leader of the Liberal Party. |
| Brucan, Silviu | Journalist, diplomat, one-time editor of the Communist Party's newspaper *Scînteia*. An important influence in the overthrow of Ceauşescu. |
| Călinescu, Armand | Lawyer. Minister of Interior 1938, Prime Minister March 1939, assassinated by Iron Guard Sept. 1939. |
| Câmpeanu, Radu | Head of the Romanian Liberal Party after the uprising of Dec. 1989. |
| Catargi, Nelly | Queen Helen's longtime faithful lady-in-waiting. |
| Ceauşescu, Nicolae | Succeeded Gheorghiu-Dej, March 1965 as First Secretary of the Romanian Communist Party. Opposed Soviet invasion of Czechoslovakia, 1968. Visited North Korea and took Kim-il Sung as his role model, 1971. Became President of the State Council and Head of State, 1974. Executed with his wife 25 Dec. 1989. |
| Ciorbea, Victor | Constantinescu's Prime Minister Nov. 1996–Dec. 1999. |
| Codreanu, Colonel | Head of the royal military household at the time of the row between King Michael and Marshal Antonescu over Mocsoni-Styrcea's posting. |
| Codreanu, Cornelia Zelea | Founder of the Legionary movement, later known as the Iron Guard. Affiliations with the National Socialists of Germany. Executed by Carol II in 1938. |
| Constantinescu, Emil | Biologist. Rector of Bucharest University. Represented the Democratic Convention in the presidential election of Nov. 1992 won by Ion Iliescu. Reformist president 1996–2000. Defeated by ingrown corruption and the infighting within the Democratic Convention. Withdrew his candidature from the presidential election of Nov. 2000 and returned to academic life. |
| Coposu, Corneliu | Maniu's secretary in the 1940s. Took part in preparations for the *coup d'état* of 1944. Secretary General of the National Peasant Party 1947. Arrested, 1948, and served seventeen years' forced labour, of which eight in solitary confinement. |

# Principal Romanians

|   |   |
|---|---|
| | After the revolution of 1989 led the National Peasant Party. Died 11 Nov. 1995. |
| Cornea, Doina | Outstanding Romanian dissident under Ceauşescu. |
| Corneliu, Zelea | |
| Coroana, General | Head of Palace Guard at the time of King Carol's abdication. |
| Cretzianu, Alexander | Minister to Turkey in Sept. 1943. Collaborated with Maniu during the war. Moved to the USA where he was active in exile politics. |
| Cristea, Miron | Romanian Patriarch. Member of Regency Council when Michael was boy King. Prime Minister, Feb. 1938–March 1939. |
| Cristescu, Eugen | Head of Romanian Security and Secret Service under Antonescu. |
| Dămăceanu, Colonel | Charged with immobilising German troops stationed in Bucharest immediately after the *coup d'état*. |
| Davidescu, Ştefan | Secretary General of the Foreign Ministry at the time of the *coup d'état*. |
| Devaux, Madame | Close friend of Queen Helen in London. Also known as Miss Thun or Mistun. |
| Duca, Ion | Leader of the Liberal Party after Vintila Brătianu's death. Formed a government under King Carol II, Nov. 1933. Assassinated by the Iron Guard, Dec. 1933. |
| Dumbrovski, General | A popular mayor of Bucharest in King Carol's time. With Maniu's agreement the King reappointed him and made him Prefect of Police in the post-*coup* government. |
| Dumitrescu, Puiu | Private Secretary to King Carol II, 1930–1933. |
| Funar, Gheorghe | Leader of the Party of Romanian National Unity, the political wing of an extreme chauvinist organisation known as Vatra Românească which operated mainly against the Hungarian minority of Transylvania. Damaged Romania's image abroad. |
| Georgescu, Rica | Active member of Maniu's Resistance movement. Ran a network of agents from Cristescu's security prison. Made Under-Secretary of State for Finance and Economy in the post-*coup* government. |
| Georgescu, Teohari | Influential member of the Communist Party. Minister of Interior, 1947. Purged 1952 |
| Gheorghiu-Dej, Gheorghe | Railway worker and member of the Communist Party. First Secretary of the Party and Minister of Communications, 1944. Head of State, 1961. Died 1965. |
| Gigurtu, Ion | Prime Minister of pro-German government which followed the loss of Bessarabia in June 1940. |
| Goga, Octavian | Transylvanian poet. Leader of the extreme right-wing National Christian Party. Prime Minister under King Carol II, Dec. 1937–Feb. 1938. |
| Groza, Petru | 1884–1958. Leader of the Ploughman's Front, affiliated to the Communist Party. Prime Minister 1945. President 1952. |

| | |
|---|---|
| Iliescu, Ion | Close friend of the Ceauşescu family in the 1960s. Secretary of the Union of Communist Youth, 1967. Full member of the Central Committee, 1968. Quarrelled with Ceauşescu over latter's adoption of the North Korean model, 1971, and removed from national politics. Led a group of recalcitrant plotters who failed to overthrow Ceauşescu in 1984. Took control of the situation left by the revolt of Dec. 1989. President of Romania 1990–1996. Re-elected in 2000. |
| Ioanniţiu, Mircea | Pupil with Prince Michael at King Carol's school and later became his Private Secretary. Took part in the *coup d'état*. Member of the Romanian National Committee in Exile, 1955. |
| Ionescu, Colonel Emilian | Officer in charge of the Palace Guard at the time of the King's *coup d'état*. |
| Iorga, Professor Nicolae | Distinguished historian. Prince Michael's teacher. Vice President of Maniu's National Party. An outspoken senator. Prime Minister 1931–1932. Assassinated by the Iron Guard, Nov. 1940. |
| Kopkov, Madame | Housekeeper of the royal palaces. |
| Lambrino, Ioana (Zizi) | 1898–1953. Married Crown Prince Carol, 13 Sept. 1918. Marriage annulled Jan. 1919. |
| Lambrino, Mircea | Son of Ioana Lambrino. |
| Lambrino, Paul | Grandson of Ioana Lambrino. |
| Lazăr, General Petre | Lecturer at the Military Academy. Member of the royal military household until removed by Antonescu in May 1942. Returned to the King's household after the *coup d'état* and in exile became the King's most valued adviser. |
| Luca, Lazlo | Of Hungarian origin. Secretary General of the National Democratic Front. One of the Moscow-trained triumvirate who with Ana Pauker and Emil Bodnăraş ruled the Romanian Communist Party until the early 1950s. Purged by Gheorghiu-Dej. |
| Lupescu, Elena | 1895–1977, King Carol II's mistress and in 1947 wife. |
| Mădgearu, Virgil | University professor of philosophy. Economist. Close colleague of Juliu Maniu. Secretary General of the National Peasant Party. Murdered by the Iron Guard in 1940. |
| Măgureanu, Virgil | A senior member of the Securitate who in April 1990 was made head of the new Romanian Intelligence Service established by Ion Iliescu. |
| Manafu, General | Commandant of the Craiova region at the time of the King's *coup d'état*. |
| Maniu, Juliu | 1873–1953. Led the Transylvanian National Party which in 1918 declared unity with the Old Kingdom. Leader of the Romanian National Peasant Party. Democrat and constitutionalist. During the Antonescu *régime* one of the prime participants in the preparation of King Michael's *coup d'état* |

|   |   |
|---|---|
| | which took Romania out of the Axis. Died in a communist prison, Feb. 1953. |
| Manoilescu, Mihai | Gigurtu's pro-German Foreign Minister. Signed the Vienna Diktat, 30 Aug. 1940. |
| Marinescu, Milica | Engineer and pilot. A good friend of King Michael who contributed to the education of the princesses when the King was particularly hard up. |
| Mihail, General Gheorghe | King Carol's Chief of the General Staff. Active in preparation for King Michael's *coup d'état*. With Maniu's agreement reinstated to previous position in the post-*coup* government. |
| Milea, General Vasile | Minister of Defence at time of the Dec. 1989 revolution. |
| Militaru, General Nicolae | A member of the 1984 group of plotters who had quarrelled with Ceauşescu and been cashiered. |
| Mironescu, Gheorghe | Foreign Minister in Maniu's government, 1928–1931. Made Prime Minister for 24 hours during 7–8 June 1930 to preside over Carol's seizure of his son's throne. Prime Minister Oct. 1930–April 1931. Resigned from the National Peasant Party, Oct. 1934. |
| Mocsoni-Styrcea, Baron Ione | King Michael's Marshal of the Royal Court for many years. A highly intelligent anglophile whom Antonescu tried hard to remove from the King's Household. After the King's forced abdication spent some years in a communist prison Exiled to Switzerland. |
| Nastase, Adrian | Born 1950. International lawyer. Joined Natinoal Salvation Front 19990. Foreign Minister 1990–1992 Prime Minister 2000–2004. When in 2004 Iliescu retired from the Presidency Nastase was defeated by Basescu in the subsequent Presidential election |
| Negel, Dumitriu | Minister of Agriculture in the post-*coup* government. Replaced Mocsoni-Styrcea as Marshal of the Royal Court on 4 Nov. 1944. |
| Negroponte, Vanya | Close personal friend of King Michael. |
| Negulescu, Colonel | Colonel of the King's Guard at the time of the *coup d'état*. Escorted Queen Helen's party from Sinaia to Bumbeşti Jiu, 24 Aug. 1944. |
| Niculescu-Buzeşti, Grigore | Head of Communications Department in the Foreign Ministry during the Second World War. Active in Maniu's Resistance and the chief liaison between the King and Maniu during preparations for the *coup d'état*. Foreign Minister in the first post-*coup* government. |
| Olteanu, Colonel | Colonel of the King's Guards Regiment which held von Gerstenberg's troops at the Baneasă bridge on the outskirts of Bucharest until the US air raid of 26 Aug., after which he recovered the Otopeni airfield. |

## Principal Romanians

| | |
|---|---|
| Pacepa, Lt General Ion Mihai | A very senior member of the Securitate who defected to the USA, July 1978. |
| Pantazi, General | Antonescu's Minister of War. Executed with the Marshal on 1 June 1946. |
| Pătrăşcanu, Lucreţiu | Communist Party link with the traditional parties. Minister of Justice in the first post-*coup* government. Suspected of Titoism and executed in 1954. |
| Pauker, Ana | Influential member of the Soviet wing of the Romanian Communist Party. Minister of Foreign Affairs, 1947. Purged by Dej, 1952. |
| Petrescu, Titel | Born 1888. Leader of the Social Democratic Party. Died in a communist prison, Sept. 1957. |
| Pleşu, Andrei | Distinguished Romanian writer. Minister of Culture and one, with Sora, of the two non-communist ministers in Roman's first government. Like Sora, he later resigned. Foreign Minister under Constantinescu's presidency. |
| Pogoneanu, Victor (Piki) | Head of cipher section of the MFA. Working in Maniu's Resistance during the Second World War. Died in a communist prison. |
| Rădescu, General Nicolae | Prime Minister, Dec. 1944–Feb. 1945. Took refuge in the British Legation. Subsequently chairman of the Romanian National Committee in exile. |
| Roman, Petre | First National Salvation Front Prime Minister, Dec. 1989–Sept. 1991. In Feb. 1992 Roman left the Salvation Front and formed his own party, the Democratic Party – National Salvation Front. In June 1993 Roman's party concluded an uneasy alliance with the Opposition parties, known as the Democratic Convention. This had a noticeable effect on the 1996 elections. |
| Sănătescu, General Constantin | Suppressed the Iron Guard revolt of January 1941. During preparations for the *coup d'état* was King Michael's head of the military household and subsequently also Marshal of the Court. Prime Minister of first two post-*coup* governments. See Bibliography. |
| Sima, Horia | Succeeded Codreanu as Leader of the Iron Guard. |
| Solescu, Rosetti | Marshal of the Royal Court, Jan.–July 1942. |
| Sora, Mihai | Minister of Education in Roman's post-revolution government. Resigned June 1990. |
| Şteflea, General | Marshal Antonescu's Chief of Staff. |
| Ştirbey, Prince Barbu | The first person to recognise Princess Marie's talent and gallantry and the great asset she could be to her country. Close adviser of King Ferdinand and Queen Marie. In the Second World War he was Maniu's emissary to the armistice talks of 1944. |
| Stolojan, Theodor | Competent economist under Ceauşescu and, after the revolution, as Minister of Finance in Roman's government. Replaced Roman as Prime Minister, Sept. 1991. |

# Principal Romanians

| | |
|---|---|
| Tătărescu, Gheorge | 1886–1961 Dissident Liberal. Prime Minister, Jan. 1934–Dec. 1937 and Nov. 1939–July 1940. Vice Premier and Foreign Minister in Groza's government, 6 March 1945–6 March 1947. Brătianu and Maniu did not forgive him for collaborating with King Carol II and later the communists. |
| Teodorescu, General | Commander of Romanian forces in Bucharest at the time of the *coup*. |
| Titulescu, Nicolae | Distinguished Foreign Minister and president of the League of Nations during the 1930s. Promoted a security network of defence treaties among the countries of Eastern Europe. |
| Tökes, Laszlo | Of Hungarian origin. Leading figure of the Reformed Church who was giving the Timişoara authorities trouble. When he resisted arrest he started the Dec. 1989 uprising. |
| Tomescu, Mircea | King Michael's ADC at the time of the Iron Guard rising of Jan. 1941. |
| Tudor, Corneliu | Leader of the Greater Romania Party, an extremist party which openly supports the rehabilitation of Ceauşescu. |
| Urdăreanu, Ernest | Minister of the Royal Court, 1933–1940. Remained with King Carol II during his exile. |
| Vaida-Voevod, Alexandru | Leader with Juliu Maniu of the Transylvanian National Party which defended the interests of the Romanian community in the province until Austro-Hungarian rule collapsed in 1918. Member of the commission which presented the Act of Union to King Ferdinand in 1919. Prime Minster for four months in 1919. Served in Maniu's government, Nov. 1928–Oct. 1930. Prime Minister under King Carol 1932–1933. King Carol used Vaida-Voevod to weaken and split the National Peasant Party during the period leading up to the Royal Dictatorship of 1938–1940. |
| Vasiliu, General 'Piki' | Marshal Antonescu's Minister of the Interior. Executed with Antonescu, 1 June 1946. |
| Vergotti, Jacques | King Michael's ADC Feb. 1941–May 1942, when posted by Antonescu to the front. Returned to the King's Household on 23 Aug. 1944 and remained with him until 1945. See Bibliography. |
| Vişoianu, Constantin | Diplomat. Protégé of Titulescu and Maniu's close collaborator. Took part in the Cairo armistice negotiations of 1944. Foreign Minister, Nov. 1944–March 1945. Escaped to the USA and was successful chairman of the Romanian National Committee for over two decades. |

# Royal Residences

**Balçic**   A small house surrounded by gardens designed by Queen Marie and built on the coast of Dobrugea. Probably her favourite house to which she often retreated during the latter part of King Carol II's *régime*.

**Bran Castle**   Medieval. Built in 1377 to protect the city of Braşov from invaders. Braşov presented it to Queen Marie in recognition of her heroic role in the First World War.

**Cotroceni Palace**   Built on a monastic site. Used by King Carol I as a summer residence while Peleş was being built in Sinaia. In 1893 additions were made for Prince Ferdinand and his wife Marie. When King Ferdinand died in 1927, Queen Marie spent much of her time there. Today it is in part the presidential palace and in part a museum.

**Elisabeta Palace**   A villa built for Princess Elisabeta, King Michael's aunt. She lent it to the King and Queen Helen after the *coup d'état* when the Royal Palace and Casa Nouă had been ruined by German bombing. Recent governments have used it to house official guests. It is now the official home of Princess Margarita and Prince Radu.

**Foişor**   A chalet built above Sinaia for use while Peleş and Pelişor were being built. Later it became the favourite summer refuge for the younger royal generation.

**Mamaia Palace**   As a boy Michael spent many holidays there. When Queen Marie inherited it from King Ferdinand she made it over to Princess Helen, who later sold it to the Government in order to buy Villa Sparta in Florence, where she was living in exile.

**Peleş Castle**   Above the mountain resort of Sinaia. Mainly German neo-Renaissance. Commissioned in 1873 by King Carol I and completed 1883. Now a museum.

**Peleişor Castle**   Built below Peleş and much smaller. Became the summer residence of King Ferdinand and Queen Marie.

**Royal Palace in Revolution Square**   Originally the residence of the Golescu family. Became the official residence of the Princes of Romania in 1834. The present neo-classical façade dates from 1937. It now houses the National Museum of Romanian Art.

**Săvârşin**   An estate in western Transylvania formerly belonging to the Hungarian Count Hunyadi. King Michael bought it in 1942. It was a charming, two-storey, eighteenth-century wooden house with a park of about twenty hectares and woods up into the neighbouring valleys. It was nationalised when the King went into exile. He has now recovered the house but not the estate.

# Notes

*Abbreviations used in the notes*

| | |
|---|---|
| AaR | Queen Anne, *Ana a României* |
| AX | Mark Axworthy, *Third Axis, Fourth Ally* |
| Bossy | Raoul Bossy, *Amintiri din Viaţa Diplomatică* |
| CAB | Cabinet papers |
| CD | Diary of King Carol II. *Între Datorie şi Passiune* |
| *Conv.* | Mircea Ciobanu, *Convorbiri cu Mihai* |
| FO | Foreign Office papers |
| FOC IC | Eleodor Focşeneanu, *Istoria Constituţională a României* |
| FOC RL | Eleodor Focşeneanu, Articles in *Romînia Liberă* |
| HD | Queen Helen's diaries |
| MA | Mark Almond, *The Rise and Fall of Nicolae and Elena Ceauşescu* |
| MC | Mircea Chiriloin, *Lovitura de stat de la 30 Decembrie 1947* |
| MF | Mark Frankland, *The Patriot's Revolution* |
| MI | Mircea Ionniţiu, *Amintiri şi Reflecţiune* |
| MR | Martyn Rady, *Romania in Turmoil* |
| MW | C.M. Woodhouse, *The Story of Modern Greece* |
| Pakula | Hannah Pakula, *Queen of Romania* |
| PREM | Prime Minister's papers |
| PRO | Public Record Office |
| RFE | Radio Free Europe |
| Scurtu | Ioan Scurtu, *Criza Dinastică din România* |
| SJ | *Jurnalul Generalului Sănătescu* |
| VA | King Michael's archives |
| VM | Jacques Vergotti, manuscript memoirs |

## Preface

1. VA Princess Helen to Queen Sophie, letter of 13 May 1921.
2. VA Queen Marie to Queen Sophie, letter of 16 May 1921.
3. VA Princess Helen to Queen Sophie, letter of 29 November 1921.
4. Pakula, p. 312.
5. VA Carol II to Grande Duchesse Georges de Russie, telegram of 27 October 1921.
6. VA Princess Helen to King Constantine, letter of 26 October 1921.
7. VA Princess Helen to her mother, letter of 29 November 1921.

8. VA King Constantine to Princess Helen, letter of 17 December 1921.
9. PRO FO 371/7698/R1385, Despatch from Sir Herbert Dering to FO of 22 January 1922.

## Chapter One

1. Talk with King Michael, 15 August 1992.
2. Duca, *Memorii*, vol. 1, p. 64.
3. Mitrany, *Land and Peasant*, quoted by Seton-Watson, *Histoire des Roumains*, p. 563.
4. CD, 22 November 1918, vol. 1, p. 68.
5. VA Ioana Lambrino to Prince Carol, letter from Cuci, 2 November 1918.
6. *Ibid.*, letter of 7 November 1918.
7. *Ibid.*, letter from Iaşi, 7 January 1919.
8. *Ibid.*, in Bucharest, 30 January 1919.
9. *Ibid.*, 7 June 1919.
10. Pakula, p. 296, citing Romanian Archives III, 117:149.
11. PRO FO 371 /4704 /C5328/5328/19.
12. VA Queen Marie to Queen Sophie, letter of 15 January 1921.
13. *Ibid.*, letter of 12 September 1920.
14. VA Prince George to Queen Sophie from Peleş, letter of 28 October 1920.
15. Pakula, p. 306, citing Romanian Archives III, 125: 26–31.
16. VA Princess Helen to Queen Sophie, letter of 14 June 1922.
17. *Ibid.*, 23 July 1922.
18. *Ibid.*, 3 September 1924.
19. *Ibid.*, 12 May 1922.
20. *Ibid.*, 8 June 1922.
21. VA Queen Marie to Queen Sophie, letter of 12 January 1923.
22. VA Queen Marie to her American friend, Hector Bolitho, *A Biographer's Notebook*, p. 43.
23. VA Queen Marie to Queen Sophie, letter of 12 August 1924.
24. VA Princess Helen to Queen Sophie, letter of 10 November 1924.
25. *Ibid.*, 14 November 1924.
26. *Ibid.*, 14 December 1924.
27. *Ibid.*, 9 September 1924.
28. *Conv.*, vol. 1, p. 133.
29. See Moats on Madame Lupescu in *Lupescu*.
30. VA Queen Marie to Prince Nicholas, letter of 4 January 1926.
31. *Ibid.*
32. VA Prince Carol to Princess Helen, letter of 12 December 1925.
33. VA Queen Marie to Prince Nicholas, letter of 4 January 1926.
34. Pakula, p. 334, citing Romanian Archives III, 154: 143–59: Prince Nicholas's published memoirs, p. 19.
35. Quinlan, *Carol II of Romania*, p. 77 citing Neagu, *Fapte din Umbra* 3: 41.
36. Scurtu, p. 43.
37. *Ibid.*, p. 50.
38. *Ibid.*, p. 43.
39. VA Princess Helen to Queen Sophie, letter of 27 December 1925.
40. VA Princess Helen to Prince Carol, letter of 24 December 1925.
41. VA Prince Carol to Princess Helen, letter of 27 December 1925.

## Chapter Two

1. VA Princess Helen to Prince Carol, letter of 3 January 1926.
2. VA Princess Helen to Queen Sophie, letter of 8 January 1926.
3. VA King George of Greece to Queen Sophie, letter of 13 February 1926.
4. Moats, *Lupescu*, p. 79.
5. PRO FO 371/11420/C3985/362/37.
6. Scurtu, p. 78.
7. Princess Helen to Queen Sophie, letter of 9 December 1926.

8. PRO FO 371/12221/C10261, Mr Gregg's despatch of 13 December 1927.
9. VA King's papers.
10. Lambrino, *King Carol II*, p. 108.
11. VA Princess Helen to Queen Sophie, letter of 8 April 1927.
12. *Ibid.*, 25 May 1927.
13. Scurtu, p. 83.
14. VA Princess Helen to Queen Sophie, letters of 9 and 11 July 1927.
15. Scurtu, pp. 100–1.
16. VA Princess Helen to Queen Sophie, 22 July 1927.
17. Bossy, vol. 1, p. 127.
18. *Ibid.*, p. 130.
19. *Conv.*, vol. 1, pp. 224–5.
20. Sub-paragraph VII (a) of the Act de Împărțeală published in *Dimineața* of 13 May 1992. I am grateful to John Wimbles for letting me see this.
21. *Le Matin* of 31 July 1927.
22. Bossy, vol. 1, p. 160.
23. Scurtu, p. 181.
24. Queen Helen herself told Arthur Gould Lee many of the details of King Michael's childhood.
25. VA HD, 7 June 1930.
26. *Ibid.*
27. Bossy, vol. 1, p. 168.
28. *Ibid.*
29. VA HD, 8 June 1930.
30. VA HD, 8 June 1930.
31. *Conv.*, vol. 1, p. 110.
32. VA HD, 8 June 1930.
33. *Ibid.*
34. VA King George II of Greece to his sister Princess Helen, letter of 13 June 1930 (dated by mistake 13 July).
35. Queen Marie speaking to the *Daily Telegraph*'s Vienna correspondent.
36. Pakula, p. 379, citing Romanian Archives III, 176: 6–19.
37. VA HD, 14 June 1930.
38. *Ibid.*, 18 June 1930.
39. *Ibid.*, 29 June 1930.
40. VA HD, entry dated 5 July 1930, probably in error for 5 August 1930.
41. *Ibid.*, 10 August 1930.
42. *Ibid.*, 20 August 1930.
43. VA Princess Helen to Queen Sophie, letter of 30 December 1930.
44. *Ibid.*, 7 November 1930.
45. *Ibid.*, 28 October 1930.
46. VA Princess Helen to Queen Sophie, letter of 30 December 1930.
47. Quinlan, p. 119 citing Queen Marie's letter to Roxana Weingartner, 19 March 1931, pp. 317–20.
48. VA King George V to Queen Sophie, 30 December 1930.
49. VA Princess Helen to her cousin Princess Olga of Yugoslavia, letter of 4 November 1931.
50. VA Prince Michael to his mother, letter written sometime in February 1932.
51. VA Queen Marie to Princess Helen from Sinaia, 14 January 1932.
52. *Ibid.*, Belgrade, 3 May 1932.
53. Bossy, vol. 1, pp. 219–20.
54. VA Princess Helen to Princess Olga, letter of 30 October 1932.
55. *Conv.*, vol. 1, p. 133.
56. VA.

## Chapter Three

1. MI p. 23.
2. Conversation with Lascar Zamfirescu, October 1991.
3. Conversation with King Michael.
4. *Conv.*, vol. 1, p. 114.
5. Baroness von der Hoven, *King Carol of Romania*, p. 204.
6. *Conv.*, vol. 1, p. 124.
7. *Ibid.*, p. 125.
8. *Ibid.*, p. 111.
9. *Ibid.*, p. 131.

10. *Ibid.*, p. 113.
11. *Ibid.*, p. 127.
12. *Ibid.*
13. My source for this information was Mr Rica Georgescu who had it from Mr Max Auşnit.
14. *Conv.*, vol. 1, p. 120.
15. Talk with King Michael, February 1991.
16. *Conv.*, vol. 1, p. 121.
17. Conversation with King Michael, February 1991.
18. *Conv.*, vol. 1, p. 112.
19. VA Queen Marie to Princess Helen, letter of 21 August 1931.
20. VA Queen Marie to Princess Helen, 14–15 September 1938.
21. VA Queen Marie's long, undated letter to Carol.
22. *Conv.*, vol. 1, p. 134.
23. *Ibid.*, p. 128.
24. *A Biographer's Notebook*, Hector Bolitho, Letter to a friend, p. 56.
25. *Conv.*, vol. 1, p. 115.
26. Talk with King Michael, February 1991.
27. *Conv.*, vol. 1, p. 155.
28. *Ibid.*, p. 119.
29. PRO FO 371/23841, Memorandum dated 20 June 1939 from Maniu and Brătianu to Argetoianu, President of the Senate.
30. Conversation with King Michael, February 1991.
31. PRO FO 371/23842, Maniu's Memorandum to the King.
32. *Conv.*, vol. 1, p. 123.
33. For an authoritative account of the Foreign Ministries of Victor Antonescu, Nicolae Comnen and Grigore Gafencu see chapters 1–3 of Haynes, *Romanian Policy towards Germany, 1936–1940*.
34. Bossy, vol. 2, pp. 278–84.
35. Hollingworth, *There's a German Just Behind Me*, p. 62.
36. *Conv.*, vol. 1, p. 120.
37. CD, vol. 2, p. 255.
38. Talk with King Michael, 7 August 1995.
39. CD, vol. 2, note 279, pp. 391–2.
40. My papers.
41. Quinlan, *Carol II of Romania*, p. 216.
42. CD, vol. 2, p. 258.
43. Conversation with King Michael.
44. CD, vol. 2, p. 258.
45. *Conv.*, vol. 1, p. 106.
46. *Ibid.*
47. Lee, *Crown against Sickle*, p. 15.
48. Quinlan, *Carol II of Romania*, p. 217 citing Buhman, *Jurnal*, p. 318.
49. CD, vol. 2, p. 261.

## Chapter Four

1. VA HD, 6 September 1940.
2. Bossy, vol. 1, p. 291.
3. *Ibid.*, p. 292.
4. *Ibid.*, pp. 293–4.
5. Manning, *Balkan Trilogy*, p. 472.
6. VA HD, 16 September 1940.
7. *Conv.*, vol. 1, p. 137.
8. *Ibid.*, p. 105.
9. VA HD, 2 October 1940.
10. *Ibid.*, 1 January 1941.
11. *Conv.*, pp. 227–8.
12. FOC p. 90.
13. VA HD, 25 October 1940.
14. *Ibid.*, 27 October 1940.
15. PRO FO 371/29990, Sir Reginald Hoare's letter to FO of 8 November 1940.
16. VA HD, 8–9 November 1940.
17. *Ibid.*, 1 December 1940.
18. *Ibid.*, 27 January 1941.
19. Colville, *The Fringes of Power*, vol. 1, p. 417.
20. VA HD, 29 January 1941.

21. *Ibid.*, 21 February 1941.
22. PRO FO 371/29991/R4768/G.
23. VA HD, 25 May 1941.
24. *Conv.*, vol. 1, p. 139.
25. AX, p. 26.
26. *Conv.*, vol. 1, p. 153.
27. VA HD, 7 July 1941.
28. *Ibid.*, 11 July 1941.
29. AX, p. 72.
30. US Foreign Relations, vol. III, p. 668.
31. *Conv.*, vol. 1, p. 149.
32. AX, p. 57.
33. *Conv.*, vol. 1, p. 141.
34. VA HD, 12–13 June 1941.
35. *Ibid.*, 5 September 1941.
36. Şafran, *Un tăciune smuls flăcărilor*, pp. 82–5.
37. Yad Vashem, Undated Memorandum on Assistance to Romanian Jews Rendered by Queen Elena during the Second World War.
38. *Conv.*, vol. 1, p. 143.
39. VM, p. 42.
40. *Ibid.*, p. 44.
41. *Conv.*, vol. 1, p. 143.
42. Hart, *History of the Second World War*, chapters 13 and 18.
43. VM, p. 50.
44. *Conv.*, vol. 1, p. 148.
45. VA HD, 28 June 1942.
46. Talk with King Michael.
47. VM, pp. 60–1.
48. AX, p. 114.
49. VA HD, 7 June 1942.
50. VA HD, 8 November 1942.
51. *Conv.*, vol. 1, p. 146.
52. VA HD, 31 December 1942.

## Chapter Five

1. VA HD, 10 February 1943.
2. *Conv.*, vol. 1, p. 157.
3. VA HD, 11 March 1943.
4. SJ, pp. 122–3.
5. SJ, Month of May, pp. 129–30.
6. VA HD, 10 May 1943.
7. *Ibid.*, 9 September 1943.
8. Talk with King Michael, 7 August 1995.
9. VA HD, 25 October 1943.
10. *Ibid.*, 21 March 1944.
11. *Ibid.*, 24 March 1944.
12. SJ, pp. 144–5.
13. *Ibid.*, p. 145.
14. FO 371/43998/R5947.
15. MI, p. 34.
16. VA HD, 11 April 1944.
17. PRO FO 371/43999/R6487.
18. SJ, p. 153.
19. VA FO 371/44000/R8341.

## Chapter Six

1. *Conv.*, vol. 1, p. 18.
2. VA HD, 4 June 1944.
3. PRO FO 371/44002/R10114.
4. *Ibid.*, R10230.
5. MI, pp. 67–9.
6. Talk with Baron Mocsoni Styrcea, 22 June 1991.
7. MI, p. 131.
8. AX, p. 165.
9. MI, pp. 37–40.
10. Talk with Baron Mocsoni-Styrcea, 22 June 1991.
11. MI, p. 43.
12. *Ibid*.
13. *Documente*, vol. 11, no. 687.
14. Drăgan, *Antonescu*, vol. 1, p. 365.
15. *Conv.*, vol. 1, p. 22.
16. Tudor Zarajanu, *Viaţa lui Corneliu Coposu*, p. 27 et seq.
17. SJ, p. 162.
18. *Ibid*.
19. MI, p. 49.
20. SJ, p. 162.
21. *Ibid*.
22. *Conv.*, vol. 1, p. 21.

23. SJ, pp. 162–3.
24. *Conv.*, vol. 1, p. 22.

## Chapter Seven

1. AX, p. 179.
2. Lee, *Crown against Sickle*, p. 77.
3. Conversation with Baron Mocsoni-Styrcea.
4. MI, p. 84.
5. HD, 23 August 1944.
6. AX, p. 185.
7. PRO FO 371/32874/N108/86.
8. AX, p. 189.
9. HD, 25 August 1944.
10. *Ibid.*, 28 August 1944.
11. *Documente*, vol. 11, no. 696.
12. Lee, *Helen, Queen Mother of Romania*, p. 235.

## Chapter Eight

1. VA HD, 15 September 1944.
2. *Ibid.*, 10 September 1944.
3. *Ibid.*, 15 September 1944.
4. *Ibid.*, 22 September 1944.
5. Talk with King Michael, 20 June 1991.
6. VA HD, 28 September 1944.
7. PRO FO 371/44044/R15980/G.
8. *Ibid.*
9. VA HD, 11 October 1944.
10. PRO PREM 3/374/13A, Cadogan Minute to P.M. of 28 October 1944.
11. PRO FO 371/44012.
12. VA HD, 4 November 1944.
13. Bossy, *Jurnalul*, 24 March 1944, p. 268.
14. PRO PREM 3/374/13A/M1070, P.M.'s personal minute to S. of S. of 4 November 1944.
15. *Ibid.*, M1083/4, P.M. to S. of S. 7 November 1944.
16. PRO FO 371/44054, FO telegram to Bucharest.
17. PRO FO 371/43989/R19568.
18. VA HD, 6 November 1944.
19. *Ibid.*, 8 November 1944.
20. *Ibid.*, 11 November 1944.
21. *Ibid.*, 13 December 1944.
22. PRO FO 371/48535/R359.
23. *Ibid.*, 48547/R1754.
24. Talk with King Michael, 20 June 1991.
25. This account of Vyshinsky's audiences with King Michael between 27 February and 1 March 1945 is based on the verbatim texts in *Conv.*, vol. 1, pp. 238–44.
26. VA HD, 2 March 1945.
27. MC Doc. 8 of 5 March 1945.
28. *Conv.*, vol. 1, pp. 39 et seq.

## Chapter Nine

1. PRO FO 371/48554/R7670.
2. *Ibid.*, 48540/R6212.
3. *Ibid.*, 48595/R9696.
4. *Ibid.*, 48554.
5. VA HD, 19 July 1945.
6. PRO FO 371/48538/R4703.
7. *Ibid.*, 48556/R13262.
8. VA HD, 14 August 1945.
9. PRO FO 371/48556/R13724.
10. *Ibid.*, 48557/R13745.
11. MC Doc. 16 Susaikov to Stalin, 22 August 1945.
12. PRO FO 371/48557/R14930.
13. *Ibid.*, 48560, Bucharest despatch 18 September 1945.
14. John Wheeler-Bennett, *King George VI, His life and Reign*, p. 618.
15. Berry, *Romanian Diaries*, pp. 274–5.
16. PRO FO 371/48563, Memorandum on the events of 8 November 1945.
17. *Ibid.*
18. CC-IFI, p. 31 et seq.
19. PRO FO 371/48562/R20715.
20. *Ibid.*, 48220/R21263.
21. *Ibid.*, R21604.
22. *Ibid.*, 59131/R1880/92/37 para. 12.

23. VA HD, 8 January 1946.
24. PRO FO 371/59131/R1880.
25. VA HD, 8 January 1946.
26. PRO FO 371/59131/R1880.
27. *Ibid.*, R2618, Le Rougetel's note to Tătărescu, 5 February 1946.
28. *Ibid.*, 59097/R2979.
29. *Ibid.*, Bucharest telegram no. 280, 26 February 1946.
30. VA HD, 26 February 1946.
31. PRO FO 371/65233/R4150 para. 9.
32. VA HD, 24 February 1946.
33. PRO FO 371/59097, Bucharest telegram no. 350, 12 March 1946.
34. *Ibid.*, 59098, Bucharest telegram no. 374, 20 March 1946.
35. VA HD, 17 March 1946.
36. *Conv.*, vol. 1, p. 161.

## Chapter Ten

1. PRO FO 371/67233/R4150 para. 31.
2. *Ibid.*, para. 22.
3. *Ibid.*, para. 34.
4. MC Doc. 20.
5. Talk with King Michael, 18 March 1992 and FO 371/59136/R17322.
6. PRO FO 371/59107, FO telegram to Bucharest no. 1285 of 21 December 1946.
7. Talk with King Michael, 18 March 1992 and FO 371/59136/R17322.
8. Lee, *Helen*, p. 262.
9. PRO FO 371/67234/R5718.
10. PRO FO 371/59135, Conversation between Mr Bevin and the Romanian Foreign Minister, 7 September 1946.
11. Talk with King Michael, 20 June 1991.
12. VA HD, 1 January 1947.
13. Berry, *Romanian Diaries*, p. 670.
14. PRO FO 371/72464, Annual Review for 1947, para. 8.
15. PRO FO 371/67240/R12221.
16. MG Doc. 27.
17. PRO FI 371/67240/R11145.
18. PRO FO 371/72464, Annual Review for 1947, para. 15.
19. PRO FO 371/67239/R11022.
20. PRO FO 371/67258.
21. PRO FO 371/67240/R11447.
22. PRO FO 371/67242, FO Memo. of 29 October 1947.
23. PRO FO 371/800 499.
24. Lee, *Helen*, p. 276.
25. Talk with Queen Anne, 5 August 1992.
26. Lee, *Crown against Sickle*, p. 159.
27. VM, p. 167.
28. PRO FO 371/67248, Bucharest telegram no. 1527

## Chapter Eleven

1. VA HD, 21 December 1947.
2. Lee, *Crown against Sickle*, p. 161.
3. VM, p. 172.
4. MC Doc. 33.
5. VA HD, 29 December 1947.
6. Talk with Queen Anne, 5 August 1992.
7. VM, pp 175–6.
8. For such details I have drawn from Arthur Lee's vivid account of the abdication written shortly after the event. My other sources were principally conversations with King Michael, *Conv.* vol. 1, ch. VII, and Mircea Ionniţiu's *Amintiri*.
9. *Conv.* vol. 1, p. 57.
10. *Ibid.*, p. 58.
11. Lee, *Crown against Sickle*, p. 167.
12. *Conv.*, vol. 1, p. 58.
13. Lee, *Crown against Sickle*, p. 169.
14. PRO FO 371/72427, Mr Snow's personal and top secret telegram from Berne to the Foreign Office, 21 January 1948.
15. *Conv.*, vol. 1, p. 59.
16. *Ibid.*, pp. 59–60.

17. Lee, *Crown against Sickle*, p. 174.
18. *Conv.*, vol. 1, p. 64.
19. *Ibid.*, p. 66.
20. Lee, *Crown against Sickle*, p. 180.
21. *Conv.*, vol. 1, p. 66.
22. *Ibid.*, pp. 66–7.
23. *Conv.*, vol. 1, p. 68.
24. VM, p. 183.
25. *Conv.*, vol. 1, p. 69.
26. *Ibid.*
27. Lee, *Crown against Sickle*, p. 184.
28. MI, p. 105.
29. *Conv.*, vol. 1, p. 71.
30. *Ibid.*, p. 70.
31. *Ibid.*

## Chapter Twelve

1. AX, p. 199.
2. PRO FO 371/72427/R535, Roderick Sarrell's despatch no. 9 of 8 January 1948.
3. PRO FO 371/72427/R1053, Telegram no. 25 of 21 January 1948 from Berne to FO.
4. FOC RL, 'O Bandă de Falsificatorii', 21 January 1992.
5. VA Letter of 3 December 1947 from King Carol II to his son.
6. VA Letter of 15 January 1948 from King Carol II to Queen Helen.
7. Talk with Queen Anne, 5 August 1992.
8. VM, p. 195.
9. Lee, *Crown against Sickle*, p. 186.
10. PRO FO 371/72427/R3090.
11. *New York Times*, 11 March 1948.
12. *Conv.*, vol. 1, p. 77.
13. PRO FO 371/72427/R4971, Lord Inverchapel's despatch no. 684 to FO.
14. *Conv.*, vol. 1, pp. 75–6.
15. *Ibid.*, p. 78.
16. Talk with King Michael, 7 August 1995.
17. Talk with Queen Anne, 5 August 1992.
18. *Conv.*, vol. 1, p. 79.
19. AaR, p. 124.
20. VM, pp. 214–15.
21. Talk with Queen Anne, 5 August 1992.
22. (a) A Clash of Legitimacy, David Horbury; lecture delivered at House of Lords, November 1995; (b) FOCRL, 31 December 1991; (c) Pacepa, *Cartea Neagră a Securității*, vol. I, pp. 139–41.
23. VM, p. 222.
24. VA Memo from FBI to CIA of 11 May 1948.
25. *Conv.*, vol. 2, p. 35.
26. VM, pp. 229–30.
27. *Conv.*, vol. 1, p. 95.
28. Talk with Queen Anne, 5 August 1992.
29. VM, p. 234.
30. VA HD, 30 March 1949.
31. *Ibid.*, 15 April 1949.

## Chapter Thirteen

1. AaR, pp. 78–9.
2. Talk with Queen Anne, 5 August 1992.
3. VA King Michael's Broadcast to Romania, 10 May 1949.
4. *Conv.*, vol. 1, Documents at pp. 231–5.
5. VA Box File 1: 1949–1955, folio 8.
6. DD, p. 15.
7. *Ibid.*, p. 22
8. *Ibid.*, p. 29 et seq.
9. Talk with King Michael, 5 August 1992.
10. VA Annex to Vişoianu's letter to Lazar of 16 February 1951.
11. AaR, p. 81 et seq.
12. VA HD, 24 December 1951.
13. Talk with King Michael and Queen Anne, 18 March 1992.
14. Sir John Wheeler-Bennett, *Friends, Enemies and Sovereigns*, p. 153.
15. Talk with King Michael, 18 March 1992.

16. VA HD, 14 July 1952.
17. Talk with King Michael and Queen Anne, 18 March 1992.
18. *Ibid.*
19. Talk with Princess Margarita, 14 May 1992.
20. Philippe Vignié Desolaces, *Domnie Întreruptă*, p. 144.
21. *New York Times*, 17 October 1950.
22. DD, p. 24.
23. *Ibid.*, p. 25.
24. *Conv.*, vol. 2, p. 42.
25. *Ibid.*, p. 52.
26. *Conv.*, vol. 1, pp. 263–84.
27. *Conv.*, vol. 2, p. 51.
28. VA Cour de Cassation, 1 December 1960.
29. *Conv.*, vol. 1, p. 198 et seq.
30. VA King Michael's letter to his mother, 15 November 1954.
31. VA HD, 23 January 1955.
32. *Conv.*, vol. 1, p. 84.
33. VA Box File no. 2, National Committee 1945–1975, folio 2.
34. Talk with Queen Anne, 5 August 1992.
35. VA HD, 19 July 1957.
36. *Ibid.*, 5 March 1963.
37. *Ibid.*, 31 December 1963.
38. Talk with Princess Margarita, 14 May 1992.
39. *Conv.*, vol. 1, p. 87.
40. VA Queen Helen to General Schyler, letter of 26 September 1965.
41. Sweeney, *The Life and Evil Times of Nicolae Ceauşescu*, p. 99.
42. VA Princess Margarita's letter of 3 November 1970 to Queen Helen.

## Chapter Fourteen

1. DD, pp. 326–9.
2. Talk with Princess Margarita, 14 May 1992.
3. VA HD, 12 December 1974.
4. Talk with Princess Margarita, 14 May 1992.
5. *Conv.*, vol. 2, p. 58.
6. *Conv.*, vol. 1, p. 10.
7. Talk with Princess Margarita, 14 May 1992.
8. *Ibid.*
9. VA HD, 18–19 October 1970.
10. *Conv.*, vol. 1, p. 321.
11. *Ibid.*, p. 314.
12. *Ibid.*, p. 324.
13. VA *New York City Tribune*, 1 August 1989. Note for publication.
14. VA AP telegram from Budapest, 3 August 1989.
15. Speech of 7 February 1990 at the Great Britain – East Europe Centre.
16. VA *The Times*, 19 December 1989.
17. VA Radio Broadcast, 19 September 1989.
18. DD, p. 314.
19. *Ibid.*, pp. 253–4.
20. MA, p. 227.
21. DD, p. 343 et seq.
22. 'Romania: The Bloody Revolution', by Jeremy Bransten, www.rferl.org/nca/special/10years/romania2.html.
23. *Ibid.*
24. During a radio interview with Brucan in Rotterdam on 30 August 1990.

## Chapter Fifteen

1. *Conv.*, vol. 1, pp. 330–1.
2. AaR, p. 109.
3. *Financial Times*, 15 January 1990.
4. *Conv.*, vol. 1, p. 181.
5. Gallagher, *Romania after Ceauşescu*, p. 146.
6. Rady, *Romania in Turmoil*, pp. 155–7.
7. According to *Romînia Liberă*, during the summer of 1998 Parliament was still debating a bill to compel the RSI to make Securitate files available to

the public and the slow pace of privatisation was a constant theme.
8. AFP, 12 April 1990.
9. ROMPRES, 11 April 1990 and *The European*, 25 May 1990.
10. *The Times*, 13 April 1990.
11. Rady, *Romania in Turmoil*, p. 171.
12. *Ibid.*, pp. 186–8.
13. Gallagher, *Romania after Ceauşescu*, p. 116.
14. VA King Michael's speech, 7 June 1990 in Brussels.
15. *Ibid.*
16. Talk with Princess Margarita.
17. RFE report of 18 November 1991 quoting AFP and Reuters of 25 December 1990.
18. *Ibid.*, quoting Radio Bucharest of 25 December 1990.
19. *The Times*, 27 December 1990.
20. *Ibid.*
21. Lost Planet in the Gutenberg Galaxy, Ursula Reston, INDEX ON CENSORSHIP, January 1991 p. 5.
22. Doamna Doina Cornea, Aurel Stroe, *Romînia Liberă*, 24 October 1991.
23. VA Speech at the Institute of International Affairs in Paris, 16 September 1991.
24. Rady, *Romania in Turmoil*, pp. 200–1.
25. *Ibid.*, pp. 201–2.
26. FOC p. 148.
27. *Ibid.*
28. *Ibid.*, p. 156
29. *Ibid.*, p. 143.
30. VA King Michaael's speech to the Council of Foreign Relations New York, 25 April 1991.
31. VA King Michael's speech at University of London, 31 January 1991.

## Chapter Sixteen

1. I owe this account of the King's Easter visit to Dr Constantin Brâncovan, who was His Majesty's Private Secretary at the time.
2. *Harpers & Queen* magazine, October 1992.
3. Letter from David Horbury of 19 June 1999.
4. *Le Figaro*, 4 May 1992.
5. *Conv.*, vol. 2, p. 20 et seq.
6. Published after the election in 22 under the title 'Cele Două Portrete'.
7. King's Papers.
8. *Cotidianul*, 21 July 1993.
9. Focşeneanu's letter of 16 July 1993 to King Michael. King's Papers.
10. *Unfinished Journey* by Sir Yehudi Menuhin (1996 edition), pp. 225–6.
11. *Romînia Liberă*, 10 March 1993.
12. AFP, 29 October 1993.
13. Declaraţie Convenţiei Democratice din România, 22 November 1993.

## Chapter Seventeen

1. *Evenimentul Zilei*, 1 July 1994.
2. Tom Barber writing in the *Independent*, 23 August 1994.
3. VA Congressional Record for Wednesday, 3 August 1994 and *ibid.*, Senate, for Tuesday 23 August 1994.
4. VA Handwritten notes entitled Colocviu (8 octombrie): 23 August./ rezumatul primei întrevederi dintre reprezentanţii fundaţiilor şi reprezentanţii puterii.
5. *Le Monde*, 8 October 1922.
6. *Harpers & Queen*, September 1992, p. 150.

7. 'King Accepts Invitation to St Paul's', Noel Malcolm, *Sunday Telegraph*, 19 March 1995.
8. VA King Michael's message, 10 May 1995.
9. Eugen Şerbănescu, Coroana la Caschetă, *Romînia Liberă*, 6 May 1995.
10. Quoted by *Adevărul*, 29 April 1996.
11. Emil Hurezeanu writing in 22, 8–14 May 1996.
12. *Conv.*, vol. 2, p. 144.
13. For an account of Prince Radu's career see his autobiography *L'Ame et Le Masque*, Les Presses de l'Avenir, first published in Bucharest, 1997, as *Dincolo de Mască*.
14. *Rador*, 14 July 1996.
15. *Rador*, 18 July 1996.
16. Micaela Grigore writing in *Romanian Press Review* by e-mail, 14 October 1996.
17. *Monarchist League News*, 29 August 1996.
18. *Romanian Press Review* by e-mail, 14 October 1996.
19. *Le Monde*, 9 November 1996.
20. The *Guardian*, 19 November 1996.
21. *Le Monde*, 19 November 1996.

*Chapter Eighteen*

1. oecd.org/sge/ccnm/oubs/rpme98/asses-rec.htm.
2. *Daily Telegraph*, 3 March 1997.
3. *New York Times*, 1 March 1997.
4. Roderick Braithwaite, 'Bringing Russia In', *Prospect*, June 1997.
5. *Herald Tribune*, 12–13 July 1997.
6. *Romînia Liberă*, 10 July 1997.
7. Octavian Paler writing in *Romînia Liberă*, 10 July 1997.
8. *Romînia Liberă*, 8 October 1997.
9. *Ibid.*, 28 August 1997.
10. *Ibid.*, 14 August 1997.
11. *Ibid.*, 24 December 1997.
12. VA King Michael's speech, 30 December 1997.
13. *Romînia Liberă*, 15 January 1998.
14. *Ibid.*
15. VA King Michael's Millennium message, 19 December 1999.
16. www.cs.kent.edu/~amarcus/Mihai.agende/en001210.html.
17. AFP, 21 May 2001.
18. These details, provided by the Romanian Cultural Centre, came from the newspaper *Ziua*, 23 October 2004.
19. See www.pressreview.ro covering the period of the 2004 elections.

# Bibliography

Almond, Mark, *The Rise and Fall of Nicolae & Elena Ceauşescu*, London: Chapmans, 1992
Barker, Elisabeth, *British Policy in South-East Europe in the Second World War*, London: Macmillan, 1976
——, *Churchill and Eden at War*, London: Palgrave Macmillan, 1978
Behr, Edward, *Kiss the hand you cannot bite: the rise and fall of the Ceauşescu*, London: Hamish Hamilton, 1991
Berry, Burton, *Romanian Diaries, 1944–1947*, The Centre for Romanian Studies, Iaşi, Oxford: Portland, 2000
Bolitho, Hector, *Romania under King Carol*, London: Eyre & Spottiswoode, 1939
Bossy, Raoul, *Amintiri din viaţa diplomatică*, vol. 1, 1918–1937, vol. 2, 1938–1940, Bucharest: Humanitas, 1993
——, *Jurnalul* (2 noiembrie 1940–9 iulie 1969), Bucharest: Editura Enciclopedică, 2001
Carol II, *Însemnări Zilnice*, Vol. 1 1904–1939, Bucharest: Editura Silex, 1995
——, Vol. 2 1939–1940, Bucharest: Editura SANSA, 1996
——, Vol. 3 1941–1942, Bucharest: Editura SATYA SAI, 1996
Ceauşescu, Ilie; Florin Constantinu; Mihail Ionescu: *200 de Zile Mai Devreme*, Bucharest: 1984
Chiritoiu, Mircea, Lovitura de Stat de la 30 Decembrie 1947, Bucuresti, Fundaţia Academia Civică, 1997
Churchill, Winston, *The Second World War*, London: Cassell, 1948–54
Ciobanu, Mircea, *Convorbiri cu Mihaiai al României*, Vol. I, 1991, Vol. II 1992, Bucharest: Humanitas
——, *Convorbiri cu Mihaiai al României*, Iaşi: Editura Princeps, 1995
Colville, John, *The Fringes of Power*, Vol. 1, 1939–1941, Vol. 2, 1941–1955, London: Hodder & Stoughton, 1985 and 1987
Coposu, Corneliu, *În Faţa Istoriei*, Colecţia 'Problemele Timpuluii', Bucharest: Editura Metropol, 1996
Cretzianu, Alexander, *The Lost Opportunity*, London: 1957
Deletant, Dennis, *Ceauşescu and the Securitate*, London: Hurst, 1995
——, *Communist Terror in Romania*, London: Hurst, 1999
Dima, Romus, *Armand Călinescu*, Bucharest: Editura Mavios-Clio, 2001
Drăgan, Josif, *Antonescu*, Vol. 1, 1986, Vol. 2, 1988, Venice
Duca, I.G., *Memorii*, Vol. 1, Neutralitatea, Partea 1, 1914–1915, Bucharest: Editura Expres, 1992

# Bibliography

Focşeneanu, Eleador, *Istoria constituţională a România, 1859–1991*, Bucharest: Humanitas, 1992
Frankland, Mark, *The Patriots' Revolution*, London: Sinclair Stevenson, 1990
Gafencu, Grigore, *Însemnări Politice*, Bucharest: Humanitas, 1991
Gallagher, Tom, *Romania after Ceauşescu*, Edinburgh: Edinburgh University Press, 1995
Giurescu, Dinu, *Guvernarea Nicolae Rădescu*, Bucharest: Editura ALL, 1996
Hart, Liddle, *History of the Second World War*, London: Pan Books, 1970
Haynes, Rebecca, *Romanian Policy towards Germany, 1936–1940*, London: SSEES, University College
Heald, Tim, *The Duke*, London: Hodder & Stoughton, 1991
Herwarth, Johnnie, *Against Two Evils*, London: Collins, 1981
von der Hoven, Baroness Helena, *King Carol of Romania*, London: Hutchinson, 1940
Hollingworth, Clare, *There's a German Just Behind Me*, London: 1942
Ionniţiu, Mircea, *Amentiri şi Reflecţiune*, Bucharest: Editura Enciclopedică, 1994
Kaplan, Robert, *Balkan Ghosts*, New York: St Martin's Press, 1993
Lambrino, Paul, *King Carol II: A life of my Grandfather*, London: Methuen, 1988
Lean, Gurth, *Frank Buchman*, London: Constable, 1985
Lee, Arthur Gould, *Crown against Sickle*, London: Hutchinson, 1950
——, *Helen, Queen Mother of Romania*, London: Faber & Faber, 1956
MacDonogh, *Prussia*, Sinclair London: Stevenson, 1994
Manning, Olivia, *Balkan Trilogy*, London: Mandarin Paperback, 1987
Moats, Alice Leone, *Lupescu*, New York: Henry Holt & Co., 1955
Nedelea, Marin, *Prim – Ministrii României Mari*, Bucharest: Casa de Editură şi Presa, Viaţa Românească, 1991
Nicholson, Harold, *King George V*, London: Constable, 1952
Pakula, Hannah, *Queen of Romania (The Life of Princess Marie)*, London: Eland, 1989
Pacepa, Mircea, *Cartea Neagră a Securităţii*, Editura OMEGA, 1999
Quinlan, Paul, *Carol II of Romania*, Westport, Connecticut: Greenwood Press, 1995
Radu, Prince of Hohenzollern-Veringen, *L'Ame de la Masque*, Bucharest: Les Presses de l'Avenir, 1997, first published as *Dincolo de Mască*
Radu, Prince of Hohenzollern-Veringen, *Ana a României*, Bucharest: Humanitas, 2000
Rady, Martyn, *Romania in Turmoil*, London and New York: I.B. Tauris, 1992
Şafran, Alexandru, *Un tăciune smuls flăcărilor*, Bucharest: Editura Hasefer, 1996
St John Stevas, Norman, *Walter Bagehot*, London: Eyre & Spottiswoode, 1959
Sănătescu, General Constantin, *Jurnal*, Bucharest: Humanitas, 1993
Săvulescu, Andrei, *Regele Mihai, Automobolist, Mechanic, Pilot, Professionalist*, Bucharest: Humanitas, 1996
Scurtu, Ioan, *Criza domestică din România*, Bucharest: Editura Enciclopedică, 1996
Seton-Watson, Hugh, *The New Imperialism*, London: 1961
Seton-Watson, R.W., *Histoire des Roumains*, Paris: Les Presses Universitaires de France, 1937
Sweeney, John, *The Life and Evil Times of Nicolae Ceauşescu*, London: Hutchinson, 1991
Sylva, Carmen, *Poveştile Peleşului*, Timişoara: Editura ARGO, 1991
Vergotti, Jacques, *Fără Drept de Înapoiere în Ţară*, Bucharest: Editura ALBATROS, 2000
Zarojanu, Tudor, *Viaţa lui Corneliu Coposu*, Bucharest: Editura Maşina de Scris, 1996

# Index

KM = King Michael

Alba Julia, 11, 23, 261, 262
Aldea, General Aurel, 100, 101, 103, 106, 108, 112 bis, 118, 161
Alexander, King of Greece, xii, 7, 8, 9
Alexander, Prince of Yugoslavia, 270
Alexander II, King of Yugoslavia, 12, 38
Alexandra, Princess of Greece, 22
Alexandra, Queen of Great Britain, 16
Alexianu, Professor Gheorghe, 158
Alice, Princess (Princess Andrew of Greece), 201
Allied Control Commission (ACC), 126, 127, 129, 136, 158
André, Prince of Bourbon Parma, 203 bis
Andrew, Prince of Greece, 13, 27, 201n
Anne, Princess Royal, 212
Anne of Bourbon Parma, Queen of Romania: early life, 173–4; meets and agrees to marry KM, 174–6; and KM's abdication, 178, 184–5, 192; visits Davos with KM, 193; problems over Catholic/Orthodox wedding, 194–5, 196, 198–200; marriage to KM, 200–1; births of daughters, 203–4, 207, 213–14, 221, 223; early married life, 205, 206; family moves to England, 211–12; market garden and chicken farm, 212–13; family moves to Versoix, 217–19; death of father, 221–2; death of brother Jacques, 223; visits to Queen Helen, 227; her old mother comes to live with them, 230–1; and fall of Communism in Romania, 239; turned back from visit to Romania, 246–7; attends Princess Ileana's funeral, 250; visits USA with KM, 250; first visit to Romania with KM, 253–6; further visits to Romania, 261, 270, 273–5, 279; normalisation of relations with Romania, 283, 285
Antonescu, Madame, 69, 85, 90, 91, 105
Antonescu, Marshal Ion, 45, 48, 50, 53, 55–9; 'Conducator' during War, 62–82 passim, 83–95 passim; deposed in coup d'état, 98–110; trial and execution, 121–2, 143, 158–9, 263–4

Antonescu, Mihai (Ica), 56, 65, 68, 78–9, 80–1, 85, 89, 92, 93, 103, 105, 108, 109, 158–9
Antoniade, Gheorghe, 275
Aosta, Duchess of *see* Irene, Princess
Aosta, Duke of (Princess Irene's husband), 166
Aosta, Amadeou, Duke of (Princess Irene's son), 206, 227, 270; Princess Claude, his wife 227
Arafat, Yasser, 234
Aspasia Manos, Queen of Greece, 9
Assembly of Captive Nations, 215–16
Association of Free Romanians, 207
Athens, 8, 128, 200
Atlantic Charter (1941), 88, 90
Atlee, Clement, 146
Austin, Warren, 206–7
Austro-Hungarian Empire, 1, 2
Averescu, General Alexander, 21, 23, 26–7
Axel, Prince of Denmark, 206, 211n, 223
Ayot St Lawrence (Herts), 212, 213, 218, 266

Badoglio, Marshal, 86
Balçic (Dobrugea), 57n
Băsescu, President Traian, 285
Baudouin, King of the Belgians, 239
BBC, 91, 115, 121, 191, 218, 231, 234
Berry, Burton, 128, 140, 149, 152, 164, 165, 209
Berthon, George, 275
Bessarabia, xiii, 1, 10, 53–4, 70–2, 74, 90, 91, 96, 102, 268
Bevin, Ernest, 146, 164, 173
Bianu (Director of Security), 175, 176, 187–8

Bistrița Monastery, 53, 55
Blăndiana, Ana, 234, 241, 248
Bodnăraș, Emil, 96, 100, 101, 106, 121, 127, 129, 136, 152, 159, 161 *bis*, 162, 169, 170, 172, 177, 185
Boissevin, Madame, 225
Boris, King of Bulgaria, 86, 199n
Bossy, Raoul, 24, 26, 30, 61–2, 120, 123, 228
Bossy, Robert, 120, 123
Bowes-Lyon, Lady Anne, 211n
Bramshill Hall (Berks), 210, 211, 212
Brandram, Major Richard, 166
Branești, 247–8
Brașov uprising, 234
Brătianu, Dinu (Constantin), 48, 52–3, 55, 56, 65, 70–1, 80, 92, 95, 96, 98, 101, 105, 107, 123, 140–1, 145, 147, 148, 153, 156, 158, 160–1, 169, 218
Brătianu, Professor George (Gheorghe), 29, 107, 109
Brătianu, Ion, 1
Brătianu, Ionel, 2, 11, 15, 18, 23, 24, 25, 146
Brătianu, Vintila, 25–6, 26, 48
British/Romanian Association, 250
Brocket, Lord, 210, 212, 218
Brown, Gordon, 228
Brucan, Professor Silviu, 234, 235, 237, 241
Bucharest, 3, 117, 118–19, 125, 150, 240, 241, 262, 264–5; Colentina Hospital, 248; Institute of Archeology, 263; Royal Palace, 46, 63, 120, 125
Buchman, Frank, 217
Buhman (Carol II's secretary), 58–9

Bukovina, 10, 53–4, 70–2, 74, 91
Bulgaria, 8, 54, 103, 118, 137, 145, 150, 152–3, 235, 250
Bumbeşti Jiu, 117–18, 120
Burenin, General, 125, 126
Buzdugan, Gheorghe, 18, 26
Buzeşti *see* Niculescu-Buzeşti
Byrnes, James, 150, 152, 156

Cadogan, Sir Alexander, 130
Cairo talks *see under* Second World War
Călinescu, Armand, 50, 53
Câmpeanu, Radu, 243, 244
Canescu, Sergiu, 243
Cantacuzino, Şerban, 233
Caranfil (Romanian exile), 205, 207, 214
Carol I, King of Romania, xi, 1–3, 225, 256n
Carol II, King of Romania: youth, 3; marriage to Ioana Lambrino and annullment, 4–7; marriage to Princess Helen, xi, 8, 9–10; renounces right to throne and lives with Elena Lupescu, 11–23 *passim*; divorces Helen, 25; returns and reigns as king, 27–41 *passim*; abdicates and leaves Romania, 56–9; after war, 130, 170, 172, 175, 193, 195, 201, 203; death and inheritance 214, 216, 259–60
Carter, President Jimmy, 226
Casa Nouă (Bucharest), 43, 63, 99, 103 *bis*, 110, 120, 125
Catargi, Madame Nelly, 39, 70, 85, 120, 123, 184, 187, 196, 220, 230

Ceauşescu, Elena, 224, 237
Ceauşescu, Nicolae, 115, 224, 226, 228, 231–7, 252, 259, 263
Celac, Marian, 234
Charles, Prince of Wales, 212, 248
Chastelain, Colonel Gardine de, 88, 94n, 116
Chirac, President, 276
*Choice, The* (play by KM and Queen Anne), 227
Churchill, Winston, xiii, 67–8, 87–8, 89, 94, 97, 130, 132, 145, 146, 157, 173
CIA, 206, 209
Ciobanu, Mircea, 98, 141
Ciorbea, Victor, 273, 274 *bis*
Civic Alliance, 245
Clark-Kerr, Sir Archibald (Lord Inverchapel), 153, 154, 155–6, 164, 196, 197, 198
Clodius, Karl, 100, 105
Cluj (Transylvania), 142, 236, 263
Codreanu, Colonel, 83–4
Codreanu, Corneliu Zelea, 10, 52, 55, 66, 67
Committee of Action to Democratise the Army (CADA), 244–5
Communist Party of Romania, 10, 96, 100, 121, 127, 129, 134, 136, 160, 224, 252
Conea, Ion, 42
Conservative Party, 10
Constantine I, King of Greece, xii, xii, 7–8, 9–10, 12, 13
Constantine II, King of Greece, 201, 223, 270
Constantinescu, Emil, 253, 262, 268, 271–2, 273, 275, 278, 279–80, 282

constitutional monarchy, 1, 2, 231, 250, 267–8, 280
Copenhagen, 175, 176, 194, 206
Coposu, Corneliu, 107, 151–2, 214, 234, 243, 249, 252n, 256, 267–8
Cornea, Doina, 234, 241, 248
Coroana, General, 57
Cotroceni Palace, xi, xii, 63, 93
Council of National Political Parties, 194
Craiova, 54, 104, 117–18
Cretzianu, Alexander, 203, 205, 207 bis
Cristea, Miron, 18, 30, 50, 51, 53
Cristescu, Eugen, 99n, 111, 112, 158–9
Curtea de Argeş, 35, 101, 245–6, 253, 256
Cyril, Prince of Bulgaria, 137
Czech Republic, 276–7
Czechoslovakia, 52, 169–70, 205, 224, 226, 234, 235

Dămăceanu, Colonel, 100, 103, 106
Damaskinos, Metropolitan, 200–1, 230, 270
Danube-Black Sea canal, 214
Davidescu, Ştefan, 104
Davos, 193–4
Deletant, Professor Dennis, 232
Democratic Convention (DC), 252, 253, 258, 261–2, 271, 272, 278–9, 282
Democratic National Salvation Front (DNSF), 252, 253 (*changes name to Party of Social Democracy of Romania q.v.*)
Democratic Party-National Salvation Front (DP-NSF), 252, 253, 258
Detroit, 198

Devaux, Madame (Miss Thun), 210
Dobrugea, 54
Dolla, Princess of Greece, 27
Domokos, Geza, 243
Droulia Company, 223
Duca, Ion, 24, 48
Duda, Dan, 270
Duda, Prince Radu, 269–71, 271n, 275, 283, 284
Dumbrovski, General, 112
Dumitrescu, Puiu, 36, 45, 46, 48, 106, 108, 109, 111

Eden, Anthony, 67–8, 93, 94, 97, 119, 131, 132, 146
Edinburgh University, 225, 228
Edward VIII (Duke of York), 12, 192
Eisenhower, President, 144, 215
Elena, Princess *see* Helen
Elisabeta, Princess (Carol II's sister), 8, 10, 24, 30, 31, 32, 39, 40, 51, 59, 65–6, 122, 126, 152, 155, 169–70, 203
Elisabeta Palace, 126, 127, 128, 274, 279, 284, 285
Elizabeth, Queen of Romania (Carmen Sylva), xi, 2, 3, 25
Elizabeth II, Queen of Great Britain, 196, 210, 212, 218, 226; wedding, 168, 170, 174
Enescu, Georges, 248
Erik, Prince of Denmark, 200, 201
Etheridge, Mark, 150, 152, 152–3
European Union, 263, 269, 274, 286
Everac, Pau,l 258
Eyal, Jonathan, 275

Fabricius (German Minister), 56, 57, 67

Farah, Empress of Iran, 270
Fărcăşanu, Mihail, 205, 207
Felix, Prince of Denmark, 194
Ferdinand I, King of Romania, xi, xii, 2, 3–4, 6, 7, 10, 11, 15–25 *passim*, 46, 187, 225
Filderman, Dr, 75
Finland, 145, 151–2, 221
First World War, xii, 2, 3–4, 7
Florence, 41, 44, 227; see also Villa Sparta
Focşeneanu, Eleodor, 185, 250, 260
Foişor (Sinaia), xi–xii, 51, 63, 101, 103, 155, 187, 284
Forman, Donald, 266
Franassovici, Richard, 172
France, 8, 195, 216, 248, 249, 250
Frederick, Prince of Hohenzollern-Sigmaringen, 52, 195
Frederick III, Emperor of Germany, 7
Frederick IX, King of Denmark, 229
Frederika, Queen of Greece, 50, 166, 201, 217, 220–1, 221, 222, 223
Free Europe Committee, 216
Free Youth, 149
Friessner, General, 100, 111
Funar, Gheorghe, 252, 253, 257, 258, 263

Gafencu (Romanian exile), 205, 207
Geer, Baron de, 230
Geneva, 199, 201, 219, 220, 221
George I, King of Greece, 7
George II, King of Greece, 7, 8, 10, 13, 20, 24, 33, 34, 50, 166, 167, 201
George V, King of Great Britain, 8, 12, 23, 33–4, 37
George VI, King of Great Britain, 49, 144, 149, 170, 173, 192, 196, 198, 211–12
George, Prince of Denmark, 211
George, Prince of Hanover, and Princess Sophie 201
Georgescu, Rica, 115, 209
Georgescu, Teohari, 131, 162
Germany, 2, 3, 10, 52–5, 234–5; see also Second World War
Gerstenberg, General von, 100, 116, 119
Gheorghiu-Dej, Gheorghe, 96, 136, 162, 167, 169–70, 177, 179–84, 193, 196, 202, 213, 224, 233
Gigurtu, Ion, 53 *bis*
Goga, Octavian, 50
Gorbachev, Mikhail, 231–2, 236
Greater Romania Party (PRM), 248, 252, 257, 258, 263–4
Greece, 7–8, 9, 13, 118, 128, 200–1, 250
Groza, Petru, 133, 134, 139–51 *passim*, 156, 158, 162, 165 *bis*, 168–87 *passim*, 193, 195, 196, 197, 202, 206
Gustav VI, King of Sweden, 229–30

Hansen, General, 116, 119
Harriman, Ambassador, 153, 154–5, 155–6, 197
Hassan, King of Jordan, 271
Helen (Elena), Princess (KM's daughter), 207, 211, 225, 253, 254, 269; daughter Karina, 269; son Nicholas, 253, 269
Helen, 'Queen Mother' of Romania: early years: Greek background, 7; meets and marries Carol II, 8–10; birth of KM, xi–xiii; early married

life, 12, 13–14, 15; Carol leaves with his mistress, 16–17, 18–19; she writes letter of reconciliation, 20; brings up KM, 21–2; death of King Ferdinand, 21, 23–4; divorced from Carol, 25; after Carol's return, 31–9; visits England and speaks to press, 39–40; Princess Elisabeta slaps her face, 40; leaves Romania for Florence, 40–1, 47–8

war years: Carol abdicates and she is invited to return, 58, 61–5; Princess Elisabeta apologises, 65–6; meets Hitler with her sister, 66–7; defence of Jews, 67, 75, 76; life during war years, 69–75 *passim*, 78, 82, 84; meets Hitler with KM, 75–6; meets Pope, 76; meets Mussolini, 76; relaxes by flying, 86; supports KM in *coup d'état*, 87, 92, 102, 103–4, 114–15; with KM in hiding, 116–18, 120, 121; life under Soviets, 122–3, 126–34 *passim*; sets up soup kitchen, 130, 132–3; receives guests, 155 *bis*; suspends writing diary, 165; attends brother's funeral, 166; attends wedding of Princess Elizabeth and Prince Philip, 170–3; and KM's engagement, 175; and KM's forced abdication, 178, 179, 183–5

exile: leaves Romania with KM, 187–8; and KM's wedding, 195, 197, 199, 200–1; visits Paris, London and USA, 195–8; and first grandchild, 204; visit from Princess Elizabeth and Prince Philip, 210; visits KM's family in England, 211; gives financial help to KM, 212; meeting with Frank Buchman, 217; financial problems, 220; visits from grandchildren, 227–8; proposal from King Gustav, 229; sells El Greco paintings, 3, 171, 185, 229–30; moves to Lausanne, 230; death, 230; 'Righteous Among Nations', 75, 249

Hill, Mr (KM's tutor), 27, 32
Hitler, Adolf, 52, 53, 54, 55, 63, 66–7, 71, 75–6, 81–2, 89–90, 91, 101–2, 107, 119
Hoare, Sir Reginald, 69
Hobbs, Mr (gardener), 212
Holman, Adrian, 163–4, 168, 169, 170, 176
Holocaust Museum, Washington, 258
Hören, Baroness van der, 43
Horthy, Regent of Hungary, 89–90
Hungary/Hungarians, xiii, 6, 54, 78, 89–90, 103, 119, 145, 152–3, 231, 232, 234 *bis*, 241, 248, 263, 269, 276–7
Hungarian Democratic Union of Romania (HDUR/HDFR), 243, 252
Hurley, General, 72–3

Iași, 3, 263
Ileana, Princess (Carol II's sister), 5, 16, 51, 152, 161, 177–8, 250; husband Anton 177–8
Iliescu, President Ion, 235, 236–7, 243–4, 249, 251, 252, 253, 257, 258, 259, 260, 261, 267,

270, 271–2, 277, 279, 282–3, 285
Independent Resistance movement, 194
Ionniţiu, Mircea, 80, 87, 99, 100, 102–3, 104–5, 106, 108, 111, 120, 122, 166–7, 171, 178, 182, 186, 187, 188, 195, 196, 209, 228
Ionniţiu, Rodica, 188, 195, 196
Ionescu, Colonel Emilian, 103, 106, 108, 110, 112, 117, 120, 187
Iorga, Professor Nicolae, 18, 27, 41, 53, 59, 66
Irene, Princess of Greece, Duchess of Aosta, 7, 8, 9, 12, 13, 66, 134, 165, 166, 171, 193, 199, 201, 206, 207, 229
Irina, Princess (KM's daughter), 213, 225, 250, 269; children Michael and Angelica, 269
Iron Guard (Legionaries), 10, 27, 48, 52, 53, 55, 56, 58, 62, 64, 66, 67–8, 127, 203, 244
Isarescu, Mugar, 282
Italy, 2, 86, 152–3, 250

Jacques, Prince, of Bourbon Parma, 173, 203, 223
Jewish people, 50, 67, 69, 74–5, 166, 197, 199–200, 248–9, 258, 263–4, 266
Jiu Valley, 234, 241, 249
John XXIII, Pope (Cardinal Roncalli), 76, 199–200, 221
Juan Carlos, King of Spain, and Queen Sophie, 221

Kalinin, Mikhail, 144
Katherine, Princess of Greece, 7, 13, 166

Khrushchev, Nikita, 224
Killinger, Baron Manfred von, 68–9, 75, 78, 79, 81–2, 84, 100, 112, 113–14, 119, 122, 134
Kim-il Sung, 224
Kiselev Palace, 41, 148, 166, 178
Kopkov, Madame, 63, 93, 121, 125, 130, 187
Korne, General, 95, 111
Kravchenko, General, 118
Kravchenko, Victor, 197
Kruger, John (Princess Irina's husband), 269

Lambrino, Ioanna (Carol II's first wife), 4–7, 9–10, 20
Lambrino, Mircea Grigore, 6, 216, 259–60
Lambrino, Paul, 259–60
Lauros, Dr, xii, 221
Lausanne, 188, 194, 199, 203, 204, 208, 213–14, 230, 270
Lazar, Gheorghe, 42, 43
Lazăr, General Petre, 69, 77–8, 171, 187, 195, 196, 197, 202, 203, 205, 209, 210, 211, 213, 214, 224
Lear, William, 217–18, 218–19, 220, 222
Lear, William Jr, 219
Lecca, Radu, 158–9
Lee, Arthur Gould, 27, 58, 122
Legionaries *see* Iron Guard
Le Rougetel, Ian, 127–8, 132, 134–5, 143, 146, 147, 148, 150–1, 152, 156
Liberals *see* National Liberal Party
Liiceanu, Gabriel, 257
Luca, Laslo, 96, 136, 140, 162, 169–70, 172, 213

Lupescu, Elena (Carol II's mistress and later wife), xiii, 12, 13, 15–16, 20, 28, 35 *bis*, 36, 42–6 *passim*, 52, 53, 55, 57, 58, 59, 62, 214
Lupu, Judge, 58, 153
Luxemburg, Jean, Grand Duke of, 174, 194

McVeagh, Ambassador, 98–9
Mădgearu, Virgil, 66
Mafalda, Princess, of Italy, 86
Măgureanu, Professor Virgil, 241, 244, 265
Maior, Liviu, 258, 263
Malaxa (industrialist), 45, 59, 203
Malaxa factory, 135–6
Malcolm, Noel, 267
Malinovski, General, 102, 131, 144, 145
Mamaia Palace, 25, 36, 41, 47
Manafu, General, 104, 117
Manoilescu, Mihai, 53, 54
Maniu, Juliu, 10–11, 21, 23, 26, 27–9, 30, 36, 40, 41, 48, 52–6 *passim*, 65, 71, 87–96 *passim*; and 1944 *coup*, 98–9, 101, 106, 107–8, 112, 113, 114, 123; and Soviet occupation, 125, 129, 131–2, 133, 134, 140 *bis*, 145, 146, 147, 148, 153, 158–63 *passim*, 165; trial and death in prison, 169, 170, 171, 218
Mardari, General, 68–9, 69 (*bis*), 77, 78
Margarethe, Princess of Denmark (Princess René of Bourbon Parma), 173, 194, 200, 203, 212, 227–8, 230

Margarita, Princess (KM's daughter): childhood, 204, 211, 212, 213 *bis*, 217, 219, 221, 222, 227–8; at Edinburgh University, 225, 228–9; Romanian government's campaign against, 265–6; marriage to Radu Duda, 201, 269–71; works for FAO, 225, 239; work for Romania, 247–8, 260, 284; lives in Romania, 285, 297; succession to KM, 253, 280; visits and other events, 242, 246, 250, 268, 274, 275, 283
Margarita, Princess of Greece, 27
Maria, Princess (KM's daughter), 223, 225, 269
Marie, Princess of France, 194
Marie, Queen of Romania, xi, xii, 2–14 *passim*, 17, 20–7 *passim*, 34, 36–7, 38, 39, 46–7, 49, 59, 187, 225; death and funeral, 51–2, 57n
Marie, Queen of Yugoslavia ('Mignon', Carol II's sister), 12, 51, 203
Marina, Princess of Greece (Duchess of Kent), 27, 172, 173, 196, 198, 218
Marinescu, Milica, and wife, 223–4, 225
Marjoribanks, James, 128
Marshall Plan, 167–8, 245
Mary, Queen of Great Britain, 33–4, 172
Massigli, Ambassador, 174–5, 195
Mathias, King of Hungary, 263
Medforth-Mills, Dr Robin (Princess Helen's husband), 253, 269
Melbourne, Roy, 146

Meleşcanu, Theodor, 264
Menuhin, Yehudi, 248, 260–1
Metravel S.A., 222
MICHAEL I, King of Romania:
  character, xiv, 12, 14–15, 38, 47,
    65, 69, 130, 148, 149, 155, 216;
    interests and talents, 14, 37,
    85–6, 87, 193
  early life: birth and baptism,
    xii–xiii; proclaimed Crown
    Prince, 18; proclaimed King aged
    five, 24–5; taught by tutor, 27;
    father returns as king, 30–41;
    palace school formed, 42–3;
    holidays with mother, 47–8; at
    Coronation of George VI, 49;
    death of grandmother, 51–2;
    outbreak of war, 53, 55
  king during war: becomes king
    aged eighteen, 57–9; his mother
    returns and provides support,
    61–3; early war years, 65–74
    *passim*; tries to defend Jews,
    74–5; meets Hitler, 75–6; meets
    Pope, 76; meets Mussolini, 76;
    visits front line, 78–9; buys
    Săvârşin, 81; calls for break with
    Germany, 81–2; learns to fly,
    85–6; rebuffs Mussolini, 86;
    hernia operation, 87, 89; makes
    plans for *coup*, 87–97 *passim*;
    1944 *coup d'état*, xiii, xiv,
    98–110, 240, 243, 256n
  king under Communist rule: after
    *coup*, 111–18, 120, 122–3,
    142–3; refuses to abdicate,
    140–1; popularity, 143–4;
    awarded Russian Order of
    Victory, 144–5; goes on strike,
    148–52, 157; and Moscow
    agreement, 152–7, 158;
    assassination plot, 157–8;
    commutes death sentences,
    158–9; continues to oppose
    government, 160–70 *passim*;
    awarded US Legion of Merit,
    167; at British royal wedding,
    170–3; meets Princess Anne of
    Bourbon Parma, 173–5;
    engagement, 175–6; forced to
    abdicate, 177–84; leaves
    Romania, 184–9
  life in exile: meets British envoy,
    192–3; considers future jobs,
    193; forms Romanian National
    Committee, 193–4; prepares for
    wedding, 194–6; press statement
    on abdication, 196; visits
    England and USA, 196–8;
    marries Princess Anne in Greece,
    198–201; stripped of Romanian
    citizenship, 201; goes to live in
    Florence, 202; birth of daughter
    Margerita, 203–4; works for
    Romanian Committee, 205–7,
    214–16; summer in Copenhagen,
    206; birth of daughter Elena,
    207; house broken into, 208;
    refuses offer of home in USA,
    209–10; establishes Paris
    University Foundation, 210–11;
    family moves to England,
    210–12; moves to Ayot house
    and keeps chickens, 212–13;
    birth of daughter Irina, 213–14;
    Mircea Lambrino wins claim to
    inheritance, 216; works for Lear
    as pilot, 217–20; family returns

to Florence, 218; new home in Versoix, 219; starts own electronics factory, 221; birth of daughter Sophie, 221; at Spanish royal wedding, 221; new work with stockbrokers, 222–3; friends provide financial help, 223–4, 225

later years: refuses to compromise with Ceauşescu government 228; death of his mother, 230; buys house in Versoix, 230–1; continues broadcasts to Romania, 231; fall of Ceauşescu, 239–40; refused visa, 242–3; visits Romania, but turned away, 245–7; lectures in London and USA, 245, 250–1; Easter 1992 visits Romania and is welcomed by people, 253–7; government campaigns against him, 257–62, 271–2; honoured by USA, 264; turned away from Romania again, 265; visits London for 50th anniversary of D-Day, 266–7; Romanian citizenship recognised by new government, 273; visits Romania again, 273–5; works for Romania's admission to NATO, 269, 275–6, 283–4; expresses wish for Margarita to succeed him, 279–80; speaks against false republicanism created to stifle democracy, 281–2; further visit to Romania, 283; 80th birthday and after, 283–6

personal relations with: Anne, his wife, 173–6, 206; Carol, his father, xiii, 19, 22, 29, 30–1, 32, 36–7, 48–9, 50–1, 57–9; Helen, his mother, 15, 33, 37, 40, 44, 47–8, 62, 64–5; Magda Lupescu, 43–5; Marie, his grandmother, 46–7, 51–2; his daughters, 205, 217, 227, 229

Michel, Prince of Bourbon Parma, 173, 174, 203 *bis*, 230
Mihail, General Gheorghe, 55, 100, 103, 112
Mihalache, Ion, 10–11, 18, 21, 29, 30, 48, 53, 105, 169
Milea, General Vasile, 236 *bis*
Militaru, General Nicolae, 237
Mironescu, George, 30–1, 36
Mitterand, President, 226
Mocsoni-Styrcea, Baron *see* Styrcea
Moldavia, xiii, 3, 74, 91, 118, 166, 253, 255
Molotov, Vyacheslav, 92–3, 99, 125, 126, 149, 153, 164–5, 171
Molotov/Ribbentrop agreement (1939), 53, 268
Moral Re-Armament, 217
Moscow Agreement, 125, 132, 152–6, 158, 161, 163–4
Moyne, Lord, 95, 96, 97, 98
Munteanu, Marian, 249
Mussolini, Benito, 54, 76, 86
Mystkowski, Casimir Wieslaw (Princess Maria's husband), 269

Nastase, Adrian, 285
National Christian Party, 50
National Council of Action against Corruption and Organised Crime, 273
National Democratic Bloc, 95–6

National Democratic Front (NDF), 129, 133, 134, 136 *bis*, 140, 148, 151, 162
National Liberal Party (NLP), 10–11, 15, 21, 25, 26, 29, 55, 96, 101, 141, 151, 153, 154, 160, 162, 218; in exile, 194, 205; after 1989 uprising, 243, 244, 249, 252, 262
National Party of Transylvanian Romanians, 10–11, 21, 27 (*becomes part of* National Peasant Party *q.v.*)
National Peasant Party (NPP), 21, 22–3, 27, 40, 50, 55, 96, 107, 129, 136, 139–40, 151, 153, 154, 156, 160, 162, 169, 170; in exile, 194, 205, 207; after 1989 uprising, 243, 244, 262, 267
National Peasant Party and Christian Democratic Party (NPP-CD), 252
National Renaissance Front (*later* Party of the Nation), 50, 52–3, 54, 65
National Salvation Front (NSF), 235, 236–7, 240–51 *passim*, 252 *bis*, 268–9 (*splits into* Democratic National Salvation Front and Democratic Party-National Salvation Front *q.v.*)
NATO, 263, 268–9, 272, 274, 275–8, 283–4
Nazi Party, 10
Negel, Dumitriu, 80, 113, 114, 131, 139, 142, 145, 148, 163, 175 *bis*, 178, 182, 186, 187
Negroponte, Vanya, 167, 178, 187
Negulescu, Colonel, 111, 114–15, 120

Nicholas, Prince of Greece, 27; Princess Nicholas, his widow, 201
Nicholas, Prince of Romania (Carol II's brother), 4, 18, 28, 29, 31 *bis*, 34, 35, 172, 195, 203
Nicodim, Patriarch, 58, 74–5
Nicolae, Metropolitan, 275
Niculescu-Buzeşti, Grigore, 80, 83, 87 *bis*, 89, 93, 95, 98, 99, 101, 103, 106, 107–8, 109, 112, 113, 116, 120, 128, 131, 133, 194, 202, 205, 206
North Korea, 224, 235
Novikov, Ambassador, 90–1, 94, 96, 97, 98–9

Oancea, Viorel, 258
Odessa, 73, 74, 79
Old Kingdom of Romania, xiii, 1, 11
Olga, Princess of Greece (wife of Prince Paul of Yugoslavia), 27, 40, 172, 201, 218n
Olga, Queen of Greece, xiii, 7, 127
Olson (comedian), 217
Olteanu, Colonel, 116, 119
Ottoman Empire, 1, 2

Pacepa, Lt General Ion Mihai, 226
Pacioga, Madame, 87, 133
Panescu (Interior Minister), 131
Pantazi, General, 112, 158–9
Paris, 195–6, 210–11, 228, 243
Parma, Robert I, Duke of, 194
Partnership for Peace, 263, 269
Party of the Nation *see* National Renaissance Front
Party of Romanian National Unity (PRNU/PUNR), 252, 258, 264, 271

Party of Social Democracy of
    Romania (PSDR/PDSR), 258,
    267, 269, 270, 271, 272, 279,
    281, 282, 285
Pătrăşcanu, Lucreţiu, 96, 99, 100,
    101, 106, 107, 112, 114, 125,
    127, 147, 177, 201, 213
Patriotic Guard, 127
Pauker, Ana, 96, 129, 134, 135, 136,
    142, 162, 169, 171, 172, 175–6,
    197, 213
Paul, Prince of Yugoslavia, 27, 218n
Paul I, King of Greece, 7, 9, 50, 166,
    199, 201, 201, 217, 220, 223
Pavlov, Alexei, 135, 147, 148
Peasant Party, 10–11 (*becomes part of
    National Peasant Party q.v.*)
Peleş Castle (Sinaia), xi, 3, 25, 130,
    169, 187, 284
Pelişor Castle (Sinaia), xi, 51, 187,
    284
People's Judges, 142, 208
Petrescu, Titel, 96, 99, 101, 106, 107,
    146, 147, 157, 160–1, 169, 229
Philip, Prince of Greece (Duke of
    Edinburgh), 27, 48, 196, 210,
    211; wedding to Princess
    Elizabeth, 168, 170, 174
Pimen, Archbishop, 253, 254, 255
Pintilie, Gheorghe (Bodnorenko), 208
Pius XII, Pope, 76, 195, 196, 200
Pleşu, Andrei, 241
Ploughman's Front, 139, 168
Pogoneanu, Victor 'Piki', 87 *bis*, 104
Poland, 169–70, 234 *bis*, 276–7
Popescu, Bibi, 188
Popescu-Tăriceanu, Calin, 285
Porter, Ivor (present author), 88, 94n,
    170

Portugal, 214, 216
Potsdam Conference, 145–7, 154
Predeal chalet, 78, 80, 178
Primakov, Russian Foreign Minister,
    268
Princess Margarita of Romania
    Foundation, 247–8
PRM *see* Greater Romania Party
Putna Monastery, 253

Racoviţa, General, 95
Rădescu, General Nicolae, 133–9
    *passim*, 141, 161, 194, 197,
    202–3, 205, 206–7, 228
Radio Free Europe, 218, 220, 231,
    234
Rainier, Prince of Monaco, and
    Princess Grace, 221
Rămniceanu, Brigadier, 5
Raţiu, Ion, 243 *bis*
René, Prince of Bourbon Parma, 194,
    195, 203, 221–2; wife *see*
    Margarethe, Princess
Reşiţa, 120, 165
Ribbentrop, Joachim von, 53, 54,
    67n, 91, 102
Rochat, Dr, 203, 204, 213
Roman, Petre, 237, 244, 246, 249,
    252, 258, 262, 272, 280
Romania: early history, xiii, 1–2; in
    First World War, 3–4; between
    wars, 18, 20–1, 25–7, 30, 48,
    50–1; at start of Second World
    War 52–5; during War, 55–97;
    1944 *coup d'état*, xiii, xiv,
    98–110, 240, 243, 256n; Soviet
    occupation, 111–59 *passim*;
    Moscow Agreement, 125, 132,
    152–6, 158, 161; rigged

elections, 160–4; Romanian Peace Treaty, 164–5, 169; communisation, 165–70; forced abdication of King, 177–84; Romanian Republic recognised by US and UK, 192; under Ceaușescu, 224, 226, 228, 231–5; 1989 December uprising, 235–7, 239–40; after 1989 uprising, 240–5, 248–9, 252–3, 257–62, 263–4, 267–8; new constitution (1991), 249–50; joins Council of Europe, 263; joins NATO, 263, 268–9, 272; Constantinescu government, 272–82 *passim*, 286
Romanian Intelligence Service (RIS), 241, 244
Romanian National Committee (in exile), 193–4, 197, 202, 205–6, 206–7, 207 (*bis*), 210, 211, 213, 214, 215–16, 219, 228
ROMPRES news agency, 242
Roosevelt, President, 72, 145, 146
Rosa (Queen Helen's maid), xii, 184, 188
Royal Foundation for Literature and Arts, 46
Royal United Services Institute (London), 245, 248 276
Rundstedt, General, 118
Russia/USSR, 1, 2, 3, 53, 97, 132; Romanian troops in invasion of, 70–4, 77, 79–80; occupation of Romania, 111–59 *passim*; *see also* Second World War

Șafran, Alexander, Chief Rabbi, 74–5, 197
St John, Miss (KM's nanny), 12, 14, 15, 41
Salic law, 221, 253, 280

Sănătescu, General Constantin, 67, 84–5, 87, 90, 91, 93, 95, 96, 98, 100, 101, 103, 106, 108, 109; Prime Minister after 1944 *coup*, 111, 112, 113, 116, 123, 129, 131 *bis*, 133
Santa Monica, 219
Săvârșin (Transylvania), 81, 83, 85–6, 87, 128, 188, 283, 285
Scanavi (Princess Elisabeta's lover), 66, 122
Schyler, General, 143, 158, 167, 223
Second World War: start of, 52–5; Romania during, 55–97; Cairo talks, 88–97 *passim*, 98–9, 102, 103–4, 116, 125–6; Potsdam Agreement, 145–8; Yalta Summit, 137, 138, 145, 154
Securitate, 208, 228, 237, 241–2, 246
Serbia, 8, 9
Sibiu (Transylvania), 120, 236
Siguranța, 99, 107, 111, 121, 208
Sima, Horia, 55, 56, 65, 67–8
Simeon, King of Bulgaria, 137
Sinaia, xi–xii, 25, 148, 186–7
Slovenia, 276
Snagov, 104, 116
Soare (caretaker), 186
Social Democratic Party (SDP), 10, 96, 101, 129, 156–7, 160, 162; in exile, 194, 205, 207; after 1989 uprising, 243, 262
Socialist Labour Party, 252, 258 *bis*
Solescu, Rosetti 'Toto', 77–8
Sophie, Princess (KM's daughter), 221, 225, 239, 242, 246, 250, 269, 271
Sophie, Princess of Greece (Princess George of Hanover), 201
Sophia, Queen of Greece, xi, xii, 7, 8, 13, 22, 38

Sophie, Queen of Spain, 221, 270
Sora, Mihai, 241, 244
Special Operations Executive (SOE), 87, 88–9, 115, 116
Speer, Albert, 118
Stahel, General, 119
Stalin, Joseph, xiii, 97, 119–20, 132, 144, 145, 146, 170, 224
Stalingrad, 72–3, 74, 80
Stana Rocată (house), 70, 81
Șteflea, General, 111
Steven the Great, Saint, 253–4
Stevenson, Air Vice-Marshal, 131, 143, 157
Știrbey, Prince Barbu, 5–6, 11, 15, 16, 17, 18, 20, 21, 51, 89–95 *passim*, 102, 104, 126, 146; wife, and daughter Katherine, 122
Stolojan, Theodor, 249
Straja Țării (youth movement), 46, 65
Sturdza, Prince George, 69
Styrcea, Baron Ion (Ionel) Mocsoni, 80, 83, 84, 86, 87, 99–108 *passim*, 117, 121, 126, 131; Bielle, his wife, 87 *bis*, 166
*Suppression of Romanian Human Rights*, 214
Susiakov, Colonel General, 135, 137, 139, 143, 144, 147–8, 150, 151, 169
Switzerland, 9, 166, 171, 175, 185, 188, 192, 199, 217, 220–1, 259

'T' Organisation, 149
Tampeanu, Lt, 16
Tătărescu, Gheorghe, 48, 50, 53, 59, 139, 142, 152, 155, 156, 164 *bis*, 167, 172, 218
Tatoi (Greece), 201, 220–1
Taylor, General Maxwell, 198

Teoctist, Patriarch, 256, 270
Teodorescu, General, 114, 116
Timișoara (Banat), 235–6, 239, 245, 258–9, 270, 275
Tîrgu Mureș (Transylvania), 241, 243, 252
Tito, Marshal, 170, 172
Titulescu, Nicolae, 33, 35, 40, 48
Tobescu, General, 112
Tökes, Laszlo, 235–6
Tolbukhin, General, 102, 144
Tomescu, Mircea, 68
Transniestria, 72, 79
Transylvania, xii, 1, 2, 3, 6, 10–11, 54–5, 73, 75, 78, 81, 104, 119, 142, 188, 236, 256n, 261, 263
Truman, President Harry, 146, 156, 167, 197–8, 198 (*bis*), 209, 214
Tudor, Corneliu, 248–9, 252, 257, 263, 265, 267, 279, 282, 285
Tudor Vladimirescu regiment, 151, 157, 177, 178, 179, 182
Turkey, 7–8, 12, 13, 105, 121; Ottoman Empire, 1, 2

Udriski (pilot), 85–6, 104, 121, 122, 166, 171, 175
Union of Moldavian Women, 255
United Kingdom, 8, 13, 23, 52, 53, 54, 87–9, 93, 97, 127–8, 130–2, 139, 140, 145–8, 150, 156, 157, 161, 163–4, 192, 266–7; KM lives in, 211–13, 218; *see also* Second World War
University Foundation, Paris, 210–11, 228
Urdăreanu, Ernest, 45–6, 51, 55 *bis*, 56–7, 58, 59, 195, 214
USA, 93, 121, 132, 156, 161, 163–4, 170, 192, 202–3, 206–7, 214–16, 226,

250, 259, 264; KM refuses offer of residence 209–10; KM visits/lives in 193, 197–8, 219, 223, 250–1; *see also* Second World War
USSR see Russia/USSR

Văcăroiu, Nicolae, 258, 263, 267, 271
Vaida-Voevod, Alexandru, 21, 40, 48, 59
Valliadis, Archimandrite, 204
Vasiliu, General 'Piki', 94n, 112, 158
Vasiliu-Rășcanu, General, 152
Vatra Romînească (nationalist group), 241, 252, 257–8, 258
Venizelos, Eleftheros, 7–8, 9, 12
Vergotti, Major Jacques, 69, 76, 77–8, 79, 115, 118, 120, 130, 167, 171, 171–2, 175 *bis*, 177, 178–9, 186–8, 193, 195, 195–6, 197, 201, 202, 207, 224
Vermehren (art expert), 230
Versoix, 218, 219, 222, 230–1, 239, 247 *bis*
Victoria, Empress (Princess Vicky), 7, 11n
*Vienna Diktat* (1940), 54–5, 87
Villa Idris (Villefranche), 203
Villa Sparta (Florence), 47–8, 48, 185, 201, 202, 206, 207, 209, 210, 218, 219, 230
Vinogradov, General, 131, 133, 134 *bis*, 135
Vișoianu, Constantin, 89, 96–7, 99, 101, 102, 131, 133 *bis*, 138, 203, 205, 207 *bis*, 209–10, 213, 215, 228
Vychinsky, Andrei, 133–41 *passim*, 142, 144, 145, 148, 153, 154, 155–6, 181, 206

Waldemar, Prince of Denmark, 194
Wallachia, xiii, 1
Warsaw uprising, 118, 119
Wilson, General, 93, 103, 104, 116
Wisner, Frank, 209

Xavier, Prince of Bourbon Parma, 194, 200, 221

Yugoslavia, 103, 118, 169–70, 209

Zamfirescu, Lascar, 42, 44
Zissu, Iancu, 205, 214
Zita, Empress of Austria, 194
Zwiedenek (head of Queen Marie's household)